D0729757

# MAGI

## The Quest for a Secret Tradition

# MAGI

## THE QUEST FOR A SECRET TRADITION

ADRIAN G. GILBERT

BLOOMSBURY

In fond memory of my parents,
Raymond Charles Gilbert
and Patricia Hilda (Lewis) Gilbert

First published 1996 by Bloomsbury Publishing Plc,
38 Soho Square, London W1V 5DF

This paperback edition published 1997

A copy of the CIP entry for this book
is available from the British Library

ISBN 0 7475 3100 5

10 9 8 7 6 5 4 3 2 1

Typeset by Hewer Text Composition Services, Edinburgh
Printed in England by Clays Ltd, St Ives plc

# CONTENTS

# PROLOGUE

T his world is full of mysteries, some large and some small. Even the most simple of people have their secrets and so too, on a larger scale, does history. Possibly the greatest mystery in the world surrounds the origins of the Christian religion. Who was this man Jesus? Where did he come from? What really was his mission? Unlike the Buddha or Mohammed, whose lives were well documented and who left writings of their own, the historical Jesus Christ continues to be an enigma.

The Biblical story is extremely fragmentary and even if we treat the Gospels as genuine biographies, the light they throw on the historical Jesus is surprisingly limited. Between the ages of twelve and thirty that is, his most formative years, we lose sight of him altogether. If Matthew, Mark, Luke and John knew what happened to him during those critical years of adolescence and young manhood, they are remarkably silent and so indeed is the Church founded in his name. Many people assume, not surprisingly given the context of the Gospels, that Christianity is simply a reformed and updated version of Judaism. After all Jesus was a Jew and indeed, if the genealogy given in the New Testament is to be believed, he was a direct descendant of the legendary King David. His three year ministry was conducted for the most part among the Jews and he was hailed by his followers as the expected Jewish Messiah. Why then, one may ask, is what he taught so very un-Jewish? As a prophet one would expect to read of him haranguing people in the fashion of a Jeremiah or Ezekiel, exhorting them to abandon false gods and to adhere to the Law of Moses. Whilst there are many references in the Gospels to the Old Testament and particularly to the prophecies of Isaiah, these are by no means important elements in the teaching of Christianity. The Jesus we read about is an intelligent, unbigoted man who heals the sick and is happy to eat with sinners. He also takes little interest in the prohibition of work on the Sabbath but rather preaches the need for tolerance, mercy and forgiveness of others. He also seems to have been on quite friendly terms with foreigners, even the Romans. Indeed one of his most important parables, that of the Good Samaritan, declares openly that a man of compassion is virtuous in the eyes of God regardless of his race and nationality. Nor does Jesus, as some suppose, seem to have been a revolutionary. In the Gospel story he walks into a trap, allows himself to be taken prisoner, is tried and crucified. Far from leading his people, Joshua like, in a great revolt against Rome, he tells his followers to render unto Caesar that which is Caesar's – hardly the words of a rebel leader. It is clear from the Gospels that Jesus was regarded as a dangerous influence by the Jewish authorities of his day. He openly derided the Pharisees and Sadducees, often making fools of them in public when they tried to trip him up with difficult questions. His flouting of their authority over such matters as the stoning of an adulteress made him even more suspect. Clearly, then, there was something about this man and his teachings that the Sanhedrin, the supreme council of high priests, found particularly obnoxious. Jesus was regarded as being a dangerous heretic; so dangerous in fact that, if the Gospels are to be believed, they colluded with the Romans in having him put to death.

Christianity is generally presented by the Church as though it were an entirely new revelation, making its appearance in the history of the world with the suddenness of a thunderbolt falling to earth. Yet is this the truth? Are there no antecedents for this most sublime religion? When the Gospel story is looked at objectively, it becomes obvious that the Jewish high priests regarded Jesus as an apostate. This was not just because he had rather flexible views concerning the Mosaic Law but because some of what he taught was clearly derived from sources outside of Judaism. However, this in turn raises a further question: what were these sources and how might Jesus have come into contact with them? This is what I wanted to find out and why I am so interested in the Magi as they seemed to be somehow connected with this secret source of wisdom.

For over twenty years, ever since visiting Bethlehem in my early twenties, I have been, on and off, on a quest to find the truth behind the legend of the Magi. For some reason the story of the three kings had imprinted itself on my mind, probably because it seemed to cloak some deeper mystery. I am reminded of the time when once, as a small boy, I cut open one of my father's golf balls to find out why it was so heavy for its size. I was amazed to discover that hidden under the tough, dimpled exterior was a mass of spun rubber, like an enormously long elastic band. This I was able to unwind, finally reaching the core of the ball which turned out to be a small balloon filled with white lead paste. Apparently this hidden, rather fragile object was the reason why golf balls had so much bounce.

For me this entirely unexpected revelation mirrors the quest for esoteric − secret − knowledge.[1] My quest for the Magi and the secret tradition from which I believe they came, has been a long drawn out affair that has required much unravelling of 'elastic' symbols and ideas to reveal what lies behind the mythology. Like the time when I cut open the golf ball I have found, hidden under many layers of symbolism, history, science and mysticism, a secret at the core of the Christian religion. This secret, a mystery within a mystery, is not made of white lead like the centre of a golf ball but of star-dust. It is my belief that Jesus, the Messiah whom much of the world has come to venerate as the Son of God, was not acting alone. He had been instructed by secret Masters of Wisdom in both the historical role he was to play − his destiny − and in certain esoteric knowledge.

Now I understand that some people, those who hold closely to what is called the 'monophysite' doctrine − that Jesus and Christ, the Son of God, are one and the same entity; that Christ's body and soul are indissolubly linked through all eternity and that the baby Jesus was therefore fully cognisant and fully conscious of his role from his time of conception − may find some of what I have to say disturbing. I can only ask such people, perhaps the majority of modern day Christians, for their indulgence and invite them to examine the evidence for themselves before dismissing what I have to say out of hand. By definition, the esoteric or secret history of the world is invisible. It is not obvious and is hard to prove. Yet, by a process of forensic science we can put together a case. It is possible to discover a hidden trail leading back to the Magi and beyond. Startling new evidence, presented here for the first time, leads me to believe that not only Christianity but Judaism too has roots going back to a secret mystery tradition lost in the mists of time. For reasons not immediately obvious, this tradition, still alive today, has always been linked with the star Sirius and the constellation of Orion. It is my contention that once the importance of this stellar connection is realized and understood, much that at present remains obscure in the Bible, and indeed in the much wider mythology of the world, becomes clear. The story, however, begins in Bethlehem.

# CHAPTER 1

✳

# A Pilgrimage to
# the City of David

It was a sunny day in early September. Light, woolly clouds were moving swiftly through the sky and the summer birds, as though sensing that the fine weather would not last, were preparing for their long flight south to Africa. I packed my rucksack in a state of high expectation, for I too was about to make a long journey – or rather I should say pilgrimage – for I was planning to cycle to the Holy Land. The previous two weeks had been a flurry of activity as my travelling companion, John, a friend of many years, and I made our final preparations to travel by bicycle not only for financial reasons but also for the sense of challenge it gave us. At the back of our minds was the image of Crusaders, saddling up their horses and setting out for Jerusalem and this somehow translated into the desire to do things the hard way, to make the journey itself something of an ordeal so that the Pilgrimage would be that much sweeter. With little money and a large measure of optimism we set out, our goal to reach Bethlehem in time for Christmas Day. Little did we know that this would be the last the Israelis were to enjoy in the comforting afterglow of their extraordinary six-day victory before the 1973 Yom Kippur War restored some level of Arab pride.

At twenty-two we were both seasoned travellers having spent two previous summers hitchhiking in Scandinavia and the summer before driven in a Mini to Spain. Nothing, however, had prepared either of us for the sheer physical challenge of the journey nor for the bad weather we encountered. For mile after mile heavy rain beat down on us as we pushed our way through the flat, Picardy countryside. We came across ghostly reminders of a tortured past as we cycled by First World War cemeteries and the grassy remnants of the trenches that had once been at the centre of the world's most terrible scrummage. At night we slept under bridges or in the wrecks of abandoned cars, our army surplus oil-skins inadequate against the non-stop rain. As we knew we could not afford to squander our scarce resources on the pleasures of the French cuisine, our diet was a 'nose-bag' of very sweet muesli. Cambrai, St Quentin, Laon, Reims . . . what had been just spots on the map turned into towns and cities before retreating behind us in a foggy haze. People hooted at us as they splashed past in their waterproof cars, we weren't quite sure whether out of irritation that we were in their way or as their expression of solidarity with lonely cyclists in the land of the Tour de France. As day followed day without any let-up, we began to doubt that the rain would ever stop. In the end we sold out to pragmatism and boarded a train to take us over the mountains to the Sâone-Rhône Valley, praying all the while for better weather ahead. Reaching Dijon, famous for its mustard and once the capital of an independent Burgundy, we allowed ourselves a break and went to visit the local cathedral.

What makes a great building is something hard to define but it has a lot to do with atmosphere and the nature of the people living in the area. Among the books that I had read in the previous year was one with the curious title *A New Model of the Universe* by the Russian philosopher and journalist, P.D. Ouspensky. In this remarkable work he had, among much else, put forward the thesis that Notre-Dame Cathedral in Paris contained a secret. Its building was not accidental, nor was it simply a matter of 'art' no matter how uplifting. He believed that the masons who built it had, at least for a short time, been in possession of a higher knowledge and were the inheritors of traditions going back to the time of the pyramids and before. How they had come by this, now lost, knowledge he did not explain but at the time I read his words, somehow what he said rang true. I felt that he was right, the mediaeval cathedrals of France and Britain were manifestations of an ancient tradition, and their builders had been in possession of secret knowledge. Dijon Cathedral, where I was now standing, belongs to the same tradition as the better known Notre-Dame and it had a haunting quality to it. It is a late thirteenth century Gothic masterpiece, which though not huge by French standards, has a character and presence all of its own. The French equivalent of the Scots, the Burgundians were always acutely aware that their fertile Duchy was something different and separate from the rest of France. Here, buried in the cathedral, were Philip the Bold and Anne, daughter of John the Fearless — their very names defiant. Their cathedral echoed this defiance and I could almost hear voices from the past saying 'Not French nor German but Burgundians we'. What, however, touched me most was the extraordinary, Romanesque crypt. Here, in a womblike, pillared chamber I felt in a state of sensory deprivation. Suddenly I realized why it was that would-be knights had to go through a period of solitary confinement and prayer, sometimes lasting several days, before they were, in great ceremony, dubbed by the monarch. Standing in the crypt I could imagine, almost remember, what it must have been like to confront in silence and seclusion the darkness inside one's own skull.

A knight from the Middle Ages did not experience the distractions we have to cope with today in our busy hectic lives. Perhaps this is why his inner life was so much richer. Religion for him meant one thing, Christianity. If he encountered any other, say Judaism or Islam, it was in the certain knowledge that only Christianity could guarantee eternal life in heaven. Though he probably had few illusions about God's representatives on Earth (like as not the local bishop was a brother or cousin) he felt confident that in the great scheme of things and provided only that he did his duty, Christ's blood had saved him from his sins. Fortified by this uncomplicated faith he could ride out to fight the enemies of the Church believing that if he should die in this holy service he would be a martyr and go straight to heaven. Our knight, though, was in all probability profoundly ignorant. He would not have read translations of the Koran, his knowledge of Ancient Greece and Rome would have been scanty, whilst all he would know of Ancient Persia and Egypt would be what was written in his Bible. Of Buddhism, Zen, Taoism or Native American traditions he would know absolutely nothing at all and, as far as he was concerned, these traditions could as well exist on other planets as on different continents.

These ideas and many others passed through my mind as I meditated in the crypt. Unlike our imaginary knight, I had practised yoga for several years, had read the Upanishads and, like many others of the 60s generation, wanted very much to go to India. I had also studied the writings of Plato and yearned to know more about the Western mystical tradition. It was this desire (which John shared with me) which drove us on our quest. Like pilgrims throughout the ages we were optimistic that we would find something in the Holy Land. There we hoped we would meet somebody or find something that would point us on the way. We were confident that we would find at least a trace of some hidden knowledge not accessible in England.

In the crypt of Dijon Cathedral I could feel the weight of time compressed into an instant moment of near infinite duration. For the first time I knew what Ouspensky meant when he wrote that there were, in reality, two histories of the world running in parallel, the one visible and endlessly reported on by the media, the other a secret undercurrent. I recalled his words:

> One history passes by in full view and, strictly speaking, is the *history of crime*, for if there were no crimes there would be no history. All the most important turning-points and stages of this history are marked by crimes: murders, acts of violence, robberies, wars, rebellions, massacres, tortures, executions . . . This is one history, the history which everybody knows, the history which is taught in schools.
>
> The other history is the history which is known to very few. For the majority it is not seen at all behind the history of crime. But what is created by this hidden history exists long afterwards, sometimes for many centuries, as does Notre-Dame. The visible history, the history proceeding on the surface, the history of crime, attributes to itself what the hidden history has created. But actually the visible history is always deceived by what the hidden history has created. [1]

I had been deeply impressed by these words when I had first read them. The idea of a hidden history behind the more visible outer events that make up what is taught to us in school made sense. Now in the dark, womblike crypt Ouspensky's words came back to me with force. I was sure that he was right and that there was an unseen, unspoken link between the cathedral builders and the ancient mystery schools of Egypt and Mesopotamia. At the time I had little idea what this meant in practice or how it might have come about but I was determined to find out. Then, my thoughts still rather vague and unfocused, I made my way out of the crypt back into the blinding sunlight now bathing Dijon town.

The next day, with a tail wind pushing us from behind, we carried on our journey down the Saône-Rhône Valley. Nuits-St Georges, Beaune, Chalon, Mâcon . . . the names reading out like a list from a vintner's catalogue. All along the sides of the road were ripening grapes and, for a time, the weather improved enough for us to enjoy something of the sights, sounds and smells around us. We had by now given up on the muesli, accepting the psychological if not physical need for a more varied diet. Stopping at a small café somewhere in Provence, we explained in broken French that we were pilgrims on our way to the Holy Land. The *patron* with a mixture of amusement and incredulity invited us in and insisted we each have a glass of his house red. A rough vintage with a kick like a mule, it was not what we had in mind at 10.30 in the morning but he insisted we empty our water-canteens and, with a flourish that reminded us of the Wedding Feast of Cana, refilled them with wine. By now his son Jean had joined us and was acting as interpreter. He explained that the grapes had been grown in their own vineyard and that his father was most anxious that we should succeed in our pilgrimage. We thanked them for the wine and promised to send Jean a card when we finally arrived in Bethlehem.

The *patron* probably didn't realize the significance of his gesture, but it meant a lot to us. At last we seemed to be touching a deeply historic vein of camaraderie between inn-keeper and pilgrim that must once have been widespread throughout Europe. Here, in a small French village, there was both acceptance and enthusiasm for what we were doing that went beyond boundaries of language and nation. As modern day heirs of countless pilgrims and Crusaders, who for centuries made their same way down the Saône-Rhône Valley, we had a status larger than our own. In offering his own wine to pilgrims the *patron* was doing something more than entertaining guests, he was partaking in our journey and linking himself to our great adventure. In this way, at least in spirit, he too was joining in the adventure. Such experiences must once have been commonplace when people journeyed by horse or on foot though not when one travels by jumbo jet. For us it was one of the highlights of the journey.

Travelling mostly by train through Italy, we then took a boat to Greece. Again like many pilgrims before us we took time out to visit Athens with its majestic past before setting sail for Israel. Our ferry, the heir to all those Venetian and Genoese merchant men that once plied between the islands of Greece and the richer heartlands of the Byzantine Empire, stopped off at Rhodes. The boat strained at anchor while more passengers were brought out by launch and I gazed at the remarkable fortress of the Knights of St John. It seemed strange to think that here, on this beautiful jewel of the Eastern Mediterranean, was fought one of the last battles of the Crusades. For on 24 June 1522, an Ottoman army with an estimated strength of 200,000 men landed on Rhodes with the intention of destroying once and for all this last outpost of Crusader power. Against them stood a force of only 500 knights, plus about 1,500 mercenaries and Rhodians, who had no intention of giving way. The battle raged on and off for six months, before the hopelessly outnumbered defenders were eventually forced to give in and accept honourable terms for surrender. On Christmas Eve, Sultan Suleiman the Magnificent, who had himself been present throughout nearly all of the siege, paid tribute to the gallantry of the knights. He allowed them and anyone who wished to go with them freedom to leave the vanquished island, even offering them use of his own ships to ferry them to ports of safety. Had he known then that in little over forty years' time the Knights of St John, ensconced in their new home of Malta, would drive his armies back and thereby deprive him of the great prize of Italy, he might not have been so generous. This however, was a separate battle, one to decide the final extent of the Ottoman Empire. To all intents and purposes, 1522 was the year that the Crusades came to an end and it happened on the beaches of Rhodes.

I did not know all this history then as I gazed out at the great ramparts of the Citadel. Yet, even so, I could feel much of the atmosphere of the place; and appreciate the strategic importance of the island for ships travelling between the ports of the Eastern Mediterranean. In one sense everything had changed over the last 450 years, yet in other, deeper ways it was still the same. There was still the same animosity between Greek and Turk, the same rivalry between East and West. History seemed to be turning full circle, for now not only were the Greeks back in control of Rhodes but a new 'crusader' state had sprung up in Palestine: the republic of Israel. Though Jewish rather than Christian it was, like the old, Frankish kingdom of Jerusalem, financed and armed by the West. All this seemed portentous, with more than a hint of the 'hidden history' about it, but of what it portended I didn't know.

Arriving in Haifa, Israel's third largest city and main port, John and I were confronted on the docks by soldiers carrying machine-guns. We felt like we had entered the camp of the Spartans, for unlike in

Northern France where the scars of the First World War though still visible were no longer septic, this place of open sores was still highly militarized. Overlooking Haifa was Mount Carmel, now incongruously dominated by a golden-domed, Bahai Shrine. Here lies the tomb of the Bab, a nineteenth century Persian prophet according to his followers. Looking at its dome glinting in the morning sunlight was a reminder that in Israel religion is no simple matter as every Middle Eastern cult claims its inheritance in what is, after all, a very small country. Carmel was once the home of the ancient school of Hebrew prophets whose books fill the Bible. Later it gave its name to the Carmelite Order of mendicant friars. This was founded in the twelfth century when a crusader called Berthold and ten like-minded companions established themselves as hermits close to the reputed cave of Elijah on Mount Carmel. Hermits were not in evidence when we visited the Mount which seemed now to be something of a garden suburb.

Leaving behind us the blue of the Mediterranean we headed inland over the craggy hills of Zafed and the parched valley of Megiddo (the Armageddon of the Bible) before dropping down to the lush Hulah Valley. Here, in something of what is an oasis of fertility, lay a number of the most affluent and productive of Israel's collective farms or kibbutzim. John and I soon found ourselves picking grapefruits for one called Kefar Szold, an old settlement with a number of survivors of the Holocaust. These people, some of them so traumatized by what they had experienced that they had long since abandoned all pretence to sanity, were a living reproach to the bestiality of mankind. It seemed a cruel irony that within yards of our huts there were fences of barbed wire. These refugees from Hitler's death camps were still on the front line.

Beyond the wire fence were the Golan Heights, a small part of Syria captured by the Israelis in the Six Day War of 1967. Here, threading through minefields and other remnants of war, there were beaten paths, which we could climb, though we were warned not to go too far and to stick always to the track. Walking up there in the afternoons as the sun was losing its heat and Mount Hermon was taking on an orange tinge, I would dream and wonder whether Jesus too had walked those same hills. Had he, as I, watched the Mountain Araxes playing amongst the rocks? Did he, too, watch vultures gathering and circling above a carcass below? Was it here that he cursed a fig tree — perhaps like the ones I saw growing wild by the roadside — for not bearing fruit? All these questions and more were suddenly alive for me in a way they had never been before I set foot in this strange country, breathed its smells and drunk its water. I took my Bible out of my bag and opened it at random. 'Seek and you will find; knock and it will be opened to you' it read, 'For every one who asks receives, and to him who knocks it will be opened.' I am knocking, I thought, I am knocking; how much louder does it have to be? From some deeper part of my soul I got the answer: Not yet, but some day. Be patient and the door will be opened; in time all will be revealed. I held these words in my heart, resolving there and then that I would never give up the search for knowledge; that one day I would find out what the Gospels were really all about and the truth about this strange man Jesus.

That Christmas John and I made it to Bethlehem and stood among the crowds in Manger Square. It was cold, snowing and not at all as we had expected, for there was crude commercialism at every twist and turn. There was a slight commotion as Harold Wilson, then Prime Minister of the United Kingdom, was escorted to the church, his famous coat tightly buttoned against the cold. Like Mary and Joseph outside the Inn, we could not follow him into the warmth within its protective walls, for there were far too many important dignitaries with precedence over mere pilgrims like ourselves. Instead we wandered over to the Post Office and sent a card to Jean from the village in France. Back in the Square, American choirs were singing endless verses of 'Once in Royal David's City' and 'We Three Kings', oblivious, it seemed to the Arab town around them. Above the Square, in tawdry imitation of the Gospel story, was an illuminated, plastic star. It glowed and shimmered like an Oxford Street illumination, so unbelievably vulgar that I didn't know whether to laugh or cry. For what seemed like an eternity I stood looking at this star with an equal mixture of revulsion and fascination. How, I wondered, could this place, supposedly the very site of the Nativity be turned into such a circus? What would Jesus himself have made of a Tabernacle choir visiting his reputed birthplace to sing hymns under a plastic star? But then something else struck me: the star was five-pointed. This I knew was traditional for the Christmas star but suddenly it seemed very peculiar. This was, after all, Bethlehem and in the Bible it is called the City of David. Yet David's star, to be seen on synagogues and on every Israeli flag, is six-pointed. This being so, why should the Star of Bethlehem be five-pointed and not six? I was to find out later that this seemingly trivial difference in design is actually quite pivotal in terms of understanding the esoteric significance of the symbol.

Looking beyond the star, I started thinking about the legend of the three Magi, usually depicted as kings and traditionally named as Caspar, Melchior and Balthasar. They were the first pilgrims to Bethlehem and we had, over the last few months, in a sense been following in their footsteps. I could remember being dressed up as Melchior at the age of six in a school nativity play but no one, then or later, had ever really explained their significance to me. Who were these kings? Where did they come from? Were they linked with some sort of mystical tradition? Suddenly, though I didn't know why, these questions seemed very important and I was keen to find someone of experience I could ask about these and many other matters. Back in England I had the name and address of one of Ouspensky's pupils and I resolved that on my return I would pay him a visit. This man was certainly one of the most extraordinary people of his generation but, as I was to discover, this was only the beginning of what would turn out to be a very long quest.

## The Gospel story of the three wise men

The story of the Magi is actually contained in only one of the four Gospels, Matthew's:

Now the birth of Jesus Christ took place in this way. When his mother Mary had been betrothed to Joseph, before they came together she was found to be with child by the Holy Spirit; and her husband Joseph, being a just man and unwilling to put her to shame, resolved to divorce her quietly. But as he considered this, behold an angel of the Lord appeared to him in a dream, saying, 'Joseph, son of David, do not fear to take Mary your wife, for that which is conceived in her is of the Holy Spirit; she will bear a son, and you shall call his name Jesus, for he will save his people from their sins'. All this took place to fulfil what the Lord had spoken by the prophet:

'Behold, a virgin shall conceive and bear a son, and his name shall be called Emmanuel.'

Now when Jesus was born in Bethlehem of Judea in the days of Herod the king, behold wise men [Magi] from the East came to Jerusalem, saying, 'Where is he who has been born king of the Jews? For we have seen his star in the East, and have come to worship him'. Then Herod summoned the wise men secretly and ascertained from them what time the star appeared; and he sent them to Bethlehem, saying, 'Go and search diligently for the child, and when you have found him bring me word, that I too may come and worship him'. When they had heard the king they went their way; and lo, the star which they had seen in the East went before them, till it came to rest over the place where the child was. When they saw the star, they rejoiced exceedingly with great joy; and going into the house they saw the child with Mary his mother, and they fell down and worshipped him. Then, opening their treasures, they offered him gifts, gold, frankincense and myrrh. And being warned in a dream not to return to Herod, they departed to their own land by another way.[2]

The role of the Magi in Matthew's Nativity story is mysterious throughout. They appear like good fairies at the birth, each offering a gift that somehow symbolizes Jesus' destiny: gold for a king, frankincense for a priest and myrrh for a healer. Whilst it can be argued that the story is pure invention on the part of Matthew (and I don't believe it is), he must have had a reason for including it in his Gospel. However we look at it, there is something very odd and esoteric about this legend.

## Constantinople and the Holy Wisdom

The story of the Magi is one of the best-loved tales in the New Testament and their 'Adoration' is one of the most frequently painted scenes of all religious art. In the Middle Ages the story of the Magi was popular, not least because it gave artists and sculptors an excuse to remind their own kings that they too needed to pay fealty to the higher authority of Christ. However, kings and emperors alike were keen to see themselves portrayed as pious followers of Christ and would often have themselves painted in the act of making symbolic offerings to either Jesus himself or the Virgin Mary. Among the finest, if not the earliest, of these is a tenth-century mosaic to be found over the gate of the vestibule in the Hagia Sophia Cathedral of Constantinople (Istanbul). It portrays two highly eminent emperors making offerings to the Virgin and Child. On the right is Constantine the Great, the first Christian emperor of Rome, offering the Virgin his new city of Constantinople and, on the left, is Justinian presenting his creation: the Hagia Sophia Cathedral itself (plate 2).

The Hagia Sophia Cathedral was consecrated on 27 December 537 AD. At the time when this mosaic was put up, some four hundred and fifty years later, it was still the largest and most imposing religious structure in Christendom and drew pilgrims from all over Europe. They were impressed not just by the size and opulence of what is still, even today, a magnificent building but by what it said about the society who created it. Western Europe was still only just emerging from the Dark Ages and there was a great sense of loss, of a cultural vacuum that yearned to be filled. In France, Britain and Germany few people could read and write, even among the aristocracy. Repeated waves of barbarian invasions: Vandals, Goths, Huns and Vikings had virtually wiped out the legacy of Rome in the West. Yet, here in Constantinople the old Empire lived on, its splendours undiminished and its Christian civilization intact. Little wonder, then, that as civilized life began to return to the West, thinking people looked to Byzantium as a source of inspiration. They also looked upon it as a treasury of lost knowledge for it contained libraries the like of which had not been seen in Europe for a thousand years. Some at least had hopes that the 'Holy Wisdom', of which the Hagia Sophia cathedral was the tangible expression, could be induced to make its home in the capitals of the West as well and thereby bring about a new enlightenment, a rekindling of Western Civilization.

In the Western mind the three kings of the Magi story represented all that was exotic and civilized. They were not merely potentates or ambassadors from the pagan East but were pilgrims of the highest order. They were holy men who recognized that great though their material wealth and power in this world may be, they were still vassals of the baby Jesus. In their art and sculpture of the Middle Ages, Western artists sought to portray this feeling of humility in the face of greater a majesty but they also borrowed from the Byzantines the idea of analogy. Just as in the mosaic over the gate of the vestibule in the Hagia Sophia, the Byzantine emperors Constantine and Justinian are seen themselves to be making offerings to the Virgin and Child, so also European kings would have themselves painted into the picture. The most famous example of this is also possibly the most esoteric painting of the Middle Ages. Close analysis of it reveals hidden knowledge and I believe points to contact between at least one of the crowned heads of Europe and a secret tradition of Christian Hermeticism that robed itself in the garb of the Magi.

## Richard II and the Wilton Diptych

In 1993, an important exhibition was held at the National Gallery, London, featuring what is considered to be the finest extant works of art from the fourteenth century: the Wilton Diptych (plate 5). This small, portable altarpiece was commissioned by one of England's least understood kings, Richard II. It is one of the world's really great works of art, standing on a par with Leonardo da Vinci's *Mona Lisa*, Rembrandt's *Night Watch* and Van Gogh's *Sunflowers*. It is Richard's misfortune that his chief claim to fame lies in the fact that it was during his reign that Parliament eventually forced a king to admit to its supremacy. He was unfortunate that he lived at the time when such matters were coming to a head, for he himself was an intelligent and sensitive man. He did not deserve to be swept away in the tide, as he eventually was, nor having already abdicated in favour of his uncouth cousin Henry IV, to be murdered at Pontefract Castle at the tender age of 33. The historian John Harvey has this to say of him:

Richard II is important because he was in the highest degree the type of his family, of the whole House of Plantagenet, and because he represented in the most personal manner the supreme case for Divine Kingship. His insistence upon the sacred and indissoluble nature of the regality conferred on him by his consecration, and upon the maintenance in full of the rights of the Crown, was due to his prescience of the nature of all that would follow, once this barrier was swept away. It is neither sentimentality nor romanticism to see in Richard a highly intelligent and supremely cultured man, fully abreast of the high intellectual attainments of his age, and gifted with a greater insight than most men, even most sovereigns, into the essential character of government.

. . . it is one of the commonest and most widely spread of errors to suppose that because a period is more remote in time, it is more barbarous, worse equipped, and less sophisticated. The flawless poise of the Greece of the sixth and fifth centuries BC, and the exquisite line of the sculpture, painting and literature of the Pharaoh Akhnaton a thousand years earlier still, are enough to teach us that. Similarly the fourteenth century saw the attainment of a supreme peak of European existence, and we shall be nearer the mark if we picture Richard II as a superman, wiser and better equipped than ourselves, than if we suppose him a crude potentate in an age of splendid savagery. It is probable that Europe proper has not, since the fourteenth century, seen any individual capable of appreciating Richard at his proper worth.[3]

In Shakespeare's play, *Richard II*, which is the first in his cycle concerning the Wars of the Roses, the king is presented as weak, effete and under the influence of unworthy, common friends with whom he is presumed to have had a homosexual relationship. This latter suggestion is almost certainly a calumny put about by his enemies to justify his overthrow. In 1382, he married Anne of Bohemia, the daughter of the Emperor Charles IV. Though the marriage remained childless, it was not loveless and he was absolutely heartbroken when she died in 1394. He may have been somewhat effeminate in appearance, indeed he was very handsome, and he was certainly more interested in scholarship than manly pursuits such as war, but that does not mean he was homosexual.

Richard's pedigree was equal to that of his queen and had they had children, the history of Europe in the fourteenth century might have taken a different turn. He was the son of the Black Prince and the grandson of Edward III, whom he succeeded to the throne. Through that side of the family he was descended from Philip le Bel of France and his half-sister, Margaret. More distantly he was descended from the Emperors of Byzantium and was related to the Hungarian Royal family. He also had a strong Welsh connection being descended from Llewellyn, husband of Joan, daughter of King John. Given his undoubted intelligence and his privileged position as the scion of so many Royal Houses, it is not surprising that he seems to have had access to secret knowledge.

The Wilton Diptych which he commissioned is a two-hinged panel painted on both sides. It has recently been cleaned and has been the subject of some extraordinary detective work since its restoration. At a surface level it is a simple, devotional device that was probably used like other diptychs as the backdrop to a makeshift altar. On the right-hand panel is a picture of the Virgin holding the baby Jesus. From head to foot she is robed in blue. Mother and Child are attended by a company of angels, eleven in all, who like her are again robed in blue and who also wear floral crowns. Most of the angels stand quietly behind her, watching in silence the unfolding scene. One to her right carries the banner of St George, emblematic of England, whilst three others, two of whom are kneeling by her side, indicate with their hands and seek to draw her attention to the unfolding scene on the neighbouring panel. Here, a young Richard II is also kneeling whilst standing behind him and evidently acting as his sponsors are three haloed saints. Two of these are former kings who ruled in England, St Edward the Confessor, who died in 1066 and St Edmund, the last king of East Anglia, who was martyred by the Danes in 870. Both of these saints had popular cults associated with them, the former's centred on his famous shrine at Westminster Abbey and the latter's at Bury St Edmunds. The third figure, the closest to the right and, therefore, to the Virgin herself is St John the Baptist.

In the painting Richard has his empty hands held out, as though he is waiting to receive something himself. This idea of a gift being given back by the Virgin Mary to the wise men, though not mentioned in Matthew's Gospel, does have an important place in another writing, an Apocryphal Gospel said to have been used by the Gnostics in the second century. This Gospel, as well as elaborating on the birth of Jesus in a cave outside Bethlehem, tells an interesting story concerning the Magi and his swaddling clothes.

> And it came to pass, when the Lord Jesus was born at Bethlehem, a city of Judea, in the time of Herod the King; the wise men came from the East to Jerusalem, according to the prophecy of Zoradascht [Zoroaster], and brought with them offerings: namely gold, frankincense, and myrrh, and worshipped him, and offered to him their gifts.
>
> Then the Lady Mary took one of his swaddling clothes in which the infant was wrapped, and gave it to them instead of a blessing, which they received from her as a most noble present.[4]

Much to the surprise of the Magi, the swaddling cloth turns out to have miraculous powers.

On their return the kings and princes came to them inquiring, What they had seen and done? What sort of journey and return they had? What company they had on the road?

But they produced the swaddling cloth which St Mary had given to them, on account whereof they kept a feast.

And having, according to the custom of their country made a fire, they worshipped it.

And casting the swaddling cloth into it, the fire took it, and kept it.

And when the fire was put out, they took forth the swaddling cloth unhurt, as much as if the fire had not touched it.

Then they began to kiss it, and put it upon their heads and eyes, saying, This is certainly an undoubted truth, and it is really surprising that the fire could not burn it, and consume it.

Then they took it, and with the greatest respect laid it up among their treasures. [5]

The interpretation offered by the National Gallery is that like Constantine on the portico of the vestibule of the Hagia Sophia Cathedral in Istanbul, Richard is presenting the Virgin with his kingdom. However, this is not the only interpretation. Unless one assumes that the banner of England held by the angel has just been presented to her by Richard, then there is no equivalent image to Constantine's gift of his city. Richard has his hands empty and appears to be preparing to receive something himself. Given that the diptych would probably have been used as an altarpiece at Mass and the posture and the body language of all concerned, it seems more than likely that he is preparing to receive the baby Jesus into his own outstretched arms. A spiritual interpretation could be that he was asking to be given the baby Jesus as a reference to his receiving communion at Mass. No doubt as a devout Catholic, he would have believed that in taking the sacrament he was indeed partaking of the body and blood of the living Christ. However, it is probable that there was another secret message intended, that he was in effect asking the Virgin to give him a son of his own. As an heirless monarch his position was threatened by the ambitions of his cousin Bolingbroke and the machinations of a number of powerful lords. Had he but had a son he could probably have faced them down.

There is however, much more to this extremely esoteric painting.

The choice of these three saints as Richard's sponsors (one could almost call them his 'guides' or guardian angels) was clearly not arbitrary. According to the book which accompanied the exhibition, it is well attested that he held these three saints in special regard. The choice of the first two is fairly easy to understand as they were both former Kings of England (or at least part of it) who had carried the same burden of responsibility as himself. His choice of St John as his third sponsor is at first sight less obvious.

Richard's birthday was 6 January and this is, of course, a major Christian feast day: the Epiphany or coming of the Magi to give gifts to the infant Jesus. Not surprisingly, therefore, the Wilton Diptych contains allusions to the Magi. The presence of three kings, with Richard as one of them, echoes the scene of countless other paintings but there is more to it than this. So important was the legend of the Magi considered to be by the Church that the Epiphany, celebrated in honour of their supposed visit, is a major feast day. However, the 6 January was not always connected with Jesus' physical birth. In the early Church, it was indeed a Holy Day but it had nothing to do with the Nativity. Rather it was considered to be the day of Christ's Baptism in the Jordan River (plate 4) and was called the 'Day of Lights', relating to the Illumination of Jesus and the Light which shone in the Jordan. We read of this event in the following chapter of Matthew:

Then Jesus came from Galilee to the Jordan to John, to be baptised by him. John would have prevented him, saying, 'I need to be baptised by you, and do you come to me?' But Jesus answered him, 'Let it be so now; for thus it is fitting for us to fulfil righteousness'. Then he consented.

And when Jesus was baptised, he went up immediately from the water, and behold, the heavens were opened and he saw the Spirit of God descending like a dove, and alighting on him; and lo, a voice from heaven, saying, 'This is my beloved Son, with whom I am well pleased'.[6]

Richard II for one evidently knew that the feast of the Epiphany, on his birthday of 6 January, had originally been celebrated in honour of Jesus' baptism in the Jordan and this explains why he regarded St John as being his own special patron saint.

That the symbolism implicit in the Wilton Diptych was of the deepest importance to Richard and his belief in the Divine Right of Kings is emphasized again in his treatment of Westminster Abbey, the venerable shrine of Edward the Confessor and the place where English kings were, and still are, crowned. Richard had a special interest in the Abbey, the northern porch was built during his reign and he contributed to the building of the nave. He often went there during times of difficulty and, on at least one occasion, had Members of Parliament swear an oath of allegiance to him in front of the shrine of Edward. He was generous towards the Abbey giving it many gifts, including banners of St Edward and St Edmund and vestments embroidered with the arms of not only these kings but also his own and those of his queen as well. On these vestments were also shown the Virgin and John the Baptist. The placing of other chapels around the Shrine of Edward the Confessor mirrors the arrangement in the Wilton Diptych. At the apex of the old church stands the shrine itself. To its north is a little chapel dedicated to St Mary and St John the Baptist, whilst on the equivalent position on the south is the chapel of St Edmund. Richard planned for his own tomb to be placed next to that of the Confessor himself and just across the aisle from the chapel of St Edmund. Clearly, then, Richard wanted to be in the same saintly company after death as he believed he was in life. However, his special devotion to John the Baptist, who on the Diptych is the saint who actually touches and presents him to the Virgin, is made clear from the inscription above his tomb: *O clemens Christe — cui devotus fuit iste; Votis Baptiste salves quem pretulit iste*. This translates as: 'O merciful Christ to whom he (Richard) was devoted, save him through the prayers of the Baptist who presented him'. This prayer, humble enough on the surface seems almost blasphemous in its implications, for, of course, the person that John the Baptist presents in the Gospels is Jesus Christ. The implication is that Richard wants to become like Jesus himself, whose ministry began with his baptism in the Jordan; he wants to become an initiate after the same order as Christ. But was this just a private obsession of a king whose birthday happened to be January 6 or is there something more to it than is apparent on the surface? Was Richard acting alone or was he indeed in touch with a secret current of ideas centred on a mystical tradition associated with the Baptist and the Magi? I believe the latter proposition to be true and that this current had its source in the Byzantine Empire and was brought back to Europe at the time of the Crusades.

## The Gothic Magi

The Crusading movement began officially in November 1095 with the Council of Clermont called by Pope Urban II. However, there is a strong tradition in Burgundy that there had already been a secret gathering of thirty-six bishops at Autun earlier in the year and that it was here that the first vows to go to Jerusalem had been made.[7] Whilst of course there were many cathedrals and large abbeys in Western Europe with foundations hundreds of years old, prior to the Crusades there were no buildings with characteristic pointed windows and doorways of the Gothic style. Older churches, such as Durham cathedral, which were executed in the so-called Romanesque or Norman style, offered limited opportunities for glasswork. The structure of the buildings was heavy with enormously thick pillars and supporting walls allowing only very small windows. They were, therefore, rather dark and gloomy places. Most decoration was in the form of murals as there was little opportunity to use stained glass. The advent of the Gothic, with flying buttresses taking the weight of the roof and much smaller columns inside, enabled the builders to make much greater use of glass. Suddenly churches became temples of light, thereby emphasizing the connection between these holy establishments and the kingdom of heaven which they were designed to represent. The light streaming through the windows was refracted in brilliant colours, changing and modifying the atmosphere inside according to the intensity of the sun and which windows it was illuminating at any given time of day. These new churches, orientated towards the east and often with large rose windows above the west portico, were de facto temples of the sun. As instruments for raising the human spirit they are unrivalled even today; yet, their appearance on the landscape of Europe was as sudden as that of the pyramids in Egypt. Clearly the impulse that brought about this development was already fully formed before the first of these temples, Chartres Cathedral, had appeared on the drawing board. The inference must be that this knowledge was brought back from the East in the twelfth century by Crusaders, the question is from where? For at the time the churches of Constantinople and Jerusalem were not of this type, they were mostly round buildings and lacked the pointed arch.

The purpose of a cathedral was multifold. On the one hand it was the seat of the local bishop and, therefore, had to reflect the dignity and prestige of his office but, on the other, it also had to function as a textbook of instruction for educating an illiterate populace. This was done principally through the imagery employed, in glass and stone, depicting stories contained in the Bible. The visit of the three kings to Bethlehem was always a favourite. At Chartres, probably the most enigmatic of all the Gothic cathedrals, there is a large stained glass window telling the whole story of the Nativity and several panels show the three kings. In the first they meet Herod, then they visit the Virgin and Child and finally, having been warned by the angel, return home by a different route. The star of Bethlehem features prominently in these windows. It is with Mary and Joseph in the stable at the time of the actual birth and it guides the Magi both to Bethlehem and, peculiarly, is still with them when they are awoken by the angel.

Probably every cathedral in Europe had, at one time, one or more windows depicting the story of the Magi but at Autun in Burgundy, where the secret convocation of bishops took place in 1095, their story is told in stone. The ground on which Autun Cathedral was to rise was given to Bishop Étienne de Bagé by the Duke of Burgundy, a cousin of the Pope Calixtus II in 1119. Work began on the site the following year in 1120 and the cathedral was finished twenty-five years later in 1145. The Magi story is charmingly represented in three different scenes carved on capitals by a great but enigmatic sculptor called Gislebertus. Little is known of him but fortunately his work, though damaged, has survived to the present day. In the first scene the Magi are shown presenting themselves to Herod. In the second they make their offerings, the frankincense and myrrh being contained in round pots whilst the gold is in a small chest. In the third, and most amusing scene, they are shown, still wearing their crowns tucked up together in bed. Above them shines the star and one of them, who unlike the others has his eyes open, is being touched on the hand by the angel, who once more is anxious to warn them to leave by a different route.

As well as stained glass windows and sculptures, cathedrals would normally have contained many pictures, either painted on the walls or on canvass. Such pictures tend to abide by a definite canon in their construction. Mary is shown seated, the baby Jesus on her lap, Joseph her husband in close attendance. They are dressed in simple clothes, hers traditionally consisting of an outer robe of blue over an inner tunic of red. Usually, she has her head covered with a blue hood or shawl but sometimes she is shown with a more contemporary head-dress. Nearly always she has a halo or golden light, indicating that she is a saint. The three Magi, by contrast, are usually shown richly adorned and dressed, with large retinues of servants and followers. Coming from the Orient, they are exotic and sometimes are accompanied by strange animals, such as tame leopards, as well as camels to show that they come from the East. In the European tradition at least, the Magi are invariably kings in their own right and they therefore wear crowns (though sometimes these are removed in deference to the King of Kings before them). One of the kings, generally the oldest, kneels before the Virgin and Child either presenting his gift or kissing the foot of Jesus. The others stand deferentially in the background, awaiting their turn to do the same thing. Again by tradition, one of them is black, either an African or an Indian from the subcontinent. Needless to say, none of these details is to be found in the Matthew account which is terse to say the least. However, the cult of the Magi though popular in France as well as in Britain was to reach its apotheosis in neither of these countries but in Germany, or rather the Holy Roman Empire. How this came about is another story and it was to be some years before I would find myself standing before what purports to be the shrine in which their very bones are housed. Long before this I was on another quest: to find out whether there were any living Masters in possession today of the secret knowledge that I believed had been the motivation behind the building of the Gothic cathedrals.

# CHAPTER 2

✴

# Meeting with a Magus

In May 1973, following my return from Israel, I found myself on a train from London to Britain's famous Spa town of Cheltenham. I was on my way to meet John Godolphin Bennett, a remarkable man whose autobiography I had read the previous year. Bennett, then in his seventies, was at that time running an experimental, esoteric school at Sherborne House, a large country mansion a bus ride from Cheltenham. Advertisements for this school indicated that it was a place where students could learn sacred dance, meditation and other techniques for personal development. I was keen to find out what these might be. I was also more than a little curious about Bennett himself as he seemed, from what I had read, to be an English gentleman philosopher and not at all like the fashionable, Indian 'gurus' of the time. In fact he appeared to belong to another age altogether.

I arrived mid-morning on a bright Saturday and was greeted affably by his wife Elizabeth, a busy lady who had something of the air of a public school matron. The building was large and old-fashioned and one could imagine country house parties having taken place there years ago. The whole place had an atmosphere of unreality, as though on walking through the gates one had been time-shifted back to the 1920s. Though the interior was rather shabby, the grounds were magnificent, with acres of carefully mown lawns and attractive flower-beds close to the buildings. I recognized that one of these was laid out in the shape of an enneagram, the nine-pointed symbol discussed extensively by Ouspensky in his last book *In Search of the Miraculous*. This didn't surprise me as I knew that Bennett had at one time been one of

Ouspensky's students. Soon we were joined by Bennett himself, a tall, rather ungainly figure with huge hands and uncontrollable white hair. In his wellington boots and tatty old clothes he looked more like a professional gardener than a philosopher. Explaining to me that he had some urgent matters to attend to, he ushered me outside, grabbing a watering can as we went. Nearby was a small rockery, a secluded area sheltered from public gaze by some trees. In front of it was a pond and it was to this that he now led me. 'Adrian' he said, 'would you be so kind as to water the rockery? I won't be long, perhaps half an hour at the outside, then you may have twenty minutes of my time to discuss whatever you wish.' With that he pressed the watering can into my hands and, leaving me to the silence of my surroundings, strode off back to the house. Somewhat peeved and not a little impatient, I filled the can from the pool and examined the serried ranks of pansies and petunias. Though I should perhaps have known better, this was not at all what I had in mind. I had travelled over a hundred miles to talk to the great man about dervishes and had expected, if not exactly red carpet treatment, at least to be given a cup of tea on arrival. Instead, I found myself all alone in a strange garden tending border plants. This was not what I had come for and, after filling the can a few times and watering those plants nearest to the front of the bed, I sat down and started thinking about what I should ask him during my twenty minutes. After what seemed like an age, he returned and immediately began an inspection of my work. Looking beyond the front rows of flowers to the back of the beds he noted the still parched conditions prevalent in that area. I flushed with embarrassment realizing all of a sudden that what I had taken to be a task of little importance, had in reality been some sort of test which I had clearly just failed.

Leaving the garden we went back inside the building for a cup of tea and the promised chat. This took place in his study, which as I remember it was a tiny room on the first floor. Inviting me in he offered me a chair next to a plain wooden desk. 'You are now sitting in the chair in which Ouspensky sat when writing *In Search of the Miraculous*. We may never meet again and you have twenty minutes of my time to discuss anything you like. So have you any questions you want answered?' I had read *In Search of the Miraculous* several years previously, whilst travelling in Sweden and been greatly interested in its contents, not least its presumption that there were still Masters of Wisdom – like the Biblical Magi – living in the East. Now, I not only found myself sitting

in its author's chair but in front of me was one of the few living people
who had studied with him personally and could tell me more about this
strange book. Where had the ideas it contained originally come from?
Did Ouspensky know more than he had written? Was there still as he
seemed to imply, a secret brotherhood of living initiates in the Near
East? All these and many more were the questions I had long wanted
to put to Bennett. However, as I sat there, my mind which till then
had been filled with ideas, now became a complete blank. I shuffled
nervously, unable now to think of a single thing, for suddenly nothing
seemed very important. As the atmosphere grew stronger, instead
of asking intelligent, philosophical questions, I burst out laughing. I
laughed not at him or at anything else in particular but simply at the
contradictions inherent in my situation. I felt like the man in the fairy
tale who when offered three wishes can think of nothing better to ask
for than a sausage. Eventually, vital minutes having ticked by, I pulled
myself together and we began to talk about destiny. At the time I did
not understand what he meant by this. It was only later when I was
able to read certain of his books that were not published during his
lifetime that I was able to grasp the true significance of what we had
discussed.

In Bennett's parlance the words 'destiny' and 'fate' have totally
different meanings. Fate, he said, includes everything that is beyond
our control and gives the framework in which our lives are conducted.
Thus, the colour of our eyes, the race, nation and family in which we
are born, our astrological horoscope, our aptitudes and talents are all
part and parcel of our fate. All this is put succinctly in the book *Deeper
Man*, which was published posthumously from his notes:

There is not only the decision to be born, but the choice of where
to be born, through which parents and with what heredity . . .
The new life that comes carries a certain pattern; it has a shape
and a form and these are inevitable limitations. The most obvious
is the genetic pattern through which the child has its hereditary
endowments, half of which come from the father and half from the
mother. At the moment that the father's seed enters the mother's
ovum, the pattern of the physical life is fixed. Then there is the
pattern of fate which does not originate from the father and mother
but is said to be fixed by the environment of planetary influences
at the moment of conception. The physical heredity and the 'astral

heredity' or fate are both fixed at the moment of conception and are the laws that govern the new life.[1]

Fate, sometimes called luck, operates throughout life bringing us opportunities, introducing us to people such as future wives or husbands, and generally shaping the way things happen. Destiny, however, was something completely different: it was, he said, our soul's task and purpose for coming into life.

> Besides the physical pattern transmitted genetically and the 'spirit pattern' or fate, there is a higher level of order that can be called *destiny* . . . The child's destiny is unique, given to the child independently of who its parents are. It does not come from them and it does not come from anything at all 'outside' of the child. We can say that it comes from God. It is to do with what he has to fulfil by being born and it is through this that there is a power to choose the corresponding conditions of life. But it does not have unlimited power. Sometimes a match cannot be made between the pattern of destiny and the conditions of life. The conception will go wrong: there is a failure to conceive, or physical difficulties or miscarriage; something which prevents the destiny from being embodied. Or it may be born and it will turn out that the fate or conditions of life do not permit the destiny to be realised. Children with very high destinies are very rare in the world and special conditions are arranged in order to ensure the conditions of their conception and birth.[2]

Success and failure in life depended on the degree to which we fulfilled our destiny, which might or might not harmonize with our fate. Destiny was something active whereas fate was in a sense passive. It was linked with the concept of personal 'Will' as the source of purpose and manifested in the individual as ambition. One of the principle functions of his esoteric school, therefore, was to awaken his students to their soul's purpose, for only by fulfilling one's destiny could one have any lasting satisfaction in life.

Bennett himself had clearly been marked with a special destiny. As a young man he had fought in the trenches during the First World War but, in 1918, was wounded and sent back to England to recover. Whilst on sick leave he learnt Turkish[3] and applied for the position of junior intelligence officer in Constantinople. From then on his life took a new turn, his close brush with death having changed his perceptions. The First World War led to many political changes not only in Europe but also in the Middle East. Throughout much of the nineteenth century the Ottoman Empire had been known as 'the sick man of Europe'. A series of wars and revolutions had already removed Greece, Serbia and a collection of other Balkan states from the control of the Ottomans and now that the sultan had made the disastrous mistake of siding with the Germans and Austrians, the Middle Eastern lands of Arabia, Mesopotamia, Syria and Palestine were also lost. These provinces now became British and French protectorates, with echoes of the old Crusader states of some 800 years earlier. Even worse for the Turks, in the aftermath of the Great War, Turkey itself was threatened with dismemberment when in 1920 a Greek army, under protection from the French and British navies, landed at Smyrna. The Greeks already occupied Eastern Thrace as far as the Chatalja Lines[4] and were pressuring the allies to allow them to take over Constantinople. Under pressure from the French and Italians, the sultan signed the Treaty of Sèvres in August of that year by which the remaining parts of Anatolia were to be divided up into 'spheres of influence' between France, Britain and Italy. This would effectively have destroyed Turkey as an independent state and naturally enough provoked outrage amongst its people. As a result the Nationalist movement, led by Mustafa Kemal (Ataturk), gained in strength. A war of independence followed, leading to the withdrawal of British and French forces and the defeat of the Greeks. On 17 November 1922, Mohammed VI, the last sultan, escaped to Malta on a British ship: the *Malaya*, and, on 29 October 1923, Turkey became a republic.

To emphasize the break with the past, Ataturk, Turkey's first president, moved the capital from Constantinople (now called Istanbul) to Ankara. He also secularized the country, creating a division between mosque and state that persists to this day. The Roman instead of the Arabic alphabet was adopted for the writing of Turkish and many other changes were made, including the abolition of the Fez and the suppression of religious movements such as the whirling dervishes.[5] Almost overnight Turkey went from being a Mediaeval to a modern state, turning its back on tradition as it did so.

It was into this mêlée that Bennett entered following his near death experience in 1918. He quickly made his mark as an intelligence officer and when British forces were withdrawn in late 1920, he found himself left in charge of all British intelligence covering the huge area of what had once been the Ottoman Empire, from the Dalmatian coast to the frontiers of Persia, Egypt and Russia. He was, in a very real sense, 'our man in Constantinople' and even though he was still only 22 years of age, had the staff rank of Lieutenant Colonel.

Whilst in the role of spy-master general for the British Empire, a job he clearly loved, he developed a strong friendship with one of the Ottoman Princes called Sabaheddin. He was the son of Damad Mahmoud Pasha, a famous Turkish reformer and vizier, who had been exiled by the despotic Abdul Hamid II. He was also a nephew of the reigning sultan, Mohammed VI. Prince Sabaheddin was a highly cultured man who preferred to speak French rather than Turkish and who had inherited his father's liberal, political views. He was also deeply interested in mysticism, had studied the Theosophy[6] of Madame Blavatsky in depth and was a personal friend of Rudolf Steiner, the founder of the offshoot anthroposophical movement. In a sense Sabaheddin represented a breed that would soon be entirely extinct. He was a living link with a past that went back to the Age of Byzantium, with a world that had all but disappeared even in 1920. Bennett, the tall, somewhat gauche, young spy, was intrigued by this small, delicate man with his exquisite manners and the feeling seems to have been mutual. Once a week they would dine together, sometimes alone, sometimes with other guests, such as Bennett's paramour and future wife, Mrs Winifred Beaumont. These meals always took place at the Palace of Kuru Chesme, for Sabaheddin never went out at night for fear of assassination, and must have been quite grand occasions. There, late into the night they would discuss philosophy and mysticism, subjects made more real by the baroque splendour of Kuru Chesme. Through Sabaheddin's influence Bennett also began to take an interest in hypnotism and other types of unexplained phenomena. It was an interest that was to change his life and ultimately to lead him some fifty years later to establish the 'International Academy of Continuous Education' at Sherborne House, which I was to visit in 1972.

## In Search of Miracles

In 1920, Constantinople, or Istanbul as it was soon to be called, was awash with refugees of all descriptions. The aftermath of the First

World War, the revolutions in Russia, political troubles in Armenia and the Greek invasion of Turkey caused large displacements of population. Many of these people, Russians, Greeks, Turks, Armenians, and others ended up in Constantinople — either as their final destination or, more usually, *en route* to somewhere else. As spy-master-in-chief for the British Empire and friend of Ottoman princes, Bennett came into contact with many colourful figures, including a recent arrival from the Soviet Union: Piotr Demianovich Ouspensky. He, even more than Sabaheddin, was to have a profound effect upon the direction of the rest of Bennett's life.

Ouspensky, a journalist from St Petersburg with strongly anti-Communist views, was a man of extraordinary intellect who possessed the rare ability of being able to make complicated ideas seem simple and simple ideas profound. Who are we? Where do we come from? What is our destiny? These were questions that bedevilled and perplexed him more than most people. He realized that we live in a world full of complexity and contradiction but he also believed in the existence of Masters. Throughout history there has been a belief that somewhere there exists a higher, yet still human, authority than the professors and politicians in our midst; a hidden school or community of the enlightened who, if they do not actually control the destiny of mankind, at least know the answers to these most pressing questions. The belief in Masters of Wisdom, for such indeed we must call them, is an important if understated part of every major religion. Yet, who were these people? Where did they come from? What evidence was there for their existence? According to Theosophy they were the instruments of God, a secret society of initiates propelling and urging the world towards its greater destiny. Yet because, unlike the Pope or Dalai Lama, these people were unknown, Ouspensky was unable to put a face to them. Like a forensic scientist he could only recognize their actions retrospectively from the traces they had left behind. He could see where they had been but not where they were now or where they were going to be in the future.

Undeterred, prior to the First World War, he set out on a quest to find the Masters for himself. He made an extensive tour of India, Ceylon and Egypt in search of whatever strange knowledge might still be hidden in those exotic countries. Like Sabaheddin and many other people of that time he had been greatly influenced by the writings of H.P. Blavatsky, the mother of Theosophy, and was hopeful that if he looked in the right places he might stumble upon her Masters, or at least meet someone who could give him directions as to where they might be found. Needless to say when he got to India he was deeply disappointed by what he found. He realized that nearly everyone engaged in so-called esoteric work, what we would now call 'New Age', was deluding both himself and others. For every half-genuine teacher of esoteric ideas there were a hundred or a thousand charlatans who preyed upon the weaknesses of others. This, he discovered, was as true of the East as it was of the West.

However, Ouspensky was not just a proto-hippy: he was also a mathematician and philosopher, who had already written a book on the recondite subject of Time and Space. This book, boldly entitled *Tertium Organum*,[7] presented extraordinary and novel ideas concerning consciousness, the reality of Higher Worlds and what this might mean in terms of the physics of time and space. Covering a vast amount of ground – everything from fourth dimensional geometry to the writings of Lao Tzu – it was a genuinely original book. Although Blavatsky's Masters had proved elusive, this book earned him recognition in Russia and was later to gain him access to London society.

Having miraculously survived the Bolshevik Revolution and its aftermath, Ouspensky arrived in Constantinople with a small entourage early on in 1920. Here he met Bennett and, through his influence, was able to get a travel permit enabling him to go to England. In August 1921, he arrived in London and, with the help of Lady Rothermere, wife of the newspaper tycoon and a fan of his *Tertium Organum*, almost immediately drew together a small circle of followers. These were mostly readers of two fringe magazines *The New Age* and *The Quest*. In 1931 Ouspensky published his second book, *A New Model of the Universe*, largely based on essays he had written during his searching days before the First World War. In the 1934 Preface to the second edition of this book, he reiterated his belief in the existence in the past (and perhaps the present) of people of Higher Mind. This (Higher Mind), he says is responsible for all the great works of art we see in the world such as the Gospels, Upanishads, the Great Sphinx of Giza and other memorials.[8] In his first chapter called 'Esotericism and Modern Thought', he goes into this subject in some depth, linking esoteric knowledge to the work of schools under the guidance of such Masters for whom Higher Mind is not just a concept but a reality. Drawing from his own experiences he makes it clear that esoteric knowledge is not lightly come by:

> Esotericism is remote and inaccessible, but every man who learns
> of or guesses at the existence of esotericism has the chance of
> approaching a school or may hope to meet people who will help
> him and show him the way . . .
> . . . For the gates of the world of the miraculous may be opened
> only to him who seeks.[9]

For Ouspensky, it was self-evident that civilization was not only caused
by the work of esoteric schools but could only continue as long as it
was sustained by continuous help from these hidden sources. Thus,
a decline in religion, that is to say in the numbers of people seeking
initiation into 'the mysteries', was bound to lead to a corresponding
decay in civilization. Scientific or technical knowledge was no substitute
for this human evolution for it was only through the latter that it was
possible to have contact with Higher Mind and without this the human
race was without guidance and therefore bound to degenerate.

It was in a later essay contained in the same book that Ouspensky
was to elaborate further on the link between esotericism and our
knowledge of what really makes up history. He had little interest in
the 'history of crime', the sort of thing contained in old newsreels and
which is presented in its unfolding every night as 'The News' on our TV
screens. He was much more concerned with the secret transmission of
ideas, the way that esoteric knowledge has passed through the ages from
one group to another, from one society, religion or even civilization
to another. This, the trace of the workings of his beloved Masters of
Wisdom, was to his way of thinking the real history of the world.

Between the wars, Ouspensky became a well-known figure in
London's rather formal esoteric circles. However, the private lectures
he gave and which were, on occasion, attended by such people as
Aldous Huxley and A.E. Waite, as well as A.R. Orage, the editor of
*The New Age*, had little to do with his own quest but were based on
ideas taught to him by another Russian: George Ivanovich Gurdjieff.
He was an Armenian-Greek who had grown up in the turbulent region
of the Russo-Turkish border during the latter part of the nineteenth
century. A great traveller and seeker after truth, Gurdjieff had wandered
extensively throughout the Near, Middle and even Far East in search of
lost knowledge. During these travels he claimed to have come across
many strange, unknown monasteries and temples preserving not only
theoretical knowledge but practical techniques for the transformation

of man. Like Madame Blavatsky a generation earlier, he now brought these ideas back to Russia proper, letting it be known that his 'work' was the real thing.

## The Master from Armenia

George Ivanovich Gurdjieff was undoubtedly one of the strangest men of this century. He was born in Armenia, which is a rugged, mountainous country sandwiched between Iran, Turkey, Georgia and Azerbaijan. As a political entity it has seldom been free from outside control and, throughout most of the nineteenth century, was bitterly contested over by Russia and the Ottoman Empire. The town of Kars, where Gurdjieff grew up, is now firmly on the Turkish side of the border but, when he was a boy, it was in Imperial Russia. It was therefore, at that time, a more favourable place for Christians than it is today and he was able to gain an education at the local Russian cathedral school. This, however, was not enough for a boy with a thirst for knowledge. At an early age he, like Ouspensky, became convinced that the ancient world had been in possession of knowledge which we have lost in our helter-skelter pursuit of materialism and he, therefore, began a lifelong quest for this antique wisdom. Over a period of years he made a series of long journeys going as far east as Tibet and India, and west as Egypt and Abyssinia. However, most of his travels were in Turkestan and Mesopotamia at the centre of this vast territory.

Gurdjieff was convinced that people of ancient times were, in some respects at least, more developed than we are today. That, whereas, we have made great technological progress over the last few centuries and learnt how to harness energies to raise our living standards, there has at the same time been a concomitant loss of other kinds of knowledge. This knowledge, connected with our spiritual, psychological and moral welfare has always been the province of religion. He was convinced that even intelligent, well-educated people living in the twentieth century are woefully ignorant about such matters when compared with their remote ancestors, that in a sense we are ourselves living in a 'Dark Age' and not a period of enlightenment as we are wont to think. Our science, though liberating us from the more disagreeable aspects of nature, is binding us ever more firmly to the material world and making it increasingly difficult for us to find our true purpose or destiny. Thus, our world and our place in it is not as we imagine.

Our values are upside down, so much so that we have stopped even asking what life is for let alone finding the answer.

All, however, was not entirely lost. Gurdjieff believed that intelligent and knowledgeable people from bygone times had anticipated that this would happen. They had expected that their own civilizations would, in time, be swept away and that profound ignorance would rule the Earth. Accordingly, they had encoded the most important aspects of their knowledge and belief systems into what Gurdjieff called 'legominisms'. Often these were material structures, such as temples or pyramids, which could be expected to stand for thousands of years. In other cases they were writings or even traditional songs and dances. There were even such legominisms as the pack of playing cards, which in its four suits of thirteen cards embodies, in shorthand, a whole range of esoteric ideas. By all of these methods he believed that knowledge had been preserved and passed on to future generations. He now set out on a series of long journeys in search of this lost knowledge.

According to Bennett, the searching period of Gurdjieff's life lasted for some sixteen years from 1891 to 1907 and culminated with his being allowed into a secret temple run by an esoteric society called the Sarmoung or Sarman[10] Brotherhood. Most of chapter 5 of Gurdjieff's semi-autobiographical book, *Meetings with Remarkable Men*, concerns his search for this mysterious brotherhood, which he believed was founded in Babylon around 2500 BC.[11] This is roughly the time when the Egyptians were busy building the Great Pyramid. In a later epoch, Bennett believed that descendants of the same secret brotherhood of the enlightened had initiated Pythagoras, the father of western philosophy, whilst he was a captive resident in Babylon. He remarks that there is an old tradition that Pythagoras travelled the world looking for knowledge. Whilst he was resident in Egypt the Persian king, Cambyses, compelled all the wise men of that country, including Pythagoras, to go to Babylon. This event is recorded in Iamblichus' (Greek Neoplatonic philosopher (c. AD 260–330)) *Life of Pythagoras*:

> . . . he [Pythagoras] visited all of the Egyptian priests, acquiring all the wisdom each possessed. He thus passed twenty-two years in the sanctuaries of the temples, studying astronomy and geometry, and being initiated in no casual manner or superficial manner in all the mysteries of the Gods. At length, however, he was taken captive by the soldiers of Cambyses, and carried off to Babylon. Here he was

overjoyed to be associated with the Magi, who instructed him in their venerable knowledge, and in the most perfect worship of the Gods. Through their assistance, likewise, he studied and completed arithmetic, music and all the other sciences. After twelve years, about the fifty-sixth year of his age, he returned to Samos.[12]

Bennett makes reference to another legend that, whilst resident in Babylon, Pythagoras may even have met Zoroaster (Zarathustra). He was the founder of the Persian religion that bears his name and is traditionally believed to have been the mentor of Cambyses' father, Cyrus. This story is contained in another *Life of Pythagoras*, this time by Iamblichus' teacher, Porphyry:

In Egypt he [Pythagoras] lived with the priests, and learned the language and wisdom of the Egyptians, and their three kinds of letters, the epistolographic, the hieroglyphic, and symbolic, whereof one imitates the common way of speaking, while the others express the sense of allegory and parable. In Arabia he conferred with the king. In Babylon he associated with the other Chaldeans, especially attaching himself to Zaratas [Zoroaster], by whom he was purified from the pollutions of his past life, and taught the things from which a virtuous man ought to be free.[13]

Earlier on Porphyry explains how the different ancient cultures excelled in one or another science and how Pythagoras learnt from them all:

As to his knowledge, it is said that he learned the mathematical sciences from the Egyptians, Chaldeans and Phoenicians; for of old the Egyptians excelled in geometry, the Phoenicians in numbers and proportions, and the Chaldeans in astronomical theorems, divine rites, and the worship of the Gods; other secrets concerning the course of life he received and learned from the Magi.[14]

Without going into details concerning his travels, it is evident that Gurdjieff modelled his life on that of Pythagoras. The legend of the father of Greek philosophy being initiated by Babylonian Magi may have been in his mind when he set out on his own quest. Certainly, according to Bennett, 'to some extent' Gurdjieff modelled his own later academy on the Pythagoras' school.[15]

In the course of his travels Gurdjieff met up with a number of like-minded people, themselves also thirsty for lost knowledge. To lessen the burden on each of them, they formed a semi-formal society called the 'The Seekers of Truth' and agreed to pool the results of their researches. One of the other members of this group was an Armenian friend of his called Pogossian. Like Gurdjieff, he was a young man with some free time on his hands and shared the former's interests in mysteries. To further this interest and in pursuit of ancient wisdom, they made several journeys together, which included a period spent squatting amongst the ruins of the ancient Armenian capital of Ani and carrying out a little archaeology of their own.[16] Today it is inconceivable that a couple of Armenian youths could amuse themselves by digging amongst these ruins but, in the 1890s, archaeology was in its infancy and still an amateur sport. It was then possible for two determined young men to set up camp amongst the old churches and palaces of their forebears and to do pretty much as they liked.

Digging around they found an underground passage and breaking through a wall at the end of this, they entered a small, arched chamber that had obviously been a monk's cell. As it turned out, there was little in the room other than some broken pots and the rotten remains of what must once have been some furniture. However, in one corner of the room there was a niche and here they found some ancient parchments. As Ani had been destroyed by the Turks in 1064, the parchments had to date from at least the eleventh century and were possibly much older. Though on being exposed to the air, some of the documents immediately crumbled into dust, most of them remained intact. With mounting excitement, they carefully gathered these up and made their way back home to Alexandropol.[17] Here, in relative comfort, they could examine their treasure and where necessary call on expert help to aid in the difficult work of decipherment.

The parchments turned out to be letters between two monks, one of whom was named 'Arem', and were written in a very old form of Armenian. Amongst this correspondence, which mostly dealt with ordinary church affairs, was included one letter that, from their point of view, was more interesting than the rest. This made mention of the mysterious 'Sarmoung Brotherhood', a name Gurdjieff had come across before in an Armenian book called *Merkharvat*, and stated that at the time the letter was written, their chief monastery was 'in the valley of Izrumin, three days' journey from Nivssi'. Pogossian and Gurdjieff

quickly worked out that Nivssi was the ancient name for the city of
Mosul in Northern Iraq. This lies near the ruins of Nineveh and, at
the time the letter was written, it was the capital of a province called
Nievi. Given the clues found in the letter, they decided it should not be
too difficult to find the valley of Izrumin and, assuming it still existed,
the mysterious monastery of the Sarmoung Brotherhood. Accordingly,
when the opportunity arose, they packed their bags and set out on
their quest.

The journey turned out to be more difficult than they had anticipated.
The usual political tensions between Turks, Armenians and Kurds meant
that they had to go the hard way to their destination over Mount Egri
Dagh, disguising themselves as Caucasian Tartars to avoid being drawn
into these local ethnic conflicts. It took them exactly two months
from the time they had crossed the Arax River, still the border

Map 1

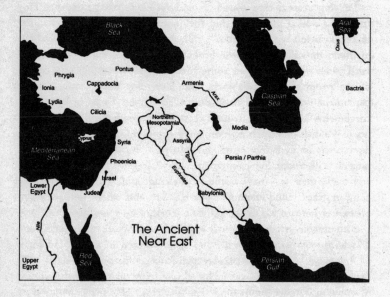

between Turkey and Armenia, to reach a town that Gurdjieff rather enigmatically calls 'Z'. Things were going well and they were nearing their destination when disaster struck:

> Exactly two months after crossing the river Arax, we finally came to the town of Z, beyond which we had to go through a certain pass in the direction of Syria. In this pass, before reaching the famous waterfall of K, we were to turn off towards Kurdistan and it was somewhere along this road that we expected to find the place which was the chief objective of our journey.
>
> In our further peregrinations, since we had by this time sufficiently adapted ourselves to surrounding conditions, everything went along fairly smoothly – until one unexpected accident changed all our intentions and plans.[18]

The accident referred to was Pogossian being bitten by a very poisonous spider. Now, instead of proceeding to the presumed location of the valley of Izrumin, they made their way to a town called 'N'. Here an Armenian priest was sympathetic to their plight and proved willing to put them up whilst Pogossian recovered from the emergency surgery that Gurdjieff had had to carry out in order to save him from the spider's bite. They ended up staying with him for almost a month and, during that time, became very friendly with the priest who confided in them that he had in his possession an ancient map. This turned out to be drawn not on paper but vellum and, according to the priest, it had been in his family for generations. When Gurdjieff first saw it he was quite overwhelmed:

> I was seized with violent trembling, which was all the more violent because I was inwardly trying to restrain myself and not show my excitement. What I saw – was it not precisely what I had spent long months of sleepless nights thinking about!
>
> It was a map of 'pre-sand Egypt'.[19]

Abandoning for the moment the search for the Sarmoung monastery, as soon as Pogossian was recovered, they set out for Egypt, bringing with them a copy of the map, which Gurdjieff had surreptitiously made whilst the priest was otherwise engaged. After various other adventures, Gurdjieff, now without Pogossian, found himself in Cairo acting as a tour guide to the Pyramids of Giza. Using his mysterious map, he made a careful study of the area, which had by now become the focus of his quest:

> It must be said that I was spending all my free time walking among these places like one possessed, hoping to find, with the help of my map of pre-sand Egypt, an explanation of the Sphinx and several other monuments of antiquity.[20]

His reasons for abandoning his earlier quest for the Sarmoung Brotherhood and his intense interest in ancient Egypt is not something he explains. Nor does he anywhere say directly that the two are connected yet. However, later on in the book he returns to Asia and, whilst resident in Bukhara, is contacted by an emissary of the Order he had been seeking. He is taken, blindfolded, to their secret monastery hidden away somewhere in an almost inaccessible valley. Whilst there he is initiated into certain secret knowledge and practices. This for him was like finding the Holy Grail.

Between 1907 and 1914 Gurdjieff seems to have largely occupied himself with putting together all the various strands of knowledge he had by then collected into an overall 'system'. This system embracing philosophy, psychology and cosmology, though in some ways similar to Blavatsky's Theosophy, was much more detailed and practical in its application. He allied this theoretical side of his work with a programme of music and dance movements, many of which he claimed to have been taught in the various secret monasteries that he had visited during his travels. It was this comprehensive programme that Ouspensky came across in Moscow in 1916 and which Gurdjieff exported first to Constantinople and then later to Western Europe and America.

Ouspensky met Gurdjieff in Moscow only a few weeks after his own fruitless journey to the East and almost immediately fell under his spell. For four years 'G', as he was known, became his mentor, teaching him many novel and extraordinary ideas. It seemed that at last he had found a genuine teacher, a real Master of Wisdom. In 1920 Gurdjieff opened an institute of his own in France at the château in the village of Avon, on the outskirts of Fontainebleau. Here he taught dance and drama as well as the sort of esoteric matters that had so fascinated Ouspensky during their time together in Russia.

Over the next couple of years Gurdjieff recruited a large number of students, many of them from America. Then, in 1924, after a serious car accident that very nearly killed him, he closed down the institute and switched his attention to writing 'legominisms' of his own. In the course of the next few years he penned three 'series' with the collective title *All and Everything*. The first of these was a doorstep of a tome in three books entitled *Beelzebub's Tales to His Grandson*. This strange work, written in a style which is both prolix and difficult to read, is in the form of science fiction. Written from the perspective of a fallen but now repentant angel, (the now elderly Beelzebub, who for the sins of his youth had been condemned to live his life in exile on the fringes of the universe in the Solar System), it describes his journey home to his own, better placed, planet: Karatas. To while away the time on this long space flight, Beelzebub amuses his young grandson, who is travelling with him, with stories about his life. In particular he talks about the history of planet Earth and why its strange people are so different from equivalent intelligent life forms on other planets in the universe. Both witty and mocking, *Beelzebub's Tales* is a clever mixture of instruction and satire which defies unravelling by all but the most persevering of readers. This is no accident. Bennett records that Gurdjieff deliberately obscured his meaning in *Beelzebub's Tales* so that only the most persistent of his readers would understand what he was saying:

> He himself [Gurdjieff] would listen to chapters read aloud and if he found that the key passages were taken too easily – and therefore almost inevitably too superficially – he would rewrite them in order, as he put it, to 'bury the dog deeper'. When people corrected him and said that he surely meant 'bury the bone deeper', he would turn on them and say it is not 'bones' but the dog that you have to find. The dog is Sirius the dog star, which stands for the spirit of wisdom in the Zoroastrian tradition.[21]

Gurdjieff's second book, *Meetings With Remarkable Men* – the one which contains the story of his search for the Sarmoung Brotherhood – is on the face of it an altogether more straightforward work. Superficially it is an autobiography but it is really more than this. Threaded into the narrative are various morality tales and object lessons on how different types of people can make best use of their talents. There are also clues, not explicitly given, as to where one might find the fount of all this wisdom. Unlike *Beelzebub's Tales*, the style is fluent and easy to read, yet *Remarkable Men* is in many ways even more esoteric. His third book *Life Is Only Real Then, When I Am* only exists in fragmentary form: he himself apparently destroyed some chapters before publication because he felt they told too much. What is left is a description of some of his teaching methods, again autobiographical, which in part explain some of his strange, and at times outrageous, behaviour towards his pupils. A short work, it contains much less of interest to the uncommitted reader than the earlier books and, indeed, was not even published until the late 1970s.

Though in 1924 Ouspensky was to break entirely with Gurdjieff, he never doubted that the teachings he had received were of value or that his former teacher had been sent as the emissary of the sort of school of wisdom which he himself had been unable to locate in either Egypt or India. Right up until his death in 1948 Ouspensky continued to give lectures on the 'System', as Gurdjieff's rather eclectic collection of ideas and techniques was known. After the Second World War, he wrote up his lecture notes, interspersed with reminiscences from his early days with Gurdjieff in the form of a book, which was eventually published posthumously in 1950 as *In Search of the Miraculous*.

The original working title of *In Search*, which was retained in the published edition as a subtitle, was *Fragments of an Unknown Teaching*. This seems to have been an oblique reference to another seminal work, *Fragments of a Faith Forgotten*, by G.R.S. Mead, the leading British Theosophist of his day. Mead was the editor of *The Quest* magazine. His monumental works, *Thrice Greatest Hermes* and *Fragments of a Faith Forgotten* were and still are seminal works on the subjects of Gnosticism and the Hermetic Tradition. Many of Ouspensky's early meetings were held at the offices of *The Quest* so the two men had close dealings. What they discussed between themselves has not been recorded but Mead, then quite an old man, seems to have been supportive towards the Russian émigré. Ouspensky, by adopting the title *Fragments of an Unknown Teaching* must have wanted to indicate to 'those with the eyes to see' the connection between the ideas he was expounding in *In Search of the Miraculous* and Mead's work on Gnostic Christianity.

Ouspensky's London groups were very successful, spawning after his death a whole series of societies and splinter groups. Bennett, following his return from Turkey, became one of Ouspensky's chief pupils and thus it was that he quite literally inherited his master's chair – the one on which I was myself to sit, rather uncomfortably, some twenty-five years later. Having been with Gurdjieff too during his dying days in 1949, Bennett himself was sure that this master's mantle had also passed to him. It seemed to him that his destiny lay in continuing their work and, to this end, he started schools of his own, first at Kingston on the outskirts of London and, later, at Sherborne.

Since his death in 1949, many books have been written about the Gurdjieff 'work' but always hanging over it has been a question mark: was he simply promoting a cult of his own invention or did he indeed make contact with a hidden source of knowledge? Was he, as he implied, the emissary of a secret Brotherhood – the Masters of Wisdom talked of by Blavatsky and searched for in vain by Ouspensky – or simply yet another charlatan? These questions, which at first sight should only be of interest to his followers, actually have a much greater significance. If he really did find the Masters, the successors of the Magi who initiated Pythagoras, then not only does it make his own work much more interesting for the purposes of objective study but it also has great implications for the rest of us.

## Gurdjieff and the Gnostic tradition

In Search of the Miraculous, Ouspensky's most famous book, continues to be the Bible of the many schools and groups flowing from the Gurdjieff tradition. A deceptively simple book it is a veritable mine of information providing not only a compendium of strange beliefs but a record of how these were originally presented. I came across these 'fragments of an unknown teaching' whilst travelling in Sweden in 1971. I had already read Tertium Organum whilst at university some months earlier but this book was clearly far more esoteric. It was not an easy book to read as the ideas it contained were unfamiliar. It carried a strange energy, the way it was written being both mystifying and enlightening at the same time. Where had these ideas come from? Had Gurdjieff indeed, as Ouspensky believed, really made contact with a secret school? These were questions that were still in the back of my mind when I cycled to Israel some two years later and had time to think about these matters in depth.

According to Ouspensky, Gurdjieff asserted that his work was really 'esoteric Christianity', that is to say derived from secret traditions that are no longer understood by the wider Church. These, he claimed, came originally from Ancient Egypt:

> The Christian church, the Christian form of worship, was not invented by the fathers of the church. It was all taken in ready-made form from Egypt, only not the Egypt that we know but from one which we do not know. This Egypt was in the same place as the other but it existed much earlier. Only small bits of it survived in historical times, and these bits have been preserved in secret and so well that we do not even know they have been preserved.[22]

The concept of esotericism in Christianity is one that today causes raised eyebrows in clerical circles. However, Jesus himself was clearly an esotericist. He taught in parables that were open to interpretation on many levels and, sometimes, he would take the apostles aside and explain the real meaning behind what he was saying. Yet, it is clear from the Gospels that Jesus did not explain everything that he was doing even to his own disciples. Many of his actions and much of what he taught was not understood by his contemporaries for they did not have 'eyes that see or ears that hear'. The ideas that Gurdjieff taught and which Ouspensky codified into a system were heady stuff and very far removed from conventional Christianity. They had a logic and authority of their own which many people, myself included, found intriguing. However, the question remained, were they simply an amalgam of ideas he had read in books blended with certain insights and wiseacreings of his own or had he indeed come across one or more secret schools in the course of his extensive travels? Whilst Gurdjieff was still alive his disciples had little cause to probe too deeply into such questions. The cult that grew up around him was, in any case, self-sufficient and few of his students had either the time or language skills needed to make a serious search of their own in the footsteps of the master. Even following his death, most were content to go on as before, reading, studying and commenting on the writings he left behind whilst building up circles of their own. Bennett, however, was not content with this approach — at least not as a long-term proposition. In the 1950s he made his own search for the sources of Gurdjieff's knowledge. He believed categorically in the existence of the Masters of Wisdom and, indeed, the title of his last book, which he was working on when I met him in 1973 and which was published posthumously in 1975, was *The*

*Masters of Wisdom.* Bennett believed that the Masters existed and that they were connected with Gurdjieff's Sarmoung or Sarman society. With his knowledge of languages he was able to throw light on the etymology of the name and to identify, at least in theory, what this group might represent:

> One such clue given by Gurdjieff is the mention in several passages of the Sarmoun (sic) or Sarman Society. The pronunciation is the same for either spelling and the word can be assigned to old Persian. It does, in fact, appear in some of the Pahlawi (Persian) texts to designate those who preserved the doctrines of Zoroaster. The word can be interpreted in three ways. It is the word for bee, which has always been a symbol of those who collect the precious 'honey' of traditional wisdom and preserve it for future generations. A collection of legends, well known in Armenian and Syrian circles with the title *The Bees*, was revised by Mar Salomon, a Nestorian Archimandrite in the thirteenth century, that is about the time of Jenghis Khan. *The Bees*, refers to a mysterious power transmitted from the time of Zoroaster and made manifest in the time of Christ.
>
> A more obvious rendering is to take the *man* in its Persian meaning as the quality transmitted by heredity and hence a distinguished family or race. It can be the repository of an heirloom or tradition. The word *sar* means head, both literally and in the sense of principal or chief. The combination *sarman* would thus mean the chief repository of the tradition, which has been called 'the perennial philosophy' passed down from generation to generation by 'initiated beings' to use Gurdjieff's description.
>
> And still another possible meaning of the word Sarman is 'those who have been enlightened'; literally those whose heads have been purified.[23]

Leaving Sherborne I had much on my mind. I had spent a weekend taking part in such things as Sacred Dance and Meditation as well as listening to lectures but I did not really feel in harmony with the work. I was also not attracted to the social ideals or the communal living that seemed to be part and parcel of the total Sherborne experience. Whilst not doubting that the school had a great deal to offer, it wasn't what I was looking for. I wanted to find out more about the Masters of Wisdom and I was not convinced that enrolling in Bennett's school would give a broad enough view on the subject. Reluctantly, I packed my bags, sure in my heart that whatever destiny might hold in store, I was not going to find it here. When I walked up the drive on my way to the bus stop I met Bennett seated on a lawnmower. The whole community was observing a day of silence, so he would not say anything as we parted but I did not feel so constrained. As I shook him by the hand and explained my reasons for leaving early he looked at me vacantly, his mind elsewhere. Though I was to meet him on a few more occasions before his death some eighteen months later and even attended some open lectures he gave in London, I was sure that I had made the right decision. Nevertheless, I felt certain that Gurdjieff's Sarmoung Brotherhood, and the strange, eastern lands of mountains and rivers from which they had come, was somehow connected with Matthew's Magi. It was to be over two decades before I could follow up on the trail myself, for whatever destiny might be beckoning, I had a lot more fate to work through first.

# CHAPTER 3

✳

# A Search among the Sufis

Following Gurdjieff's death in October 1949, Bennett, who had spent much time with him during his final months decided to go on a journey to the East in search of the mysterious Sarman Brotherhood. Being fluent in Turkish, the lingua franca of not just Turkey but all of what had once comprised the Ottoman Empire, he determined to concentrate his search in that region. Setting out from his old stamping ground of Istanbul, where he had once worked as a British spy, he was to journey to Konya, Damascus, Jerusalem, Baghdad and Old Babylon before making his way back to Europe.

Bennett was extremely interested in Sufism, the mystical heart of Islam. He records in his autobiography *Witness* how, in 1920, he visited the Constantinople *Tekke* of the Mevlevi, or whirling dervishes, perhaps the most famous of the Sufi Orders.[1] He must have been one of the last Western visitors to see the Mevlevi in practice in Constantinople as soon afterwards their Order, like all the others, was banned by the modernizing Ataturk. At the time he witnessed it, the whirling dance of the felt-hatted dervishes didn't mean very much to him but when, in 1953, he returned to Turkey, one of the first things Bennett did was to revisit the long abandoned *Tekke*. Believing there might be some hidden knowledge contained in its dimensions, he set about measuring the *Sema Hané* or dancing room. He writes:

As I stood on the dust-laden floor and looked at the crumbling woodwork, I saw what the dervish attitude to life had meant to the Turks for more than seven centuries. They had been the leaven of practical mysticism that had saved the religious life of Turkey from degenerating into formalism.[2]

His mystical insights into the power and purpose of Turkish religious architecture was heightened when he visited the Holy City of Konya and there visited the original Mevlevi *Tekke*, where Djellaludin Rumi, the founder of the Order, is himself buried.[3]

> Every day that I spent in Konya I went to the great Mevlevi *Tekke*, the home of the poet Djellaludin Rumi – founder of the order of Mevlevi dervishes. The *Sema Hané* was built in the twelfth century under the direction of his son, Sultan Veled, by the Seljuk Kings of Konya. It is the prototype of three hundred and sixty-five similar buildings, distributed throughout South-west Asia. As I studied it, I became convinced that the size and proportions of the building were derived from some lost art of creating a concentration of psychic energies, that could influence the inner state of those who met in it to worship God.[4]

Inspired by his visit to Rumi's mausoleum but still with no definite itinerary, Bennett proceeded to Adana and then, leaving Turkey for Syria, went on to Aleppo and Damascus. By now he had decided to 'travel and live like a Turk, with little money to spend' and he, therefore, avoided other westerners. In Syria, he visited more *Tekkes* and Holy shrines this time meeting living representatives of the Mevlevi Order, who because they were outside of Turkey were not subject to Ataturk's ban. However, though impressed by the simplicity and religious commitment of the dervishes, he nonetheless felt the calling to move on. He was as anxious to meet the past as the present and was keen to see some of the important archaeological sites that litter this part of the world. Making his way from Syria to Iraq he spent time amongst the ruins of ancient Babylon, the setting of many of Gurdjieff's *Beelzebub's Tales* but his most significant discovery in Iraq was to be a lost valley called Sheikh Adi, the chief sanctuary of a little known people called the Yezidis, though they are sometimes called Yesevis.

Sheikh Adi derives its name from the 'saint' whose shrine it is and who is believed by the Yezidis to have lived thousands of years ago

– perhaps around the time of Abraham. Bennett spent a day visiting the shrine and questioned its custodian, through a Kurdish interpreter. Summing up his impressions in his diary of the time he writes:

> It is my belief that they [the Yezidis] are descended from the ancient Chaldeans. Their own tradition is that they migrated from the South, and they may well be the lost remnants of the Babylonian Magi who disappeared after the time of Alexander of Macedon. [5]

Leaving Sheikh Adi, Bennett made his way back to Constantinople and thence to London. Though for the rest of his life he maintained close relations with various Sufi groups and was deeply attracted by the Islamic religion, he couldn't quite bring himself to cross the divide that lies between cross and crescent and ended his days as a Roman Catholic. Even so, he retained a fascination for another religion that predated both Christianity and Islam and which left a lasting imprint on both: Zoroastrianism. This, the religion of his Babylonian Magi, was he believed, if not the greatest of all the worlds revelations, the one that most nearly succeeded in its practical application. He believed that its teachings were a major element in Gurdjieff's philosophy of self-transformation, as is implied by the latter's remark about Sirius and burying the dog star not the bone. Bennett was also convinced that Zoroaster, the founder of this religion, was the real identity behind a character that Gurdjieff calls 'Ashiata Shiemash' in his book *Beelzebub's Tales*, who succeeds in persuading people to give up animal sacrifice. This, according to Gurdjieff, was a practice that in Asia at one time reached epidemic proportions.

Whether or not the 'Babylonian Magi' were the ancestors of the Yezidis, they were clearly of importance in Bennett's search for Gurdjieff's Masters but could they be connected with the mysterious Sarmoung Brotherhood? This was a question which concerned me greatly but to which Bennett himself provided no clear answer. However, it is obvious that if there is any truth in Matthew's legendary Magi, then there must be some sort of link between them and Zoroastrianism, the religion of the people that the Greeks called *Magoi*. Accordingly, I decided now to investigate what these connections might have been.

## The Good Religion

Though there is some uncertainty about this, Zoroaster seems to have been born somewhere in what is now the borderlands between Iran and Azerbaijan on the banks of the Arax river.[6] He is generally believed to have been born around 630 BC[7] and the religion that he founded is unashamedly dualistic.

Like Egypt and Mesopotamia, Persia is a very ancient country. Its religious roots are very deep, going back to the dawn of civilization. In that antique period, before the pyramids were built and long before Abraham made his epic journey from Ur of the Chaldees to Hebron, there were already people of Indo-European extraction living in both Iran and India. These people, the ancestors of both modern Persians and Europeans were organized on tribal lines with dynasties of kings ruling over them. Their religion seems to have been cultic with many elements still recognizable in the contemporary cultures of the region today. At the root of their worship was a veneration of the elements, particularly fire and water, and a desire that these be kept 'pure'. Their rituals involved both the pouring of libations and animal sacrifice – usually bulls.

Zoroaster was an anointed priest of this earlier religion but he had an almost Biblical calling to become a prophet. According to the legends preserved in the Gathas,[8] at the age of 30 he had a vision in which he met Ahura Mazda, the high god of the Iranian pantheon. Unappreciated amongst his own people, Zoroaster went to the court of a neighbouring king, Vishtaspa and converted him to the new religion. According to Bennett the priests of the older, pre-Zoroastrian religion were already called Magi and their acceptance of the new prophet was crucial:

> The Magi were members of a caste or class that existed in central Asia before the time of Zoroaster. They accepted Zoroaster when he came to the court of King Vishtaspa, the Bactrian king of Khorasmia. Two Magi were given the task of testing Zoroaster's credentials and found that his initiation went beyond anything they themselves knew of. The king was converted on their advice.[9]

The religion that Zoroaster promulgated and which the Persian kings were now to embrace was, however, a radical departure from the earlier cults, for he taught that the world, though fashioned by God, was created to be a battleground between good and evil. According to Zoroaster, the Good God, Ahura Mazda (or Ohrmazd as he is called in later texts) existed as eternal light, and time. However, his enemy Angra Mainyu (later called Ahriman), the spirit of all darkness and evil also existed, if only as a potential. Realizing the danger that evil posed to the purity of his eternal being, Ohrmazd conceived a plan to trap and destroy Ahriman. This trap was our material world; one which, because it is subject to space and time, would force the enemy to come into the open. Ohrmazd knew that the evil Ahriman would seek to destroy this world but, unlike his adversary, he could see ahead of time and knew that in trying to do so, the Devil would become ensnared in time and space. Thus, although evil might win some early victories and thereby cause suffering in the world, in the long term it would be defeated and good would triumph.

In the Zoroastrian tradition, the prototype man (the equivalent of the Biblical Adam) was called Gayomart. He, along with a heavenly bull and the first plant, was created on the sixth day. Ahriman responded to Ohrmazd's challenge by breathing death upon these first creations of life. However, though they themselves succumbed, they gave forth their seeds a thousand-fold; from the bull were generated all the other animals, from the plant all other plants and from man the human race. Thus, though Ahriman had brought death into the world he could not destroy life itself. The battle between God and Devil, good and evil, life and death was going to be ongoing.

According to Zoroaster, Mankind had a special role to play in this protracted war against evil, his soul being the primary battle ground for the struggle between these two forces. Ohrmazd knew from the beginning of time that Ahriman would tempt Man into sin and thereby cause him to die. However, though in the short term Man would inevitably fall, eventually he would remember his divine origins and act as God's agent in the physical world. For the devout Zoroastrian the life, work and teaching of the prophet surpassed everything that had gone before and provided the reference points for the conduct of an ethical life. He looked forward to a time, at the end of the age, when Saoshyans[10] would be born. Then the Devil would be destroyed for once and for all, evil would be banished and the world would be put to right. In the meantime, the wise man kept to the precepts laid down by Zoroaster, fought the good fight and above all tried to keep both himself and his world pure.

For some two hundred and fifty years the Magi ministered to the religious needs of their people. However, the invasion of Alexander the Great in 334 BC caused enormous upheavals throughout what had been the Persian Empire. By the time when the Gospel Magi are supposed to have journeyed to Bethlehem to witness the birth of Jesus, Zoroastrianism as a religion was in a state of near total eclipse. Though it was later revived and would indeed experience its golden age under the Persian Sassanian Dynasty, this was still far into the future.

In the first century BC most of Mesopotamia was incorporated into the Parthian Empire,[11] this was not as centralized as either the Achaemean Empire that preceded Alexander's conquest nor the Sassanian Empire (c. AD 224–651) that was to come later. Before the Romans took control of the area, there was considerable freedom, religious as well as political, for a number of small states both in Eastern Turkey and Mesopotamia. In these looser circumstances, many local cults were able to flourish, most importantly that of Mithras, a god who was venerated by the Aryans[12] long before the birth of Zoroaster. The existence of these cults on the fringes of the Parthian Empire, led me to suspect that the Gospel Magi didn't come from Persia as such but rather from Mesopotamia. I was now anxious to investigate further the Mithras connection.

## Mithras the hero

When J.G. Bennett made his visit to the shrine of Sheikh Adi in 1953 he was looking for something more than an old tomb. He suspected that the Yezidis were in possession of ancient knowledge and may well have been one of Gurdjief's most important sources. He had good reason for thinking this as Gurdjieff himself refers to the Yezidis in *Meetings with Remarkable Men*. There he describes how he witnessed that if a circle is drawn on the ground around one of them, he cannot of his own volition leave it. The circle becomes a cage which, try as he might, he cannot escape.

Some strange force, much more powerful than his normal strength, keeps him inside . . .

If a Yezidi if forcibly dragged out of a circle, he immediately falls into a state of catalepsy, from which he recovers the instant he is brought inside. But if he is not brought back into the circle, he returns to the normal state, as we ascertained, only after either thirteen or twenty-one hours.

To bring him back into a normal state by any other means is impossible. At least my friends and I were not able to do so, in spite of the fact that we already possessed all the means known to contemporary hypnotic science for bringing people out of the cataleptic state. Only their priests could do so, by means of certain short incantations. [13]

If Bennett had been harbouring any hopes of seeing similar phenomena he was disappointed. Either his hosts at Sheikh Adi avoided standing inside circles or, more likely, they kept this sort of esoteric performance to themselves. Unfortunately, whatever he may have thought about the significance of the Yezidis and their strange cult, he did not take them up on an offer made to him to come and stay with them for a while and learn about their inner mysteries. He could say little more other than that he believed they were a surviving link of ancient cults that prefigured early Christianity.

> Their cult is a hotchpotch of Sabean, Christian and Islamic traditions – probably various legends were borrowed from time to time to link up their beliefs with those current in the surrounding world. The Yezidis may also be connected with the old Mithraic cult. If we compare the symbols outside the sanctuary at Sheikh Adi with those in the temple at Hatra, [14] we can recognise the serpent and perhaps also the scorpion. [15]

Mithraism is generally regarded as being a heretical offshoot of Zoroastrianism but this is a gross oversimplification. The relationship between the two religions is really much more complicated than this and in many ways parallels that between Christianity and Islam. For just as in some ways Islam is a reformed version of Christianity, yet is also a radical redefinition of the Old Testament approach to God by way of submission to His Will in daily life, so Mithraism was in many ways a return to a pre-Zoroaster past.

In the Persian, Aryan tradition that preceded Zoroaster's reformation, there was already a Mithras [16] who, along with Varuna and Indra, was one of the great gods. He was closely associated with the concept of justice and was invoked to witness cases of ordeal by fire, when the accused had to run along a narrow space between two blazing piles of logs. The link between Mithras and fire became strengthened as time went on and, rather like the Christian archangel Michael with whom he may be compared, he became a solar deity. He personified the burning heat of the sun as well as its light. Thus, on an exoteric or ordinary level of teaching, Mithras was a fiery Sun-god, lord of covenants and a personification of the abstract quality of justice. This, however, was not what drew his Roman adherents to become followers of his cult. For them he was the personification of the hero archetype. His cult, which spread like wildfire throughout the Roman Empire in the first and second centuries AD, was more subjective than Classical Zoroastrianism. For the Greeks and Romans, Mithras was a heroic, anthropomorphic deity to be equated with Hercules as well as the Sun-gods Apollo and Helios.[17]

Unfortunately, little in the way of writings concerning Roman Mithraism have come down to us although there are a number of reliefs and statues still in existence that give us the broad outlines of what the cult was about. Its central legend has clear links with both Zoroastrian and Biblical creation myths. Mithras, like Gayomart, is a divine child. He is born out of a rock beside a sacred stream at the foot of a tree.[18] But he is also an 'Adam', who eats of the fruit from the tree and fashions clothes from its leaves. As Joseph Campbell, the great mythographer comments, there is no sin attached to his eating of the fruit.

In the Persian Mithra the two Adams are united;[19] for there was no sin, no Fall, involved in his enactment of the deeds of a temporal life. With his knife the child culled the fruit of the tree and fashioned clothing of its leaves: once again like Adam – but without sin. And there is another scene, which shows him shooting arrows at a rock, from which water pours to refresh a kneeling suppliant. We do not possess the myth, but the episode has been compared to that of Moses producing water from the rock in the desert with his rod (Exodus 17:6). However, Moses sinned, for he struck twice, and consequently was denied entrance to the Promised Land – as Adam sinned and was denied paradise. But the saviour Mithra both ate the fruit of the mother tree and drew the water of life from his mother rock – without sin.[20]

Fig. 1                              Fig. 2

Mithras stele, obverse.          Mithras stele, reverse.

The Mithras legend is best known for its connection with the fate of the heavenly bull. Unlike the Zoroastrian Creation story, in which this first bull simply dies as a result of the activities of Ahriman, in Mithraism it is sacrificed. For reasons which are not clear Mithras has to capture the live bull and carry it back to his cave on his shoulders. Here, in a famous scene, which is represented on countless statues and stelae like the one in the Louvre, he sacrifices it. This event is pregnant with symbology:

> The primal bull was grazing on a mountainside when the young athletic god, seizing it by its horns, mounted, and the animal, wildly galloping, presently unseated him, but, clinging to its horns, he was dragged until the great beast collapsed. He then seized it by its hind hoofs, which he hoisted to his shoulders, and this so-called transitus, or difficult task of hauling the live bull, head down, along the way of many obstacles to his cave, began. This painful ordeal both of hero and of bull became symbolic both of human suffering in general and the specific trials of the initiate on his way to illumination — corresponding (though with hardly comparable force) to the *Via Crucis* of the later Christian cult. When he had reached his cave, a raven sent by the sun brought the saviour word that the moment of sacrifice had arrived, and, seizing his victim by the nostrils, he plunged the knife into its flank . . . Wheat sprang from the bull's spinal cord and from its blood the vine — whence the bread and wine

of the sacramental meal. Its seed, gathered and purified by the moon –
as in the orthodox Zoroastrian myth – produced the useful animals by
which man is served . . . the animals of the goddess-mother of death
and rebirth arrived to perform their several tasks: the scorpion, dog
and serpent.[21]

This description of the god dragging the primal bull back to his cave
and sacrificing it was undoubtedly paralleled by rites in the practices
of the cult. One can imagine 'rodeo' events with brave young men
fighting with bulls – perhaps even dragging them back to a cave
to be sacrificed. Such bull sacrifices were, of course, commonplace
throughout the ancient world and we can still see the last vestiges of
this in the Spanish bullfights of today.

In the Bible Moses calls down the wrath of God on the heads of
the Israelites when he witnesses them worshipping and dancing round
the golden effigy of a bull. This was not something of their own
invention, they got the idea from the Egyptians who, at that time,
also worshipped a sacred bull called Apis. The centre of the Egyptian
bull-cult was at Memphis and the Apis, of whom there was only one
at any given time, was kept in luxury whilst he lived. After death
his body was mummified and buried in a gigantic mausoleum called
the Serapeum. This is near the Royal cemetery of Saqqara and is a
labyrinthine network of catacombs containing the immense sarcophagi
in which the mummified bodies of the bulls were once housed. It was
rediscovered in 1850 by the eminent French archaeologist, Auguste
Mariette, revealing to the modern world the full extent of the Egyptian
obsession with their Apis. Each sarcophagus is three metres high, two
wide and four long and is carved out of a single piece of granite.
The labour that must have gone into cutting and moving each – and
there are dozens – testifies to the power the cult once held over the
Egyptians.

In Persia things took a rather different turn. The exact form of
Indo-Iranian beliefs before the birth of Zoroaster is not definite but
it is known that they too had a bull cult which involved the sacrifice
of these animals. Originally this was a very holy act and not done
lightly but, by the time that Zoroaster was born, probably around 630
BC, a certain decadence had set in and huge numbers of bulls were
being sacrificed unnecessarily. The Zoroastrian reform of the earlier,
primitive religion of Iran, which seems to have centred on the worship

(or at least propitiation) of elementals and nature spirits, had far reaching consequences. In particular it called into question the whole practice of animal sacrifice, which as far as Zoroaster himself was concerned, had no place in religion. As Professor R.C. Zaehner writes:

> 'Thus the Zoroastrian reform demonized that class of deity which was called *daeva* and eliminated the other class of deity called *ahura* by the Iranians and *asura* by the Indians with the single exception of Ahura Mazdah (later called Ohrmazd) who was elevated to the status of the one true God from whom all other divinities proceeded. Over against this God stood Angra Mainyu (Ahriman), the Destructive Spirit; and life on earth is represented as a battle between Ahura Mazdah and his attendant Powers on the one hand and Angra Mainyu and his demonic hordes on the other. For Zoroaster it was a very real battle since the worshippers of the *daevas* were still the representatives of the traditional religion, and these he roundly identified with all that is evil. Among their practices seems to have been an animal sacrifice in which a bull was the victim; and this sacrifice Zoroaster vigorously attacks.'[22]

Given that Zoroaster himself was so against animal sacrifice, it seems very strange that it should play such a central role in Mithraism. The answer seems to be that the latter was not, as is generally assumed and is repeated endlessly in every textbook on the subject, a heretical derivative of Zoroastrianism. Rather they are both descended, albeit with some mutual interactions, from the same original proto-religion but evolved down different, parallel paths. There was, we know, an Aryan religion of great antiquity – believed by some to date back to the last Ice Age – which was practised throughout the Middle East and Northern India long before the time of Zoroaster.[23] However, the oldest references to the Vedic or Aryan gods are found neither in Persia nor India but in what is now Turkey.

In one of the great migrations of history, at a date around 2200 BC, if not before, a people called the Hurrians moved down from the hill country surrounding Lake Urmia into the fertile plains of Northern Mesopotamia. Like the Persians these people were Aryans and they brought with them a then novel invention: the war chariot. This light-weight and highly manoeuvrable vehicle had its origins in the steppes of Southern Russia and up until then it had not been seen by the peoples of the old civilizations of Egypt and Babylonia. Armed with the new machine of war, the ancient equivalent of a tank, the Hurrians were able to drive all before them and establish a kingdom, called Mitanni, in what is now loosely called Kurdistan. They carried on their conquests and by 1800 BC had reached the Persian Gulf. From there they moved west into Syria and Palestine, mixing in with the already settled Semites of the region. In a treaty signed around 1400 BC between the Mitanni and their neighbours the Hittites, who may have been related, mention is made of five Aryan gods: Indra, Mitra (Mithras), Varuna and the two Ashvins. Thus, the god Mithras was a known deity in Eastern Turkey long before the advent of Zoroaster, who is generally believed to have been born around 630 BC.

Bennett's suggestion that today's Yezidi religion might have descended, at least in part, from the cult of Mithras was for me extremely relevant in my own quest for the Magi tradition. Mithraism was a subject that I myself had become increasingly interested in over the years and I had come to see that not only was it one of the sources of Gurdjieff's knowledge but it had deeply influenced the development of early Christianity. Indeed, it seems that even the 'mitre', the characteristic hat of a Christian bishop, is named after Mitra, an alternative spelling of Mithras. That this should be so is not really surprising, for the emergent religion of Christianity took over more than funny hats from Mithras. Embarrassingly for Christians, there are many parallels to be found between his cult and Roman Catholicism, not least the choice of 25 December, the birthday of Mithras, as Christmas. In fact, there is even a chapel dedicated to Mithras hidden in the catacombs beneath the Vatican in Rome. Whilst the exact nature of the ceremonies that went on inside such Mithraic grottoes is unknown, enough has come down to us to show that it had much in common with its later rival, Christianity.

## Christ and Mithras

As I looked into the matter it became clear that Christianity itself was more than a little indebted to Mithraism. At the time I could not see why this should be other than the fact that both early Christianity and Mithraism were Asiatic cults with, presumably, certain ideas in common. However, as I went into the subject deeper it became clear that there was more to it than this. Not only that, studying Mithraism threw light upon certain 'Christian' ceremonies.

Mithraism, like other cults with their roots in the Middle East, was closely identified with astrology. Whilst little has been preserved of the writings of the Mithraists, we are able to understand quite a lot about the cult by studying surviving sculptured reliefs from their temples. It seems that like modern Freemasonry, it was based on the idea of progressive initiation. According to one modern author, quoting a treatise entitled *Le Culte de Mithra* by M. Layard, there were twelve of these.

> These degrees were divided into four stages, Terrestrial, Aerial, Igneous, and Divine, each consisting of three. The Terrestial comprising the Soldier, the Lion and the Bull. The Aerial, the Vulture, the Ostrich and the Raven. The Igneous, the Gryphon, the Horse, the Sun. The Divine, the Eagle, the Sparrow-Hawk, the Father of Fathers.[24]

Quite how most of these names arise is a mystery but what is clear from the reference to the four elements and the three degrees appropriate to each is that we are dealing here with a zodiac. However, according to Joseph Campbell the zodiac represented the unchanging background against which the planets moved.

> . . . the zodiac had come to represent the bounding, ever-revolving sphere of time-space-causality, within which the unbounded Spirit operates – unmoved yet moving in all. The orbits of the seven visible spheres – Moon, Mercury, Venus, Sun, Mars, Jupiter, and Saturn – were conceived as so many envelopes around the earth, through which the soul had descended when coming to be born.[25]

There were seven degrees, or initiations, to be passed on the way to becoming a Master and these corresponded to the seven planetary spheres. The first degree was called *Corax*, (raven) and symbolized the sphere of the Moon. The second initiation was called *Cryphias* (the hidden master) and was associated with the sphere of Mercury; the third was *Miles* (the soldier) the sphere of Venus; the fourth was *Leo* (Lion) the sphere of the Sun; the fifth *Perses* (the Persian) the sphere of Mars; the sixth was *Heliodromus* (the courier of the Sun) the sphere of Jupiter; the seventh and last was *Pater* (Father) the sphere of

Saturn. Whilst we can only speculate on the mystical significance of these names or what graduation ceremonies were carried out, we do know that candidates for initiation dressed up in appropriate costumes. What is important is their astrological connection and the belief that it was possible to climb the ladder of the heavens, ascending as it were through the planetary spheres. This is a common conception to be found in many secret traditions, not least, Kabbalah, the mystical inner path of Judaism.[26] According to the Kabbalah, the seven lights of the seven-branched Jewish candlestick, or Menorah, represent the seven planets or 'wanderers' (including the sun and moon).

The movements of the planets were carefully monitored by priests and astrologers throughout the ancient world because it was felt that they controlled human fate. It was thought that they imbued men and women with astral power according to their own nature. However these 'gifts', which manifested as inborn talents, were double edged: they could be virtues or vices depending upon how they were used.[27] Self-development at the astral or planetary level meant learning to recognize one's own planetary type, i.e. which 'gods' or lights were predominant in one's own nature, then developing the self-discipline needed to control the way such forces were used, so that they manifested in a positive rather than negative way. However, the real aim of such esoteric cults as Mithraism was, like Bennett's school at Sherborne, to teach the individual how to rise above this level altogether. The seven-stepped ladder of initiation was intended to free the soul from the forces of what was often symbolized as a seven-headed dragon. Then, after death, his soul would be able to leave the solar system altogether and journey to a heaven beyond the stars. As Campbell puts it:

> The individual had derived from each (planetary sphere) a specific temporal-spatial quality, which on the one hand contributed to his character, but on the other was a limitation. Hence, the seven stages of initiation were to facilitate passages of the spirit, one by one, beyond the seven limitations, culminating in a realization of the unqualified state.[28]

In Christianity there is a similar conception of the planetary or astral world as being the source from which we draw both our talents and shortcomings. This is most clearly shown in the Book of Revelation, the last book of the Bible. Here, the seven planets are represented as seven stars which are held in the right hand of 'one like unto the Son of Man'. They are related to seven candlesticks and seven archetypal churches:

> The mystery of the seven stars which thou sawest in my right hand, and the seven golden candlesticks. The seven stars are the angels of the seven churches: and the seven candlesticks which thou sawest are the seven churches.[29]

The seven churches of Asia Minor, to whom the first part of the Revelation is addressed, have each of them a particular strength, for which it is praised and a weakness that is tending to lead it into sin. Like Mithraism, its great rival of the first and second centuries AD, Christianity offers seven initiations, called sacraments, to aid the soul in its struggles to attain salvation. The seven sacraments can be seen as a sort of ladder and once more correspond with the planetary spheres. Thus we have Baptism, (the Moon); Penance, (Mercury); Marriage, (Venus); Communion, (Sun); Confirmation, (Mars); Holy Orders, (Jupiter); and Last Rites, (Saturn).

With all these parallels between Christianity and Mithraism, it is tempting to think that the latter must have been the stellar religion of the Magi. However, there are other arguments against this assumption, not least that Christmas Day, was not celebrated on 25 December until AD 353, when it was declared such by Pope Liberius. Before then the major Christian feast of the season was the Baptism of Christ, and this was held on 6 January. The choice of this date for such an important feast seems to have its antecedents neither in Persia nor Mesopotamia but in Egypt.

## The Aeon and the Christos

During Roman times there was, in the port city of Alexandria, a very large temple called the Koreion. Here on 6 January was celebrated the birth of the Aeon.[30] As this is recorded in the writings of Saint Epiphanius (c. 315–402), the pagan feast of the Aeon must have still been marked even in his day. He writes:

> . . . at Alexandria, in the Koreion, as it is called – an immense temple, that is to say the Precinct of the Virgin – after they have

kept all-night vigil with songs and music, chanting to their idol, when the vigil is over, at cock-crow, they descend with lights into an underground crypt, and carry up a wooden image lying naked on a litter, with the seal of a cross made in gold on its forehead, and on either hand two similar seals, and on either knee two others, all five seals being similarly made in gold. And they carry round the image itself, circumambulating seven times[31] the innermost temple, to the accompaniment of pipes, tabors and hymns, and with merry-making they carry it down again underground. And if they are asked the meaning of this mystery, they answer: 'Today at this hour the Maiden (Kore), that is the Virgin, gave birth to the Aeon.'[32]

This startling evidence for a connection between a Virgin birth and the Feast of Old Christmas, which we in the West now celebrate as the Epiphany, points the finger at Ancient Egypt as an alternative source for the legend of the Magi. This is not as unlikely as it at first seems. At the time of Jesus, Alexandria was possibly the most civilized city in the world and home to a large Jewish community. Its greatest philosopher was also a Jew, a pre-eminent citizen named Philo (c. BC 30 − AD 45), whose brother Alexander was banker to the Caesars. In Philo's voluminous writings, one of the best contemporary records to have come down to us, he tells us much concerning the beliefs and practices of the 'wise men' of his day. Amongst these are numbered the Magi of Persia: 'who by their careful scrutiny of nature's works for purpose of the gnosis of the truth, in quiet silence, and by means of [mystic] images of piercing clarity are made initiates into the mysteries of godlike virtues, and in their turn initiate [those who come after them].'[33] But Philo was not just an observer of exotic religions, it would seem that he was on close terms with, and perhaps a member of, a community of mystics called the Therapeuts. They had their centre to the south of Alexandria and much of what Philo has to say about them and their beliefs curiously prefigures Christianity.

As a philosopher Philo has much in common with both Bennett and Mead, who in his *Thrice Greatest Hermes* analyses Philo's work in depth. For Philo it was self-evident that the work of a philosopher had no purpose outside of a religious framework. This framework was closely allied to the idea of initiation, kept secret from the masses because it would not be understood. Thus he writes:

These things receive into your souls, ye mystae, ye whose ears are purified, as truly sacred mysteries, and see that ye speak not of them to any who may be without initiation, but storing them away in your hearts, guard well your treasure house; not as a treasury in which gold and silver are laid up, things that do perish, but as the pick and prize of possessions – the knowledge of the Cause [of all] and Virtue, and of the third, the child of both.[34]

This sentiment, of not revealing holy mysteries to the uninitiated is repeated in Matthew's Gospel: 'Give not that which is holy unto the dogs, neither cast ye your pearls before swine, lest they trample them under their feet, and turn again and rend you.' One of these great secrets, as far as Philo is concerned, is the doctrine of the Logos as Son of God. He writes:

Moreover God, as Shepherd and King, leads [and rules] with law and justice the nature of the heaven, the periods of sun and moon, the changes and progressions of the other stars – deputing [for the task] His own right Reason (*Logos*), His First-born Son, to take charge of the sacred flock, as though he were the Great King's viceroy.[35]

Mead, in his commentary on this passage discusses how this 'Heavenly Man' was for Philo the Celestial Messiah of God. He goes on to quote another passage which at the time I read it was most mysterious but, as I was later to discover, is the key to very much indeed.

Moreover, I have heard one of the companions of Moses uttering some such word [logos] as this: 'Behold Man whose name is East' – a very strange appellation, if you imagine the man composed of body and soul to be meant; but if you take him for that Incorporeal Man in no way differing from the Divine Image, you will admit that the giving him the name of East exactly hits the mark.

For the Father of things that are hath made him rise as His eldest Son, whom elsewhere He hath called His First-born, and who, when he hath been begotten, imitating the ways of his Sire, and contemplating His archetypal patterns, fashions the species [of things].[36]

These words are remarkably similar to the beginning of St John's Gospel, which used to be read at the end of every Catholic Mass:

> In the beginning was the Word (Logos), and the Word was with God, and the Word was God. The same was in the beginning with God. All things were made by him; and without him was not any thing made that was made. In him was life; and the life was the light of men. And the light shineth in darkness; and the darkness comprehended it not. [37]

Thus, in Philo's philosophy, as in St John's Gospel, the Son of God, that is the Primary Logos, is responsible for creating the visible universe according to the image and archetypal patterns laid down by his Father. The 'life which is the light of men' and which 'shineth in the darkness' is, of course, the sun. How Jesus Christ, the Logos or word made flesh, is connected with the sun is one of the great mysteries of Christian esotericism. Philo, however, postulates a 'star of stars', that stands at the centre of creation and gives light to all other bodies, including the visible stars, our sun, moon and planets.

> [This Light] is the [One] star, beyond [all] heavens, the Source of the Stars that are visible to the senses, which it would not be beside the mark to call All-brilliancy, and from which the sun and moon and the rest of the stars, both errant and fixed, draw their light, each according to its power. [38]

As can be seen from all of the above, Philo was fond of allegory – so much so indeed that at times he becomes almost unintelligible. What is clear from his writings is that there was a strain of Jewish thought in Alexandria that bore close relationship to another Egyptian school that was flourishing around the same time, that of Hermes Trismegistus. This, as I was to discover, continued to be deeply influential on Western thinking right up to the time of the Renaissance and beyond. Could Philo's idea of a 'master star', one which gives its light to all others, be connected with the ancient Egyptian veneration of Sirius, the brightest star in the sky? If so, this would provide an interesting link between Egypt and the Magi story, for as I was to discover the writings of Hermes survived not in Egypt but in Mesopotamia, the place where Gurdjieff had sought his Sarmoung Brotherhood.

# CHAPTER 4

✳

# Hermes Trismegistus

In 1986, some twelve years after Bennett's death in 1974, I came across an old edition of a very strange book. Called *Hermetica* it was a collection of ancient writings translated from Latin and Greek. These included a series of essays or *libelli*, known as the *Poimandres* or *Corpus Hermeticum*. In many ways these resembled the dialogues of Plato except that they were Egyptian in origin and the teachings were not those of Socrates but Hermes Trismegistus, a Greek name given to Thoth, the Egyptian god of wisdom. At that time philosophical alchemy was a subject which greatly interested me and indeed in my first book[1] I had been writing about it in the context of astrology. I had seen many references in alchemical writings to Hermes Trismegistus, the supposed author of these texts but I had not realized that there was in existence such a selection of works by the master himself. Destiny or fate, this was to turn out to be the key for which I had been searching for very many years and renewed my interest in the subject not just of Egypt but also of an invisible college of Masters. These Hermetic writings were also to provide many clues to the true identity of Gurdjieff's sources and to where I should look if I wanted to find traces of the Gospel Magi.

Little is known about the origins of the *Hermetica* other than that they probably emanated from Alexandria around the beginning of the Christian epoch. Because they are mostly written in Greek and their subject matter is often recognizably similar to that under discussion in the works of Plato, they have tended to be dismissed by modern scholars as 'Neoplatonism' and therefore unworthy of serious analysis.

Yet, this is a misunderstanding of the situation. Whilst it is probably true that the essays contained in the *Corpus Hermeticum* are of fairly late provenance and in style, being conversations between a master (usually but not always Hermes himself) and one or more of his pupils, resemble Platonic dialogues, the teachings they embody are of very much greater antiquity.

The Greeks of the time of Plato, Socrates and even earlier looked up to the Egyptians as the custodians of the ancient wisdom. Many of the greatest Greek philosophers journeyed to Egypt for initiation into their secret rites, the cults of Isis and Osiris. For them the hippy trail led not to Katmandu but to Sais. Indeed it was the priesthood of Sais who, according to Plato, instructed Solon (*c.*638–588 BC), in the mysteries and who told him the story of Atlantis that Plato was later to repeat in the *Timaeus* and *Critias*. Herodotus (*c.*484–425 BC), the 'Father of History', visited the Temple of the Phoenix in the city of Annu, later to be called Heliopolis, around 450 BC. Plutarch (AD 46–120), the Greek biographer and miscellaneous writer, certainly visited Egypt and based his account of the story of Isis and Osiris on what he was taught by the priests there. Pythagoras (sixth century BC), the father of all Greek philosophy was also an initiate of the Egyptian schools, and no doubt it was there that he developed his interest in geometry, a subject which they invented. He probably even learnt the theorem which carries his name from the Egyptians!

That the Egyptians were keen on writing down all forms of knowledge is not just hearsay. Alexandria housed the greatest library in the ancient world until it was burnt down by the Romans (*c.*47 BC) in an act of vandalism worthy of Mao Tse Tung's Red Guards. Contained in the library were texts from all over the known world and, of course, thousands from Egypt itself. Could it not be possible that rather than the Egyptian writers of the *Hermetica* plagiarizing Plato that it was the other way round? That Plato (or rather his teacher Socrates) derived much of his philosophy from Egyptian sources? This is not to say that the writings contained in the *Corpus Hermeticum* predates Plato but rather that they both draw on a common source, a secret teaching handed down from the most ancient antiquity by Egyptian initiates.

The history of how the *Corpus Hermeticum* came to the West is itself a fascinating story and one worth retelling. Egypt, and more particularly Alexandria, was very early on home to a Christian community. This was scarcely surprising given the large numbers of Greeks, Jews and other immigrants living in the country and the free movement of peoples between her and the Levant. The Christians did not want to seem out of place in this cosmopolitan region so, at first, the early Church made use of parallels between its own doctrines and those of the ancient mystery cults as a means of attracting recruits. This ecumenical approach meant that Egypt developed a hybrid, Gnostic Christian tradition of its own that drew as much upon the mysteries of Memphis as those of Calvary. By the second century AD this open-minded approach was becoming an embarrassment for a Church whose teachings were beginning to solidify into fixed doctrines. The Egyptian Gnostics were reviled by such church fathers as Iranaeus and once Christianity was accepted as the religion of the Roman Empire, persecuted. In AD 390 an edict was passed banning paganism in Egypt, the important temple of Serapis in Alexandria having already been seized and turned into a church a year earlier. The pagan books, like the *Corpus Hermeticum*, contained in its library were looted and burnt by the mob. When Alexandria, along with the rest of Egypt, was taken by the Arabs in AD 641, its libraries, or what was left of them, were destroyed completely. Indeed, it is said that books were used to heat the public baths of the city for six months. Though this story is now considered to be apocryphal on account of the wide scale destruction of books that had already occurred in earlier centuries, there is no doubting that from this date Alexandria itself fell into terminal decline and any Hermetica would have disappeared in their entirety were it not for another accident of history that saw their preservation outside of Egypt in the unlikely situation of Northern Mesopotamia.

It is mentioned in the Bible that Abraham (Abram), the patriarch of all the Hebrews, was born in a city called Ur of the Chaldees before he and his family emigrated from there to eventually take up residence in the Promised Land of Canaan. The early part of this journey was at the instigation of his elderly father, Terah, who died and was buried *en route*. The story is told in the Book of Genesis:

> And Terah took Abram his son, and Lot the son of Haran his son's son, and Sarai his daughter in law, his son Abram's wife; and they went forth with them from Ur of the Chaldees, to go into the land of Canaan; and they came unto Harran and dwelt there.
>
> And the days of Terah were two hundred and five years: and Terah died in Harran.[2]

Now Harran, the city where Terah was buried, lies on a small tributary of the Balikh River, itself a tributary of the mighty Euphrates, in south-eastern Turkey, a few kilometres north of the present Syrian border. For thousands of years it was an important location, guarding as it did the trade routes between East and West. It was a large city, fortified with a perimeter wall several miles in length and surrounded by open fields. Harran features again in the Bible when Abraham, now resident in Hebron, sent his servant there to seek out a bride for his son Isaac. The servant sat down by the city well, having made a bargain with God that the first young woman to answer his request for water and to offer to water his camels too, should be the one to wed his master's son. This turned out to be Rebekah, Nahor's grand-daughter and therefore Abraham's great-niece. In the next generation, Jacob, the son of Isaac and Rebekah, was also sent to Harran to find a wife. He ended up spending fourteen years working for his uncle Laban, Rebekah's brother, and marrying both of his cousins. Thus the city of Harran, has a special place in the Bible as Abraham's homeland, the place where his extended family dwelt.

Yet, Harran was not a Jewish city, in the religious sense of the word, and neither did it ever become fully Christian. With a tenacity almost unparalleled anywhere else in the mediaeval world, it remained true to more ancient traditions than these and stayed stubbornly pagan. Right up until its destruction by the Mongols in AD 1259 the majority of the people there continued in their worship of stellar gods, the most important religious building of the city being not a church or synagogue but the temple of the Mesopotamian Moon-god, Sin. In one of the curious turns of history, this conservatism was to ensure that the Egyptian Hermetica survived the Dark Ages to rekindle the fires of the European Renaissance.

This might not have happened had fate taken a slightly different course. Harran was seized by the Arabs in their conquest of Syria and Mesopotamia between AD 633 and 643. As before, when nominally under the Christian rule of the Byzantine Empire, the majority of the people refused to convert to the new religion and carried on as pagans, no doubt paying taxes for the privilege. Everything went on peacefully as before until in AD 830 the Caliph al-Mamoun, the same who had in AD 820 ordered the opening of the Great Pyramid of Giza, passed by the city *en route* to fight the Byzantines. Noticing that many of the people were strangely dressed, he enquired of them to which religious group protected by the law did they belong? They answered that they were Harranians. They were then asked were they people of the book, either Christians, Jews or Magians? In each case they had to answer no. On being asked whether they had a holy scripture and a recognized prophet, they were evasive. By this time the caliph was losing his temper and announced that if they had not by the time he came back become either Moslems or one of the other religions recognized in the Koran, he would have no hesitation in having them all put to death as infidels and idolaters.

With this threat ringing in their ears, many of them became either Christians or Moslems but some still held out. Though Caliph al-Mamoun died shortly afterwards whilst still on campaign and never returned to carry out his threat, they realized from this incident how precarious their position was should it ever be challenged again. They, therefore, announced that they were Sabians, the name of an allowed religion to be found in the Koran, and that their prophet was none other than Hermes Trismegistus, whose writings they possessed in the form of the *Corpus Hermeticum*. Fortunately nobody, least of all the Moslems, knew who or what the Sabians were, still less what they believed, so this was enough to ensure them protection under the law. Thenceforward the Sabians of Harran were a recognized group with their own religion.

Though many, if not most, of the Harranians were simple pagans for whom religion meant little more than maintaining the temple rituals, there were others amongst them of a more philosophical nature. These men were well-educated and it was they who had had the intelligence to name a recognized collection of *Hermetica*, or discourses of Hermes, as their holy books. As far as the Arabs were concerned, Hermes was to be identified with Idris, their name for Enoch, whilst Agathodaimon, also spoken of in the *Hermetica* and really a name for Osiris, was identified as Seth, the third son of Adam. With this arrangement everybody was satisfied and for the next two centuries the Sabians of Harran were more or less left in peace by the Moslems to follow their own teachings. With this new understanding, some of them moved from Harran to Baghdad. The leader of this faction, Thabit ibn Qurra, became a well-known teacher, writing works in Arabic and translating many others from Greek and Syriac into that language. For the next century and a half, the Sabians, still a separate sect, enjoyed a privileged position in Baghdad society becoming a conduit for the transmission of ancient wisdom to the Arabs.

However, this happy state of affairs was not to last for ever. The golden age of the Caliphate was passing and the empire over which such rulers as al-Mansur, al-Rashid and al-Mamoun had ruled was disintegrating. The caliphs of Baghdad lost power to provincial governors and Turkish generals, who were only nominally their vassals. With the ascendancy of the Buwayhids as 'Mayors of the Palace', the caliphs became little more than shadowy pontiffs. As time went on, so the forces of religious orthodoxy grew in strength at the expense of the more liberal outlook that had allowed such groups as the Sabians to flourish. This process was accelerated when the Seljuk Turks, at the 'invitation' of the Caliph, effectively took over Baghdad in 1055 and their leader, Tughril Bey, was made king of East and West. Unfortunately for the Sabians, as champions of Sunni orthodoxy, the Seljuks did not look kindly upon Hermetic philosophers.

Many of the writings contained in the *Hermetica* had by now been translated into Arabic but it would seem that at least some of the Sabians, either in Baghdad or Harran itself, still understood Greek and had in their possession the texts in their original language. Fearing persecution, or perhaps because of it, they now made their way westwards to Constantinople. Here there was something of a Platonic revival under way led by the great teacher and later prime minister, Michael Psellus. Somehow, either through direct or indirect contacts with these Sabian refugees, he came into possession of a collection of *Hermetica*. These he copied and put back into circulation with an added scholion of his own.[3] It would be some four hundred years more before the *Hermetica* would once more be back in the news, this time in Italy.

## Hermes Trismegistus and the Florentine Renaissance

Possibly the greatest and most traumatic event of the whole fifteenth century, at least as far as the Christian West was concerned, was the capture of Constantinople by the Turks in 1453. It is difficult for us today to appreciate just how serious an event this was but perhaps the seizure of Tibet by the Chinese in 1950 offers some sort of comparison. The Byzantine Empire had, of course, been in terminal decline for centuries. Following the defeat of the Emperor's

forces at Manzikert in 1071, an appeal had been sent to the Pope for
Western support against the Turkish menace. The resulting Crusades,
though far from ideal from the Eastern Empire's perspective, relieved
some of the immediate pressure. However, by 1453, the Crusader
states and their armies were long gone and the Holy Land was back
firmly in Islamic hands. Constantinople itself was a pale shadow of its
former glory and surrounded on all sides by hostile forces. Bereft of
its empire on which its wealth and strength ultimately depended, its
end as a Christian city was inevitable. The siege lasted several weeks
and its end was brutal. For the customary three days, the city was
wantonly sacked so that at the end of it even the conquering sultan
wept as he left saying 'What a city we have given over to plunder and
destruction'. Churches were looted for their gold and once more, as
so often happens on such occasions, whole libraries of precious books
were put to the torch. The surviving Greeks, some 50,000 of them,
were mostly enslaved though the sultan did free a few and some escaped
West. Not a few of these émigrés ended up in Florence, where they
were given a ready welcome. How the *Corpus Hermeticum* survived the
disaster is not clear but it had probably already been taken out of the
city before the siege. At any rate, this priceless collection of Hermetic
writings was one refugee that made it to the West.

In 1460, a Greek monk named Fra Lionardo del Pistoja was sent by
Cosimo de Medici, Duke of Florence, to Macedonia. Cosimo had long
been in the market for the works of Greek philosophers such as Plato
and rumour must have reached him that an important manuscript of
this type had come onto the black market. Pistoja was sent to retrieve
it. When he returned he brought back with him what was, as far as the
Florentines were concerned, a treasure beyond belief: the complete
Greek text of the *Corpus Hermeticum*. Unable himself to read Greek
and knowing that he did not have long to live, Cosimo immediately
ordered his chief translator, Marsiglio Ficino, to put aside the works
of Plato on which he had been working so that he could get on with
this new work.

Platonism, or rather Neoplatonism, was then fashionable in Italy but
though this label was later to be attached to the *Hermetica* themselves,
this was not the reason for Cosimo's interest. He, like everyone else,
believed in a lost golden age, a time when mankind was more enlightened
than today. In the Bible it was clear that Adam and the later patriarchs
were often on speaking terms with God. Unlike today, where the latest

opinion on any subject is considered to be the best answer available, in Cosimo's time antiquity added value. Like good wine, philosophy and philosophers improved with age. The more ancient the philosopher, or so it was held, the nearer he was in time to the golden age and therefore the closer he was to the source of real knowledge. By this analysis the works of Moses were of greater value than those of Plato, who in turn was senior to Aristotle, Seneca, Marcus Aurelius, St Augustine and so on. However, Hermes Trismegistus, the presumed writer of the *Hermetica* was in a different category altogether. He was the Egyptian prophet and god known as Thoth (Tehuti) who was credited with the invention of the mysterious hieroglyphs and with teaching the ancient Egyptians such sciences as pyramid building. Not only that but he was also equated with the Hebrew prophet Enoch, who though he gets the briefest of mentions in the Bible as the father of Methuselah and as having 'walked with God', was also known to the early Church Fathers from the Apocrypha. In fact, as we now know from studying the Dead Sea Scrolls, the so-called 'Book of Enoch' was highly esteemed by the Essenes at the time of Jesus. The belief by Cosimo, rightly or wrongly, that he had in his hands the lost works of such a venerable sage, one moreover who was only removed from Adam by seven generations, must have been almost too much to bear. For in the conventional hierarchy of ideas, this work by Hermes also known as Thoth who is equated with Enoch not only surpassed Plato but also Moses and even Abraham. Little wonder then that he had Ficino set about translating this remarkable work with all possible haste.

Though few today would support the notion that the extant *Hermetica*[4] are of really great antiquity, they are still extraordinary documents. Their immense influence on Renaissance thought is beyond question and they still have a resonance and depth of feeling that is unmatched by any other works of ancient philosophy. Almost certainly the Hermetic writings, which include others such as the *Asclepius*, which Cosimo would have already had possession of in the form of a Latin translation, and the *Kore Cosmu*, part of another collection of Hermetica known as the *Stobaeus*, were the lecture notes of an esoteric school – the sort of school that Gurdjieff was looking for in the late nineteenth century.

Old Cosimo was able to read early drafts of Ficino's Latin translation of the Greek *Corpus Hermeticum* before his death in 1464. The elder Medici's enthusiasm for the project, however, was just the start of a

Hermetic revival that was to have a profound effect on the direction of the Renaissance that was now sweeping not just Florence but the whole of Italy. The new translation, published in 1471, was greeted with rapture by the young Platonists of the Florentine academy, such as Pico della Mirandola, who amalgamated the teachings of Hermes with ideas on 'Christian Kabbalah'[5] to produce a new, occult philosophy or 'magia'. This secret undercurrent of occultism, a subject studied in depth by the esteemed historian Dame Frances Yates, runs through much of the art and science of the sixteenth, seventeenth and eighteenth centuries.

Astrology, which like today enjoyed one of its periodic renaissances, was the language of the occult philosophy. A whole science of correspondences was developed; a 'natural magic' relating plants, herbs, stones, symbols and temperaments to the planets. Whilst these ideas were published openly in books written by magicians such as Cornelius Agrippa and Dr John Dee, they also formed the basis of a subtle language of artistic allusion. For example, the three graces to be seen dancing in such paintings as the *Prima-Vera* of Botticelli represent the benign influences of the Sun and the planets Jupiter and Venus.[6] Possibly the best known and influential of all Hermetic documents was a short, mystifying document entitled: *The Emerald Table of Hermes Trismegistus*, which presents in shorthand the Hermetic philosophy as it applies to alchemy. It begins:

> True without deceit, certain and most true.
> What is below is like what is above and what is above is like what is below, for the performing of the marvels of the one thing.

According to Ouspensky this document was frequently mentioned by Gurdjieff to his groups in St Petersburg and Moscow. He was fond of quoting a later verse concerning philosophical alchemy – 'You shall separate the earth from the fire, the subtle from the gross' – as the basis of the work that he was himself teaching. Thus he was in a very real sense a 'Renaissance man', a teacher in the tradition of Ficino and Pico della Mirandola.

Needless to say, the rediscovery of the Hermetic philosophy and its associated magical sciences of astrology, numerology and divination was not to everybody's taste. Whilst it was tolerated by the Church under the stewardship of Popes Leo X and Clement VII, both grandsons of

Cosimo and educated by the Florentine academy, it was not without its opponents. Giordano Bruno, a former Dominican friar and travelling missionary for the Hermetic movement sailed too close to the wind both politically and theologically. Had he stayed in Germany or England where he had friends and the Reformation had seen off the Inquisition, he might have escaped persecution; however in 1591 he made the fatal mistake of returning to Italy. Within a year he was imprisoned in Venice, betrayed to the Inquisition by a former sympathizer who suspected him of treasonable association with Henry of Navarre, now King of France and at that time a Protestant.

The Catholic Church was still suffering the humiliation of the Reformation and had proved unable to force the straying sheep of northern Europe back into the fold. The defeat of the Spanish Armada by the English in 1588 and the rise of the House of Navarre in France seriously jeopardized the Pope's control of Italy itself. Whereas a century earlier Bruno might have been regarded as a harmless eccentric, attitudes were now hardening and the Church was on the defence against anything that might further undermine its authority. Among his crimes was his belief that the Christian symbol of the cross owed its origins not to the crucifixion of Jesus but to the much earlier symbol, the crux ansata or *ankh* of the Egyptians. Frances Yates writes of this and quotes from documents relating to the Venetian Inquisition:

> Very important, among the new documents in the *Sommario* are the indications of Bruno's view of the cross as really an Egyptian sacred sign. A fellow-prisoner reports him as having said that the cross on which Christ was crucified was not in the form shown on Christian altars, this form being in reality the sign which was sculptured on the breast of the goddess Isis, and which was 'stolen' by the Christians from the Egyptians. In reply to an inquisitorial question about this, Bruno acknowledged that he had said that the form of the cross on which Christ was crucified was different from the way in which it is usually 'painted' adding these significant words:
>
> 'I think I have read in Marsiglio Ficino that the virtue and holiness of this character (*carattere*, by which he means cross) is much more ancient than the time of the Incarnation of Our Lord, and that it was known in the time in which the religion of the Egyptians flourished, about the time of Moses, and that this sign was affixed to the breast of Serapis.'[7]

Such ideas might have won him plaudits at the court of Queen Elizabeth I when he visited England in 1583, but they cut no ice with his inquisitors. He was kept in gaol for a further nine years until, on 17 February 1600, in the Campo de' Fiori in Rome, he was burned at the stake as a heretic. He was one of the last of the Hermetic philosophers to flaunt his ideas openly. Thenceforward the movement went underground.

In England Elizabeth, the 'Faerie Queen', was seen by others, and probably by herself as a living embodiment of Isis. A cult grew around her that positively embraced Egyptianism as a counter-weight to papal authority. She recognized the importance of archetypes and successfully promoted herself in the affections of her people as a substitute for the Virgin Mary. As long as she was alive, hermetically inspired philosophers such as Dr John Dee were protected. However, with her death in 1603 and the accession of James I on the English throne, a less favourable atmosphere prevailed. The new king was against astrology and magic, which he regarded with abhorrence. Dee, who could now no longer rely on the patronage of the old queen, died in poverty in 1608. His passing marking the end of an age.

However this was not enough. The king and his supporters, who wanted a pure Protestantism free from any taint of Egyptianism, realized that if this were to be achieved then the *Hermetica* themselves needed to be discredited. Fortunately James had a willing accomplice in one Isaac Casaubon, the most brilliant Greek scholar of his day. By means of careful analysis of the original Hermetic texts and their comparison with other Greek writings of various ages, he was able to date the *Corpus Hermeticum*. Far from being works of hoary antiquity, dating from before the time of Methuselah, he found that they were probably written during the early centuries of the Christian Era.

This shattering revelation gave weight to those who wanted to see in all the *Hermetica* nothing more than a regurgitation of Platonism, spiced up with borrowings from the Bible and cast into an Egyptian framework. It now could and was argued that the unknown authors of both the Greek *Corpus Hermeticum* and the Latin *Asclepius*, another important Hermetic writing, lived in Alexandria during the second and third centuries AD and were simply pagans trying to turn back the tide of Christianity. From then on this became the standard academic attitude towards the *Hermetica*, which became little more that curiosities of interest only to scholars investigating the fringes of Neoplatonic philosophy. This, the now received opinion, was well summed up in the Introduction to the 1924 Walter Scott translation which had now come into my hands:

> By what sort of people, and in what circumstances, were our *Hermetica* written? That question may be answered as follows. There were in Egypt under the Roman Empire men who had received some instruction in Greek philosophy, and especially in the Platonism of the period, but were not content with merely accepting and repeating the cut and dried dogmas of the orthodox philosophical schools, and sought to build up, on a basis of Platonic doctrine, a philosophic religion that would better satisfy their needs. Ammonius Saccas, the Egyptian teacher of the Egyptian Plotinus, must have been a man of this type; and there were others more or less like him. These men did not openly compete with the established schools of philosophy, or try to establish a new school of their own on similar lines; but here and there one of these 'seekers after God' would quietly gather round him a small group of disciples and endeavour to communicate to them the truth in which he had found salvation for himself. The teaching in these little groups must have been mainly oral, and not based on written texts; it must have consisted of private and intimate talks or the teacher with a single pupil at a time, or with two or three pupils at most. But now and then the teacher would set down in writing the gist of a talk in which some point of primary importance was explained; or perhaps a pupil, after such a talk with his teacher, would write down as much of it as he could remember; and when once written, the writing would be passed from hand to hand within the group, and from one group to another.
>
> . . . In the first place, it may be asked whether there is anything in the *Hermetica* that is derived from the indigenous religion of Egypt. As far as definite statements of doctrine are concerned there is very little . . . the Egyptian ingredient in Hermetic doctrine still remains comparatively small in amount; the main bulk of it is unquestionably derived from Greek philosophy.[8]

Reading this I was immediately struck by the similarity between the type of esoteric school he was describing and Ouspensky's account of talks given by Gurdjieff in Moscow. Yet, I couldn't understand why he was so sure that these Egyptian Masters were so under the influence of Greek philosophy. Granted that the Greeks, especially Plato, developed the idea of written philosophical dialogue but the most important ideas at the root of his philosophy are unquestionably Egyptian.

Perhaps because of G.R.S. Mead's Theosophical connections, Scott makes no mention of his 1906 translation of the *Hermetica* entitled *Thrice Greatest Hermes*. Mead was an expert on the writings of the early Church and like Scott was able to read Greek and Latin with ease. Whether the two men met is not recorded but it would have been interesting to hear them discussing the *Hermetica*. Unlike Scott he did not believe that the *Hermetica* were Neoplatonic forgeries but like me felt they represented the last outpourings of a native Egyptian tradition. Mead, perhaps more aware of the inner meaning of the *Hermetica* than Scott, quotes in their defence an article by a French author called Artaud:

> We have heard from Champollion, the younger, giving expression to the formal opinion that the books of Hermes Trismegistus really contained the ancient Egyptian doctrine of which traces can be discovered from the hieroglyphics which cover the monuments of Egypt. Moreover, if these fragments themselves are examined, we find in them a theology sufficiently in accord with the doctrines set forth by Plato in his *Timaeus* – doctrines which are entirely apart from those of the other schools of Greece, and which were therefore held to have been derived by Plato from the temples of Egypt, when he went thither to hold converse with its priests.[9]

Mead pursued the argument further, exploring the works of many German commentators and the various spurious arguments that had, in the past, been put forward to discredit the *Hermetica* before reaching his own conclusion that these writings were of the utmost value.

> The more one studies the best of these mystical sermons, casting aside all prejudice, and trying to feel and think with the writers, the nearer one is conscious of approaching the threshold of what may well be believed to have been the true Adytum[10] of the best in the mystery-traditions of antiquity. Innumerable are the hints of the greatnesses and immensities lying beyond that threshold – among

other precious things the vision of the key to Egypt's wisdom, the interpretation of apocalypsis by the light of the sun-clear epopteia of the intelligible cosmos.

Such greatnesses and such mysteries have a power and beauty which the most disreputable tradition of the texts through unknowing hands cannot wholly disguise, and they are still recognisable, even though clad in the rags of their once fair garments, by those who have eyes to see and ears to hear.[11]

Mead was right. The *Hermetica* is indeed an extraordinary collection of writings but reading them for the first time, I was amazed to discover how deeply personal and modern they seemed. Their philosophy was not abstract like that of Plato or Aristotle but referred to a real though secret, initiatory tradition of great antiquity. Philosophical debate was not for them a matter of open discussion but the process whereby a Master could instruct his pupils in the necessary knowledge for their own religious development. They taught that the most important goal in life was to achieve personal *gnosis*, that is to say knowledge of things divine. It seemed that everything else was preparatory to this moment of illumination when the student would perceive for himself the divine truth of the *gnosis* of God. According to the *Hermetica* the first person to have achieved this had been the god Hermes, the founder of the school.

And as long as the Craftsman who made the universe willed not to be known, all was wrapped in ignorance. But when he determined to reveal himself, he breathed into certain godlike men a passionate desire to know him, and bestowed on their minds a radiance ampler than that which they already had within their breasts, that so they might first will to seek the yet unknown God, and then have power to find him. But this, Horus my wondrous son,[12] it would not have been possible for men of mortal breed to do, if there had not arisen one whose soul was responsive to the holy Powers of heaven. And such a man was Hermes, he who won knowledge of all. Hermes saw all things, and understood what he saw, and had power to explain to others what he understood — [yet he did not make the truth known without reserve] for what he had discovered he inscribed on tablets, and hid securely what he had inscribed, leaving the larger part untold, that all later ages of the world might seek it.[13]

The way that this happened is described in the first book in the *Corpus Hermeticum*, the *Poimandres* (in English 'shepherd of men'). The *gnosis* was revealed to Hermes when he had had some sort of out-of-the-body experience.

> Once upon a time, when I had begun to think about the things that are, and my thoughts had soared high aloft, while my bodily senses had been put under restraint by sleep, yet not such sleep as that of men weighed down by fullness of food or by bodily weariness, methought there came to me a Being of vast and boundless magnitude, who called me by my name, and said to me,
>
> 'What do you wish to hear and see, and to learn and come to know by thought?' 'Who are you?' I said. 'I,' said he, 'am Poimandres, the Mind of the Sovereignty.' 'I would fain learn,' said I, 'the things that are, and understand their nature, and get knowledge of God. These,' I said, 'are the things of which I wish to hear.' He answered, 'I know what you wish, for indeed I am with you everywhere; keep in mind all that you desire to learn, and I will teach you.'[14]

This chapter goes on to describe how the universe was created by God out of a primordial substance from which he also made souls. It seems that these pure souls originally lived with God in the highest sphere, that is to say in a region of creation beyond time, space and the conditioning influence of the planets:

> But Mind the Father of all, he who is Life and Light, gave birth to Man, a Being like to Himself. And he took delight in Man, as being His own Offspring; for Man was very goodly to look on, bearing the likeness of his Father. With good reason then did God take delight in Man; for it was God's own form that God took delight in. And God delivered over to Man all things that had been made.

However, man became bored and restless, wanting to be a creator himself. According to *Poimandres* it was this desire that was to inevitably lead to his 'fall' and the incarnation of souls to become physical men and women. The description of the fall of man is similar to that to be found in Genesis, yet somehow the story as told here in symbolic fashion is more profound.

And Man took station in the Maker's sphere, and observed the things made by his brother (viz. the demiurgic power or Solar Logos that created the seven administrators or lights of the solar system), who was set over the region of fire; and having observed the Maker's creation in the region of fire, he willed to make things for his own part also; and his Father gave permission, having in himself all the working of the Administrators; and the Administrators took delight in him, and each of them gave him a share of his own nature.

And having learnt to know the being of the Administrators, and received a share of their nature, he willed to break through the bounding circle of their orbits; and he looked down through the structure of the heavens, having broken through the sphere and showed to downward-tending Nature the beautiful form of God. And Nature, seeing the beauty of the form of God, smiled with insatiate love of Man, showing the reflection of that most beautiful form in the water and its shadow on the earth. And he, seeing this form, a form like to his own, in earth and water, loved it, and willed to dwell there. And the deed followed close on the design; and he took up his abode in matter devoid of reason. And Nature, when she had got him with whom she was in love, wrapped him in her clasp, and they were mingled in one; for they were in love with one another.

It is not surprising that the Biblical account of Adam and Eve is similar as Moses, who is said to have written the first five books of the Bible himself, was also said to have been schooled in the wisdom of the Egyptians. This could only mean that he had been initiated into the Hermetic tradition and that he would have studied a creation myth similar to that found in the *Poimandres*. However, the story as told by Moses in Genesis, takes on a patriarchal twist. The Fall of the divine Adam is blamed not on the enticements of nature but his wife, the first woman, Eve. When I realized that Adam is the Hebrew word for man and Eve means 'mother of all things' it became clear to me that in the Genesis story there had to be a corrupted version of this original, Egyptian creation myth. I was both amazed at the profundity of the teachings given in the *Poimandres* and the way that its creation myth seemed to be so much richer in meaning than Genesis.

Having described the attraction of Man for nature, the *Poimandres* went on to tell of his fate:

And that is why man, unlike all other living creatures on earth is twofold. He is mortal by reason of his body; he is immortal by reason of the Man of eternal substance. He is immortal, and has all things in his power; yet he suffers the lot of a mortal, being subject to Destiny. He is exalted above the structure of the heavens; yet he is born a slave of Destiny.

This, it seems, would be man's fate for all eternity were it not for the intercession of the gods. In a later *Hermeticum* called the *Kore Cosmu*, or 'Virgin of the World', it is taught how because mankind had polluted the world with his incessant warfare and vice, the earth herself appealed to heaven for help.

Next Earth stood forth, in bitter grief; and [when she was given leave to plead] my glorious son, she thus began: 'O King and Father, President of the over-arching spheres of heaven, and Governor of us, the Elements, that stand before thee . . . I am dishonoured; trouble has risen up against me from mankind. Having naught to fear, they commit all manner of crimes; slaughtered by every sort of cruel device, men fall dead on my plains, O Lord, and I am soaked through with the juices of rotting corpses. Henceforward, Lord, since I am forced to contain beings unworthy of me, I wish to contain, together with all the things which I bring forth, God also. How long shall thy terrestrial world, peopled with mortals, have no God? Bestow upon Earth, if not thy very self, – that I ask not for I could not endure to contain thee, – yet at least some holy efflux of thee.[15]

In answer to her prayers, the Father god, Atum, sent his great grandson, Osiris, along with his wife Isis, to bring about civilization: the method by which mankind would be brought back to a state of holiness and thereby eventually regain his freedom from the material world:

. . . God filled the universe with the sound of his holy voice, and said, '. . . Another shall now come down to dwell among you, an efflux of my being, who shall keep holy watch on men's deeds. He shall be judge of the living, – a judge that none can deceive, – and a terrible king of the dead; and every man shall meet with such retribution as his deeds deserve.'

Thereupon Horus said: Tell me then, mother, how did Earth attain to that happy lot of receiving the efflux of God? – And Isis answered: Mighty Horus, do not ask me to describe to you the origin of the stock from whence you are sprung; for it is not permitted to enquire into the birth of gods. This only I may tell you, that God who rules alone, the fabricator of the universe, bestowed on the earth for a little time your great father Osiris and the great goddess Isis, that they may give the world the help it so much needed.

It was they that filled human life with that which is divine, and thereby put a stop to the savagery of mutual slaughter.

It was they that established upon the earth rites of worship which correspond exactly with the holy Powers in heaven.

It was they that consecrated temples and instituted sacrifices to the gods that were their ancestors, and gave to mortal man the boons of food and shelter.

. . . It was they that, having learnt God's secret law-givings, became law-givers for mankind.

It was they that devised the [initiation and training] of the prophet priests, to the end that these might nurture men's souls with philosophy, and save their bodies by healing art when they are sick.

When we had done all this, my son, Osiris and I, perceiving that the world had been filled with blessings by the gods who dwell in heaven, asked leave to return to our home above.[16]

Reading this it was clear that the ancient Osiris religion of Egypt had a tremendous amount in common with Christianity. Not only did both religions talk about the need for mankind to be redeemed from their sinful ways but they also talked of God sending his 'efflux' or seed, to bring about change in the world. Recognizing the importance of these texts, I felt that it was time a new edition was published, one that would be more accessible to the general public than the over-scholarly edition of Scott's translation that I had in my possession. Accordingly, I set to work editing his tome, smoothing the text and removing much of the impediments to clear reading. As I wanted people to read these documents with excitement and not in the clinical way of scholars, I front-ended the book with a Foreword of my own, drawing attention to their esoteric value. I hoped the book would be successful and would revive interest in the whole subject of the Hermetic philosophy. However, when I finally published this new edition in May 1992 I had no idea that it was going to lead me into the greatest adventure of my life to date.

# CHAPTER 5

# The Orion Mystery

It was now some five months since the publication of my new edition of the *Hermetica* and I just happened to be at my Bath distributors for the day sorting out some problems they had with their computer system. Suddenly the phone rang and, much to my surprise, the call turned out to be for me. At first I thought it must be my wife, for who else would know I was at Ashgrove that day. However, any worries that may have sprung to mind concerning car problems or other difficulties necessitating an emergency phone call by her in the middle of the day were quickly dispelled when I heard an unfamiliar male voice on the other end of the line.

The caller turned out to be a Robert Bauval, a Belgian-Alexandrian construction engineer who, having been expelled from Egypt during one of Nasser's purges of foreigners, now lived in England. He, it turned out, had been looking for Scott's translation of the *Hermetica* for some time but at every shop he had tried he had been told it was out of print and unobtainable. Then, a week or two before his call, he had chanced to visit a rather old-fashioned booksellers in Oxford. They, much to their own surprise, discovered my new Solos Press edition on their microfiche. He had promptly ordered two copies — one for a friend of his — and these had duly arrived a few days later. Our conversation went on and he explained the reason he was calling was that he had been intrigued by my Foreword with its references to a connection between the Alexandrine school of Hermes Trismegistus and the IVth Dynasty pyramid builders. This, it seemed, was a major field of interest of his own and indeed he had written an unpublished book on the subject. We talked about this for maybe an hour and a half, the conversation ranging over a wide range of subjects, everything from the work of Dame Frances Yates, to the Battle of the Pyramids, the Osiris religion and the astronomy of the constellation of Orion. He asked me if I would be interested in seeing his book, with a view to publication, and a few days later it arrived in the post.

The work when it arrived was far ranging in its implications revealing the workings of an extraordinary mind. I was used to seeing strange manuscripts and sometimes it seemed that the world was entirely populated by closet eccentrics churning out the most bizarre theories in the mistaken belief that they would ever find a publisher willing to put them into print. However this author, even if clearly driven, was no eccentric. What he had to say on the subject of the pyramids, though completely unorthodox, was well-argued and backed up with painstaking researches that must have taken years to put together. Despite the fact that the book covered too much ground and was, to my way of thinking, too academic in its style of presentation to appeal to a wide readership, I was sure it contained at least one potential best-seller. We therefore arranged to meet up and a week or two later I found myself on his doorstep.

Robert Bauval turned out to be a man in his mid-forties, lean and with all the excitability of a Mediterranean. Extensively travelled, he had lived and worked in Africa and the Middle East on some of the largest construction projects this century. His Egyptian background coupled with his knowledge and experience concerning the practicalities of building had led him to re-examine current theories on the purpose of the Giza pyramids. It seemed to him that there was an exactness to their execution that was at odds with accepted academic opinion that these were merely individual tombs of powerful pharaohs. With his builder's eye he could see that there was more to it than this and that even if they were tombs, their positions and sizes were dictated by some overall scheme. Quite what this scheme was and why it should have been chosen was not at first apparent but he was determined to find out, convinced by now that it concealed some very important secret.

At first his interest in the pyramids had been merely a hobby but gradually, over the years, it had become more and more of a consuming passion. He had by now put together an extraordinary jigsaw puzzle revealing that the IVth Dynasty pyramids of Giza were built to represent the stars we know today as the Belt of Orion. Not only that but other pyramids, built around the same time, represented other neighbouring stars whilst the Egyptians conceived of their River Nile as an earthly counterpart of the Milky Way. It was an astounding conception that most academics he had approached had been keen to dismiss out of hand. Yet he had been able to back his conclusions with other data, lending support to this new stellar theory. He had found many references in the Pyramid Texts, the oldest corpus of religious writings in the world, stating that dead pharaohs believed they would be reborn as stars in Orion. There were many representations of Orion to be seen on the walls of later tombs and inscribed on the captones of pyramids and it was well established by Egyptology that this constellation was associated with Osiris, the god of the dead. As if this were not enough, there was also the matter of certain 'air-shafts' in the Great Pyramid, one of which had been discovered in 1964 to have been directed at the culmination of Orion's Belt[1] at the time the pyramid was built. All this had to be more than coincidence and indicated a need for a complete rethink concerning the Egyptians' astral religion.

Sitting in Robert's kitchen, he bombarded me with facts, figures and dates with hardly a pause for breath. My head was aching from the intensity of our discussion when I left for home some six hours later. What he had had to say was so extraordinary and important I knew that, come what may, it had to be published. I was also aware, as one is on these occassions, that for both of us this was a matter of destiny. He was like an unexploded bomb, containing a critical mass of uranium that could explode at any moment. I knew that it was my duty to make sure that this material detonated in a controlled fashion. Between us we had to make sure that the electricity generated by these radioactive ideas would reach as wide an audience as possible.

In the weeks that followed we worked closely together on the project. We decided to write a book together that would be entitled *The Orion Mystery*, which we would publish jointly through Solos Press. However, destiny had more tricks up her sleeve when we became embroiled in events surrounding the discovery of a secret 'door' inside the Great Pyramid itself.[2] We were persuaded that it would be better not to publish the book ourselves but to put it in the hands of a large publisher. This proved to be a wise decision as, following the broadcasting of a documentary called *The Great Pyramid — Gateway to the*

*Stars* that we made for the BBC, and only some fourteen months after Robert and I had first met over the phone, *The Orion Mystery* became a UK number one best-seller.

## Harran and the Magi

Whilst writing *The Orion Mystery*, and indeed from the very beginning of our association, Robert and I would often dicuss the subject of the Magi. We both believed that the star described by Matthew in his Gospel was unlikely to have been a supernova. It was much more likely that it represented Sirius, the brightest star in the sky, which was venerated throughout the Near East and which the Egyptians closely associated with the birth of kings. Matthew wrote his Gospel a generation after the events he describes and his expected readership was probably more Gentile than Jew. He needed to prove to the Egyptians, Greeks, Syrians and others that his Messiah, the Jesus of his Gospel, was not just a Jewish prophet but a universal saviour. He needed to have established credentials and part of this was the association of the Messiah with Sirius, the royal star of Isis and Horus. The Egyptians based their Sothic calendar on the movements of Sirius which they called Spdt, rendered into Greek as Sothis. It was linked with their most popular goddess, Isis and her son Horus, who according to legend was conceived miraculously from the seed of her dead husband Osiris. The Egyptians believed that all their pharaohs, whilst alive, were incarnations of Horus. After death they went through a series of rituals, including mummification, designed to transform them into an 'Osiris'. They were then able to ascend to heaven and become a star in the constellation of Orion. As part of the funeral ritual, Isis had to 'give birth' to a new Horus. This required the performance of further rituals involving the star Sirius and, at one time we believed, the Great Pyramid.

Isis as mother was a popular icon in ancient Egypt. It is very clear to anyone making a study of the subject that this symbol of Isis, the widowed mother of the divine child Horus, passed into Christian iconography as the Virgin with Child. There are countless figurines in existence showing Isis with the young Horus suckling one of her breasts or, more esoterically, sitting on her lap with one finger to his lips – a gesture meaning 'keep the secret'. With the advent of Christianity, Isis, the mother goddess who was popular not only in Egypt but throughout the Roman Empire, became Mary the Queen of

Heaven. The latter's title of *stella maris*, 'star of the sea', betrays the origins of her cult. The 'sea' in question was not the Mediterranean but the ocean above, that is to say the sky. The 'star of the sea' was and is Sirius, the brightest star of our skies and for millennia considered to be the star of Isis. Mary did indeed inherit the blue mantle of Isis.

The idea of Magi following the movements of Sirius was certainly not an invention of Matthew's. The skies in Mesopotamia are generally clear and it was normal for travelling caravans to move at night. All the peoples of the Near East were expert astronomers and around Christmas time Sirius would rise around sunset and set not long before dawn. For anyone skilled in navigation and knowledgeable of its movements, it would indeed have been an ideal guide star. Given all of these connections, religious and navigational, it was not hard to see that Matthew's story of a star guiding the Magi would have had an immediate resonance in Egypt. The question remained, however, was Matthew's story, elaborated as it no doubt is, based on a real event? Had real Magi from the East, as pictured on millions of Christmas cards, visited the manger at Bethlehem? I believed that they had and that they were emissaries of a secret school active in Mesopotamia and Persia. However, the first piece of evidence was not to be found in Palestine or even in Mesopotamia but in Egypt, the land from which Moses had once led his people, where I believed the Magi also had connections.

## The Temple of the Phoenix

In March 1993, Robert and I, along with my wife Dee, went to Egypt to carry out some last minute research and to take pictures for our forthcoming book. Whilst there we took the opportunity of visiting Heliopolis, now a suburb of Cairo but five thousand years ago the spiritual heart of Egypt. Called Annu (the On of the Bible) Heliopolis, the 'city of the sun', was sacred to Atum, the Father of the gods. Though he himself was, like the Christian God-the-Father, the invisible power behind creation, he was usually worshipped as Atum-Ra, the setting Sun. Heliopolis was built on top of a hill overlooking the River Nile and, as the abode of the Father of the Gods, had the same sort of meaning for the Egyptians as Mount Sinai would later have for the Israelites. In ancient times there were many temples on the Hill of Heliopolis, representing the different schools and cults popular at different times. However, the most important of these and the focus of our interest was the remains of the Temple of Atum itself. This, possibly the oldest religious site in Egypt, had once housed a stone pillar sacred to the Father god. According to Egyptian mythology, Atum created the universe out of his own semen and his pillar, a proto-obelisk which probably had similar associations to the altar stone later raised by the Hebrew patriarch Jacob seems to have represented his phallus. Also kept in the same temple was an object called the Benben stone. It probably stood on top of the pillar and seems to have been either brightly polished or covered in gold so that it gleamed in the sunlight. In *The Orion Mystery* Robert and I followed up clues linking the Benben of Heliopolis with a wider meteorite cult that was once prevalent throughout Egypt and the Near East. Much to my regret the scope of *The Orion Mystery* and its archaeological nature did not allow us to pursue more esoteric ideas concerning its symbolism. At some time during the Pyramid Age (*c.*2700–2180 BC), the Benben stone went missing. It was Robert Bauval's belief that it had found its way into the Great Pyramid, hidden there by the pharaoh Khufu who either feared for its safety or simply wanted to keep its powers to himself for all eternity. Whether this is indeed so we may never know for sure, but the discovery in 1993 of what looks to be a closed aperture leading into a secret chamber lends weight to this hypothesis.

The building of the great pyramids of Giza and Dashour by the IVth Dynasty pharaohs Sneferu, Khufu, Khafra and Menkaura was a major undertaking – no less than the creation of a heaven on earth. However, the cutting, dressing and laying of millions of tons of limestone to make these structures seems to have taxed both the resources and patience of the people. With the passing of Menkaura there seems to have been some sort of rebellion and power passed to a new dynasty of pharaohs, three of whom were said to have been the triplet sons of a priestess from Heliopolis. These pharaohs of the Vth Dynasty seem to have been content to build much smaller pyramids than their forebears which are today little more than rubble heaps. Unas, the last pharaoh of the Dynasty had his pyramid raised in the original royal cemetery of Sakkara, close to that of the IIIrd Dynasty pharaoh Zoser who had started it all with his revolutionary Step-pyramid. This pyramid is different from all of its predecessors as Unas' priests came up with the radical scheme of having the inside walls of his burial chambers inscribed with hieroglyphics. These 'Pyramid Texts', as they are called, form the oldest corpus of religious writings in the world. They tell us much about the royal cult of the pharaohs and their belief that after death they would travel to the stars.

Following the death of Unas power changed hands again with the start of the VIth Dynasty. These pharaohs continued to build pyramids at Sakkara, most of which also carry hieroglyphic texts. However, at the end of the VIth Dynasty, around 2180 BC, Egypt seems to have been convulsed by some sort of revolution. The Golden Age of the pyramid builders came to an abrupt end and Egyptian civilization went into sharp decline. Pyramids, temples and tombs were robbed and the country went into the 'Dark Age' known to historians as the First Intermediate Period. During this period of turbulence pharaohs and dynasties continued to come and go but little is known about them. Then, around 1990 BC, with the advent of the XIIth Dynasty, there was something of a renaissance and Egypt regained its self-confidence. One of the pharaohs of this Dynasty, Sesostris I (also called Senusert I) set about rebuilding the temple of Atum at Heliopolis and it was largely his handiwork that we had come there to see.

Following the death of the last XIIth Dynasty pharaoh c. 1786 BC, Egypt plunged into another Dark Age. This time the cause does not seem to have been internal revolution but rather the invasion of the country by a mysterious peoples called the Hyksos. These foreigners, called variously the 'Shepherd Kings' or 'Sea-Peoples', controlled the country for some two hundred years. There is much debate over who they were or where they came from but judging from extant reliefs, they were of Semitic extraction, their homeland being almost certainly Syria and south-east Turkey. This is very interesting from the Biblical point of view, for if there is any truth in the story of Abraham's migration and the subsequent settling of the children of Israel in Egypt, then it has to have happened around this time. In fact this dating fits in with Matthew's chronology. At the start of his Gospel he spells out the genealogy of Joseph, Jesus' adoptive father, and concludes by telling us:

> So all the generations from Abraham to David are fourteen generations; and from David until the carrying away into Babylon are fourteen generations; and from the carrying away into Babylon unto Christ are fourteen generations. [3]

Since we know that the fall of Jerusalem and the exile of the Jews to Babylon took place in 586 BC and that the birth of Jesus probably took place in 7 BC, then it is a matter of simple arithmetic to conclude that for Matthew a generation lasts approximately forty years. Projecting backwards from the birth of Jesus by 42 such generations takes us to a date of c. 1684 for the beginning of the generation of Abraham. This is in the Second Intermediate Period of Egyptian history at around the time of the Hyksos invasion.

During the Hyksos period Egypt was ruled by foreign kings and it could have been one of these who was the pharaoh that Abram (Abraham) met and to whom he pretended his wife Sarai was only his sister:

And there was famine in the land: and Abram went down into Egypt to sojourn there; for the famine was grievous in the land. And it came to pass when he was come near to enter into Egypt, that he said unto Sarai his wife, Behold now, I know that thou art a fair woman to look upon: Therefore it shall come to pass, when the Egyptians shall see thee, that they shall say, This is his wife: and they will kill me, but they will save thee alive. Say, I pray thee, thou art my sister: that it may be well with me for thy sake; and my soul shall live because of thee.

And it came to pass, that when Abram was come into Egypt, the Egyptians beheld the woman that she was very fair. The princes also of Pharaoh saw her, and commended her before Pharaoh: and the woman was taken into Pharaoh's house. And he entreated Abram well for her sake: and he had sheep, and oxen, and he asses, and menservants, and maidservants, and she asses, and camels.

And the Lord plagued Pharaoh and his house with great plagues because of Sarai, Abram's wife. And Pharaoh called Abram, and said, What is this thou hast done unto me? Why didst thou not tell me she was your wife? Why saist thou, She is my sister? so I might have taken her to me to wife: now therefore behold thy wife, take her, and go thy way. And Pharaoh commanded his men concerning him: and they sent him away, and his wife, and all that he had.[4]

This story, probably apocryphal, reflects better on the Egyptians than it does on Abraham who comes over as not only cowardly in hiding behind Sarai's skirts but deceitful in accepting gifts for her dishonour.

Joseph, Abraham's great-grandson, fares rather better. Brought to the country as a slave, in the Biblical narrative he rises to become chancellor over all the land after he correctly interprets the pharaoh's dreams. Even today, in Egypt he is widely credited with having built the canal, the Bahr Yussef, that connects the River Nile with Lake Moeris (Birkat Qaroun), enabling large areas of extra land in the Fayum to be irrigated. To reinforce his place as a very senior official, Joseph marries the daughter of the chief priest of On (Heliopolis), who would almost certainly have been of royal blood.

> And Pharaoh said unto Joseph, I am Pharaoh, and without thee shall no man lift up his hand or foot in all the land of Egypt. And Pharaoh called Joseph's name Zaphenath-paneah; and he gave him to wife Asenath the daughter of Poti-pherah priest of On.[5]

Asenath, later bears Joseph two sons, Mannaseh and Ephraim, who even though they are half-Egyptian, receive a special blessing from their grandfather Jacob (Israel). He adopts them into his own family as the equals of their uncles, the eldest of whom, Reuben, has disgraced himself by sleeping with Bilhah, his father's concubine.

> And one told Jacob, and said, Behold thy son Joseph cometh unto thee: and Israel strengthened himself and sat upon the bed. And Jacob said unto Joseph, God Almighty appeared unto me at Luz in the land of Canaan and blessed me, And said unto me, Behold I will make thee fruitful, and multiply thee, and I will make of thee a multitude of people; and I will give this land to thy seed after thee for an everlasting possession. And now thy two sons, Ephraim and Manasseh, which were born unto thee in the land of Egypt before I came unto thee in the land of Egypt, are mine; as Reuben and Simeon,[6] they shall be mine.

Jacob goes on to lament to Joseph the death of his favourite wife Rachel, the latter's mother, on the way to Bethlehem.

> . . . And as for me, when I came from Padan,[7] Rachel died by me in the land of Canaan in the way, when yet there was a little way to come unto Ephrath: and I buried her there in the way of Ephrath; the same is Bethlehem.[8]

Evidently the beautiful Rachel, for whose hand Jacob had sacrificed fourteen years of his life working for his uncle in Harran, died whilst giving birth to Joseph's only full-blooded brother, Benjamin. He was the youngest of the sons of Israel and it was on him that Joseph played a trick before revealing himself to his brothers; he had his own silver cup hidden in Benjamin's sack of grain so that he would unwittingly steal it and the party would be forced to return when this was later discovered by the Egyptian guards. This, it seems, was a test to see if his other half-brothers, who had previously betrayed Joseph, would be prepared to abandon Benjamin too. They do not and indeed Judah, who previously had sold Joseph for twenty pieces of silver, even offers his own freedom in return for that of the boy. Accordingly, they are received back with much jubilation by Joseph and later rewarded by Pharaoh with land-holdings in Egypt.

Walking round what remained of the Temple of the Phoenix with its huge obelisk of Senusert I (plate 11), I couldn't help but wonder what Joseph must have thought of it. I could imagine him discussing the phoenix legend with his father-in-law, who as high priest here would have had the title 'chief of the observers'. As chancellor of all the land of Egypt, the man without whose permission no one could 'lift up hand or foot in all the land of Egypt', Joseph would have had responsibility for maintaining shrines such as the Temple of the Phoenix. He would have seen the brightly gleaming obelisk and no doubt would have had its symbolism explained to him.

The Hyksos lived largely in the Delta region with only nominal control over Upper Egypt. Gradually a new native Egyptian power base was consolidated around the city of Thebes (Luxor) and an independence movement gained in strength. The Hyksos period came to an end around 1567 BC when they were eventually defeated by this new, upsurgent power and the New Kingdom was born. With their defeat it would seem that the remaining Hyksos, presumably including the Israelites, now became slaves.

During the New Kingdom, Egypt attained its greatest worldly power under the militant pharaoh Tuthmosis III. He made war on his neighbours, taking his army as far north as Carchemish on the Euphrates and extending the Egyptian Empire to include large areas of the Near East, including Palestine. Though the capital of Egypt had moved south from Memphis to Thebes, the temple precinct of

Heliopolis was now refurbished. To celebrate his victories and no doubt as a thanksgiving to the sun-god Atum-Ra, Tuthmosis furnished his temple with at least four obelisks. The biggest of these, which at thirty-two and a quarter metres was the largest ever erected, was removed by the Romans. It was transported to Rome by Constantine the Great and today it stands in the Piazza of St John Lateran. A second of Tuthmosis' obelisks was taken in AD 390 to Constantinople by the Byzantine emperor, Theodosius, and re-erected on a marble base in the Hippodrome. It still stands there to this day, though unlike the obelisk itself, which is still in pristine condition, the base is now badly eroded. The last two, falsely known as Cleopatra's Needles, were taken by the Roman emperor Augustus to adorn the Caesareum Temple in Alexandria. They were removed again in the late 1870s to London and New York respectively, where they stand on the Thames Embankment and in Central Park to this day.

The New Kingdom was in many ways Egypt's most glittering period. It left us the priceless paintings of the Valleys of the Kings and Queens, the massive Temples of Luxor and Karnac, not to mention the tomb of the boy king, Tutankhamun. Pharaoh Rameses II erected enormous statues of himself throughout the land, including a huge, now recumbant figure at the Old Kingdom capital of Memphis. One of the obelisks that he placed in front of the Temple of Amon at Luxor is now in the centre of Paris, marking the spot where the guillotine once stood. If he erected others at Heliopolis, they have long since disappeared. Today the Middle Kingdom obelisk of Senusert I stands in splendid isolation, as indeed it did before the advent of the New Kingdom.

Just when Moses and the Israelites made their historic crossing of the Red Sea is not known from the Egyptian records. However, if we apply the Matthew rule of roughly 40 years to a generation and accept that Naasson, son of Aminadab and father of Salmon is the same person as Nashon, the brother-in-law of Aaron,[9] then we can say that the Exodus occured eight generations or roughly 320 years after the time of Abraham. This gives us a date of c.1364 BC, which puts the Exodus into the frame of the New Kingdom XVIIIth Dynasty.

The Exodus may indeed have occurred, as many people believe, during the period of unrest following the rule of the famous New Kingdom pharaoh Akhenaten. He moved the capital of Egypt from Thebes to a new site at Tell el-Amarna and instituted monotheistic worship of the Sun's disk, called the Aten, in place of the older cults of the gods. The experiment was not a success and following his death, his heir, Tutankhamun, was forced to come back to Thebes and reinstitute the old ways. He died whilst still a boy, to be followed first by a general called Horemheb and then by one of Egypt's greatest rulers, Seti I. His carefully decorated tomb in the Valley of the Kings, now sadly vandalized, is considered to be one of the greatest artistic achievements of all time. Its ceiling decorations, showing constellations such as the Hippopotamus goddess Tuart holding an anchoring post, reveal that the Old Kingdom stellar religion was still alive one thousand years after the pyramids were built. The ancient wisdom of Egypt had not been forgotten.

The Biblical story of Moses in the bullrushes, which precedes the Exodus itself, has parallels with the earlier story of Horus, the son of Isis, who also had to hide amongst the papyrus groves of the Delta marshes lest he should be murdered by his wicked uncle Sett. In the case of Moses the threat comes from Pharaoh, who like Sett, is a cruel tyrant and in an attempt at population control has ordered that all newborn male Hebrew children are to be killed at birth. To circumvent this edict, Moses' mother hides him in an ark amongst the reed beds at the edge of the Nile.

And there went a man of the house of Levi, and took to wife a daughter of Levi. And the woman conceived and bare a son: and when she saw him that he was a goodly child, she hid him three months. And when she could no longer hide him, she took for him an ark of bulrushes, and daubed it with slime and with pitch, and put the child therein; and she laid in the flags by the river's brink. And his sister stood afar off to wit what would be done to him.

And the daughter of Pharaoh came down to wash herself by the river; and her maidens walked along by the river's side; and when she saw the ark among the flags, she sent her maid to fetch it. And when she opened it, she saw the child: and behold the babe wept. And she had compassion on him, and said, This is one of the Hebrew's children. Then said his sister to Pharaoh's daughter, Shall I go and call to thee a nurse of the Hebrew women, that she may nurse the child for thee? And Pharaoh's daughter said to her, Go. And the maid went and called the child's mother. And Pharaoh's daughter said unto her, Take this child away and nurse it for me, and I will give thee thy wages. And the woman took the child and nursed it. And the child grew and she brought him unto Pharaoh's daughter, and he became her son. And she called his name Moses: and she said because I drew him out of the water.[10]

The daughter of Pharaoh, like Isis with Horus, protects the child until he is old enough to take on the establishment and, like Horus, reinstitute the rule of law amongst his people. The Biblical narrative seems to be making the point that in this sense Moses is the legitimate 'Pharaoh' sanctioned by God. He, like Horus son of Isis, has had to endure the indignity of being hidden amongst the rushes before, at last, in the name of God he is able to take on Pharaoh and win the freedom of his people.

As any reader of the Bible will know, that freedom was short lived. Within a few centuries the Israel of the Old Testament went from being a powerful nation state to a divided kingdom split between the northern realm of ten tribes with its capital of Samaria and a southern realm of two tribes, Benjamin and Judah still centred on Jerusalem. Crushed between the great powers of Egypt and first Assyria and then Babylonia, these little states could not long endure. The ten tribes of Israel, that formed the original Kingdom of Samaria, were taken captive by the Assyrians and transported to Asia:

The king of Assyria came up throughout all the land, and went up to Samaria, and besieged it three years. In the ninth year of Hoshea[11] Assyria took Samaria, and carried Israel away into Assyria, and placed them in Halah and Habor by the river of Gozan, and in the cities of the Medes.[12]

The cities of the Medes were south of the Caspian Sea in what is now north-west Iran. Gozan was much closer to home for the now enslaved Israelites. It was a region of Northern Mesopotamia watered by a tributary of the Euphrates called the Khabour. The ten 'lost tribes' of Israel, including those of Ephraim and Manasseh, the sons of Joseph, disappear from the Bible at this point, though their fate is again mentioned in I Chronicles:

And the God of Israel stirred up the spirit of Pul king of Assyria, and the spirit of Tiglath-Pileser king of Assyria, and he carried them away, even the Reubenites, and the Gadites, and the half-tribe of

Manasseh, and brought them unto Halah, and Habor, and Hara, and to the river Gozan, unto this day.[13]

According to Young's Concordance, Hara may be the same place as Harran, the ancient city where Abraham's father was buried, which lies on the Belikh river, another tributary of the Euphrates and also at that time controlled by the Assyrian Empire:

> 'Hara . . . A place utterly unknown unless it is identified with Haran or Charran, the city of Mesopotamia to which Abraham came from Ur. Haran was known to the ancients as *Carrhae*. Hence we may conclude that a portion of the Israelites carried off by Pul and Tiglath-Pileser were settled in *Harran* on the *Belik*, while the greater number were conveyed to *Chabora*.'[14]

The exact locations of Halah and Habor are less clear but the first seems to be the unexcavated mound of earth called *Gla* near the confluence of the Khabour and Jerujer rivers. The city of Habor could be near modern day Nusaybin.

Having lost the ten tribes of northern Israel, the Bible now concentrates solely on the fate of their southern brethren, who were in the main descendants of the two tribes of Judah and Benjamin and are referred to from now on as the Jews. Though some of them also were transported by the Assyrians, they were finally removed from Jerusalem by the Babylonians who in 586 BC stripped the Temple of Jerusalem and burnt it down along with most of the rest of the city. Nearly all the people, excepting the poorest peasants who were left to 'be vinedressers and husbandmen', were taken captive to Babylon. This is not the end of the story, as a small civil war then took place amongst those who were left behind. Against the warnings of the prophet Jeremiah, the survivors decided to flee to Egypt to escape the wrath of the Babylonians. Needless to say they were, as Jeremiah predicted, not safe there either as this was the next target for Nebuchadnezzar. Amidst his terrible prophecies of destruction for the Jews, Jeremiah now made one for the temple of Heliopolis:

> And I will kindle a fire in the houses of the gods of Egypt, and he shall burn them and carry them away captives: and he shall array himself with the land of Egypt, as a shepherd putteth on

his garment; and he shall go forth from thence in peace. He shall break also the images of Bethshemesh ['the house of the sun' i.e. temple of Atum-Ra in Heliopolis], that is in the land of Egypt; and the houses of the gods of the Egyptians shall he burn with fire.[15]

The Babylonian invasion of Egypt seems to have taken place at some time around 580 BC. Whether the temple of Atum was actually sacked is not recorded but it is a likely supposition.

In 539 BC Babylon fell to the united armies of the Medes and Persians led by Cyrus the Great. He is best remembered as the king who released the Jews from their Babylonian captivity and allowed them to go home to rebuild the Jerusalem temple. By 525 BC the Persians already controlled most of Asia, including the best part of Anatolia, and they were looking to expand their empire westwards. With the help of Phoenician and Greek mercenaries, Cyrus' son, Cambyses, successfully invaded Egypt. Had he been content with merely robbing the country and demanding tribute he would probably have been accepted as no worse than any other foreign conqueror, however he scandalized the Egyptians by killing the sacred Apis Bull of Memphis.

The Egyptians used to keep these bulls, there being only one at any given time, in great luxury. They were believed to be incarnations of Osiris and after death were embalmed and buried in giant sarcophagi at the Serapeum, an enormous underground necropolis at Saqqara. As far as the Persians were concerned, this was mere superstition and Cambyses probably wanted to drive home the point that he was now master of the country and could do as he wished. However, for his sin against the Apis Bull, he is said to have been cursed and the Egyptians would not have been surprised by his subsequent madness and suicide.

This first Persian Empire, for all its might, did not last very long. In the spring of 334 BC, backed up by an army of 30,000 to 40,000 men, Alexander the Great invaded Asia Minor. Arriving at Gordium, the Phrygian capital, he solved the riddle of its famous knot by cutting through it with his sword. The following year he crossed the Taurus Mountains and passed through the Cilician Gates to defeat the Persians near the town of Issus. Marching down through Syria and Phoenicia, he arrived in Egypt in 332 BC. Unlike Cambyses he had considerable respect for the Egyptian religion and, indeed, wanted himself to be recognized as the son of a god. He believed the tale of his mother,

Olympias, that he was born after she had been ravished by Zeus, whom the Greeks equated with the Egyptian god Ammon. He therefore behaved very properly in Egypt, sacrificing to the gods at Memphis and making a famous pilgrimage to the cult centre of Ammon at the Oasis of Siwa.

Alexander's death in Babylon at the youthful age of thirty-three cut short the most glittering military career in all history. We can only guess at how both he and the world might have developed had he survived into old age. As it was his vast empire, which stretched from the Eastern Mediterranean to Northern India was doomed to fall apart. It was divided between his generals, Egypt falling to the lot of Ptolemy, who established his own dynasty in the new capital of Alexandria. This line continued to rule Egypt with varying fortunes for three hundred years. Meanwhile Palestine and Syria were taken over by Seleucus, another of Alexander's generals, and he established his own line: the Seleucids. Then in 30 BC, following the naval battle of Actium, Octavius Caesar, later to become the first Roman emperor, Augustus, invaded Egypt. Cleopatra, the last of the Ptolemies, committed suicide, her lover Mark Anthony having already fallen on his sword. The long line of pharaohs, going back to the Ist Dynasty of around 3100 BC, was brought to an end. No longer an independent power, Egypt became a province of the Roman Empire administered by a governor. This did not mean that the Romans were wholly unsympathetic to its glorious past. On the contrary they allowed the Egyptians to continue to worship their chosen gods, especially Serapis (a late version of Osiris) and his consort Isis. So popular were these gods that they found many followers amongst the Romans themselves and their cults were exported throughout the empire. Indeed there were soon temples of Isis as far away from Egypt as Cologne and Paris.

The Jews, meanwhile, had for a time succeeded in throwing off all foreign yokes. Under the Maccabee leader, Judas ben Mattathias, they had risen in revolt against their Seleucid ruler Antiochus IV. He had greatly insulted the Jews by proscribing circumcision, overturning their laws and encouraging Gentile forms of worship in the temple. His greatest crime, believed by many to be alluded to as the 'abomination of desolation' by the prophet Daniel, was to sacrifice a pig on the High Altar:

> For the ships of Chittim [Cyprus] shall come against him:[16] therefore he shall be grieved, and return, and have indignation against the holy

covenant. And arms shall stand on his part, and they shall pollute
the sanctuary of strength, and shall take away the daily sacrifice,
and they shall place the abomination that maketh desolate.[17]

The Jewish war of independence raged on for a generation, the
Seleucid garrison being finally removed from Jerusalem in 141 BC.
The Maccabees, or Hasmoneans as they are known, attempted to
combine the roles of high priest and hereditary monarch with only
partial success. Though they successfully conquered virtually all of
what had historically been the twin kingdoms of Judah and Israel,
along with the east banks of the Jordan River and Dead Sea, they
were opposed by the Pharisees, who disputed their claims to the high
priesthood. These divisions eventually led to the fall of the Hasmoneans
and the usurpation of the state by the party of the Idumaean Antipater,
who acted as adviser to John Hyrcanus II.[18]

By now the fate of Judea was inextricably mixed up with the destiny
of the Roman Empire. Following Antipater's death, his sons Herod and
Phasael were nominated as heads of state by Mark Anthony, thereby
displacing Hyrcanus. The change in dynasty was confirmed by the
Roman senate in 40 BC when Herod was confirmed as King of Judea.
He, at least in his own eyes, legitimized his claim by taking as his
second wife a princess called Mariamme, the last of the Hasmoneans.
Her brother, Aristobulus was made high priest but fearing that he was
becoming too popular, Herod had him put to death in 35 BC.

Herod's title was again ratified by Octavius in 31 BC, following the
Battle of Actium, the former's opposition to Cleopatra making up for
his earlier allegiance with Mark Anthony. Secure in his support from
Rome, Herod now felt free to execute Hyrcanus. He was, nevertheless,
hated as well as feared by his subjects who regarded him as a foreign
usurper. Never able to trust anyone, he murdered Mariamme as well
as his own two sons by her. Even on his death bed he didn't feel entirely
safe and, discovering that his eldest son Antipater was plotting against
him, had the latter executed just five days before he himself died.

Given this track record of one of history's most infamous dictators,
it is not surprising that the Holy Family should have found it advisable
to flee Judea. It is clear that if Herod had got wind of the birth of any
child with a half-legitimate claim to the throne, he would immediately
have ordered his execution.

Herod went to Egypt and visited Cleopatra whilst on his way to

Rome to secure his throne. It is unlikely that he went up the Nile to Heliopolis but had he done so, he would no doubt, like Cambyses, Alexander and Augustus, have marvelled at the strange beauty of the Heliopolitan obelisks, the enigmatic needles of the Sun-god.

## Heliopolis and the tree of the Virgin

Arriving ourselves at Heliopolis by car we made our way through a gate into a small park which is all that remains of the once sacred enclosure. It was not very large and was separated from neighbouring fields and blocks of flats by an ugly wire fence. The temple itself, or at least what remains of it, looked rather like an empty swimming pool; I could imagine it being filled with water and a fountain playing in the middle. It was difficult to believe that this rather plain structure had once been the most important temple in Egypt but then one had to remember that that was over five thousand years ago – a lot can happen in five millennia. In front of us and above the temple rose an enormous obelisk. A plaque in front of it informed us that it was raised c.1940 BC by Senusert I. Today it stands alone, mute witness to the former greatness of Annu but once it was surrounded by a positive forest of obelisks as well as elaborate buildings.

At first it seemed that our trip to Heliopolis was going to be something of an anti-climax but then we accidentally stumbled upon something else which was to turn out to have been very important in the context of the Magi story: a Christian church called the Materiya.

Egypt was one of the first countries in the world to become Christianized. Its large, cosmopolitan community at Alexandria where Greeks rubbed shoulders with Jews, Syrians, Romans and others made it an ideal recruiting ground for the new faith. When, on the orders of Constantine the Great, Christianity became the state religion of the Roman Empire, Alexandria was already one of the major patriarchates. With the closure of the pagan temples, the Church consolidated its power. Its dominant position in Egyptian life was not, however, to last. In 640 AD a Moslem Arab army under the command of a general called 'Amr invaded the country. In July they defeated the Byzantines at Heliopolis and went on to lay siege to Fortress Babylon, in what was to become Cairo. On Good Friday, 6 April 641, the garrison surrendered and 'Amr, was able to march northwards to Alexandria.

It was treacherously surrendered by the patriarch, Pkauchios, who may even have been a covert Muslim himself. Thus, it was that in little over a year and with minimal opposition, one of the richest provinces in the Roman Empire was lost to Christendom. Within a very short time, either through immigration or by conversion, the majority of Egyptians became Moslem, Christians becoming a shrinking minority.

A few days before going to Heliopolis we had visited the Greek orthodox cathedral and the so-called 'Hanging Church' of St George's that stands on the former site of Egyptian Babylon. The churches were magnificent but we were appalled to see how the graveyard had recently become the target of vandals and robbers. Many of the tombs, some of them quite new, had been plundered for whatever trinkets they might contain, the bones of the deceased being scattered in the process. Whilst we knew, of course, that grave-robbing has been practised in Egypt since before the time of the earliest pharaohs, it was still a shock to see modern sepulchres, some of them still carrying the pictures of their owners, torn apart in this way. Looking at the shattered crosses and whitened bones gave us pause for thought. It made one realize just how vulnerable civilization is and how poverty will drive people to the extremes of anti-social behaviour.

What interested me more, though, and my reason for visiting the churches was not the adversities of the dead but the fate of the living. I felt sure that the Coptic Christians were in possession of certain secrets concerning the origins of Christianity and its links with the old Egypt before the time of Christ. Whilst I didn't know what these might be, I was confident that at the heart of this mystery was the story of the Flight to Egypt.

Now when they [the Magi] had departed, behold, an angel of the Lord appeared to Joseph in a dream and said, 'Rise, take the child and his mother, and flee to Egypt, and remain there till I tell you; for Herod is about to search for the child, to destroy him'. And he rose and took the child and his mother by night, and departed to Egypt, and remained there until the death of Herod. This was to fulfil what the Lord had spoken by the prophet, 'Out of Egypt have I called my son'.[19]

As one might expect, for Egypt's Christians this is one of the most popular stories in the New Testament, and in the Church of St George we had seen paintings celebrating the event. Though nothing more is said concerning this journey, it is noteworthy that this is the only Gospel record we have of Jesus ever going out of the Holy Land and this is a matter of great pride to the Egyptians. In our discussions with the clergy at the cathedral we learnt that local traditions state that on arriving in Egypt the Holy Family stayed for a while in Heliopolis, before going on south to Assyut, where they lived for several years. Apparently a church, called the Materiya, now stood on the site where they had stayed.

Our curiosity aroused, we decided, when chance would permit, to look for this church. Leaving the obelisk of Senusert, we drove the short distance back into the heart of what are, by Cairo standards, quite affluent suburbs. Many of the people living in today's Heliopolis are Christian Copts, and like the Greeks and Armenians, they have a reputation for being good at business. Perhaps for this reason the shops and houses had a different feel to them from the rest of Cairo. There was also an even stronger French influence in evidence than in the rest of Cairo, the centre of which has a certain *Belle Époque* splendour, so that Heliopolis itself felt more like Marseilles than Egypt. Here in the centre of this thriving community we found what we had been looking for, the church of the Materiya (plate 13). Passing through the gates we were confronted with a small, yellow painted building surrounded by a peaceful garden of cacti, palms and other exotic plants that insulated the church from the noise and pollution outside. The present building was only about one hundred years old and had been erected by the French. Over the double doorway was a Latin inscription reading 'SANCTAE FAMILIAE IN AEGYPTO EXSULI'. Inside, the church walls were decorated with six large murals telling the story of the Flight. The first of these, on the left-hand side and nearest to the door carried the legend '*Massacre des Innocents*'. It illustrated the story from Matthew's Gospel:

> Then Herod, when he saw that he was mocked of the wise men, was exceeding wroth, and sent forth, and slew all the children that were in Bethlehem, and in all the coasts thereof, from two years old and under, according to the time which he had diligently inquired of the wise men.
>
> Then was fulfilled that which was spoken by Jeremiah the prophet,

saying in Rama was there a voice heard, lamentation, and weeping, and great mourning. Rachel weeping for her children, and would not be comforted, because they are not.[20]

The picture showed brutal soldiers carrying out Herod's orders, whilst the mothers of the slaughtered infants cried in anguish. Rachel, the favourite wife of Jacob, is in a sense the patron of Bethlehem because she died in childbirth on her way there. Naturally she laments the death of the innocent children, especially as the tribe of Benjamin, supposedly the descendants of her younger son, made up half of the Jewish nation named after Judah. Esoterically she prefigures Mary because her first-born son Joseph was sold by his brothers to the Ishmaelites, at the instigation of Judah, for twenty pieces of silver. Later on in the Gospel, Jesus is likewise betrayed to his enemies by another 'Judah' – Judas Iscariot – for thirty pieces. Prophetically this seems to be the greater cause of Rachel's lament and the reason why Matthew makes reference to it here.

The second mural shows Joseph and Mary on separate beds inside a stone-built cellar. He is awakened by an angel who tells him that they must flee to Egypt (plate 15). The execution of the picture was very moving, in particular the sensitive figure of the angel. He was painted so thinly that, like a ghost, you could see through him to the wall behind. The third mural, and the last to deal with events in Judea, shows Joseph leading Mary seated with the baby on the back of a donkey. Behind them stand the walls of Bethlehem, ahead the flat expanse of the unforgiving desert they must cross if they are to get to Egypt.

Crossing the aisle of the church seemed to be symbolic of traversing the Sinai for the next mural, on the right-hand side and nearest to the altar, shows the Holy Family resting by the Nile. Mary sits on one of a row of crumbling sphinxes with birds gathering round her feet. She is discreetly feeding the baby Jesus whilst in the distance Joseph is watering the donkey at the Nile's edge. The sphinxes seem to represent the enigma that is Egypt, ancient even before the birth of Abraham. Perhaps the esoteric significance of this painting is that Egypt is both a resting place and a source of nourishment for the young Messiah, that his mother, like Isis so many millennia before, is able to find sanctuary here both for herself and her newborn baby.

The next picture concerns a local legend and is, as far as the church of the Materiya is concerned, the most important of all. Near the church, in a little courtyard of its own, stands an old sycamore tree, which today is propped up on crutches as, unaided, it is no longer strong enough to support the weight of its venerable limbs (plate 17). I had visited this tree before going into the church, though the warden there, would only allow me to take still photographs and, as I don't speak Arabic, he was unable to tell me anything much about it other than to point at a nearby stone trough containing some water. This, as I later discovered, is central to the legend which states that Mary and Joseph either rested under or planted this very tree. The story is contained in an old, Gnostic Gospel first translated and published by a Mr Henry Sike in 1697:

> Hence they went to that sycamore tree, which is now called Matarea; And in Matarea the Lord Jesus caused a well to spring forth, in which St Mary washed his coat; And a balsam is produced, or grows, in that country from the sweat which ran down there from the Lord Jesus.[21]

Evidentally the old warden wanted me to understand that the water trough was the very one in which Mary had washed the coat. The connection between the Materiya and a spring of water is not an invention of the Gospel writers. The old Arabic name for Heliopolis, *Ayin esh Shems*, which means 'the fountain of the sun', seems to be derived from this legend of Jesus causing a spring to issue forth in the city of the sun.

In the 'Lost Books of the Bible' there is a note giving a little more detail to the tree side of the story:

> Cheminitius, out of Stipulensis, who had it from Peter Martyr, Bishop of Alexandria, in the third century, says, that the place in Egypt where Christ was banished is now called Matarea, about ten miles beyond Cairo; that the inhabitants constantly burn a lamp in rememberance of it; and that there is a garden of trees yielding a balsam, which were planted by Christ when a boy.[22]

The church mural of the event (plate 16) had a very good likeness of the old tree as it looks today and showed Joseph standing and Mary sitting in its shade. They appear relaxed, perhaps relieved that their long journey is nearly over and they are safe. Yet I could not help but feel there was more to this story, an esoteric meaning over and above the association of Jesus with a healing balsam that could presumably be made from the sap of such a sycamore tree. In pre-Christian times the sycamore was sacred to the goddess Hathor, who is often depicted as a cow hiding amidst its branches. She, like Nut the mother of Osiris, was a sky goddess. Each day she gave birth to a son called Ihy who is identified with the rising sun.

There was, however, another tradition, about a Mother Goddess, which was probably ignored or suppressed during the Old Kingdom but emerged in the Coffin Texts . . . The heavenly ocean was imagined as a 'great flood' — worshipped in several places as a cow whose starpecked belly formed the sky . . . Hathor is the face of the sky, the deep and the lady who dwells in a grove at

Map 2

The Flight to Egypt

the end of the world. Her son is Ihy, the child who emerges from his mother every day at dawn as the new sun . . .

Ihy is the light-child, a symbol for the first emergence in its freshness and potentiality . . . The rose hue of the dawn sky, whether on the first morning or every day, is the blood emitted by Hathor or Isis – the names are interchangeable – when she bears her son.[23]

The mythological connection between Mary as mother of the living Jesus and Hathor as mother of the rising sun, both of whom rest in a grove of sycamore trees, would have appealed to Gnostic Egyptians. But could there be some message in the symbol of the Mary tree that was even more esoteric?

Throughout the Bible, trees symbolize families, not least the original Royal House of the Kings of Israel. This family tree takes it root from Jesse, the father of King David. It was symbolically cut down at the time when Jerusalem fell to the Babylonians and the sons of the last king of Judah, Zedekiah, were slain in front of him before he himself was blinded and taken in chains to Babylon. In Isaiah there is a messianic prophecy concerning a regrowth of this tree, with a sucker coming up from its roots:

And there shall come forth a rod out of the stem of Jesse, and a branch shall grow out of his roots: And the spirit of the Lord shall rest upon him, the spirit of wisdom and understanding, the spirit of counsel and might, the spirit of knowledge and the fear of the Lord . . . And in that day there shall be a root of Jesse, which shall stand for an ensign of the people; to it shall the Gentiles seek: and his rest shall be glorious.[24]

This prophecy has always been understood by Christians as referring to Jesus, Jesse being one of the ancestors of Joseph listed at the start of Matthew's Gospel. This prophecy, with its positive message for the Gentile nations, is quoted by St Paul in his Epistle to the Romans in support of his mission to the Gentiles.[25] Could it be then that the Virgin Tree is meant to symbolize the Royal House of David and Jesus' destiny to be the rod coming from the root? That had to be one explanation but I wasn't entirely satisfied with it. Had the Materiya been near Jerusalem then a symbolic reference to Jesus as a relation of King David would have made more sense. It seemed to me that the family tree in question, assuming that was what the ancient sycamore symbolized, was older than this and connected with Egypt. The references to Rachel seemed to be an oblique indication of this. In other words it was not the tree of Jesse but that of his ancestor Joseph, the patriarch with the many-coloured coat. It seemed to me that the message of the Virgin Tree was that by coming to Heliopolis Jesus was making contact with a very ancient connection dating from long before the birth of Moses and that this would be fortunate for him.

The sixth and last of the murals took this Heliopolitan connection one stage further (plate 14). It showed Mary with the baby riding through an archway into the old city, a scene that in some ways prefigures the story of Jesus' later fateful ride into Jerusalem on the first Palm Sunday. To the side of the painting were several Egyptian columns, one of which was falling over and losing its capital. Again this might refer to events contained in the non-canonical Gospels where the arrival of Jesus in Egypt causes idols to fall down. This seems to symbolize the ending of one epoch, the ancient world of which Egypt was the cradle and the beginning of the next, the Christian era. In the background of the picture is the lone obelisk of Senusert, its narrow shaft piercing the sky.

Looking at this picture I was more and more coming to the conviction that Christianity, as we know it, has strong links with the mystery traditions of the ancient world, especially Egypt. How or why this came about was not clear but it obviously had something to do with the sojourn of the Israelites prior to the Exodus of Moses. I was beginning to realize that if I was to have any chance of untangling this mystery, then it was neccessary to look behind the mythological framework of the Old Testament and to try to understand the symbol of the obelisk.

The Persian invasion of 525 BC had important consequences beyond the killing of the Apis bull: it brought Egypt into a larger empire that embraced most of the Middle East and opened it up to foreign travellers. One of these was the Greek historian Herodotus who around 450 BC visited the Temple of the Phoenix. There he talked with the priests and they told him of their legends concerning the mythological *bennu* bird. This Egyptian phoenix (plate 12) has the hieroglypic form of a grey heron and is frequently depicted on papyri in the company of Osiris, the god of the dead, whose soul it is said to represent. It would seem that it occupied a role in Egyptian thinking somewhat analogous to the

European stork. According to the priests it was an infrequent visitor, only putting in an appearance once every five hundred years. It came from Arabia and would bring with it the body of its parent, wrapped up in a ball of myrrh, which it would then bury in the temple.

Looking into the etymology of the name, the word *bennu* seems to be linked to the Semitic root word *ben* meaning 'son of'. As Nu or Nut was the sky goddess of ancient Egypt and the company of anthropomorphic gods, Osiris, Isis, Seth and Nephthys, were said to be her children, it could be that *bennu* means 'son of Nut'. This would be an appropriate term for Osiris. However, according to Egyptologist R.T. Rundle Clark, the *bennu* is not only closely linked with Osiris as the embodiment of his soul but also represents the 'word of God' or Logos. Its visit to the temple at Heliopolis initiates a new world age or aeon, thereby giving order to time. In this sense it is a messenger of heaven. He writes:

> 'The phoenix, therefore, embodies the original Logos, the Word or declaration of destiny which mediates between the divine mind and created things . . .
>
> Underlying all Egyptian speculation is the belief that time is composed of recurrent cycles which are divinely appointed: the day, the week of ten days, the month, the year – even longer periods of 30, 400 or 1460 years, determined according to the conjunctions of sun, moon, stars and inundation. In a sense, when the phoenix gave out the primeval call it initiated all these cycles, so it is the patron of all division of time, and its temple at Heliopolis became the centre of calendrical regulation.'[26]

The *benben* stone that once stood in the Temple of the Phoenix appears to have symbolized, or perhaps was believed to be, the actual 'egg' of the phoenix. As the capstones, or pyramidions, put on the tops of pyramids were also called by the name *benben*, it seemed clear to Robert and I that they were symbolically linked with the original *benben* of Heliopolis. Also, since the sharp, pyramidal tips of obelisks were also called by the name *benben't*, it seemed that this symbol was of wider significance. It appears, then, that the pyramid shape had an analogous place in Egyptian religion to the cross in Christianity. For like the cross it represented death and resurrection, the divine word of God, the incarnation of a saviour and the birth of a new age. If Jesus really had come to Heliopolis as the Egyptians believe, then he was fulfilling not only the prophecies of the Jews, who were expecting their Messiah to be born in Bethlehem but those of the Egyptians as well.

Leaving Heliopolis and the Materiya we went back to our hotel. Our trip to Egypt had been a great success and we were confident that *The Orion Mystery*, when it came out, would be a great success. However, my mind was now moving ahead, from Egypt to Mesopotamia. I remembered at the back of my mind the story of how Gurdjieff had found somewhere in what is now Kurdistan his map of 'pre-sand Egypt' and how this map had ultimately led him to meet up with a secret brotherhood. I was beginning to suspect that this brotherhood might have had some connection with the Magi in Matthew's Gospel. Anxious to dig deeper into this mystery, I ransacked my library for further clues. In the end it became clear that there was only one course of action to be taken, I would have to follow in Gurdjieff's and Bennett's footsteps and have a look for myself. It was to turn out to be an adventure with interesting ramifications.

# CHAPTER 6

✴

# A Search for
# the Secret Brotherhood

Working on the Orion project was both stimulating and exciting, more importantly it got me thinking hard about Egypt and the pyramids. The layout of the pyramids as a gigantic map of the sky was something extraordinary and at first hard to comprehend. Yet the idea had the ring of truth about it and I was sure that Robert Bauval was correct, at least in broad terms, in his deductions. It was then that I remembered what I had read many years earlier in *Meetings with Remarkable Men* about Gurdjieff discovering a map of 'pre-sand Egypt' in the course of his travels. I couldn't help wondering whether he too had stumbled upon the Orion correlation. Had he found an old and secret document laying bare the secret of the Orion correlation (map 3)? If so, where had this map come from and where had he found it? Intrigued, I decided to look into this matter more deeply and reread the section of his travels covering this period very carefully.

It became clear almost at once that whilst he was clearly leaving a trail for others to follow after him, it was not quite as straightforward as it at first appeared. Bennett's assertion that the secret valley of Izrumin[1] was to be equated with that of Sheikh Adi I found rather suspect. After all, in the story of his travels contained in *Meetings* Gurdjieff never actually arrived at Izrumin; his search for the secret monastery that he believed had once stood there being cut short by Pogossian's accident with the spider and the need to nurse him back to full health. If Gurdjieff had meant to indicate the Yezidis as the source of his knowledge about the Sarmoung, as Bennett seems to have believed, I felt he would have done this in a more direct and tangible way. In fact most of what he says about them is hardly flattering, indicating that they were involved in some sort of primitive Voodoo over which they had no control.[2] Though Gurdjieff may have made a study of the Yezidi religion, I didn't feel that this was the true source of his knowledge nor did I feel that the Yezidis of today were the living custodians of the tradition that most interested him.

Bennett's search for the heirs to the Sarmoung among the Sufi Orders of Central Asia, I also felt to be misdirected. There could be little doubting that Gurdjieff had visited Sufi *Tekkes* where he had learnt not only much about breathing techniques but also certain sacred dances. These he brought to the West and announced that they came from Central Asian, dervish monasteries. His writings too implied a certain feeling for places such as Bukhara, Balkh and Samarkand and he

Map 3

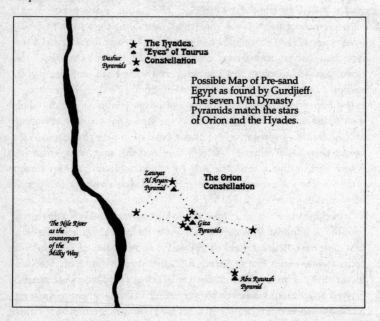

The Hyades.
"Eyes" of Taurus
Constellation

*Dashur Pyramids*

Possible Map of Pre-sand
Egypt as found by Gurdjieff.
The seven IVth Dynasty
Pyramids match the stars
of Orion and the Hyades.

*Zawyat
Al Aryan
Pyramid*

The Orion
Constellation

*The Nile River
as the
counterpart
of the
Milky Way*

*Giza
Pyramids*

*Abu Ruwash
Pyramid*

did seem to have imbibed much concerning the secret traditions of those places. Yet, though quite clearly a keeper of ancient traditions and with a long pedigree, I felt that Sufism was essentially a development from a different line of transmission. I couldn't see that these Orders were really the descendants or inheritors of the Sarmoung Brotherhood, which seemed to be closely connected with Egypt and the pyramids rather than Bactria and the blue-tiled archways of the Mongol revival. I was sure that Gurdjieff had got his major insights much closer to home than this, in what had been in his day the Ottoman Empire itself.

Getting out a suitably large scale map of the Middle East and matching it with the descriptions he gives in *Meetings*, I started to trace his probable route. I suspected that where Bennett had gone wrong and what had mistakenly led him to Sheikh Adi, was that he had been preoccupied with following what Gurdjieff had said was his intended route rather than where he actually went. The logical thing was to follow his footsteps, not his journey plan, and to see where these led (map 4).

Gurdjieff tells us that two months after crossing the River Arax he came to the town of 'Z'. Bennett, I believed correctly, identified this with Zakho in Iraqi Kurdistan. It is a border town, close to both Turkey and Syria and stands on one of the tributaries of the Tigris River. They then went off through a certain pass in the 'direction of Syria'. In this pass they were to reach a waterfall called 'K' before turning off for Kurdistan. Now looking at the map it seemed strange that he would talk about turning off for Kurdistan since they were already in it. Also, going towards Syria didn't make sense if their goal, as Bennett thought, was a valley in the vicinity of Mosul. This city lies much further down the River Tigris and, crucially, in the opposite direction to Syria. My feeling was that they were headed north-east from Zakho, up not down the Valley of the Tigris, towards the town of Cizre. Just above here, on my modern map of Eastern Turkey, the Tigris had been dammed, thereby creating a large, multi-fingered lake in the valleys above. I couldn't find any references to waterfalls in the area but as the Tigris in this region is swiftly flowing through deep gorges, it seemed likely there had been one above Cizre before the dam was built. On my map, much further to the south-east of Zakho was marked in Turkish the name Çukurca. On a British map of the area this town is called Kirkuk. If Cizre could have an alternative spelling as Kizre, then it was clearly Gurdjieff's town of 'K', where they had to turn off in a different direction.

The next event was the biting of his friend by a poisonous spider.

We are not told where this incident took place but we are informed that they now abandoned their search for the valley of Izrumin and went instead to a town called 'N', where they stayed in the house of an Armenian priest. It was here that they found the ancient map of 'pre-sand Egypt'. Looking at my map of the area it was quite clear that this town had to be Nusaybin, a very ancient city on a tributary of the Chabour River. Crucially Nusaybin lies directly west of Cizre (or Kizre). Had they been proceeding north along the Tigris from Zakho, they would have reached the waterfalls above Cizre and then turned west to go towards Nusaybin. This fitted the pattern of the journey as described and, crucially, it meant that they had never intended to go to Mosul or Sheikh Adi as Bennett imagined.

I now began to suspect that the identification of 'Nivssi' with Nineveh and therefore Mosul was a blind put into the story by Gurdjieff to throw casual seekers off the scent. I could find no reference to Mosul or Nineveh ever being called Nivssi, though as it lies in Iraqi Kurdistan I wasn't about to go there and check it out on the ground. What I did find was that Nusaybin itself used to be called Nisibis, a near anagram of Nivssi, and that it had once housed a famous academy. This institution had owed its eminence, if not its origins, to an event that occurred in AD 449 at the city of Edessa,[3] some 190 kilometres further east. At that time a great debate raged in the Eastern Church concerning the nature of the divinity of Jesus Christ. Two schools of thought, loosely labelled Diophysite and Monophysite,[4] were in open contention. Proponents of the first school held, in essence, that Jesus was born man and became joined to God. Its most extreme proponent was Nestorius (d, c.AD 451), a Syrian ecclesiastic who became patriarch of Constantinople from AD 428–431. The Monophysites taught that Jesus was born God, was one in substance with God, always was and always will be God. This is pretty much the orthodox teaching of the Church today, Diophysitism having been suppressed as heresy. However, it flickered on as an underground movement even though Nestorius himself was declared a heretic and exiled to Upper Egypt.

In the middle of the fifth century, there were at Edessa, now called Urfa, one of the most important Sees in the world, three theological schools: the Armenian, the Syrian and the Persian. The last of these was considered one of the very great centres of learning not just in Edessa but in the whole world. However, it was not popular with the local bishop, Cyrus, on account of its Nestorian leanings. In AD 489, at his prompting the Emperor Zeno closed it down and the teachers were expelled. Many of them went over the border into what was then Persia and settled in Nisibis, either starting or invigorating a school there. Since Nisibis in the second century was also home to the most important Jewish community and school in the region, it seemed more than likely that it was Gurdjieff's Nivssi and that his lost valley was somewhere in the region.

All of this made sense and a pattern was beginning to emerge. In Northern Mesopotamia, just forty kilometres to the south of the city of Edessa was the ancient city of Harran, which had once been home to the patriarch Abraham and where, according to the Bible, his father Terah was buried. This was also the city where the *Hermetica* had been preserved throughout the European Dark Ages and right up to a time not long before its destruction by Genghis Khan in the thirteenth

Map 4

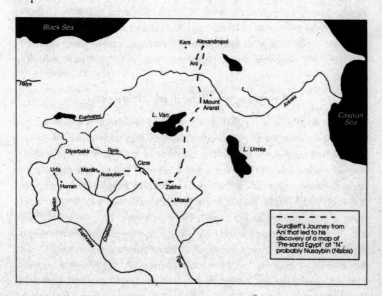

century. If Gurdjieff really had found a map of 'pre-sand Egypt' in the house of a priest at Nisibis, then it seemed likely that this was in some way connected with the school of Persians that moved there in AD 489. This school owed its origins to Edessa and was almost certainly in contact with whatever school had once existed in Harran. The conclusion seemed obvious: if I was going to search for traces of Gurdjieff's Sarmoung Brotherhood, then this region just to the north of Syria was a good place to start.

There was, however, somewhere else that had caught my attention and which I also wanted to investigate. This was the lost kingdom of Commagene which lay to the north of Edessa. Here I knew there was a remarkable monument built just before the time of Jesus which I had a strange suspicion was somehow connected with the Magi story. I didn't know what this connection was but it seemed that this monument, a sort of Turkish pyramid, contained a deep secret, worthy of investigation, of its own. I also suspected it might be linked with Gurdjieff's Sarmoung Brotherhood, though again what this link might be was at this time a mystery. As Nusaybin, Harran and Commagene were all in Turkey, they were reasonably accessible and therefore, unlike Iraq, open for research. The sensible thing, therefore, was to go and have a look.

## Commagene, the lost kingdom

I had no doubt in my mind that the Magi of Matthew's Gospel had connections with Egypt. However, the question still remained: where exactly had they come from? The assumption that they were Persian is not very helpful as, at the time of Jesus, all of Mesopotamia and much of Anatolia were nominally at least in the Parthian Empire and, therefore, 'Persian'. The Magi didn't need to come all the way from Parthia itself to be regarded as Persians. Indeed, it would be surprising if they had. It was much more likely that they had come from Mesopotamia, that they were 'Babylonian Magi' to use Bennett's terminology. The Abrahamic as well as the Hermetic connection suggested Harran as a likely candidate for being their point of departure and I decided that I would have to pay it a visit but there were other places to be considered as well.

The Magi were also unlikely to have been orthodox Persian priests as in the first century BC the Zoroastrian religion was in a state of eclipse. They could, however, have been members of a secret school and this could have had links with other cults and movements, such as Mithraism, prevalent in Eastern Anatolia and Mesopotamia. Realizing I knew little about the region, I began to study its history. I quickly realized that there was a lot going on in the valleys of the two rivers at the time of Christ, particularly the Euphrates, and that further investigation was called for. Much to my surprise I discovered that Mesopotamia was, at that time, still outside of the Roman Empire and that it was home to a number of interesting star-cults involving Magi. One of the most important of these, if only because it has left many traces, was the royal cult of the kings of Commagene, a small state on the Upper Euphrates. Could Commagene then have been the place from which the Gospel Magi had come? I decided to look into the matter.

Though frequently invaded by foreign powers, Commagene was a very old country with a pre-history and civilization going back to before the rise of Assyria. Kutmuhi (or Kummuhu) as it was known to the Assyrians seems to have been first conquered by Adad-Nirari I, (c.1300 BC) and seems to have remained a vassal state until the fall of Assyria in 612 BC. The Assyrians, as the Bible testifies, were utterly ruthless imperialists. They were always making war on their neighbours from whom they demanded heavy tributes in return for peace. Around 1100 BC, at the beginning of the reign of Tiglath-Pileser I, the Kutmuhi became involved in a revolt, perpetrated by the Mushki (Meshech of the Bible). This was put down savagely by the Assyrian king, who boasts of his victory upon a clay prism now preserved in the British Museum:

In the beginning of my reign, twenty thousand men of the land of Mushki and their five kings . . . in their own strength they trusted and came down and seized the land of Kutmuhi. With the help of Assur[5], my lord, I gathered my chariots and my troops. With their twenty thousand warriors and five kings I fought in the land of Kutmuhi and I defeated them. The corpses of their warriors I hurled down in the destructive battle like the Storm-(god). Their blood I caused to flow in the valleys and on the high places of the mountains. I cut off their heads and outside their cities, like heaps of grain, I piled them up. Their spoil, their goods, and their possessions, in countless number, I brought out. I carried off six thousand [men], the remainder of their troops, who fled from before my weapons and had embraced my feet, and I counted them as inhabitants of my land.[6]

The people of Commagene were evidently not merely victims but active participants in the revolt, for having dealt with the miscreant Mushki, he now turns his attention to punishing them.

> At that time also I marched against the land of Kutmuhi, which was disloyal, and which had withheld tribute and tax from Assur my lord. I conquered the land of Kutmuhi in its length and breadth. Their booty, their goods, and their possession I brought out. I burned their cities with fire, I devastated, I destroyed them. The rest of the people of Kutmuhi, who had fled from before my weapons, crossed over to the land of Shereshe [a city in the region of modern Diyarbakir], which is on the further banks of the Tigris, and made that city their stronghold. I took my chariots and my warriors and over the steep mountain and through their wearisome paths I hewed my way with pickaxes of bronze, and I made passable a road for the passage of my chariots and troops. I crossed the Tigris and conquered the city of Shereshe, their stronghold. I scattered their warriors in the midst of the hills like—, and made their blood to flow in the Tigris and on the high places of the mountains.[7]

Today Tiglath-Pileser and most of the other Assyrian kings would be regarded as war criminals. Reading his boasts concerning his campaigns in Commagene and elsewhere, I couldn't help but think of recent television pictures of Kurdish villagers being driven out of their homes and into the hills by the ruler of modern Assyria, Saddam Hussein. The 'history of crime' at least, it would appear, constantly repeats itself. The effect of Tiglath-Pileser's war must have been to cow Commagene, for though it features in the records of other Assyrian kings, it is nearly always in the context of paying taxes. One interesting entry concerning tribute paid to Shalmaneser III (c. 857 BC) is included the so-called 'Monolith Inscription' engraved on a stele from Kurkh, a city twenty miles south of Diyarbakir. This is now also in the British Museum:

> 'Katazilu of Kummuhu,—20 minas of silver, 300 cedar logs, yearly I received (from him).'[8]

With the fall of the Assyrian capital of Nineveh in 612 BC, Commagene seems to have passed first into Babylonian control and then, with the victory of Cyrus, into the Persian Empire. The subsequent story of Commagene, with which I was by now well familiar, makes one of the most curious footnotes to the history of the Middle East. In 334 BC Alexander the Great, then King only of Macedonia, crossed the Hellespont and invaded Asia Minor. Arriving at Gordium, the ancient capital of Phrygia, he made his way to the temple of Zeus where a strange cart was kept. According to legend Zeus had once, through an oracle, instructed the Phrygians to take as their king the first man to ride up to his temple on such a cart. The lucky man was a peasant named Gordion and he was indeed made king, his vehicle being taken into the temple. This cart was very special for it was held together by a strangely knotted length of cornel bark. As a further twist to the tale a prophecy was made that whosoever should succeed in untying this knot would become master of all Asia. Of the many who must have tried and failed to untie the complex knot, history has no record but Alexander is said to have wasted no time trying to unravel it but to have chopped it in half with his sword. Thereafter and in fulfilment of the prophecy, he did indeed become master of Asia, going on to conquer Egypt, Persia and even penetrating into India. Though he died in 323 BC at the tender age of thirty-three and was, therefore, unable to consolidate his empire, his conquests were to have a profound influence on the future development of the region.

Following his death, the empire was divided between his generals: Ptolemy taking Egypt, Antigonus most of Asia Minor and Seleucus Babylonia, Persia and north-east India. The inevitable wars that followed left Seleucus in charge of Syria as well, now with access to the Mediterranean. The Seleucid Dynasty was to retain control over Syria, Babylonia and the western parts of Persia for several centuries more before its eventual collapse under pressure from Rome in the west and Parthia in the east. Seleucus himself founded the new city of Antioch, named after his father Antiochus, on the coast, close to Issus where Alexander had won his famous battle against Darius. This city was to become the Syrian capital and the focus of Hellenistic culture in the region long after Babylonia and Persia were lost.

Further north the kingdom of Antigonus rapidly fragmented, partly through internal pressures and partly as a result of an invasion by Gauls. Small successor states formed, giving only nominal allegiance if any to either the kings of Macedonia, Persia or Syria. The most important of these was Pontus, an area of Cappadocia that lay east of the Halys river and south of the Black Sea, Galatia, which occupied most of what had been Phrygia and the coastal city state of Pergamum. For several centuries this continued to be a politically very unstable part of the world until the *Pax Romana* was eventually imposed by Pompey.

The situation, however, did have its advantages. The decline of Seleucid power offered Commagene in particular the opportunity to gain independence for the first time since the Assyrian invasions centuries before. Early in the third century BC, a king named Samos established a power base in Commagene and built a capital called Samosata. His son, Arsames, moved the capital up the Nymphaus, a tributary of the Euphrates, to a more defensible position: a place called Arsameia-ad-Nymphaeum. Arsames, like his father, was still a vassal of the Seleucids but in 162 BC his grandson, Ptolemy, revolted and declared Commagene an independent state. His son, Samos II made peace with the Seleucids, part of the settlement being that his son and successor, Mithridates [Mithridates I Callinicus] married Laodice, the daughter of the Syrian king Antiochus VIII. By all accounts the marriage was happy and the fruit of the union was Commagene's most famous king, Antiochus I Epiphanes, who seems to have succeeded to the throne some time before 69 BC.

Antiochus was a king who took his religion, a Hellenized form of Zoroastrianism, very seriously. Fortunately he left behind a large number of Greek inscriptions, so we know quite a lot about the royal cult that he promoted. The kings of Commagene, perhaps to legitimize their authority with a mixed population, claimed descent from both the Greek and Persian royal houses. Accordingly, the gods that they worshipped were a curious syncretism of more generally recognized Greek and Persian deities. The royal cult was clearly astral in nature as the gods were also personifications of the sun, moon and planets. Antiochus built a number of monuments, but the most important, which has now become an important tourist attraction, is his so-called hierothesion. First investigated by a German team in 1883 following its accidental discovery during a land survey, it was this I now wanted to see.

## An adventure in the land of Kummuhu

In April 1994, my wife Dee and I at last had time to visit Northern Mesopotamia, which I was beginning to suspect may at one time have been the headquarters of the mysterious Magi of the Gospel legends. Flying to Western Turkey was both cheap and easy, but reaching the south-east of the country turned out to be more problematic. This is difficult at the best of times and was made more so by the tense political situation. Only a few weeks before we set out the Turkish airforce had been busy bombing Kurdish villages around Cizre, just to the east of the region we wished to visit. We were repeatedly warned off from going there by well-meaning Turks, for whom, travelling anywhere east of Ankara was like going to Outer Mongolia. Without denying the wisdom of what they were saying and realizing that there probably was some risk involved in going outside of the normal tourist areas, we decided we would not be that easily deterred. This, however, was not the only problem. As we were not going to be part of a tourist group, we had to find our own means of getting there. Time was limited and, cheap and efficient as Turkish coaches are, we could not afford to waste time – we had to go by air. We discovered that there were a couple of flights a week going from Ankara to Urfa, the nearest town to Harran, and booked our return tickets. Little did we realize what an adventure this would turn out to be.

The Kurds, who make up the bulk of the population of south-east Turkey are a rugged, handsome people. Unfortunately for them they were losers in the treaties signed between the Allies and the Turks following the First World War and in the dismemberment of the Ottoman Empire, the territories they occupied ended up divided between Turkey, Iran, Iraq and Syria. Today the Kurdish region of northern Iraq has a quasi-autonomous status which will last as long as American, British and French warplanes patrol their skies. The bombing of their villages by the Turkish airforce had been done ostensibly to punish Kurdish terrorists though to the outside world it seemed like a sledgehammer being used to crack a walnut. In the volatile atmosphere that existed in Northern Mesopotamia following the Gulf War, nobody was taking any chances with the status quo.

Given this tense atmosphere, we were a little hesitant about going into what was presented on television as a war zone. As we got off the plane a group of what we presumed were secret servicemen unbuttoned their jackets to reveal shoulder holsters. With all the nonchalance of tourists checking through their duty free whisky, they drew their well-used automatics and had them checked through customs. As nobody batted an eyelid, we presumed this was normal behaviour

Map 5

The kingdoms of
Commagene and
Osrhoene

and this only added to our concern that we were entering a region where guns were the law. We needn't have worried, though, as our fears were to prove unfounded. Everyone we met, Turks and Kurds alike, whatever their own differences, proved to be most friendly towards foreigners. However, when arriving in Urfa, the ancient city of Edessa, it was still a shock to discover how backward this part of Turkey was. Here most of the women were still wearing traditional dress and were veiled. Many men likewise wore the baggy trousers and the loosely tied turbans of the area, though, incongruously, these were generally accompanied not by the brightly coloured waistcoats of old but by drab, western style jackets.

Taking the airport bus, we made our way to the centre of town. Urfa, or rather Sanliurfa as it is now called,[9] turned out to be a curious hybrid between a mediaeval centre and a suburban sprawl of 1960s style high-rise flats. There was an atmosphere of dereliction about it with street after street of crumbling buildings. Looking out of the windows of the bus we could see that the pavements and tea shops were teaming with people either engaged in business or simply passing time. The market that we drove past, according to our guidebook the largest outside Istanbul, was filled not with tourist goods but with the essentials of life: food, spices, pots, pans and cloth. Sanitation in this part of town was clearly primitive, as on disembarking from the bus a smell of drains and worse assailed our nostrils. Yet, for all this Urfa was a lively place. Around us there were people speaking in Turkish, Arabic, Kurdish and probably a dozen other eastern languages and dialects we couldn't make out. All looked at us in amazement as though we had come from another planet, for in truth Europeans are seldom seen in these parts and we were as much a novelty for them as they for us. We did not have time to take in very much more as we were anxious to press on to Adiyaman and from there to proceed to Kahta, gateway to the lost kingdom of Commagene.

We boarded a dolmus, the ubiquitous minibus/taxi of the Middle East and shortly afterwards found ourselves tearing through the Mesopotamian countryside. Soon the near desert around Sanliurfa gave way to greener pastures as we entered the foothills of the Anti-Taurus Mountains. On the tops of many of the peaks were the ruins of old castles, possibly at one time Crusader fortresses dating from the time when the whole region was in the front confrontation line between Christendom and Islam. Now everything seemed peaceful as farmers, many of them brightly dressed women, tended their fields of tobacco, cotton, wheat and vegetables. The men were mostly to be seen driving tractors whilst it was left to the children to look after little flocks of sheep and goats. It was a truly Biblical setting and soon we found ourselves crossing the great River Euphrates, for many centuries the boundary between the Roman Empire and the lands ruled over by the Persians.

Yet looks can be deceiving, this is not a land that is standing still. There were bright, new signposts at various points along the way to Turkey's newest wonder: the Ataturk Baraji or dam. This massive civil engineering project, holding back and redistributing the waters of the mighty Euphrates, would have made even Tiglath-Pileser jealous. Unfortunately the large lake that it has created, though providing many obvious benefits, has drowned out along with many other sites in the area, the original Commagene capital of Samosata. We could only sigh and hope that the benefits would be worth it for the local people and wildlife and that the damming of such a major river wouldn't cause too many problems for others downstream.

Adiyaman, when we got there, turned out to be a shabby town in the midst of a gold rush. Recent finds of oil in the vicinity have produced a local, probably unsustainable boom to its economy. This could not hide the fact that its previous dollar earning industry, tourism, had all but died from the bad publicity surrounding the Kurdish troubles. This did have one benefit in that it was relatively easy for us to find a room in the town's one reasonable hotel. Over breakfast the following morning we were offered a lift by a friendly company representative to Kahta, the jumping off point for tours around the Commagene National Park. Before long we found ourselves bumping along the narrow cobbled track that leads up to Mount Nimrod, the highest peak in Commagene and our intended destination.

Our suspicions about the lack of tourists were confirmed by our guide, a Kurd who spoke broken English and ran a local hotel. He for one deeply regretted that hot-head elements of the PKK (the Kurdistan Workers Party) had taken several foreigners hostage earlier in the year, ostensibly to put pressure on the Ankara regime by threatening the lucrative tourist industry. The threat had been almost totally effective with the result that his hotel was now empty and he faced bankruptcy. Needless to say he was more than willing to put on a private, guided tour to all the antiquities in the region, chartering a minibus for the purpose. Leaving Kahta we climbed steadily for several hours, passing through villages alive with chickens and children before eventually reaching the top of the mountain. We were now standing before an impressive peak of white limestone under which are buried, somewhere, the mortal remains of Antiochus Epiphanes I, the most important of Commagene's minor kings.

The tumulus, which in many ways resembles a pyramid, is one of Turkey's most famous monuments: they like to refer to it as the eighth wonder of the ancient world. It was built on top of Mount Nimrod, the tallest mountain in the area, and is constructed out of fist-sized rocks piled up in a great heap. Clambering up the pathway to the foot of the tumulus took about fifteen minutes, leaving us breathless when we arrived at the top. It was a truly awesome scene that greeted us, for all around were mountain peaks, stretching off into the distance as far as the eye could see. However, we had not come for the view but to see something else: a curious collection of colossal statues that for over two millennia have stood guard over the mountain, watching the daily risings and settings of the sun.

As we came round the corner onto the east terrace we were suddenly confronted by the first group of these, a tableau of decapitated colossi (plate 18). Their heads, toppled by earthquakes, lay at their feet gazing eternally towards the dawn. The central figure of five seated gods was Zeus, the Father of the Greek pantheon whom Antiochus equated with Ohrmazd. He was enormous and standing by his feet, even though I am over six feet tall, I didn't reach up to his knees (plate 19). Next to him on his left-hand side was the only goddess in the group. She was once thought to have personified the goddess of fate, who in Greek was called Tyche and in Persian Ashi but is now believed to be the fertile country of Commagene. On her other side was Apollo-Helios, who was wearing a Phrygian cap and, as god of light, was identified with Mithras in the Persian pantheon. On Zeus/Ohrmazd's right-hand side was the youthful figure of Antiochus himself. Though slightly smaller in size than his illustrious companions, he evidently believed that in death if not in life he was going to sit at the right hand of the Father. To his right was the figure of Heracles, who, to judge by the number of times he is depicted in Commagene reliefs, was one of their favourite gods. He was identified with the Persian god of victory called Verethragna (Artagnes). These five gods were flanked on each side by paired statues of an eagle and lion, the heraldic beasts of the Royal House of Commagene.

In front of the statues was a fairly large ledge, at the east end of which was a low, stepped platform. It was square in shape of side 13.5 metres and though it looked like a helipad, and is indeed sometimes used as such, according to the guidebook it was a Zoroastrian fire altar. On the north and south sides of the ledge and in a line more or less perpendicular to the row of colossi were sockets that once carried a series of reliefs. Some of these lay nearby, flat slabs sculpted with the images of Persian and Greek nobles: Antiochus' ancestors. Other reliefs were of the 'shaking hands' variety, a favourite device of the Commagenes indicating what good terms they were on with their gods.

The whole effect of this eastern terrace was stunning, made all the more so by the huge pyramid of stones behind the seated statues of the gods and the panoramic views in every other direction. This glimpse of divine majesty, however, was only the beginning. Following the path around the north side of the tumulus, we came to the western terrace. Here there was the same group of gods sitting on their thrones, once more flanked by reliefs of ancestors and more images of Antiochus shaking hands with the gods. There were, however, some notable differences: there was no fire altar and the colossi, though not much smaller than their eastern counterparts, were arranged in a slightly different order. However, there was something else of great interest and unique to this terrace: an astrological frieze representing the constellation of Leo (plate 21). Seeing it now for the first time was a thrilling experience as I had read about it. It had been the subject of detailed research by the famous archaeo-astronomer, Otto Neugebauer, who had determined not only that it symbolized Leo but that it was, in fact, a horoscope.

It was very cold and on this side of the tumulus, snow still lay in pockets on the ground even though it was now the beginning of May. There was no one else around apart from us and the total silence was broken only by the sound of the wind screeching through cracks in the colossal statues. Somehow the power and presence of the statues spoke down to us through the ages but the feelings they expressed were not what one might have expected. Antiochus did not come over as a cold, ruthless egomaniac, even though the placing of a statue of himself at the right hand of Zeus suggested a certain vanity. True the cost in terms of his people's labour must have been enormous for creating such a remarkable monument and one could only sympathize at the effort involved in quarrying and raising the large blocks of stone needed to make the colossi. But the work needed to build the tumulus, which at 50 metres high is not much smaller than the pyramid of Mycerinus,[10] was probably voluntary. I could imagine teams of workers hewing away at the limestone cliffs further down the mountain and breaking up large boulders into small, manageable fragments. There would have been an endless procession of people carrying baskets of these chippings on their heads as they slowly made their way back up to the summit to deposit their loads on the growing heap. If the tumulus so raised was to be his final resting place, as most archaeologists believe, then building it out of rubble in this way was a clever idea. So far no one has discovered his burial chamber and, short of removing the entire heap, it seems unlikely that they ever will. Unlike the Egyptian pharaohs who trusted their mortal remains to more elaborate pyramids, Antiochus is able to rest in peace under his tumulus of small boulders.

According to inscriptions that he had carved on the backs of the colossi, he had built his hierothesion for a purpose. It was not constructed as a simple tomb but to be a place where he could gather his people for religious festivities connected with either his birthday or coronation. As aware of the power of symbols as any Pope, he had built a temple of the gods on top of the local equivalent of Mount Olympus. Here, they evidently venerated the planetary gods as well as celebrating the mysteries of dawn and sunset. As the highest point of his kingdom, it was symbolically the closest point to heaven, the place where gods and men could mingle. However, I suspected that it was even more than an elaborate tomb with Olympian pretensions. It had a strange atmosphere somehow reminiscent of the Egyptian pyramids. Could this complex, like Giza, be what Gurdjieff termed a 'legominism'? In short did it contain a secret message for the future? There was much to suggest that this might be so, not least the curious Lion Horoscope. I determined that I would look into this once I returned home.

Descending Mount Nimrod by the same pot-holed road we had come up, we made our way to another important Commagene sanctuary at Eski Kale (the old fortress). Here we visited what had probably once been the main spiritual shrine of ancient Commagene as it was much more accessible to the capital of Arsameia-ad-Nymphaeum and, unlike the peak of Mount Nimrod, could have been visited all year round. Making our way up a steep path on the side of a cliff, we were greeted by magnificent views, this time over the valley of the River

Nymphaeus (plate 22). Nearby was a broken relief of Antiochus shaking hands with a god who has been identified with Apollo-Mithras. Further up the hill was a cave, that archaeologists believe may have been the tomb of his father, Mithridates I. The cave itself was rather uninteresting except for a blind passage, function unknown, leading down from its rear. Just in front of the cave and on the edge of the escarpment were fragments of a relief that seem to represent father and son together, perhaps at one time also shaking hands.

Leaving this first cave, we made our way back and further up the hill to what was evidently the most important and certainly the best preserved sanctuary on the hill. Here there was another large relief of a Commagene king, either Mithridates or Antiochus shaking hands with Heracles (plate 23). As on the reliefs at Nimrod the latter was shown as a powerful, naked and bearded man with a large club in his left hand. Next to the relief, carved into rock is a Greek inscription – the longest in Asia Minor. This explains how Antiochus had built the site as a memorial to his father, Mithridates, and how he had arranged for certain ceremonies to be carried out there monthly in honour of him. Below the inscription was another blind passage cut into the hillside (plate 24). This tunnel, which was cleared by German archaeologists between 1953 and 1956, is 158 metres long and slopes at an angle of 35 degrees. If the Germans had been hoping, at the end of all their hard work, to find Mithridates' tomb, Egyptian style, at the bottom of the shaft, they were disappointed. Its purpose remains an enigma, nobody knows what it was for, but the suggestion that it is unfinished and was intended to be an escape route from the castle above is now discarded in favour of some unknown ritual significance. Examining the shaft for clues, I had to admit I was baffled. But remembering *The Orion Mystery* and how the so-called 'air-shafts' inside the Great Pyramid had ritual significance in that they pointed at certain stars, it crossed my mind that this might also be the case at Arsameia.

Leaving this site we made our way back downhill and once more boarded the minibus. The landscape that surrounded us had a certain magical beauty and we could imagine Mithridates, Laodice and Antiochus living very pleasantly in these surroundings. What was noticeable, though, was the lack of large trees. If the Commagenes today had to pay a tribute to the Assyrians of 300 logs a year they would be hard put to find them. The loss of forest cover, as in so many other parts of the world, has had damaging consequences. It means that the hills have been badly eroded so that now away from the river margins little grows but scrub. Even this is regularly pollarded to provide emergency winter feed for goats, so that there is little chance for the forests that must once have graced the bare hills to grow back. It was all rather tragic and in stark contrast to Bennett's description of the valley of Sheikh Adi, where as late as the 1950s living trees were considered sacred by the local populace of Yezidis and it was forbidden to cut them down. They were therefore plentiful, providing shade, retaining soil and adding to the beauty of the valley.

Leaving the hill country behind, we came to a bridge over the Cendere Creek, a tributary of the Nymphaeus. This remarkable construction, which is 7 metres wide and 120 metres long, was put up at the orders of the Roman Emperor Septimus Severus (AD 193–211). At either end of it he had paired pillars raised, to himself and his wife, Julia Donna, at one end and to their two sons, Caracalla and Geta, at the other. After Severus' death, there was a battle for the throne and Caracalla had Geta killed. As a consequence the latter's pillar was also thrown down, so that now there are only three. Looking at this bridge was another lesson in how so often vanity, architecture and politics go hand in hand. Nevertheless it said a lot for Roman engineering that it was still standing intact after some 1800 years of steady use.

Before leaving Commagene on our way back to Urfa we visited another strange tumulus, this one believed by some researchers to have been the burial place of the royal womenfolk. Others believe that it was used for rituals during the winter months when the other sites higher in the hills were not accessible. Either way, it was still quite impressive, even though at about 35 metres it is lower than the tumulus on top of Mount Nimrod. However, here there were no seated statues of the gods but instead a collection of upright columns. These were originally arranged in equidistant groups of three on the south, north-east and north-west sides of the tumulus. Their ritual significance is unknown but four of them are still standing. Standing on top of one is an eagle (giving the site its Turkish name of 'Karacus' or blackbird), on another is a headless lion, whilst on a third is a 'shaking hands' scene of what is possibly a queen with one of the gods.

Leaving all these curious monuments to a lost civilization behind us, we once more found ourselves back in Kahta. By now it was late in the day and we were keen to get back to Urfa. However, what had still then been a pleasant, if sometimes overcast day turned into something else. Dark clouds now filled the sky and on the bus journey from Adiyaman we were treated to the full might of a Mesopotamian storm. Great lightning bolts streaked across the sky and rain poured down in bucket-loads. Pretty soon the road was completely awash as though the Ataturk Dam itself had been ruptured. Arriving in Urfa the main street, inevitably called Ataturk Boulevari, which the day before had been dry and dusty, was now a river. It was an inauspicious start to the second leg of our trip as cold and bedraggled we checked into the only decent hostelry in town: the Hotel Harran.

That night I was struck violently sick. I had turned down the offer of barbecued chillies so kindly proffered by our Kurdish guide and throughout the week that we had now been in Turkey, I had carefully avoided Doner kebabs. Whether it was the freshly baked pitta bread from a village bakery near Kahta, or the cool, spring water from half-way up Mount Nimrod, or perhaps something not quite so fresh at the hotel in Adiyaman, we will never know. What was clear was that I was very ill and we had foolishly left our medicine bag, along with half our clothes, at the hotel near Fethiye into which we were booked when we returned from the east. It was now Friday evening and everything, including the pharmacy next door, was closing. Desperately we rushed down there and I tried to explain what I wanted and they, equally desperate, tried to understand. But there was a language barrier between us and try as we might we couldn't get them to understand. In the end they sold us what turned out to be indigestion tablets and a bottle of aspirin. Not at all what was required. As I have insulin-dependent diabetes, it was not only an inconvenience but a positively dangerous situation to be in. With the pharmacies now shut for the weekend and with no possibility of getting the right medicine, I was having to balance my blood glucose on an empty stomach. What was even worse was that our return flight to Ankara, and thence to Fethiye, was on the following Tuesday. Come what may we had to be on that flight and as Saturday turned into Sunday, and Sunday into Monday and still I was no better, we realized we were not only going to miss going to Harran but probably not even look around Urfa.

That evening, as I lay on my bed for the third night, I became quite delirious. I began to hallucinate wildly, seeing vivid scenes in my mind's eye of sumptuous palaces, churches and castles. In this dream state I was greeted by a man, who seemed to be a monk. He led me up a spiralling staircase to show me what he said were the wonders of Edessa, the ancient name for Urfa that I had all but forgotten. The staircase, the balustrades and much else besides were made from the most delicate filigree, of carefully carved timbers inlaid with mother of pearl. It was like the Baghdad kiosk, the most beautiful of the sultan's pavilions in the Topkapi palace of Istanbul, only larger and even more ornate. This, he explained, is what Edessa had once been like, a city whose magnificence had been the envy of the world.

I began to realize that hidden here, beneath the dusty streets and broken masonry, was a mystery that I would have to seek. A secret was concealed that could now be brought to light. However, whatever was hidden here, I would not find it on this occasion. This journey had, it seemed, been for the sake of Commagene only. The 'monk' informed me that for now the gates of Edessa were closed to me but if I returned next year, better prepared than I was at present, then I would find what I was looking for. With that I woke up, or rather came back to my senses, bathed in sweat but with the fever broken. Feeling like Sir Percival who, when shown the Grail, forgets to ask the right question and as a consequence misses the opportunity of catching more than a glimpse of the magic cup, I was once more confronted with the drab, brown decor of our hotel room and the incessant din of traffic outside. The Grail analogy, as I was to discover later, was entirely apt for what had happened.

The next day, feeling right as rain, I was able to partake of some breakfast, my first food for three days, before we once more headed off for the airport. We had had no time to visit the fish-ponds of Abraham, to look at the castle, the market, the ruined church of St John or any of the other wonders of ancient Edessa. It was just as the archetypal monk of my fantasies had said, the doors were closed to us on this occasion. We had come, unknowingly, to one of the most extraordinary cities on earth and I had not even realized it until it was too late. Yet, just as the story of Galahad has its sequel in that he receives a second chance to put right his mistake, so I knew that come what may we would be back in Urfa. Next time I would be better prepared and would ask the right questions of the guardian at the gate: what is this city and who is its keeper? These questions, however, would have to wait. First I had to unravel the mystery of Commagene and Antiochus' strange cult of the gods. I had no idea what this would lead to but I did have a hunch that it would be something exciting.

# CHAPTER 7

✳

# The Lion of Commagene

eturning home from Urfa I had a lot to do. Whilst in
Commagene we had bought two small guidebooks, the only
sources of information in English that we could find concerning
Antiochus and his curious monuments. These mentioned the pioneering
work of Otto Neugebauer on the Lion Horoscope. I had come across
his name before in connection with *The Orion Mystery*: he, along with a
colleague called Richard Parker had worked for many years as a team at
Brown University, Rhode Island, and they were both acclaimed experts
on Egyptian astronomy. They had been the first to recognize that the
anthropomorphic *Sahu* figure, to be seen on the ceilings of Egyptians
tombs and inscribed on the capstones of pyramids, represented the
constellation of Orion.[1] I was therefore very interested to see what
he had to say about Commagene. The best source for this sort of
information seemed to be the British Museum, so a few weeks later
I got in touch with the Department of Western Asiatic Antiquities to
see if they could help. I was referred to one of their assistant keepers,
a very helpful lady named Dominique Collon. She knew exactly what I
was after and very kindly offered to send me a photocopy of an article
by Neugebauer (this time teamed up with another colleague, H.B. van
Hoesen) entitled 'Greek Horoscopes', as well as a useful bibliography
for other sources on Commagene should they be required. Thanking
her for her trouble, I waited eagerly for the package to arrive.

The material when it came turned out to be quite extraordinary.
Neugebauer and van Hoesen had carefully analysed the star patterns
on the Lion stele of Antiochus' hierothesion, which everyone seemed

to agree represented some sort of horoscope, and pinpointed it to a date in 62 BC. The body of the lion has a number of stars emblazoned on it, indicating that it is meant to represent the constellation of Leo. Neugebauer was clear about this, contrasting it with the Catasterisms of Eratosthenes:

> That the lion represents the constellation of 'Leo' cannot be doubted since the 19 stars which are depicted on and near the body of the lion agree very nearly with the positions of the 19 stars assigned to this constellation in the so-called Catasterisms of Eratosthenes.[2]

The connection with Eratosthenes (c.276–c.194 BC) was very interesting. He was a scientific writer of great genius from Alexandria, his greatest achievement being his measurement of the earth's circumference. Learning that at the summer solstice the sun shone straight down a well without casting a shadow at Syene, on the Tropic of Cancer, he measured the angle of the sun at noon on the same day at Alexandria. As it was known that the distance from Syene was 5,000 stadia, he was able to calculate that this corresponded to $\frac{1}{50}$ of a great circle round the earth, which therefore had a circumference of 250,000 stadia.[3] He later corrected this to 252,000 stadia. Neugebauer's suggestion that the stars depicted on the lion figure corresponded to Eratosthenes' star-atlas suggested that whoever had it sculpted had this book in his possession – not at all unlikely given that the royal house claimed Greek ancestry. Later, I was to discover that this was almost certainly true and had other surprising ramifications.

Neugebauer and van Hoesen then went on to discuss the three larger, more elaborate stars that stand above the lion's back. These are labelled on the relief with names that give their identity as Jupiter, Mercury and Mars – with the first mentioned nearest to the head. Beneath the head of the lion, hanging on its neck is a crescent moon. This, the authors felt, was the most significant feature of all, for whereas the stars and lion could, perhaps, be explained away as being merely symbolic of royal power or the patronage of favourite gods, the moon, normally speaking, has no connection with the sign of Leo. Its presence on the lion sculpture indicated that the whole thing is a horoscope, the constellation of Leo playing host to the three planets and the moon. The number of possible dates when such a pattern might have been present in the sky is not as high as one might at first think. Jupiter is a fairly slow moving planet; its cycle of twelve years means it will only be present in Leo for one out of every twelve years. Whilst Mercury will put in an annual appearance, Mars is slower and will only cross Leo for approximately two months once every two years. To narrow things even further, the moon takes only 29½ days to make an entire cycle of the zodiac. It will therefore only be in Leo for about 2½ days. Taking all of these factors into account and backtracking the skies over Commagene to the appropriate epoch, Neugebauer and van Hoesen were able to pinpoint five possible dates at around the right time to fit the horoscope. These were:

a) −108 July 15
b) −97 July 16
c) −61 July 7
d) −61 August 4
e) −48 July 13[4]

As the Lion Horoscope does not include either the sun or the planets Venus and Saturn, a), d) and e) can all be excluded. This leaves only the dates in −97 July 16 and −61 July 7. Since the horoscope is believed to refer, somehow, to Antiochus' coronation, −97 can be written out as too early. This leaves just c) which, written in Gregorian terms as opposed to astronomical, is 7 July 62 BC.

Interpreting what this date means, however, is not as straightforward as one may think. Historical evidence shows that Antiochus was already king of Commagene in 69 BC, when he was forced to surrended to the Roman general, Lucullus. If the Lion Horoscope represents his coronation day, then it was a re-crowning. In support of this the authors point to the fact that following Pompey's reorganization of the East, Antiochus was re-confirmed by the Romans and allowed to keep his little kingdom as a buffer state. This re-confirmation of Antiochus on his throne, they argue, is what the horoscope refers to and a matter for some celebration.

Reading through their detailed arguments and testing them out using a computer running the SKYGLOBE simulation program, I had to agree that they were probably right as regards the date in 62 BC, though 6 July rather than 7 July would seem to be more appropriate as on this day the moon would indeed be below the 'head' of Leo rather than half way down the lion figure. Yet, I couldn't believe that Antiochus would want to celebrate the Romans' interference in the internal affairs of Commagene. Still less would he want to advertise, assuming that it was indeed the case, that he owed his throne, on which he had already sat for many years, to Pompey. There had to be more to the hierothesion than this and I was still convinced that it contained some sort of esoteric message; a deep secret written in stone. As the first place to look for this hidden code seemed to be the statues themselves, I went back to the guidebooks and the video pictures I had taken myself to see what clues might be revealed.

Looking at the western terrace, where the Lion Horoscope stands, I counted the statues. There were five in all (not counting the paired eagles and lions), which were named as Zeus-Ohrmazd, Aries-Hercules-Artagnes, Apollo-Helios-Mithras-Hermes, Commagene and Antiochus himself. Whilst the first two were clearly Jupiter and Mars, something was wrong with the third. Whilst it made sense for Antiochus to syncretize Apollo with Helios and Mithras – they were all gods of light connected with the sun – Hermes was a misfit. In Greek mythology he was god of roads, writing, mathematics and medicine. His planet was not the sun but Mercury, which is of course his Latin name. Why had Antiochus made so obvious a mistake, I asked myself. Why confuse Hermes with the Sun-god by whatever names they are known? Then there was the question of the goddess Commagene. Was

Fig. 3

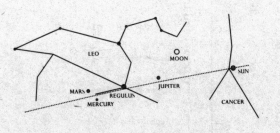

Actual horoscope for 6th July 62 BC as viewed from Arsameia.

she simply the spirit of the land or was she too to be equated with a celestial body? If this were the case then there were really only two candidates to consider: Venus and the moon. As the moon appears in the Lion Horoscope and Venus doesn't, I was inclined to think that that body was the one most closely identified with Commagene. This also made sense as the moon in mythology is nearly always not only connected with the feminine side of life but with water. I had seen for myself how Commagene was a country dominated by its rivers which, though peaceful and slow moving in summer, at other times could swell to become torrents. Melting snows in the Anti-Taurus Mountains combined with rain could easily cause not just the Euphrates itself to flood but its smaller tributaries too. Little wonder then that they worshipped the moon and sought to propitiate her lest she have one of her angry moods.

Accepting that the statue of Commagene was symbolic of the moon, it became obvious that the one of Antiochus himself and not the Sun-god Apollo-Mithras must really represent Mercury. This, it seemed likely, was the esoteric secret of the statues: they all represented celestial bodies and with the addition of the sun, they were the same ones as were inscribed on the Lion Horoscope. To confirm this, I now

Fig. 4

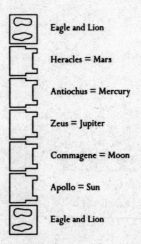

Eagle and Lion

Heracles = Mars

Antiochus = Mercury

Zeus = Jupiter

Commagene = Moon

Apollo = Sun

Eagle and Lion

Eastern terrace of the Hierothesion of Antiochus Epiphanes I of Commagene viewed from above. Date equivalent to 12 July 98 BC.

looked at the order of the statues on their thrones. This is different
on the east and west terraces and, because the statues have all lost their
heads, there is some disagreement between experts as to exactly what
this order should be. However, according to Akgurkal and most other
writers other than Dörner, the order as one faces the statues on the
west terrace is Apollo, Commagene, Zeus, Antiochus and Heracles.
This, viewed from behind, i.e. from the perspective of the tumulus
under which Antiochus is presumably buried, is exactly the order of
sun, moon and planets on 6 July 62 BC. Yet the question remained:
why had he chosen this day and what did it signify? Whatever Antiochus'
reasons might have been for building his hierothesion, it was likely that
clues were to be found in the writings he left behind explaining his
intentions to future generations. I decided I had better have another
look at these.

## Scriptures for a new age

We are fortunate that Antiochus, like certain of the Egyptian pharaohs
with whom he might be compared, left behind a huge number of
inscriptions. The most important of these are written on the backs
of the Nimrod colossi and were translated in 1883 by two Turkish
scholars: Osman Hamdi Bey, director of the Ottoman Imperial Museum
and Osgan Efendi of the Faculty of Fine Arts. These epigraphs reveal
that Antiochus was not a tyrant but an intensely religious man, who
saw himself as being protected by the gods. He writes:

> I have always believed that piety is, of all the virtues, not only the
> one of which possession is most sure, but also the one where the
> pleasure is most gentle for mortals; it is piety which constitutes the
> happiness of power and which makes its use enviable and, during all
> of my life, I have been seen to have respect for the gods, like the
> most faithful guard of my royalty, and as an incomparable delight
> for my heart.

After more pious words he explains what he is doing in building his
hierothesion.

> Thus I justify my intention in erecting, close to the celestial thrones
> and on foundations inaccessible to the ravages of time, this tomb

where my body, after having aged in the midst of these blessings, will sleep in eternal rest separated from the pious soul flying off towards the celestial regions of Jupiter-Oromasde.

I resolve to consecrate this place to the erection of seats for all the Gods alike, in order not only to raise there in the memory of my ancestors monuments which you see, but also so that devout people dedicated to superior spirits, will constantly have before their eyes, as a witness of my piety, this same place, where they will have the same feelings. It is thus why I have erected these statues in divine forms which you see, to Jupiter-Oromasde, to Apollo-Mithras-Helios-Hermes, to Artagnes-Hercules-Aries, and to my homeland, the fertile Commagene . . .'

After explaining how he has set up a special priesthood 'with robes of the Persian race' to administer sacrifices and set aside land in perpetuity to pay for their services, he dedicates his birthday on the 16 Aydnaios and coronation day on 10 Loos as new feast days to be celebrated *ad eternam*. This is spelled out on the pedestal of the statue of Zeus at the hierothesion:

'I have therefore dedicated the date of my birth which is the 16 Aydnaios and the day of my coronation which is the 10th of the month of Loos, to pious demonstrations to the great gods who have always served as my guide during my happy reign and who have been the unique cause of general well-being throughout all my kingdom and, considering the abundance of the sacrifices and having established that each of these two days will be designated for annual fetes, I have conveniently divided up the whole expanse of my empire for reunions, fetes and sacrifices, and I have ordered that the towns celebrate the fetes in the nearest temples and which, for the same reason, are found to be most convenient for them. As for the rest of the year, I have decreed that the priests honour the 16th and 10th day of each month as the anniversary of my birth and of my coronation.'

Neugebauer and van Hoesen argued that it was the feast day of 10 Loos that was represented by the Lion Horoscope and that it was this day that was symbolized by the seated gods on the west terrace. They arrived at this deduction because they believed that the calendar used by Antiochus was the same as that of later Roman Asia, which would put the month of Aydnaios in December-January and Loos in midsummer:

> Finally there comes the question of the calendar. We know that the time of year must be about July because with Mercury in Leo the sun must be in or close to Leo. On the other hand we know that Antiochus was born on Aydnaios 16 and that his coronation fell on Loos 10. As Puchstein remarked, the horoscope could not have been cast for the day of birth because the Aydnaios in the Roman calendar of the Province Asia (coastal area of Western Turkey) corresponds roughly to the month of December . . . one must take the date of Loos 10, the date of coronation, as the date of the horoscope because Loos corresponds roughly to the month of July as required by the horoscope.

Whilst agreeing with them that the western terrace, with its symbolic date of 6 July 62 BC inscribed on the lion and represented by statues represented a date in July, according to our modern calendar, I was not entirely satisfied with their arguments. Consulting the *Encyclopaedia Britannica*, often a fount of information, I discovered an entry on the subject of calendars that seemed highly relevant:

> Also important for late times is the Macedonian calendar, originally twelve lunar months called Dios, Apellaios, Audynaios, Peritios, Dystros, Xanthikos, Artemisios, Daisios, Panemos, Loios, Gorpiaios, Hyerberetaios. At about the beginning of our era this calendar, which was in common use in Asia Minor and Syria, was reformed on Julian lines.

Now, since Commagene was outside of the Roman Empire until AD 17 and not even a client state until Pompey's reorganization in 62 BC, it would seem that in Antiochus' day the Macedonian calendar that the Commagenes were using would still be lunar. Since twelve lunar months of 29½ days each comes to 354 days, the lunar 'year' lags behind the solar year of 365¼ days by 11¼ days. This means that without some means of rectification, the start of each month drifts backwards, year by year by 11¼ days. Thus Puchstein's 'remark' can be comfortably ignored concerning the month of Aydnaios. It didn't have to be around December but, like the Moslem Ramadan and for the same reason, could have begun at any time depending on which year you looked at.

Realizing this, I was confident that whatever the western terrace represented, the eastern terrace ought to be his birthday. The order of statues is different here from in the west, but the same planets still seem to be involved. Looking at them they are arranged as follows going from left to right: Apollo, Commagene, Zeus, Antiochus and Hercules. I had a suspicion that Antiochus' birthday might have been around Neugebauer's date b), i.e. 16 July 98 BC. Freed from the constraint that the month of Aydnaios had to be in mid-winter, this was quite possible. We know he was already king (and probably had been for some time) in 69 BC. We also know he died as an old man some time between 35 and 31 BC. A birthday in 98 BC would have been about right.

Using the SKYGLOBE program, I once more tracked back through the centuries. I found that the best fit was not for the 16th but the 13th of July. On this day the favoured planets were in the right order if viewed from the tumulus. Even more startling was the horoscope for this day: one for which anyone would be proud. Antiochus had in

Fig. 5

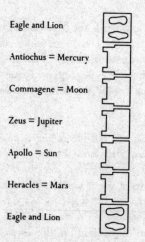

Eagle and Lion

Antiochus = Mercury

Commagene = Moon

Zeus = Jupiter

Apollo = Sun

Heracles = Mars

Eagle and Lion

Western terrace of the Hierothesion of Antiochus Epiphanes I of Commagene viewed from above. Date equivalent to 6 July 62 BC.

his chart what astrologers term a 'stellium' involving his natal Sun
in exact conjunction with Mars and Jupiter in the sign of Cancer but
constellation of Leo.[5] Only about 11 degrees in front of this grouping
were his Mercury and Moon, themselves conjunct in Cancer.[6] This,
as any astrologer would know, is a remarkably powerful horoscope
indicating an individual with great charisma, drive, a good mind and
love of home, whilst giving a tendency to vanity. From what we can
tell from this distance in time, this admirably describes Antiochus. The
missing factors in his horoscope appear to be the planets Venus and
Saturn. This could be explained if these were below the horizon when
he was born, for astrologers of his day tended to ignore planets that
had not yet risen when interpreting horoscopes. As Saturn set around
7.15a.m and Venus didn't rise till about 8.30a.m., it would seem that
if this really is his horoscope, that he was born some time in between

Fig. 6

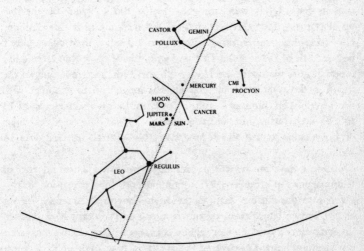

Horoscope for Antiochus Epiphanes I of Commagene, based on the pattern of the eastern terrace.

these two times. All of this fitted beautifully with the placement of the gods on the eastern terrace of his hierothesion.

All this might seem fanciful were it not for something else. It would seem that his 'birthday' of 16 Aydnaios, which he tells us was of such importance, was not his real nativity but a date of his own choosing, rather like the Queen of England's 'official' birthday in June. This birthday he shares with his father, Mithridates I, and it seems to be a sort of royal birthday of the kings. This is made clear from a long inscription in the high canyon at Arsemia that details the responsibilities of his priests.

> . . . I had statues made of the older people, my paternal grandfathers and myself approximately fitted to the real measurements and in accord to Gods. In addition I had priests and sisters come and wanted them to look at the exalted places. Later I said that the day of sacrificing for Gods, the day of the faith meeting and the birthday of my father and mine would be on the same day of the month and this day would be celebrated as a public festival.

Going back to the computer I noticed something very peculiar. If we assume that 13 July was Antiochus' real birthday (which fits the line up of statues), then this occurred around the time of the new moon. However, if he was working with a lunar calendar, then this couldn't be the 16th of the month. That day would have to be just after a full moon. But if we count on 16 days to the 29th, then not only is the moon in the right place but the sun has moved on to conjunct with the heart of Leo, the star Regulus. Could Antiochus real birthday of 13 July 98 BC have that year corresponded to a lunar date on his calendar of 1 Aydnaios so that this second date, his 'official' birthday was 16 Aydnaios?

I didn't have an answer to this until we made a second trip to Commagene, in October 1995.[7] Our purpose for going back was to investigate the curious shaft in the High Canyon at Arsemia. As we hadn't known it was there on our first visit and couldn't have guessed its significance, we hadn't brought a compass with us. However, when on returning home I discovered that it sloped at an angle of 35 degrees, I tried out the computer to see where it might be pointing at in the sky. To do this I made an assumption that it was orientated due south, like two of the shafts in the Great Pyramid. Much to our surprise it seemed that it was aligned to the culmination point of the star Sirius for the epoch in question. Naturally we were elated and couldn't wait to get back to test this hypothesis. However, reality turned out not to be so simple. The shaft didn't after all face south but was pointing due west. The Sirius alignment had to be abandoned. However, what was obvious is that there would be at least one day in the year when the sun would shine down the narrow shaft, illuminating its bottom. Somewhat dejected by the failure of what had been a promising hypothesis, it was a while before I tried out the real alignment on the computer. Once more I set up SKYGLOBE to run, this time with the cursor elevated to 35 degrees and a western orientation. I let the sky tick round minute by minute to see when the sun would align with the shaft, the day of illumination of the well below. To my utter amazement it turned out to be 29 July, the very day I was hypothesizing that Antiochus had set up as his (and his father's) official birthday. On this day the sun would conjunct with the brightest star in Leo, the star Regulus, 'the little king', and in the afternoon shine down the shaft. This was all too much to be a coincidence, it had to be the 'Royal Birthday' of 16 Aydnaios.

Exciting though this discovery was, it was by no means the end of the story. Tracking the day back from the afternoon, when the alignment with the shaft would occur, to sunrise, there was another surprise in store. On this very day would have occurred another event that the Egyptians would have recognized only too well: the heliacal rising of Sirius. That is to say it was the day when Sirius would make its first appearance in the dawn sky after 70 days of invisibility. This day started the Egyptian year and was connected with the idea of the birth of Horus, the Sun-king. This had astounding implications for it meant that what Antiochus was doing with his deep shaft was not constructing a dead-end escape route from the castle of Arsemia, or digging a burial pit for his father Mithridates but setting a new calendar. He was fixing the start of the Commagene year, which hitherto had been based on the movements of the moon, to the Sothic (Sirius) cycle, long used by the Egyptians as the basis of their calendar. To the ordinary people, those who were not initiated into the Mysteries, he was merely changing his birthday and honouring the gods, the sort of thing kings are required to do. In reality he was not only practising astrology of a very esoteric kind but laying the basis for a calendrical reform of great significance.

\*       \*       \*

Looking again at Antiochus' hierothesion, I began to appreciate it in a different way. All of it, and of course with the ravages of time it is no longer complete, had deep symbolic significance. It has long been established that the rows of figures carved on stele on the north and south sides of the terraces represent his ancestors. According to F. Karl Dörner, who has studied them for many years, those on the 'father's' side represent the Persian line of descent from Darius I (AD 522–486), through such kings as Xerxes to Rhodogune. The 'mother's' side is Greek and runs from Alexander the Great through Seleucus I Nicator (who was actually the son of another Antiochus, a general of Alexander's father Philip), through the Seleucid Dynasty to Antiochus' own father Mithridates Callinikos, whose mother Laodice was, of course, the daughter of the Seleucid king Antiochus VIII. It

Fig. 7

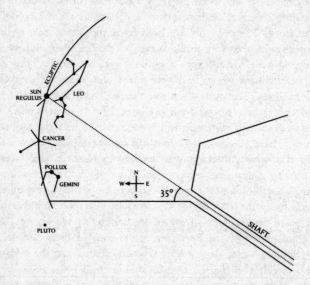

The alignment of the shaft at Arsameia with Regulus on the 'official' birthday of the Commagene kings, 29th July.

ends with a frieze of Antiochus himself. He was telling the truth when he wrote at Arsemia:

> '. . . I had statues made of the older people, my paternal grandfathers and myself approximately fitted to the real measurements and in accord to Gods.'

This seemed to throw some light on the curious, heraldic eagle and lion sculptures that stand together in pairs, framing the seated statues of the gods. Perhaps the lions represent the Persian line and the eagles the Greek. More esoterically it could be that these, like the gods, represent celestial bodies, the lion being the star Regulus and the eagle Sirius that between them give birth to the new king.

The digging of a deep shaft to observe the sun on a certain date adds

Fig. 8

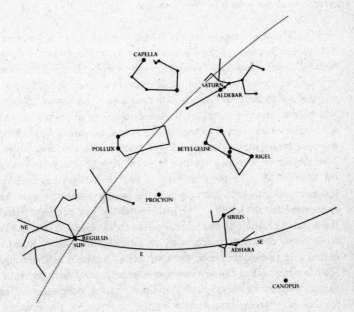

Eastern Sky at dawn on the 'official' birthday of the lion-kings of Commagene.

weight also to Neugebauer and van Hoesen's assertion that the pattern of stars on the Lion Relief was based on an illustration of Eratosthenes. It seems likely that Antiochus knew of his experiment involving the deep well at Syene and adapted the idea to his own latitude by having an angled shaft constructed that would carry out the same function of providing a shadowless tube on a particular day. This Alexandrian connection, along with his adoption of the date associated in Egyptian minds with the birth of Horus, would suggest that Antiochus was at least knowledgeable about, if not fully initiated into, the Hermetic tradition.

Other evidence for this is to be seen in the various 'hand-shaking' stele. Astrally these could represent conjunctions of the planets but more likely is a Hermetic interpretation based on the idea of the soul descending to earth through the spheres of the gods and receiving gifts from each one. These, according to the Hermetic writings, have to be given back at death. The dexosis or handshake that Antiochus gives to each of the gods of his birth, that is the planets above the horizon at his nativity, is him greeting the gods and returning their gifts. This doctrine is put very well in the *Poimandres*:

'Full well have you taught me all, O Mind,' said I, 'even as I wished. But tell me furthermore of the ascent by which men mount; tell me how I shall enter into Life.' Poimandres answered, 'At the dissolution of your material body, you first yield up the body itself to be changed, and the visible form you bore is no longer seen. And your vital spirit you yield up to the atmosphere so that it no longer works in you; and the bodily senses go back to their own sources, becoming parts of the universe, and entering into fresh combinations to do other work. And thereupon the man mounts upward through the structure of the heavens. And to the first zone of heaven (Moon) he gives up the force which works increase and that which works decrease; to the second zone (Mercury), the machinations of evil cunning; to the third zone (Venus), the lust whereby men are deceived; to the fourth zone (Sun), dominating arrogance; to the fifth zone (Mars), unholy daring and rash audacity; to the sixth zone (Jupiter), evil strivings after wealth; and to the seventh zone (Saturn), the falsehood which lies in wait to do harm. And thereupon, having been stripped of all that was wrought upon him by the structure of the heavens, he ascends to the eighth sphere, being now possessed of his own proper power;'[8]

Having ascended the ladder of the crystal spheres to the highest heaven, he is now free to enter Olympus, symbolized by his white tumulus. That Olympus stands above the planetary spheres is also made clear in the *Hermetica* when it says: 'There are seven wandering stars which circle at the threshold of Olympus, and among them ever revolves unending Time.'[9] In building his burial tumulus above the level of the seated gods, Antiochus was making a statement. He was announcing to the world his intention of rising above the crystal spheres to enter Olympus itself, symbolic of the higher heaven that stands above the planetary worlds. He was not a megalomaniac who built colossi for the sake of boasting but rather an initiate with a message. Like the pharaohs in Egypt he made his tomb into a book that could be read by generations to come.

## The Hero of the World

Leaving the tumulus on Mount Nimrod, I now turned my attention back to the other principal archaeological site in Commagene, Arsameia. Here there were to be other surprises in store that I wasn't expecting. The most prominent feature of the remains of what must have at one time

Fig. 9

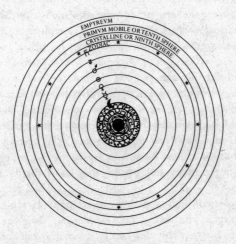

Traditional diagram of the spheres of the planets, the zodiac and the higher heavens.

been a significant complex surrounding the mouth of the shaft was the near perfectly preserved relief of a Commagene king, either Antiochus or his father Mithridates I, shaking hands with the god Heracles (or Hercules to give him his more popular Latin name). Now although on the hierothesion it would seem that Hercules was associated with the planet Mars and that the 'handshake' represented his soul passing back through the crystal spheres after death, I had a feeling that there was also some deeper mystery implied here. If the royal cult of Commagene was anything like that of Mithras, then there would have to have been at least seven levels of initiation. It was obvious that more highly initiated members of the inner circle, such as Antiochus himself, would be privy to deeper secrets than those understood by the general populace. One of the more esoteric teachings seemed to concern the god Hercules, whose image and 'handshake' were to be seen all over the place. True, he could be equated with Aries, the god of war, but Hercules, though a great fighter, was not that simple a character. Rather he was the most popular of the Greek heroes, a sort of Superman whose cult was celebrated throughout the Macedonian Empire. Suspecting that there might be something more to this legend than meets the eye, I decided to take another look at his myth.

Hercules, like many other heroes, was a divine twin. His father was said to be Zeus who, attracted to Alcmene, the wife of the king of Tiryns,[10] made love to her in the form of her husband, Amphytrion. She gave birth to twins: Iphicles, who was the mortal son of Amphytrion and Zeus' son Hercules. Unfortunately for the latter twin, his father's adultery had not gone unnoticed on Mount Olympus; Zeus' own wife, the goddess Hera, was profoundly annoyed and became the sworn enemy of the young hero. When the babies were still only eight months old, she sent two poisonous serpents into their cot. Iphicles saw them first and screamed but Hercules, unafraid even at that tender age, took them one in each hand and throttled them. On hearing the scream Amphytrion and Alcmene burst into the room and seeing the young Hercules with the snakes in his hand, they knew that he was the son of Zeus.

Though blessed with superhuman strength Hercules' life was essentially tragic. His first wife was Megara, daughter of Creon, the King of Thebes. He died whilst Hercules was away and his throne was seized by a Euboean called Lycus. He was preparing to murder Megara and her three sons, rightful heirs, when Hercules unexpectedly returned to the city. He quickly dealt with the usurper but at the celebrations which followed, in a fit of madness brought on by Hera's machinations, he himself killed his sons and their mother who tried to shield them. Consulting the oracle at Delphi he was told that as a penance he must go to Tiryns and do whatever tasks were given to him by his bitterest enemy, Eurystheus king of Argos. The latter set him a series of challenges, of the hardest and most dangerous sort, hoping that he would fail. These became the twelve labours of Hercules and were: 1) Slaying the Nemean Lion; 2) Slaying the Hydra of Lerna; 3) Bringing back alive the Cerynitian Hind; 4) Bringing back alive the Erymanthian Boar; 5) Cleansing the Augean Stables; 6) Driving off the Stymphalian Birds; 7) Bringing back alive the Cretan Bull; 8) Bringing back alive the man-eating mares of Diomedes; 9) Bringing back the girdle of Hippolyta, queen of the Amazons; 10) Bringing back alive the cattle of Geryon; 11) Bringing back the Golden Apples of the Hesperides; 12) Bringing back Cerberus, the three-headed hound of hell.

Naturally Hercules, as well as carrying out many other heroic deeds, succeeded in all these tasks and was therefore able to go free. He married again, this time a beauty called Deinara. When a centaur called Nessus tried to carry her off one day, Hercules shot him with an arrow poisoned with the blood of the Hydra of Lerna. This was to be his undoing, for as the centaur died he lyingly told Deinara to save his, now poisoned, blood as a love-philtre. Unknown to Hercules she did so and later, when she was afraid she was losing his affections to Iole, whom he had won in an archery contest, she dipped his shirt in it. When Hercules put on the shirt it burned him and in agony he tore it off, taking the skin with it. Realizing now how she had been tricked by the centaur, Deinara hanged herself. Hercules, knowing that this was his pre-destined end, had a funeral pyre built for him. As it burned his body a bolt of lightning shot forth and was taken into Olympus, where he became a god and was at last reconciled with Hera. Zeus, proud of his son, named a constellation after him.

This in its barest bones is the myth of Hercules and as I looked at it certain things became immediately obvious. It was clear that the twelve labours of Hercules relate somehow to the course of the sun through the twelve signs of the zodiac. Some of the signs associated with his tasks were easy to identify. His killing of the Nemean lion was obviously a reference to the sun passing through Leo.[11] The Cretan bull had to be Taurus and Hippolyta, the virgin queen of the Amazons had to be Virgo. Similarly the Hydra, with its poisonous blood, was probably Scorpio and the centaur who brought about his death Sagittarius. The order of the labours and the signs they represented didn't exactly fit but I was in no doubt that the cycle of twelve represented the year.

Similarly the birth and death of Hercules represented the solstices. He and Iphicles were twins, only one of whom was immortal. This was a clear reference to the Gemini or Dioscuri, for in this pairing only Pollux (or Polydeuces) was born immortal, though later he shared his immortality with his brother Castor. In Greek times the summer solstice took place with the sun clearly in the constellation of Gemini.[12] Conversely the winter solstice in Graeco-Roman times took place when the sun was placed between the constellations of Capricorn and Sagittarius.[13] Thus the centaur Sagittarius would 'kill' the sun in the last day before its rebirth on the first day of the next cycle.

All these connections implied that Hercules, whilst alive, was a solar not a martian deity. He was associated with the birth and death of light, with the cycle of the year and the labours of the twelve signs. Looking at these I could see clear parallels between him and the Persian Mithras. Both were demi-gods sent to earth, both had to carry out near impossible tasks and both were 'born' at one or other solstice.[14] The connection between Mithras and astrology is clear from the many representations of him sacrificing the bull of heaven. In these the god stands with right leg outstretched, holding down the right foot of the bull. With his other leg he half kneels on the bull's back. He grabs the unfortunate beast by its nostrils with his left hand and plunges his knife into its flank with the right. Blood, sometimes represented as ears of wheat, flows from the wound in the bull's side to be lapped up by a dog. A snake too sidles up to take its share whilst a scorpion attacks the bull's heavy testicles.

Dozens of statues depicting this rather gruesome event have been found all over Europe, a particularly fine specimen being that currently on display in the Roman galleries of the British Museum. Some other versions show, in addition to all the above details, two small acolytes standing by the bull's tail, one of them helping Mithras to hold it down. On a stele now on display in the Louvre at Paris (fig. 4), the Sun-god Helios and the Moon-goddess Selene watch over the scene. They presumably approve of the sacrifice, for on the other side of the stele, Helios is

seen bestowing power on Mithras which he is then able to use to
control the serpent, symbol of man's lower nature. These scenes are
clearly rather intimate to the cult and must refer to some aspect of
initiation. What is more obvious to the casual observer is that above
this scene and on the the same panel, Mithras is shown by Helios' side
and, like the Sun-god himself, carries a long wand of office crooked
in his left arm.

The astrological symbolism behind all these scenes is very clear.
The bull of heaven is clearly Taurus. The scorpion who attacks the
very symbols of potency is Scorpio, the opposite sign to the bull. For
just as Taurus stands for spring, the time of fertility and birth, so
Scorpio stands for autumn, death and the retreat of the powers of
nature. The two acolytes are clearly the Gemini twins, who stand
next along from Taurus in the order of the zodiac. This leaves Mithras
himself with his attendant dog. He, it would seem, stands not only for
the light of the sun but also for the constellation of Orion. His dog
is Orion's attendant, Canis Major, whose bright star Sirius stands for
illumination in the Zoroastrian tradition.

The equation of Orion with Mithras has clear implications for the
'real' constellation of Hercules.[15] In the 'shake-hands' relief at Arsameia
the king (Antiochus or Mithridates) carries a long staff crooked in his
left arm, just like Mithras in the Louvre. He is dressed in what must
have been his most formal costume. He wears an elaborate crown, that
seems to have five, sunray-like feathers coming out of it, a waistcoat
with a complex design of diamonds and stars and an under tunic,
raised up between his legs by some sort of draw-cord attached to
his belt, to reveal his trousers beneath. Hanging from his right hip is
a ceremonial dagger and attached to its sheath are five lion-heads –
perhaps symbolizing that his official birthday is in Leo, the fifth sign
of the zodiac.

All the symbolism of this royal figure seemed to point to the equation
of royalty with the sun-god. It seemed to be stating that the king, like
the hero Mithras after his elevation, was imbued with solar authority.
I could see that he was, to use a title borne by Egyptian pharaohs,
a 'Son of the Sun'. In this case why was he shaking hands with
Hercules, who could also be equated with Mithras and with Orion?
Once more I went back to the SKYGLOBE program and had another
look at the point in the sky indicated by the shaft. I already knew that
the sun's conjunction with Regulus was one of the things it indicated

but I was keen to see what the other point on the ecliptic was that passed directly over it.[16] Tracking once more round the sky I found this other point on the ecliptic that would align with the shaft. To my amazement it turned out to be the very day on which the sun would stand directly above the outstretched right arm of Orion. On this day the sun would be quite literally 'shaking hands' with Orion and therefore with Mithras-Hercules (fig. 10). This had to be the meaning behind the sculpture and gave me a third date: 26 May.

The symbolism implied here was astounding. Remembering that this monument was built in honour of Antiochus' dead father Mithridates, then if the date of 29 July represented the official birthday, the 26 May had to be the official 'death' day. Now in ancient Egypt, whilst a pharaoh was alive he was considered to be the living embodiment of a Sun-god. He was the Horus of the time, the Son of the Sun. In Commagene this

Fig. 10

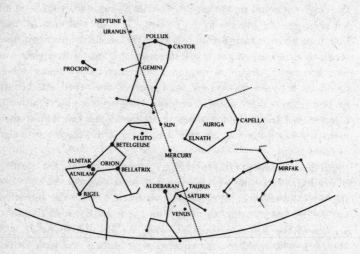

The sun 'shaking hands' with Orion in alignment with the shaft, May 26th 62 BC.

corresponded with the official birth of the king as an Apollo-Mithras, obviously the Graeco-Persian equivalent of Horus. After he died, an Egyptian pharaoh's mortal remains were mummified and various rituals were carried out to enable his soul to join the god of the dead, Osiris, who was believed to reside in the constellation of Orion. All this is very clear both from the Book of the Dead and from the architecture of the pyramids, which seem to have acted as a sort of launch pad for the soul during the Old Kingdom.[17] The connection between the Arsameia shaft and Orion seems to indicate a similar doctrine. The Commagene kings, like the pharaohs of ancient Egypt, wanted to be translated to the stars of Orion after death. Perhaps this shaft in the hills of Commagene, like the southern air-shaft of the King's Chamber in the Great Pyramid of Giza, was used as a sort of 'super-gun' to fire the soul of Mithridates I into the sky where he would 'shake hands' with Hercules and join him in his celestial home of Orion.

This, or something like it, seems to be what Antiochus had in mind and probably he too was 'loaded' into the cannon when his time came before his body was taken up Mount Nimrod to be buried in his hierothesion. If this is so then his Mount Olympus, like the Egyptian 'heaven' which they called the *Duat* was to be found in the region of the sky marked by Orion. Like an Egyptian pharaoh, he built a pyramid to house his mortal remains and hoped to go to heaven, where he would join Zeus-Ohrmazd. At the eastern end of his funerary monument, his birth horoscope is laid out to honour the gods of his nativity. Sculptures of his illustrious ancestors are presented on parade by his side, as he no doubt hoped they would be after he passed over. To the west of the monument he salutes the gods, perhaps for confirming him on his throne. On 6 July 62 BC (Loos 10th), the date recorded on the Lion Horoscope, he seems to have undergone some sort of coronation ceremony. Unlike Neugebauer, I do not think this was directly related to his confirmation as king by Pompey. As will become apparent, it is more likely that this was some sort of initiation connected with the esoteric side of his religion. Significantly this was the first time since his nativity that the planets, or gods, of his birth were gathered together again 'in council' in the same, royal region of the sky – Leo. Again his ancestors pay homage, lining up by his side.

At the centre of the monument is his tumulus representing Olympus, the final summit of heaven that stands above the ruling planets of the lower spheres. Somewhere in this mound of broken limestone, probably fairly high up, he is buried. However, it may only have been his bones that were placed here.[18]

Remembering now what Bennett had written about the Sarman Brotherhood and how the name implies that they were 'the chief repository of the tradition', which has been called 'the perennial philosophy' passed down from generation to generation by 'initiated beings', I could see that Antiochus fitted this description. Not only that but he claimed royal descent from the Persian kings and was indeed from a most 'distinguished family or race' such that he was in possession of an important 'heirloom', namely the perennial philosophy. Looking again at the Lion Horoscope with its date of 6 July 62 BC, I now found something else that seemed to clinch the connection between Commagene and Gurdjieff's Sarmoungs. On that day the sun, which is in the middle of the constellation of Cancer, stands directly below the cluster of stars which has always been known as the 'Bee-Hive'. Since the word Sarman (Sarmoung in Gurdjieff's Armenian dialect) means both those 'who preserved the doctrines of Zoroaster' and 'bee' in old Persian, then it is quite clear that in 62 BC the 'hive', the place of gathering of the bees, was Commagene.

It would seem that on 6 July that year a group of 'wise men', or Magi, gathered together at the court of Antiochus in Commagene. They had a lot to talk about, not least the real threat posed to the Zoroastrian tradition by the steady advance of Rome into Anatolia and Mesopotamia. The convocation probably included several kings of neighbouring territories as well as Antiochus. He, I would suggest, was elected and crowned as leader of the brotherhood, which must have been a sort of Masonic society. This, not his 'confirmation' by Pompey, is signified, I believe, by the Lion Horoscope. He was charged with preserving the Zorastrian tradition by showing its connections with the Greek and therefore Roman pantheon. Thus he gave the gods dual names, in Greek and Persian, and created the curious syncretism that was the state religion of Commagene. In this way it was hoped that, even if the Romans did conquer Mesopotamia, they would leave the people alone to practise a religion which would not seem too foreign to them. In fact, with some modifications, the Romans embraced this new religion themselves and it became the Mithraism which spread throughout their empire, reaching as far as Britain and Germany.

How much they understood of its esoteric significance is certainly open to question but it did provide a moral force in the life of the Roman legions and in some ways prepared the ground for the greater revelation of Christianity.

How much of this Antiochus himself foresaw is unknown. He did, however, leave a message, a 'legominism' as Gurdjieff would have put it, in the form of his monuments. He seems to have wanted us to know that he was a Hermetic scholar who strove during his life to be a good ruler. His final words at Arsameia make a fitting epitaph:

> 'Let everybody and those who try to perform religious works look at the face of the Gods, following the happy natures of the lucky believers as a consolation; and let them have a good life.'

Reading this and having visited what seems to have once been his happy kingdom, one can only feel respect for the man who died only about thirty years before Jesus was born. He was undoubtedly himself a Magus and it is not at all unlikely that it was from the little kingdom of Commagene that at least one of Matthew's Magi came.

Having discovered what I believed to be at least part of the mystery surrounding Commagene, I now felt free to turn my attention back to Urfa/Edessa, little realizing what extraordinary mysteries I was to stumble on there too.

# CHAPTER 8

✳

# The City of
# the Patriarchs

U rfa was once a beautiful city, the 'eye of Mesopotamia'.
Situated on a craggy outcrop of the Anti-Taurus mountains
to the north and seasonally refreshed by the Daisan, a tributary
of the Balikh River – itself a tributary of the mighty Euphrates – it was
also well placed on the trade routes running from far off India to the
fleshpots of Alexandria, Antioch and Constantinople. These factors
alone, though, were not sufficient to raise it above its neighbours. It
had two other strategic advantages that made it an ideal location to
build a fortress and establish a capital: it had a useful hinterland for
growing arable crops and all year round springs of water beneath
its citadel, so that its defenders could withstand a protracted siege.
Unlike its near neighbour, Harran, its name has not been found in
Assyrian records. Nevertheless, there is little doubt that this prime
location was settled as far back as the bronze age and probably much
earlier. This is reflected in local legends that maintain that it was first
founded by the Biblical Nimrod, the son of Cush and great-grandson
of Noah, the citadel being known as the 'Throne of Nimrod'. He,
we are told in Genesis, was a 'mighty hunter before the Lord' and
in Turkey he is often associated with old ruins, especially those on
high places such as Mount Nimrod in Commagene. Nimrod was
also, according to the Bible, the patriarch of the Babylonians and
Assyrians. He is said to have founded the cities of Babel, Erech,
Accad and Nineveh to name but a few. According to its modern
day citizens, Urfa should be added to this list.

Whatever its past as an Assyrian or pre-Assyrian city, Urfa was refounded by Seleucus in c.302 BC and given a new, Greek name: 'Antioch Kallirhoe', meaning 'Antioch by the beautiful flowing water'. This name seems to be a reference to the springs which, flowing out from caves beneath the citadel, feed the fish-pools for which the city is famous even today. More often it was known as Edessa, perhaps named after the Macedonian capital from which Greek immigrants had come or maybe derived from a Hellenization of the name of the River Daisan which flowed in a loop through it.[1] However, the local, non-Greek population called their city Orhay and Urfa, the current name for the city, is derived from this.

Edessa-Orhay did not stay long under Seleucid control. In 130 BC the army of Antiochus Sidetes was defeated by the Parthians. This was the final straw as far as the Seleucids were concerned and thereafter they did not attempt to control regions east of the Euphrates. According to Syriac chroniclers it was just before then, at around 132–131 BC, that the dynasty of Aryu[2] took the throne of Edessa. These kings, or rather phylarchs, were of Nabotean, that is to say Arab, stock.[3] As a dynasty they were remarkably successful in hanging on to power throughout difficult times in what was a highly unstable region. Though much official business was done in Greek, their native language was Syriac. This, though written in a peculiar script of its own, was a branch of Aramaic: the language of Syria and Palestine at the time of Jesus.

With the retreat of the Seleucids to regions east of the Euphrates, the phylarchs, most of whom seem to have been called Abgar, were able to assert their authority over the city of Edessa (Orhay) and its principality. Like its neighbour Commagene, Osrhoene, as the state was called, was a buffer between Parthia to the east and, first, Seleucid then, later, Roman Syria, to the west. Politically the Abgars had to balance the interests of both sides by playing one power off against the other. This was not always easy to do, especially when one or the other was intent on expanding its influence.

In many ways the experience of Osrhoene, at least in the early days, mirrored that of Commagene. When the Romans defeated Tigranes of Armenia in 69 BC, the Edessan king, like Antiochus of Commagene, found himself on the losing side. Likewise in 62 BC Abgar II, who was probably the son of the defeated king, was, like his neighbour Antiochus, confirmed as ruler over his territory. Tigranes, Antiochus and Abgar had much in common. All three were kings as a result of the break-up of the Macedonian inheritance, they were all notionally clients of Parthia but they all also had to take into account the growing military menace of Rome, which had already swallowed Pontus and Syria west of the Euphrates. The failure of Mithridates and his allies, first against Lucullus and then Pompey had shown that military resistance was not a feasible alternative against what was by now a superpower. They had little alternative but to accept Rome's terms, at least until such time as Parthia might come to the rescue.

Partial reprieve was not to be long in coming. In November 55 BC, the Roman Triumvir Crassus, who along with Pompey and Julius Caesar dominated the Roman political scene, set out for the East. He was jealous of the victories gained by both Lucullus and Pompey and coverted the booty that the former had brought home to Rome. Although the Parthians had given Rome no cause for alarm, he was determined to make war against them to enhance his prestige. Since

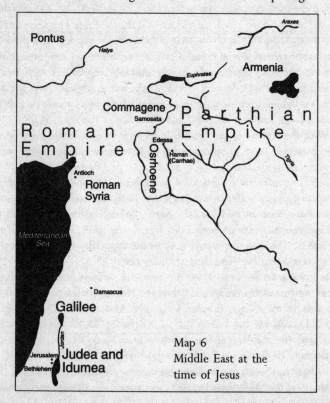

Map 6
Middle East at the
time of Jesus

Caesar, the third Triumvir, had also been successful in winning new
territories for the Roman Republic and thereby gaining kudos for
himself, Crassus needed victories of his own to show that he was the
equal of his partners.

Arriving in Syria he marched east and spent much of the following
summer making a thorough nuisance of himself wasting Mesopotamia.
The following year, after spending the winter in Syria and plundering
the temple in Jerusalem, he went back across the Euphrates with
seven legions, totalling some 35,000 foot soldiers and 4,000 cavalry.
He was greeted civilly by Abgar the phylarch of Edessa who, outwardly
at least, acted like a Romanophile. This, however, was just an act as he
was not keen to have his principality annexed like Syria to the west
of the Euphrates. Crassus lacked both the charisma and military genius
of Pompey that both instilled respect and went some way towards
alleviating the humiliation of having been 'confirmed' by him. In the
eyes of Abgar he was just a greedy Roman plutocrat out to steal,
for his own benefit, whatever he could get his hands on. In these
circumstances it is natural that his loyalties should be highly suspect.
He did what he had to do and led the Romans into a trap. The story
is told by Plutarch.

'. . . there came an Arab phylarch, Ariamnes by name,[4] a crafty and
treacherous man, and one who proved to be, of all the mischiefs which
fortune combined for the destruction of the Romans, the greatest and
most consummate . . .

. . . coming to Crassus, the barbarian (and he was a plausible
talker too) lauded Pompey as his benefactor and congratulated
Crassus on his forces. But then he criticised him for wasting time
in delays and preparations . . .

At this time, therefore, after the barbarian had persuaded Crassus,
he drew him away from the river [the Balikh] and led him through
the midst of the plain, by a way that was suitable and easy at first
but soon became difficult when deep sand succeeded, and plains
which had no trees, no water and no limit anywhere which the eye
could reach, so that not only did thirst and difficulties of the march
exhaust the men but also whatever met their gaze filled them with
obstinate dejection . . .

Cassius . . . privately abused the barbarian. "Basest of men", he
said, "what evil spirit brought you to us? With what drugs and

jugglery did you persuade Crassus to pour out his army into a yawning abyss of desert and follow a route more fit for a nomad robber chief than for a Roman Imperator?"

But the barbarian, who was a subtle fellow, tried to encourage them with all servility, and exhorted them to endure a little longer; and as he ran by the side of the soldiers and gave them his help, he would laughingly banter them and say, "Is it through Campania that you think you are marching, longing for its fountains and streams and shade and baths (to be sure!) and taverns? But remember you are traversing land on the borders of Assyria and Arabia!" Thus the barbarian played the tutor with the Romans, and rode away before his deceit had become manifest, not, however, without the knowledge of Crassus – he even persuaded him that he was going to work in his interest and confound the councels of his enemies.'

Meanwhile, the Parthians had mobilized. Though they had in the main accepted the status quo following Pompey's settlement of the east, they were not going to sit idly by while Rome annexed what, in theory at least, were their western provinces. To do so would have been foolhardy as, by the domino effect, they would soon find Roman armies knocking at the gates of their own cities. Under the direction of their general Surena and probably with the connivance of Abgar, they now arrived on the scene. Their force, unlike the Roman legions, was composed entirely of horse-archers. They now surrounded Crassus and his men to pour down a continuous rain of arrows onto the heads of the Romans. Whenever the Roman cavalry sought to counter-attack they would simply melt away, firing backwards at their pursuers (the so-called Parthian shot) as they went. Eventually the main body of the Roman cavalry was drawn off and destroyed to leave the foot soldiers totally unprotected on the wide open plains. At nightfall the much depleted Roman army sought shelter within the walls of Carrhae, the Latin name for the ancient city of Harran. They stayed there the next day and the following night tried to retreat back to the Euphrates. It was no use, the distance was too great and morning found them once more exposed to the withering rain of arrows. The army was utterly routed in what was Rome's greatest ever defeat and Crassus himself was killed during negotiations for surrender.

The Battle of Carrhae, as it came to be called, made a deep and lasting impression on the Romans. It was their most humiliating defeat since Cannae in 216 BC when the Carthaginian general, Hannibal, had virtually annihilated the entire Roman army. Much of the blame must sit fairly and squarely on the military incompetence of Crassus. The flat plain around Harran is not the forbidding desert that Plutarch makes out nor is water as scarce, especially in May when the land is quite verdant. The truth is that for this kind of warfare the Romans were no match for the Parthians and even Julius Caesar, a far more skilled general than Crassus, would have been hard pressed to extricate himself from such a trap. The immediate aftermath of Carrhae was to cause the Romans to scale down their ambitions in Mesopotamia, thereby giving the little kingdom of Osrhoene a breathing space. From the point of view of the Romans, Abgar, the cunning Aramean phylarch, was the treacherous villain who had led brave but foolish Crassus and his men into the trap. From his own perspective and that of the party which he represented, Abgar was undoubtedly a hero who had successfully played off the Romans against the Parthians and ensured the continuance for the time being of the quasi-independent principalities of Northern Mesopotamia. He had played the game of poker and this hand, at least, he had won.

It would not be for another 167 years, until AD 114 that Edessa would once more be threatened with the Roman mailed-fist. This time it was the emperor Trajan who was out to settle the 'Eastern Question'. An embassy from Edessa was sent to Antioch by Phylarch Abgar VII with costly presents and protestations of friendship for the Romans. Yet it was only five years previously that he had 'bought' his kingdom from the Parthians. Evidently it was an expensive business being sandwiched between two empires. Trajan went on to annex the neighbouring principality of Anthemusia, whose capital was Batnae and then pressed on with the main business of invading Parthia and seizing its capital, Ctesiphon. Insurrection in Northern Mesopotamia, including Edessa, brought him swiftly back, though he soon retook the city, its king dying in the general disorder.

Trajan's victories were to be short-lived. He left behind a Roman Empire that was greater in its reach than ever before or since but much of which was in revolt and resources were over-stretched. His successor, Hadrian, took a pragmatic view of things in the East and decided that the best solution was to give up pretensions east of the Euphrates and come to an accomodation with the enemy. Briefly a Parthian prince was put on the throne of Edessa but in AD 123 the old line of Abgars was restored with the accession of Ma'nu VIII. Unfortunately, only a generation later, the Parthians went on the offensive themselves, crossing the Euphrates and invading Syria proper. Ma'nu now looked to Rome for protection after he was deposed in favour of a more Parthianophile pretender. In AD 165 the Romans retook Edessa, the citizens having slaughtered the Parthian garrison and opened the gates. Ma'nu was restored and given the title Philorhomaios.

Thirty years later, there was more trouble when another Abgar laid siege to nearby Nisibis, which at that time was under Roman protection. The plan failed and he and his allies were defeated. Even so, he somehow managed to get back on good terms with the emperor, Septimus Severus, even getting his throne back. His new found loyalty was put to the test in AD 197 after the Parthians again laid siege to Nisibis. This time he aided the Romans offering to supply them with skilled archers. It paid off for, after the Romans had gained an easy victory, he was invited back to Rome itself and entertained lavishly as a 'king of kings'.

This Abgar VIII, known as the Great, probably died around AD 212. Although he was succeeded by his son, the great days were almost over as far as independent Edessa was concerned. However his rule coincided, or so respected historians such as J.B. Segal believe, with the adoption of Christianity as the state religion of the city. In AD 213 or 214 Edessa was proclaimed a *colonia* and though the kings continued to rule until about AD 240, this was really only in name. Thereafter the city was incorporated into the Roman first and then the Byzantine Empire – not without some pain it has to be said – until the advent of the first Moslem Empire.

## The letter of Abgar and the miraculous image

Edessa was to enter the history books for other reasons than its fish-ponds and strategic location; during the first millennium it was famous throughout Christendom for being the sacred city of the Mandylion: a miraculous image of Jesus Christ himself.

The story goes that whilst Jesus was preaching in Galilee, word got back to the reigning King Abgar V concerning this miracle worker and his wondrous powers of healing. Hearing that Jesus was receiving a poor reception from the Jewish authorities, he wrote him a letter inviting him to take up residence at Edessa. As the reply to this letter was the only example the Church had of the Master's own correspondence, the story was held in great esteem and copies of the letter were taken all over Europe. Abgar supposedly sent his lettter to Jerusalem via a footman named Ananias. It goes:

> Abgarus, king of Edessa, to Jesus the good Saviour, who appears at Jerusalem, greeting. I have been informed concerning you and your cures, which are performed without the use of medicine and herbs. For it is reported that you cause the blind to see, the lame to walk, do both cleanse lepers, and cast out unclean spirits and devils, and restore them to health who have been long diseased, and raisest up the dead;
>
> All of which when I heard, I was persuaded of one of these two, viz: either you are God himself descended from heaven who do these things, or the son of God.
>
> On this account therefore I have wrote to you, earnestly to desire you would take the trouble of a journey hither, and cure a disease which I am under. For I hear the Jews ridicule you, and intend you mischief. My city is indeed small, but neat, and large enough for us both.

Jesus' reply, sent back by the same footman, is courteous but negative. He is unable to go to Edessa because he has a destiny of his own to fulfil; but he will send help in due course. He writes:

> 'Abgarus, you are happy, forasmuch as you have believed on me, whom ye have not seen. For it is written concerning me, that those who have seen me should not believe on me, that they who have not seen might believe and live.
>
> As to that part of your letter, which relates to my giving you a visit, I must inform you, that I must fulfil all the ends of my mission in this country, and after that be received up again to him who sent me. But after my ascension I will send one of my disciples, who will cure your disease, and give life to you, and all that are with you.'[5]

Whether the story was true or not is open to question but the letters are quoted by Eusebius, who was Bishop of Caesarea in Palestine in the early years of the fourth century. He claimed to have found the story in the city archives of Edessa. So the deception, if such it was, is extremely old. Certainly the idea of a sick king sending a message to Jesus in the hope of a cure is not impossible and it agrees with the Matthew Gospel which tells us the latter's fame spread throughout all Syria, which in a larger geographical sense included Osrhoene.[6]

According to the legend, the outcome of Abgar's request was that after the crucifixion and resurrection, the apostle Thomas sent one of the seventy,[7] a man named Thaddaeus to go and visit Abgar. The story is told by Eusebius:

Now after the ascension of Jesus, Judas who was also Thomas, sent Thaddaeus to him [Abgar] as an Apostle, being one of the seventy, and he came and stayed with Tobias the son of Tobias. Now when news of him was heard, it was reported to Abgar, 'An Apostle of Jesus has come here, as he wrote to you'. So Thaddaeus began in the power of God to heal every disease and weakness so that all marvelled.

And when Abgar heard the great and wonderful deed that he was doing, and how he was working cures, he began to suspect that this was he of whom Jesus had written saying, 'When I have been taken up, I will send to you one of my disciples who will heal your suffering'. So he summoned Tobias, with whom Thaddaeus was staying, and said, 'I hear that a certain man of power has come and is staying in your house. Bring him to me'. Tobias came to Thaddaeus and said to him, 'The toparch Abgar summoned me and bade me bring you to him in order to heal him'. And Thaddaeus said, 'I will go up since I have been miraculously sent to him'.

So Tobias rose up early the next day and taking Thaddaeus came to Abgar. Now as he went up while the king's grandees were standing present, as soon as he entered a great vision appeared to Abgar on the face of the Apostle Thaddaeus. And when Abgar saw this, he did reverence to Thaddaeus, and wonder held all who were standing by, for they had not seen the vision which had appeared only to Abgar. And he asked Thaddaeus, 'Are you of a truth a disciple of Jesus, the son of God, who said to me "I will send you one of my disciples who will heal you and give you life?" ' And Thaddaeus said, 'Since you have had great faith in him who sent me, I was sent to you for this reason. And again if you believe in him, the request of your heart shall be to you as you believe'. And Abgar said to him, 'I have had such belief in him as to have wished to take force and to destroy the Jews who crucified him, had I not been prevented from this by the Roman Empire'. And Thaddaeus said, 'For this cause I put my hand on you in his name'. And when he did this, immediately he was healed from the disease and suffering that he had . . . These things were done in the 340th year.[8]

The story of the healing of Abgar and the introduction of Christianity to Edessa had wide currency in the early Church. Copies of the letters were made and were to be found as far away as Spain. There was, however, another tradition linked to this story of even greater import: the legend of the Mandylion or portrait of Jesus.

There is a Syriac document called the *Doctrine of Addai* which tells another version of the legend, Addai being an alternative form of Thaddaeus. According to this document, which probably dates from around AD 400,[9] on hearing about Jesus, Abgar sent two of his courtiers along with his secretary, Hannan, to visit the Roman governor of Syria. From there they went to Jerusalem and saw Jesus, recording all that they witnessed before returning home. Hannan was then sent back to Jesus with the letter, explaining Abgar's predicament and inviting him to come to Edessa. However, in this version of events the secretary, Hannan, is not only a man of letters but also the court artist. He paints a picture of Jesus 'in choice colours' and brings this back to Abgar, along with Jesus' reply, and he places the portrait 'with great honour in one of the rooms of his palace'. Now although it is easy to dismiss such a story as a late invention, there is no reason why it should not have been true. Abgar would undoubtedly have wanted to know what this man looked like and since he was evidently ill, could not make the journey to Jerusalem himself. We know from examples of surviving coffin tops, like those from Alexandria in the British Museum, that there were skilled painters around at that time. There is every likelihood that Abgar would have had at least one such skilled individual in his court and it is not at all unlikely that he would have been sent to paint Jesus' portrait.

Whatever the truth behind the story, the portrait of Jesus at Edessa became legendary. As time went on, so details were added and changed as Professor Segal puts it:

. . . in the early fifth century, the portrait has a comparatively minor role. But an analysis of later allusions to the portrait shows that gradually it increased in sanctity. In the earliest version, it was the work of the painter Hannan, in later accounts it could be painted only with the assistance of Jesus, finally it was wholly the work of Jesus himself. It had now become the impression of the features of Jesus which he had himself left on a kerchief, and it was divine — 'not the work of mortal hands', as it was termed, a phrase that may occur for the first time in 569.[10]

Other traditions state that the Mandylion — a name meaning a piece of cloth that could be used as a headscarf or kerchief — was the towel used by Jesus after his baptism in the Jordan. It is also clearly the origin of the tradition that when a St Veronica wiped the face of Christ with her veil as he paused on his way down the Via Dolorosa to his crucifixion, his image was miraculously transferred to it. Though this miraculous event is celebrated as the sixth station of the cross and is represented in picture form in Catholic churches throughout the world, there is no evidence of there ever having been a 'St Veronica'. She is not mentioned anywhere in the Gospels and the name, if such it is, is derived from the Greek '*Veron Ikon*', meaning 'True Likeness'. As many copies were made of the Edessa Mandylion and at least one of these made its way to Rome, it is almost certain that the Veronica Veil was one of these. Nevertheless, if it is true that the original Mandylion was a genuine portrait by Hannan, Agbar's secretary, then these also were indeed 'true likenesses' of Jesus and therefore worthy of veneration in their own right.[11]

Following his miraculous healing, Abgar was dutifully converted to Christianity, so Edessa became the first truly Christian city in the world. That it was able to do so without incuring the wrath of Rome lay in the fact that it was at that time the capital of a buffer state. Agbar was not, however, able to stop his successors backsliding. He died in AD 50 and was succeeded by his eldest son. After he died in AD 57, Abgar's second son took the throne as Ma'nu VI bar Abgar. He, it seems, was hostile to the new faith and restored the old paganism. Though the Christians were persecuted, they managed to hide their most treasured possessions, the letter of Jesus and the Mandylion, in the stonework of one of the gates of the city. There they lay undisturbed for nearly three centuries, the city in the meantime being re-Christianized some time between AD 177 and AD 212 during the reign of Abgar VIII, known as the Great. It was not until a flood in

AD 525 causing widespread damage to this gateway that it again was to see the light of day.

The recovery of the Mandylion was the biggest event in the history of Christian Edessa. News of it travelled fast and within a very short time the city, which already attracted pilgrims on account of its associations with the patriarch Abraham and the prophet Job,[12] had become an even more major centre of pilgrimage. By this time Edessa was inside the Byzantine Empire, exciting envy on account of its precious relic. By now the history of Edessa was closely tied in with that of the Roman Empire and it would not be long before Byzantium, as Constantinople was known to the Greeks, would set claim over such an important relic.

## Byzantium, the Imperial legacy

Throughout the period of Europe's darkness, when what culture there was lived in seclusion behind monastery walls, the eastern branch of the twin-headed Roman Empire lived on in Byzantium. Though often under attack from outside and subject to periodic insurrection within, it was a truly millenarian state that was to survive for over a thousand years after the sacking of Rome in AD 410. While barbarian Vandals, Saxons, Visigoths and Huns raped and pillaged what was left of the West Roman Empire, the East, with its magnificent capital of Constantinople, evolved a Christian civilization of great sophistication. Its churches and palaces were the largest in the world, its libraries contained the most books, its markets the highest quality produce, its people wore the finest clothes and they had time enough to engage in philosophy. Little wonder, then, that men of the West looked with awe and wonder, perhaps tinged with envy, at this glittering jewel.

But looks can be deceptive. Byzantium had many enemies nibbling at its borders and one implacable foe that Rome had never been able to conquer: Persia. Though Alexander the Great had in 331 BC defeated Darius and taken Greek civilization all the way to India, his empire soon crumbled and by AD 224, Persia had re-emerged as the Sassanian Empire. The Persians were devoutly religious and the Sassanian kings revived Zoroastrianism, the religion of their forefathers, that had gone into decline following the invasion of Alexander. For centuries Zoroastrian Persia and Christian Byzantium fought inconclusively over the border areas of Armenia, Syria and Upper Mesopotamia, neither side securing a final victory. Then, in AD 610, while Byzantium was in turmoil with serious internal problems, the Persian King Chosroes II launched a massive invasion. In a campaign lasting twelve years he overran large parts of the Empire, taking Anatolia, Syria, Egypt and even Jerusalem. The Christian inhabitants of the Holy City, maybe 60,000 in all, were massacred and what was believed by all to be the holiest relic in Christendom, the True Cross on which Jesus was crucified, was sent back, along with 35,000 slaves, as booty to Persia.

The devastation in the wake of the Persian army was immense. Everywhere churches were looted and burned. All except, that is, for the little church of the Nativity in Bethlehem. This the invaders spared on account of its mural showing the Magi in Persian costume paying homage to the newborn saviour. This war, however, was not to be the end of the Byzantine Empire. Solemnly pledging to fight the powers of darkness, to bring back the cross and retake the Holy places, the emperor Heraclius set out on what was, in effect, a Crusade. After a long and gruelling campaign, he eventually, in December 627, defeated the Persians at Nineveh. Chosroes was murdered soon afterwards and the Persians, themselves war-weary, at last sued for peace. The Holy Cross, which symbolized so much for Christians East and West was restored to Heraclius who was now able to bring it with all due reverence back to Jerusalem.

These events etched themselves deeply into the minds of Christians everywhere when, some 450 years later the Empire was faced with similar perils. The role of the cross was not forgotten as the all powerful emblem of Christendom at war as well as peace and it was to be invoked again. Unfortunately the jubilation after Heraclius' victory was to be short-lived. Both empires had exhausted themselves in their titanic struggle and had failed to pay attention to what was happening further South in Arabia.

It is said that even as the emperor was celebrating in Constantinople and receiving congratulations from all over the Christian world, he received a letter from an Arab declaring himself to be the prophet of God and urging the emperor to join his new faith. Similar letters had also gone out to the Persian emperor and the governor of Egypt and one can imagine only too well the sneering derision with which they were received. However, all three leaders were to learn soon enough that this was no joking matter, for Mohammed had arrived and he was intent on spoiling the party. By AD 632 Moslem armies controlled Arabia and by AD 645, following a series of brilliant campaigns by his successors, the Arabs controlled Palestine, Syria and Egypt. However, they did not stop there but carried on pushing out the frontiers of Islam in all directions. Thus by AD 717, less than a century after the cross had been returned to Jerusalem, there was a massive Islamic Empire of the crescent stretching through Spain, North Africa, Palestine, Mesopotamia and Persia right through to Northern India.

Christendom had by now shrunk to Europe (those parts which were not either Islamic or pagan) plus Anatolia – what we would now call Turkey. However, this did not mean there were suddenly no Christians in the new Arab Empire nor that everyone who lived within those lands had to become a Moslem. Christians, Jews and Zoroastrians were, as 'people of the book' allowed to carry on practising their own faith as long as they paid special taxes and did not seek to make converts. In fact Islam was not as foreign a religion as many in the West imagined. In many ways Islam was a reform movement of Christianity itself, Mohammed being a sort of early Protestant fundamentalist. Whilst rejecting the, for him, absurd belief of Christians that Jesus was the Son of God, he revered him as a prophet.

For Christians the new political situation was one they had to come to terms with. The East, the fertile ground in which Christianity had been born, had always been more intellectual than the West. It was from Antioch, Alexandria and Edessa that most of the early teachers had come from as these places had a long tradition of philosophy going back to times before the age of Moses. Also in the East there were a number of small, heretical sects such as the Nestorians or Jacobites that were virtually unknown in Europe where the Roman Catholic Church had a monopoly over theology. Under Islam these fringe Churches were able to carry on their traditions without interference from the orthodox authorities so that for them, at least in part, Islam was something of a blessing. However it also meant that there was no chance of reconciliation between the different Churches, which would arouse Arab fears and lose whatever historical privileges they possessed were they to reunite. Thus it was that following the conquest of Islam they were now, as it were, preserved in amber. The heretics could carry on being heretical as long as they kept their heresies to themselves. They were now by definition esoteric societies, passing down the knowledge and traditions of their sects through their own generations and not openly advertising these ideas to outsiders.

The most important form of esoteric Christianity had long been anathematized by both Popes and emperors alike and went by the blanket term of Gnosticism. It had effectively been suppressed as an open movement by the orthodox Catholic Church during the fourth century but it continued as an underground current, especially in cosmopolitan centres such as Alexandria and Edessa. It was precisely in these places that the earliest Churches had their roots, amongst the communities of Jews, Essenes and Greeks that were first instructed by the Apostles. It is therefore more than likely that a lot of what was regarded by the Latin Church as heresy was, in fact, part of the early, secret teachings of Jesus himself. Gnostic traditions, ideas and writings were preserved by the unorthodox communities of the East in spite of persecution by the 'Church Fathers'. The continued existence of Gnosticism was to be of profound significance for the future development of Europe when, through the Crusades, the Franks were to find themselves in Northern Mesopotamia.

Among the cities of Asia Minor that were first devastated by Chosroes and then seized by the Moslem Arabs was Antioch. It was one of the most important cities in the world and like Alexandria in Egypt owed its origins to the conquests of Alexander the Great. It was founded in 307 BC by Seleucus Nicator on a site that could conveniently control the trade routes between Upper Mesopotamia, Egypt, Palestine and Asia Minor but rose to prominence under Antiochus I. He made it the capital of the western part of the Seleucid Empire and the residence of the Seleucid kings themselves. As a Hellenistic city it prospered greatly and was well known for its arts as well as its relaxed ways. Unlike its contemporary and rival, Egyptian Alexandria, it didn't have the weight of an enormously antique civilization resting on its shoulders and was in some senses, more free to experiment. It therefore took to Christianity enthusiastically and after the destruction of Jerusalem in AD 70 became, in effect, the mother city of the Church.[13]

It was not until the Council of Nicaea in AD 325, of course, that a fixed Creed, to be adhered to by the whole Church, was laid down at the behest of Constantine. Prior to this date there was as much disagreement as agreement between the different Churches as to what constituted orthodoxy and even after the promulgation of what came to be called the Nicene Creed, matters were far from settled. It would seem that it was at this time that much of the esoteric understanding concerning Christianity, especially its connections with earlier astral religions was lost. This situation is well put by William Kingsland, who was himself both a professor of Astronomy and, like Mead, a Theosophist:

> The study of Christian origins is a very large and controversial question . . . but it is quite evident that the literalization of these narratives [the Bible] was due to the fact that those who ultimately obtained the ascendancy in the Church Councils, and were the framers of the Creeds which have been current for so many centuries, were *not* those who were instructed in the Gnosis. They were in fact miserably ignorant, not merely of that Gnosis which . . . lies at the heart of all the allegories, myths and fables in the Christian as in other ancient and pre-Christian Scriptures, but also of geographical, astronomical and anthropological facts well known to other peoples for thousands of years prior to the Christian Era, and which, when known – as they were to the *initiated* Church Fathers, who were, however, declared to be *heretics* by these same creed-makers – entirely alter the whole structure of the traditional Creeds.[14]

Within the early Church, Antioch and Alexandria came to represent two opposing views concerning the nature of Christ and his mission. The Antiochene school tended to stress the human as opposed to the divine nature of Christ. They saw in the man Jesus the exemplar rather than the saviour of the human race. According to this view Jesus, though highly gifted, was born as a mortal man and it was only in the course of his life that he developed his higher faculties and reason to become divine – the culmination of this process being his resurrection from the dead. His victory over death, though of immense significance for the human race, was no guarantee of salvation for his followers. People needed to follow in his footsteps themselves and, with Christ's help, attain eternal life. It would, however, be largely by their own efforts and without these there would be no personal salvation.

The Alexandrian school, by contrast, stressed the divine nature of Jesus from birth as the incarnation of the Logos or Aeon. It was much influenced by the legacy of paganism, both that of ancient Egypt itself and of the Neoplatonic schools, such as the Therapeuts, that drew heavily on the Greek philosophical tradition. The Alexandrians were concerned to develop a Christology that fitted with traditional philosophy and to this end tended to interpret the Bible in a more allegorical manner. For them the man Jesus was of much less import than the fact that he was the incarnation of the second person of the Trinity. The divinity of Jesus the Christ as the Aeon or Logos[15] was not in question but the Alexandrians were, at least in the view of the Antiochenes, in danger of losing the significance of the historical man Jesus.

The tension between these two, polar schools of thought was the driving force behind much of the Church politics of the fourth century, often to the bafflement of the Roman Church which, unlike its Greek cousins, was little interested in academic theology and more concerned with power. Both schools were, though they often couldn't see it themselves, aspects of the same Gnostic view of Christianity. Their differences stemmed from their viewpoints, the one considering life from the position of man as a created yet imperfect being and the other centred on the ideal: the perfected man in the image of God. The Nicene Creed tended to favour the Alexandrian view with a highly abstract definition of the Trinity as a mystery impossible of human comprehension. This satisfied the Latin Church but caused deep discomfort in Antioch, eventually resulting in schism as various heretical movements, such as the Arians and Nestorians, split off from the main body of orthodox catholicism.

Edessa was caught up in these conflicts and, as we have seen, in 489 the school of the Persians, which was identified with Nestorianism, was closed down and its teachers expelled to Nisibis. This, however, did not mean that the remaining Christians in the city were united in the face of Islam. The Monophysites were still divided into three mutually suspicious sects: the Melkite or Orthodox Greek Church that was loyal to the emperor, the Jacobites, who were largely Syrian in nationality as well as being strongly Monophysite and finally the Armenians. Each Church had its own archbishop or patriarch as well as its own cathedral and each had its own Mandylion. Naturally they disagreed as to who was in possession of the original and it is quite possible that all three were copies.

The capture of Edessa, along with the rest of Northern Mesopotamia, by the Arabs in AD 639 meant that the Mandylion was now once more outside of the Empire. This was intolerable for the Byzantines, who collected ancient relics with a passion that would do justice to a modern archaeologist. In 943 they mounted a siege of Edessa demanding the surrender of the Mandylion in exchange for Moslem prisoners of war and a payment of 12,000 pieces of silver to the Church.[16] Though the Christians of Edessa were most unwilling to part with their most cherished icon, their Moslem masters could better see the value of a bargain that would free several hundred of their co-religionists in return for a rag of dubious provenance. In the end the Edessans, though not without a struggle, were persuaded to surrender the Mandylion and it was taken back in triumph to Constantinople to be displayed in the Hagia Sophia Cathedral before being taken for safe keeping into the Imperial Palace. Though they left with what they were convinced was the genuine article, it is not unlikely that the Byzantines were palmed off with one or another old copy. One thing is certain and that is that the Edessans would not and did not part with it willingly as one of the superstitions associated with the Mandylion was that as long as it was in the city, they were protected by Christ from invasion. That this protection had demonstrably failed to keep out the Arab Moslems did not diminish their faith. Two hundred years later the Edessans would be sorely in need of any protective powers they could lay their hands on.

Assuming it still exists today, the whereabouts of the Byzantine Mandylion is a mystery. It was certainly counted amongst the imperial treasures up until the sacking of Constantinople in 1204 by the Fourth Crusade. Thereafter it went missing and it is not impossible that it exists to this day hidden in some château or museum if not stored safely in some corner of the Vatican. The theory put forward by Ian Wilson that the Turin Shroud and Mandylion are really one and the same, though always suspect, is now completely discredited as the former has been proven to be a mediaeval fake.[17] This does not mean that the Mandylion itself was a forgery. Some of the other points that Wilson made in his book *The Turin Shroud* are still valid. It is, as he says, noteworthy that it was not until after the Mandylion was rediscovered in 525 that portraits of Christ began to show him in familiar fashion as a man with long hair and a bifurcated bearded. The belief that the Mandylion was an original portrait or true likeness does not rest on the supernatural nor is it dependent upon the veracity of the Turin Shroud. It could well be true that Hannan's rough picture was a genuine portrait of Jesus and that it still lives on as the archetype of countless icons and paintings. If so then there is a chance that this portrait of Christ still exists.

Having now learnt about Urfa's surprising past, Dee and I were keen to pay the city another visit. I remembered the strange dreamlike vision I had had whilst ill on our previous trip and how the monk had said the city contained secrets. I was now beginning to see what some of these might be and was also suspecting a connection with both the Magi story and Gurdjieff's Sarman Brotherhood. With these thoughts uppermost in our minds, we made our arrangements and set off once more for Northern Mesopotamia.

# CHAPTER 9

✳

# A Tale of Two Cities

Having studied Gurdjieff's journey plan in detail, I was sure that he must have visited Edessa. In his book *Meetings with Remarkable Men* he tells us that after finding the map of 'pre-sand Egypt' in the house of the Armenian priest at 'N', he and his friend Pogossian had other adventures on their way to Smyrna (Izmir), before they took a ship to Alexandria. To get to Smyrna they would have had to pass through Urfa and, given its Hermetic connections, they would almost certainly have wanted to visit nearby Harran as well. Whether he would have gone on north to Commagene is less obvious but since Antiochus' hierothesion had received wide coverage following its discovery only a few years earlier and given Gurdjieff's evident interest in cultural ruins, it is not unlikely.

We, too, were excited at the prospect of going back to Urfa. Since our last trip in April 1994, I had read nearly everything I could find about the city. I now knew that the strange, dream-like vision I had had of palaces and churches gracing the old city was not entirely fantasy: that once Edessa had indeed once been the 'eye of Mesopotamia'. However, I felt sure that there was still some great secret contained there that was not to be found in books. Dee and I wanted to get back there to take another look for ourselves just as soon as pressure from other work would allow. Thus it was that in September 1995, we once more found ourselves on a plane bound for Turkey. This time I was determined not to fall ill or to fail in the quest. I would ask the right questions for, come what may, I was determined to find out what the great mystery was about Urfa and what connection, if any, it had with the Magi legend.

Arriving this time at Diyarbakir, the old fortress city on the Tigris 183 kilometres to the north-east of Urfa, we found ourselves a taxi. Soon we were tearing through the countryside, a desolate landscape of scattered, mostly black, rocks and scrub fit only for the grazing of the hardiest sheep and goats. Here and there amongst this wilderness were little patches of green where the immediate availability of water from a nearby well made it possible to grow the odd crop of tobacco or cotton but, for the most part, the land was little better than a desert with not a tree nor even a shrub in sight. Once more our driver was a Kurd and as we bumped along the open road he played us a cassette of Kurdish music. However, clearly afraid of the military, whenever we came to a roadblock (and there were several in the course of the journey) he would hastily pull out the cassette and hide it from the prying eyes of the soldiers. It seemed the situation was still tense and we felt grateful that we would not be staying long.

Arriving in Urfa, we went straight to the Hotel Harran, scene of my discomfort the previous year. This time we were well prepared with a medicine kit that would have done justice to an expedition up the Congo. Thankfully, as it turned out, we never needed to use it. Soon, after greeting Mustafa who remembered us well from the previous year and who had now been promoted to manager, we found ourselves walking down towards the old market. Somehow the dust, the smells, the crowds of people did not seem so alien this time. Now that we had a better grasp of the history of the city, it all made much more sense. Whereas last time we had been almost entirely detached from the life around us and therefore unable to make much sense of it, this time we ourselves were a part of it. In some small way, by virtue of our having made the effort to return, Urfa was now our city and we had earned the right to learn something of its secrets.

At the top of a small hill, we found the ruins of what must once, as it covered at least an acre, have been a very large building. One corner of it had evidently until quite recently been used as a mosque as its walls were painted turquoise. Now gutted and without a roof it was an empty shell. The rest of the complex was mostly below the present ground level and though the centre of the area was now being used as a storage depot for building materials, there were still underground crypts inviting exploration. These, featuring Gothic arches and fenestration, were clearly of very ancient construction – going back, we thought, to at least Crusader times if not earlier. Could this shabby, neglected ruin have once been one of Edessa's famed cathedrals? There was nothing to tell us and it was not mentioned in any guidebooks but it certainly looked as though it might.

Around the corner from the 'cathedral' were two interesting bridges, one of them obviously Roman, over the currently dried up bed of the River Daisan. Flanking it on both sides were tenement blocks, home to some of the city's teaming population. Even so, these tangible remains of former empires were still impressive not least because they were still of use. Walking down the hill in the direction of the Citadel, we passed many more relics of the past. What is now recognized as having been an ancient church of St John is visible from the street. Unroofed and open to the elements, its columns and Gothic windows clearly revealed its former ecclesiastical use even though it would appear to have more recently served as either a house or shop. Near to this church were several other small, open-fronted shops of the sort that are totally extinct in Western Europe. In one of these three small boys were turning large, economy-size tins into colanders. It was a simple process of making nail holes in the bottom of the tins but, nonetheless, an ingenious example of recycling. Further down the hill were the beginnings of the covered market proper. Here, Ali Baba style, was a warren of streets and alleys, each dedicated to its own type of merchandise. In one you would find food merchants, in another cobblers, in a third carpenters and a fourth jewellers. It was just as it must have been for a thousand years and, I imagined, would have probably seemed quite familiar to King Abgar the Great. By now exhausted, we decided to return to the hotel to freshen up before supper. We wanted to save Urfa's most important sites for when we were fresh enough to properly take them in.

The following day we made our way straight down to the market and proceded from there to the foot of the Citadel, where once the Abgars had had their palaces. According to local people, 'Urfa' is derived from the original name for the city from long before the Greeks arrived and renamed it Edessa. They relate it to a city called 'Ursu', mentioned in Akkadian, Sumerian and Hittite texts and assert that it is the place referred to in the Bible as Ur of the Chaldees. According to these traditions the patriarch Abraham was born in a cave at the foot of the Citadel. Today this cave (plate 30) is an important centre of pilgrimage for devout Moslems who make up the bulk of Urfa's tourism. They come not just from Turkey but from Syria, Iraq and other countries too.

After paying a small entrance fee, Dee and I made our way into the cave. It is, in fact, divided into two by a partition wall, with a room for each sex, for as is usual in Moslem countries, men and women pray separately. I went through the entrance into the men's cave, which turned out to be a small, airless chamber. At the back of it was a metal grill and beyond this, where it could be seen and not touched, was a pool of shallow water fed by a natural spring. To the right of the room was a tap where pilgrims could draw off water for drinking but this did not seem to be the main purpose of a visit; the men I saw were so busy prostrating themselves and practising their *zikr* that they didn't seem to need the water nor even notice my entrance. Slightly embarrassed at intruding on such private moments, I stayed only a short time before tiptoeing out. Dee likewise had felt the same inhibitions on her side of the party wall, with the additional problem of overcrowding. As in general there seemed to be five women pilgrims for every man, and as many of them had young children with them as well, there was barely room for everyone to squeeze into the small room let alone to practise the required prostrations.

Feeling virtuous now after paying our respects to Abraham, though wondering slightly why his mother had chosen such a wet cave in which to give birth, we made our way over to the fish-ponds themselves. These are set in a small park and are one of the greatest delights of Urfa. Fed by the springs we had just seen, their water would be fit to drink were it not for the thousands of tame carp that swim in great shoals in search of food. This is bought from vendors and fed to the fish by pilgrims and other visitors such as ourselves. As the carp are sacred they are never eaten and therefore grow to great size. The park was pleasantly shaded by plane trees and though the Pool of Abraham (plate 31) itself is flanked on one side by a mosque and is therefore reserved for quiet contemplation, its neighbour, the Pool of Zulha, is set in a tea-garden. Here we were able to drink endless glasses of *cai*, feed the fish and contemplate our next move.

Leaving the tea-gardens and with the aid of two young guides, we made our way up to the Citadel (plate 29). This imposing castle dominates the entire city below. Set on a natural eminence, with wells to provide water and very smooth walls that would have been difficult to climb, it was obvious how it had withstood so many determined sieges in the past. As Count Joscelin, the last of the Frankish rulers found to his cost, a well-victualled garrison could hold out here for a very long time. There were various ruins on the summit, mostly dating from the Ottoman or Seljuk periods but here and there were traces of Greek or Roman structures. To the west end of the summit were the remains of a building that incorporated several blocks with Corinthian decoration, evidence of a recycled past. The most significant remains though and what we had principally come up to see were two, remarkably well-preserved columns (plate 28).

These columns, which are fifteen metres high, are as emblematic of old Urfa/Edessa as Tower Bridge is of London. A Syriac inscription on one of them indicates it was dedicated to Queen Shalmath, who may have been the wife of Abgar the Great. He died in AD 212 and was the last of the independent kings of Edessa prior to the Romans' annexation of the city as a *colonia*. This therefore dates the columns to the end of the second and beginning of the third centuries AD. It was during his reign, in AD 201, that a great flood occurred, destroying a large part of the city and killing over two thousand people. Abgar ordered the people not to build 'booths' (presumably shops) close to the river and had a new palace erected on the Citadel mount though he also seems to have had another one below which enclosed the site of what is now the area of the fish-ponds and their associated mosques. This palace included a temple to the Moon-god, Sin, as well as a structure, which was known later as the 'Tower of the Persians' (plate 32). According to local legends, it was so named because it was later part of the building occupied by the famous 'School of the Persians' before that institution was closed down and its teachers expelled to Nisibis in AD 489.

The association of the Moon-god with the springs and pools of Edessa seemed entirely appropriate. Always in ancient civilizations the moon is associated with water, whether it be clouds, rain, rivers or the sea itself. The source of the springs in the caves under the Citadel Mount must always have been a great mystery. Unlike the unpredictable Daisan, they never dried up and the water they produced was both sweet and pure. Little wonder then that they were regarded as a gift of the gods and in particular of the moon, which ruled over all water. However, I suspected there was more to it than this – a suspicion which was to increase a few days later after a trip to the Moon-god's most famous sanctuary, Harran.

Leaving behind the fumes and dust-laden atmosphere of Urfa, our taxi sped through the North Mesopotamian plain. However, unlike the regions to the south of Diyarbakir this land was not only composed of good, brown soil but is now extremely fertile. This is no freak of nature but is largely due to the hands of man. A couple of days earlier, whilst on our way to Commagene[1] we stopped off and saw what is undoubtedly one of the wonders of the modern world: the Ataturk Dam. This enormous concrete structure, built with American help and know-how, now holds back the mighty Euphrates, flooding the valley behind to give birth to a large lake. Hydro-electric power is only part of the reason why the dam has been built. As important is the water itself which is now being taken off in aquaducts to irrigate the fields around Harran. The result of all this work was now clearly visible in the form of crops, mainly cotton, growing in the very fields where once Crassus and his legions had thirsted. It was clear that this area, which Jacob calls in the Bible 'Padan Aram' is rapidly turning into a new garden of Eden, a transformation that would no doubt have surprised not just Crassus but Abraham too.

The effect on Syria and Iraq of reducing the flow of the Euphrates is yet to be seen; maybe it won't make much difference. But the blooming around Harran once more indicates how important water has always been to this isolated city. The nearest river to the city, the Balikh, is some ten kilometres away and though an aquaduct was built in ancient times, the water it brought to the city was brackish at the best of times. This supply could easily be cut off in times of siege making Harran vulnerable to attack in a way that Edessa was not. For the most part the inhabitants had to rely on wells[2] and these were inclined to run dry during the hot summer months.

Yet, for all this Harran was from time immemorial the most important shrine of the Moon-god, Sin. During Assyrian times the city was almost uniquely privileged as it didn't have to pay taxes. Not only that but the Assyrian kings took a personal interest in its welfare as a holy city and sanctuary of the gods. On one of the Khorsabad Bulls Sargon, the oppressor of Israel who carried off the Samaritans, boasts of how Harran is under his 'protective shadow' at the desire of Anu and Adad: two of the principal Assyrian gods.[3] Prior to this Shalmaneser III, who is recorded on the famous 'Black Obelisk'[4] as receiving tribute from the Israelite King Jehu, son of Omri, had previously built a temple to Sin at Harran. This was evidently a very large, elaborate structure. It was restored by Assurbanipal (668–626 BC), who takes time out from boasting about his military conquests to tells us all about it.

At that time Ehulhul, the temple of Sin in Harran, which Shalmaneser, son of Assurnasirpal, [a king who lived before my time], had built, – [its foundations] gave way, it had become old and its walls had caved in. I restored its ruins and laid its foundation platform . . . The whole structure of that temple I built to a height of 30 *tipki*. (An addition,) 350(?) (cubits) long, 72 (wide), running to the east, I added to it . . .

Great cedars, which had grown exceedingly tall in Mount Lebanon, cypress (logs), whose odour is pleasant, which Adad(?) had made beautiful(?) on Mount Sirara, which the kings of the seacoast, my vassals, had felled . . . and had laboriously dragged out of their mountains, a wearisome region, to Harran, – with these I roofed Ehulhul, the abode of gladness, and . . . Great door-leaves of cypress I bound with a band of silver and set them up in its doors. At the beginning of my reign I completed the building of the whole of this splendid temple.[5]

The great hall, Ehulhul, evidently housed an idol representing the Moon-god as Assurbanipal later describes how: 'I grasped the hands of Sin and caused him to enter amid rejoicing and caused him to take up his abode.'[6]

Walking round the ruins of Harran today there is no trace of Ehulhul or even any other Assyrian structures. It is probable, though, that the city walls (Harran's most striking feature) are the same that faced the Caliph Al Mamoun when he demanded to know of the Sabians what religion they professed. Within their protection – now from sand-storms rather than invading armies – are today huddled numerous bee-hive huts and other simple dwellings of the town's Arab population. They, though, are not the descendants of the original Harranians, who abandoned the city after its destruction by the Mongols in 1260, but rather local Bedouin. Several of them volunteered to act as our guides, showing us the remains of the castle, a caravanserai and, what must once have been a very beautiful building: the Islamic school or Medrese.

Walking around the dusty ruins of the old city it was hard to imagine it as a bustling metropolis even though the sheer size of the area enclosed by the walls indicated what a considerable settlement it must once have been. Situated on a prominent hill overlooking the plains below, it would, provided its wells didn't run dry, have provided a welcome place of refuge for travellers. One could see why

Abraham's aged father Terah might have decided to finish his days here rather than trek on to Canaan. The daunting thought of mile after mile of semi-arid desert between here and the Levant would be enough to put off all but the most intrepid emigrant. Better by far to stay here, amongst those who spoke the same language and worshipped the same gods than to plunge into the unknown. Our guides were in agreement with this sentiment and showed us the site, or so they said, where Terah was buried before taking us outside the walls to the very well where Rebekah met the servant of Abraham. Any idea of a picturesque old brick-well with a bucket and chain was soon dashed when we saw it. It now looks more like a Second World War 'pill-box' than a well, shrouded as it is in a casing of cast concrete. We were rather more interested to hear from our guides about an Arab merchant in Urfa who had in his possession a strange statue that they said he would be keen for us to identify for him. There being nothing more of interest to see in Harran itself, we took his address and headed back to our hotel in Urfa.

The next day, bright and sunny as usual, we went down to the market where the Arab had his shop. Tactfully, as the situation was rather delicate, we asked him about the statue and after several cups of *cai* and preliminary chat, he agreed to show it to us. Suddenly I understood how Gurdjieff must have felt when first shown the map of 'pre-sand Egypt' by the Armenian priest at Nisibis. As he unwrapped it our eyes fell upon what was undoubtedly a genuine antique (plate 25). Examining it closely I could see that it was made of a hard stone similar to the Black Obelisk of the British Museum. It was shaped rather like a piece of Edam cheese, with a curved back and triangular section. The carving itself was of a limbless, bearded man robed with tapering leaves and with a fish's head instead of feet. In his navel (or what would have been his navel had he had a body as such) was drilled a hole. This was perhaps a centimetre in diameter and a little deeper. Feeding into this hole was a narrow channel coming from the fish's mouth, though its function was not at all obvious. Our host suggested that this might be so that a piece of leather or string could be threaded through it, enabling the statue to be worn round the neck, but I was not so sure.

Our host was keen to know what we thought the statue might be and, more to the point, what it might be worth. We were unable to enlighten him on the second point, still less to make an offer. With dubious provenance and the likelihood that he had obtained it illegally, it would obviously be stupid to buy the little statue tempted as I was. He did, however, agree to let Dee take pictures of his treasure, a service for which he was generously rewarded with 'Backsheesh'. This I was keen to do as I was pretty sure that it was Assyrian, represented the Moon-god, Sin, and was probably some sort of votive lamp. In profile it looked like a crescent moon and I could imagine that if a wick were threaded through the fish's mouth and the hole in the navel filled with olive oil, it would function as a little lamp. I could believe him, therefore, when he said it had come from Harran as it could easily have belonged to the temple there as a gift of Assurbanipal at the time he rebuilt the temple. It was possible, of course, that it was even older and went back to the time of Shalmaneser III or even earlier. However, without other objects of a similar type and no knowledge of its exact site of discovery, there was no way of knowing for sure when it had been made.

That night I pondered the matter deeply. Somehow the little 'Aladdin's lamp' or whatever it was, seemed important to our quest but I wasn't sure why. Unable to sleep, I got up and paced the room. Suddenly it struck me: the statue of the Moon-god was really more appropriate to Edessa than Harran. The head represented the 'man in the moon' as it shines down on the Citadel, the garment of foliage the trees below and the fish-head at the bottom the ponds with their carp at the bottom. We know that there was indeed a temple of the Moon in Edessa that stood guard over the fish-ponds where the Abdurrahman Mosque is today. The kings of Edessa, certainly up until the end of the reign of Abgar the Great in AD 212, kept the temple of the Moon in operation long after they formally adopted Christianity. While other temples were torn down or turned into churches, this one building, safe within the precincts of the palace, carried on the old religion. Later, it seems, the site was occupied by the 'School of the Persians', whom even their enemies acknowledged as being very knowledgeable. A tower, said to have been used by them, still stands between the ponds to this day. Thinking about this it became clear, that the tower was probably used for watching the phases of the moon – possibly by looking at its reflection in the pool below. This would have been a necessary and vital task for a people whose calendar was lunar.

The Moon-god was important because for the Mesopotamians he represented water and therefore fertility. More than this he was the giver of time and therefore the principal ambassador of the unseen god, whom they seem to have called Marilaha 'lord of all' or Be'elshamin, 'lord of the heavens'. All ancient religions, however polytheistic they might appear on the surface, had at their root the understanding that above and beyond the visible universe resided an unseen god, the original cause of all that manifests. In Egypt he was called variously Atum or Amun, in Persia Ahura Mazda and in Mesopotamia Be'elshamin. However, because people find it hard to think about the unthinkable or to imagine the unimaginable, the unseen god becomes, by a process of objectification, identified with one or another celestial body. In Egypt this was the Sun so that Atum was worshipped as Atum-Ra, the setting Sun. In Mesopotamia it was the Moon and Sin became known as Sin-Marilaha. The Temple of Sin at Urfa/Edessa, therefore, had the same sort of significance for the Mesopotamians as the temple of Atum-Ra at Heliopolis did for the Egyptians. More importantly the migration from Ur and the burial of Abraham's 'father' at Harran seemed to indicate a cultural transference. If it is true that Abraham was born at Urfa, the real Ur of the Chaldees, then this, not Harran, had to be the original home of the Moon cult. Given the presence of the springs at Edessa contrasted with the dryness of Harran, this made sense. Suddenly, perhaps under the guidance of the 'Genie of the Lamp', I was beginning to understand the significance of Edessa and why nine hundred years ago, during the First Crusade, it had been considered of great importance.

## The Pilgrims' Progress

For Western Christians the Islamic conquest of the Holy Land offered opportunities as well as posing serious practical problems. For centuries there had been quite considerable friction between the Pope, who saw himself as the successor of St Peter and head of the entire Christian community, and the Patriarchs of the East, who regarded themselves and their churches as autonomous equals of the Holy See. The loss of Syria, Palestine and Egypt to Islam, whilst an enormous calamity for Constantinople, gave Rome the opportunity to assert itself as the protector of Eastern as well as Western Christians. As the Patriarchs of the East lost power and influence, so the Pope gained in authority. This expressed itself in the building of new hostels in Jerusalem and in greatly increased numbers of Western pilgrims to the city.

A major concern for the Pope and for all Western Christians was the free movement of pilgrims and their access to the Holy Places. From the very earliest days, pilgrims had made their way to the Holy Land so that they could visit the sites associated with Christ's ministry. The most important of these were the Church of the Holy Sepulcre at Jerusalem and the Church of the Nativity in Bethlehem. With the decline of Byzantine power and the rise of the Holy Roman Empire of Charlemagne in the eighth century, the Latin Church took the opportunity of establishing new, Catholic hostels in Jerusalem. However, the great age of pilgrimage did not properly begin until the tenth century, when improving economic conditions at home and a reasonably peaceful accommodation between the Christian Empire of Byzantium and the Islamic world allowed for a free flow of Europeans to both Constantinople and the Holy Land itself. This happy state of affairs was to endure until nearly the end of the eleventh century when disaster once more struck the Eastern Empire.

For some time the Byzantines had been under pressure in the East from new neighbours who had come from Central Asia. These people, the Turkomans or Turks were nomads who had been converted to Islam and had already overrun Persia. They were now intent on invading the Empire. For centuries Armenia had acted as a useful buffer state between Anatolia proper and the wilder areas to the east of the Arax River. However, with the fall of Persia to the Turks and the establishment of their new capital at Isphahan plus the acknowledgement by the Caliph of Baghdad of the Seljuk Turkish leader, Tughril, as champion of Sunni Islam and king of East and West, the situation became much worse for the Byzantines. By 1054 the Turks were raiding deep into Armenia and, in 1066, they sacked Caesarea, the principal town of Cappadocia. The situation was dire for the emperor, Romanus, made worse by the policies of his predecessor Constantine X who had seriously reduced the armed forces. Even so he realized that the Turkish threat would have to be faced and, putting together an army largely made up of Frankish, Norse, Norman and Turkish mercenaries, set out in spring 1071 to reconquer the lost territory of Armenia. On 26 August, near Manzikert, a fortress on the southern branch of the Upper Euphrates, he was confronted by the army of the Seljuks under their leader Alp Arslan, who had hastily marched north to meet him. If there had been any doubt as to how the battle would turn, it was removed with the desertion of Romanus' Turkish troops to the standard of their kinsman and the refusal of the West European mercenaries to take part in what they could see would be a losing battle. Not surprisingly, Romanus and his remaining forces of Greeks and Armenians were routed, he himself being wounded and taken prisoner. News of this devastating defeat sent a shock wave that was to be felt throughout Christendom. It was suddenly realized that the Roman Empire (for such indeed was Byzantium still considered to be), facing its greatest threat since the advent of Islam, was in no fit state to defend its territories. The way was now open for full-scale Turkish migration into Anatolia made easier by the the fact that much of the land had been depopulated through an earlier, short-sighted clearance policy.

However, Turkish expansion was not confined to Anatolia. Since 1055, when Tughril had first entered Baghdad, pressure had mounted on the Holy Land. In 1071, Jerusalem was taken by a vassal of Alp Arslan and this was quickly followed up by the seizure of Damascus, Aleppo and other Syrian cities. Though the region's Christians were not badly treated, the instability and uncertainty that now bedevilled the Holy Land and the risk of banditry now inherent in travelling overland through Anatolia, made life difficult for pilgrims. In 1073, the new Emperor, Michael VII, realizing the need for Western support if the menace from the Seljuks was to be met, wrote to Pope Gregory VII, congratulating him on his inauguration. He drew attention to the sorry plight in which the Empire found itself and asked for help. The Pope was sympathetic to his request realizing that this offered a golden opportunity to impress upon the orthodox Churches the need to come under the umbrella of Rome. Little did Michael know that his simple call to arms would result in one of the greatest, military adventures of the Middle Ages: the First Crusade.

## A Crusade for the Holy Land

In November 1095, the next Pope, Urban II, called a Council at Clermont in France. Here he laid out his plans to retake the Holy Places and invited volunteers to go on a Crusade to the East. The response was overwhelming and, before long, several unruly armies of mostly Franks and Normans were on their way to Constantinople. The nobles who led these forces were younger brothers and sons of the French aristocratic houses, anxious for adventure and hopeful of profferment. Foremost amongst them were Godfrey of Bouillon, Duke of Lower Lorraine; his brother Baldwin, later to be crowned King of

*Plate 1*. Adoration of the Magi (Ducal Palace, Dijon)

*Plate 2*. Emperors Constantine and Justinian giving gifts to the Virgin (Hagia Sophia, Istanbul)

*Plate 3*. The Shrine of the Magi (Cologne Cathedral)

*Plate 4. The Baptism of Jesus,* Piero della Francesca, c 1450 (National Gallery, London)

*Plate 5. The Wilton Diptych,* c 1395 (National Gallery, London)

*Plate 6.* The pyramids of Giza

*Plate 7.* The Great Sphinx of Giza

*Plate 8.* Khafra (Chephren) embraced by Hawk

*Plate 9.* Hawk-headed Sphinx

*Plate 10.* Osiris (Orion) with Isis (Sirius) and Nephthys (Procyon) in attendance

*Plate 11.* Obelisk of Senusert I (Heliopolis)

*Plate 12.* The Egyptian Phoenix or 'Bennu' bird

*Plate 13.* The church of the Materiya, Heliopolis

*Plate 14.* The Holy Family arrive at Heliopolis

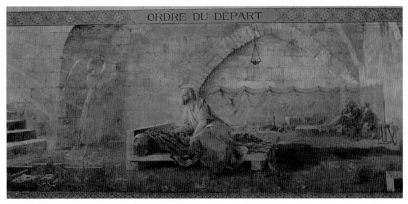

*Plate 15.* Angel waking Joseph (Materiya Church)

*Plate 16.* Mary and the Tree (Materiya Church)

*Plate 17.* The 'Virgin Tree' today. Heliopolis

*Plate 18.* The Hierothesion of Antiochus Epiphanes (eastern terrace)

*Plate 19.* The author by the throne of Zeus (eastern terrace)

*Plate 20.* Fallen heads of the Gods, Hierothesion of Antiochus Epiphanes (western terrace)

*Plate 21.* Lion horoscope with twin Eagle and Lion statues (western terrace)

*Plate 22.* Arsamia

*Plate 23.* 'Shaking Hands' relief at High Canyon, Arsamia

*Plate 24.* The author measuring the angle of the shaft at High Canyon

*Plate 25.* The 'Alladin's Lamp'

*Plate 26. St Veronica with the Sudarium.* c 1420 (National Gallery, London)

*Plate 27.* Roman follis of Justinian I from Edessa

*Plate 28*. The Corinthian pillars of Edessa

*Plate 29*. The Citadel of Edessa with pillars, viewed from below

*Plate 30.* The cave of Abraham (Urfa)

*Plate 31.* The Pool of Abraham
(Urfa)

*Plate 32.* The Tower of the Persians
(Urfa)

*Plate 33*. Harran, the Castle

*Plate 34*. Relics of St John (Topkapi Museum, Istanbul)

*Plate 35. Beheading of John the Baptist* (Ducal Palace, Dijon)

*Plate 36.* Star-correct *Adoration of the Magi* by Bengt Alfredson

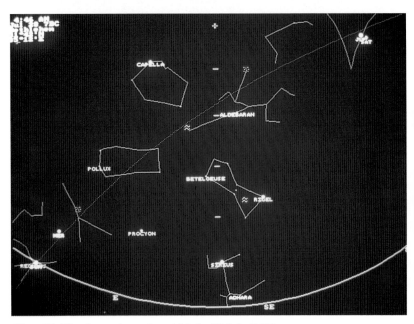

*Plate 37.* The dawn sky at Jesus' birth, 29 July 7 BC

*Plate 38. The Annunciation,* Fra Filippo Lippi, c 1450 (National Gallery, London)

*Plate 39.* The 'Smiling Angel' on Reims Cathedral

*Plate 40.* Sagittarius statue on Reims Cathedral

*Plate 41.*
Heavenly lilies
in the Egyptian
afterworld

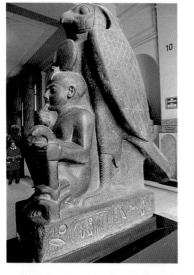

◀ *Plate 42.* Horus as a child, protected by Hawk

▼ *Plate 43.* The Fleur-de-Lys

*Plate 44.* Maat over-
seeing 'The Weighing
of the Heart'

Jerusalem; Count Raymond of Toulouse, whose lands were already home to heretics in the form of the Albigenses; Robert, Duke of Normandy, the eldest son of William the Conqueror; Bohemond, Prince of Taranto and his nephew, the ever energetic Tancred. These nobles plus hundreds of other knights and thousands of retainers, not to mention ordinary pilgrims, formed several armies that now marched through the Balkans to Constantinople. There they joined together to form a great expedition intent on not only the retaking of Jerusalem but also the creation of principalities and dukedoms for themselves.

There had, of course, been countless expeditions mounted before against the Turks and others by the Byzantines. Many of these, such as that of the ill-fated Romanus, had involved Frankish, Norman, Anglo-Saxon and other mercenaries. What made this adventure different and the reason why it is still of interest to us today was both its religious intensity and the fact that it was independent of Byzantine leadership. After an epic journey with many hardships and not a few delays, the Crusaders at last reached Jerusalem on 7 June 1099. As it had taken them fifteen months to take Antioch and they were in no mood for further delays outside the walls of Jerusalem, they immediately set siege. On 17 July the city's Moslem garrison surrendered but this proved to be a futile gesture. In one of the most infamous attrocities in history the Franks slew almost the entire Moslem and Jewish population sparing only the Christians, who must themselves have been absolutely terrified by what they had witnessed. This appalling massacre sent another shock wave, this time throughout the Moslem world, that in time would have repercussions for the descendants of the Crusaders themselves. For whereas before these horrible events Jerusalem's Christians, Jews and Moslems had been able to live side by side in relative amity, after this holocaust there would be far more suspicion.

This First, the only truly successful, Crusade, was to have a profound effect upon European thinking. Jerusalem, 'ethnically cleansed' of its Jewish and Moslem inhabitants, was now a Christian city and it was soon to have a Frankish king: Baldwin I.

## The High History of the Holy Grail

Right from the start of the campaign the Crusaders had been infused with a fervour more akin to the warriors of Islam than Christians.

They believed that they were carrying out a Holy War and that if they died on the battlefield or even off it, provided it was in the service of their calling, then they were guaranteed a place in heaven. Though such beliefs might seem naïve today, at the time and in this context they were considered perfectly normal. One reason for this was a growing mystical sense that would soon find its expression in another important tradition of the Middle Ages: the religious quest. This had its origin not in Byzantium but in far off Britain, which following William of Normandy's conquest in 1066 had intrigued the Normans with its cycle of Arthurian Romances.

In 1091, Robert Fitzhammon, who was the Earl of Gloucester and a close relative of William the Conqueror, unexpectedly seized the castles of South Glamorgan. Though Wales was very far from subjugated, this delighted William II (Rufus), the brother of Robert Duke of Normandy, and was enough for Fitzhammon to be given the titles of Conqueror of Wales and Prince of Glamorgan. Unlike in England the Normans were relatively well received in Wales and almost immediately began marrying into the leading families of the area. As many of them were themselves descended from the Bretons of Northern France, they were fascinated to hear about the history of Britain at the time of the Saxon invasions and how during this period Brittany and Normandy had been settled by emigrants from Britain. The Normans were quick to realize that this Breton connection gave them some sort of legitimate claim to Britain itself. Welsh tales concerning King Arthur, who reigned in Britain during the sixth century, went down well with the Norman court. For just as Arthur had defeated the Saxons in the Battle of Badon, so their own Duke William had again destroyed an English army at Hastings. Viewed in this light William had not usurped the throne of Britain but restored it into rightful hands. The Normans also assimilated other aspects of Welsh, mystical folklore including legends concerning events following the Crucifixion. According to various accounts a cup, known by the title of the 'Holy Grail' and believed to have been that used by Christ at the Last Supper, had been brought to Britain by Joseph of Arimathea shortly after the resurrection. This cup was believed to have miraculous properties and its subsequent loss by the British was deemed to have had disastrous consequences for King Arthur's kingdom.

Though the Grail legend in the developed form in which we have it was not written down until the mid-twelfth century and therefore some fifty years after the First Crusade, there can be little doubt that the idea of the religious quest was already, in 1097, a motivating force for the Frankish aristocracy. Conversely the experience of the Crusade and its aftermath had a profound effect upon the development of Arthurian mythology. One of the most important events of this Crusade happened during the long and gruelling siege of Antioch, for during this campaign a spear, believed by many to be that used to pierce the side of Christ, was discovered under the floor of St Peter's Cathedral.

The story goes that a man named Peter Bartholomew, the servant of a Provençal pilgrim named William Peter, had had a vision during which he met up with St Andrew. During the vision the saint took him in spirit into the church of St Peter, which at that time was still in Turkish hands and being used as a mosque. He showed him an area of the floor in the South Chapel where, he was told, lay hidden the spear which had been used to pierce the side of Christ. He was then instructed to tell the story to the Bishop of Le Puy and Count Raymond of Toulouse, his own overlord. Much taken aback by this curious, clairvoyant experience and not a little afraid of the reception that he, a humble peasant, would receive if he presented himself to such noble gentry with such a story, Peter Bartholomew was at first unwilling to do as the saint had requested. Further visions, however, made this imperative and, in the end, he did as he was told. Eventually, the city having by now been captured, the floor was excavated and he was able to pull the spear out of the ground. As it turned out, its discovery was the turning point of the Crusade, which up until then had had little success. Peter's visions and the discovery of the spear where he said it would be lent heart to the by now flagging Crusade. Carrying it as a talisman the Franks attacked a relieving army of Turks, who were now in turn besieging them, and succeeded in gaining victory against the odds. This was enough to ensure the acceptance of the spear as genuine by all but the most hardened sceptics in their midst.

The story of Peter Bartholomew illustrates the way that the Crusade was itself driven by mysticism and the prominent role given to the Lance of Longinus in the later Grail legends almost certainly derives from this real experience of real knights. It is also not inconceivable that at least some of the Crusaders were actively seeking other paraphernalia of the Crucifixion, including the Grail itself, as part and parcel of their work. This, I believe, was the main reason why a contingent of knights under Baldwin of Boulogne (later to become the first king of Jerusalem) and

Tancred, the nephew of Bohemond, left the main body of the army as it took up position outside Antioch and went east to seize Edessa. This famous city claimed to have been the first to be converted to Christianity and, as we shall see, has particular significance for the Grail legend.

After Constantinople and Antioch, Edessa was the third greatest Christian city of the Byzantine Empire. Situated in a perilous position on the fringes of the Empire in Northern Mesopotamia it was always vulnerable to attack. It had been seized by the Persian King Chosroes in 609, won back by Heraclius in 628 only to be lost again to the Moslem Arabs in 639. At the time of the First Crusade it was, for the moment, back in the hands of Christians and had an Armenian governor named Thoros. He was nominally the vassal of the Byzantine emperor but, in practice, felt pretty much free to do as he liked. His position, though, was tenuous, the small principality being surrounded on all sides by a sea of hostile Moslems. He therefore looked upon the presence of a large Crusader army in the region as a godsend. As an old man with no heirs to worry about he was only too willing to share power with Baldwin in exchange for Frankish protection for the city and on these terms invited the Franks to join him at Edessa. Baldwin, with Tancred (later to become Prince of Galilee and Regent of Antioch), plus their accompanying knights, arrived in Edessa to a rapturous welcome. In a bizarre ceremony that involved Baldwin stripping to the waist and rubbing his bare breast first against that of Thoros and then of his wife, he was adopted as their son and heir. Shortly afterwards the Armenian was murdered by an angry mob and Baldwin became the *de facto* Count of what was now to become the first Crusader state.

The historical view that the Crusades were simply a cloak of respectability to cover the naked ambitions of young French knights, intent on carving out principalities and dukedoms for themselves, is no longer in vogue. This view, formerly championed by Lord Runciman (author of the famous historical trilogy on the Crusades) is debunked by Jonathan Riley-Smith, editor of the recent *Oxford Illustrated History of the Crusades*. He writes:

> But while intellectual developments [after the Second World War and Nuremburg Trials] may have been predisposing people to look more empathetically at crusaders, most explanations of the involvement of so many men and women in the movement were

still that they had lacked sophistication or had desired material gain; and the latter view gained powerful support from a clever, but very narrowly based, suggestion that crusaders were generated by family strategies for economic survival . . .

In fact it was hard to credit sincere men and women with an ideology as repugnant as crusading; it was easier to believe that they had been too simple-minded to understand what they were doing or to argue that they had been motivated, whatever they might have said, by desire for land or booty, although the latter explanation should have been hard to sustain. Everybody knew that medieval warfare had been costly and a mass of material was already in print, even if unread, which demonstrated the financial sacrifices men and their families had to make to take part in crusading.[7]

Crusading was a time-consumming and expensive business, the costs involved generally outweighing any material rewards that might be forthcoming. Not only that but all too often the experience ended in death. It is clear that Crusading, at least in its early days, was essentially an act of penance. It combined armed service with pilgrimage and as such had great appeal for a nobility whose favourite literature concerned the doings of King Arthur and his Knights of the Round Table. To go on Crusade was a way to enter fully into the Romance, to actually emulate the likes of Gawain, Lancelot and, of course, Arthur himself.

The more I looked at the story of Baldwin at Edessa, the more I began to see that there was more to this episode than meets the eye. For the Crusade as a whole, Edessa was of little strategic value and its defence stretched resources. It was on the wrong side of the Euphrates, a formidable barrier when it came to sending reinforcements, and it was surrounded by Moslem principalities on all sides. Once in Edessa itself retreat would be difficult. Like Crassus at Carrhae in 53 BC, the Franks could expect little protection if things went wrong and they found themselves stranded out in the open. From a military point of view it would have been better by far to have drawn a line down the east bank of the Euphrates and held this securely, seizing Aleppo, Damascus and the other cities of Syria, rather than trying to hold on to this distant outpost. Yet, this is exactly what Baldwin did. The only conclusion must be that Baldwin's motives for going to Edessa were not so much political as religious. He cannot have failed to know something of the city's extraordinary history and maybe Thoros told him something else: that the Mandylion was still there.

The Holy Grail might have been lost to Christendom but the Mandylion of Edessa was one very ancient object which was well known to Christians throughout the world. Though it probably was (and maybe still is) a simple painting of Jesus by Hannan, Abgar's secretary, in mediaeval Europe it was believed to have been caused by Christ wiping his face on a towel prior to his crucifixion. This made it a uniquely important relic as it was the only known object in existence (besides the fabulous cup of the Last Supper the whereabouts of which was anyone's guess) believed to be impregnated with the very blood of the saviour. Not only that, it was a 'True Icon', the face of God as man, and therefore an object worthy of worship in its own right. In the super-heated religious atmosphere of the late eleventh century, this was a treasure beyond price — far surpassing in value the cruel Lance of Longinus. For a Christian knight, the recovery of the Mandylion would have been a supreme achievement of as great, if not more, importance than clearing Jerusalem of infidels.

Looked at in this way, it becomes clear that the Crusaders' principal motivation in going to Edessa was probably more spiritual than temporal. To get Baldwin and Tancred to leave the main body of the army and come to Edessa, Thoros the Armenian must have promised them a reward that meant something. Now J.B. Segal writes that around AD 700 the Edessans, when required to pay taxes that they could not afford, were blackmailed by a certain Athanasius into pawning the Mandylion to him in exchange for 500 dinars.[8] He then had a copy made by a skillful painter, who was able to make it look exactly like the original. This copy he returned to the Edessans when they repaid their loan, keeping the original himself. He was a devout Jacobite[9] and later, with the caliph's permission, built a new baptistry. In this he apparently placed the Mandylion. As we have seen, by the time the Byzantines arrived in AD 943 demanding the Mandylion in exchange for Moslem prisoners of war, there were at least three credible 'Mandylions' venerated at Edessa — one for each of the principal sects: Melkites,[10] Jacobites and Armenians. What happened after that is not exactly clear but it seems some sort of 'beauty contest' was held. The Byzantines, no doubt advised by their friends the Melkites, took the one they believed to be genuine and returned the other two. In this game of 'find the lady', it is not impossible that they were deceived and took the wrong one. It is also quite probable that all the Mandylions they were shown, indeed all the ones on public display, were fakes; the real one being carefully concealed. After all, if Athanasius could have one convincing forgery made he could have had several – and he may not even have had the original in his possession to start with.

Whatever the truth, and we will probably never know it for certain, it seems likely that in 1098 Thoros had a Mandylion – possibly even the real one – in his possession. As ruler of the city he had access to many hidden treasures gathered over the centuries and, as Baldwin was later to find out, these were considerable. It is therefore not at all unlikely that at least one Mandylion was included in these. Even so, if Thoros did have the real one in his possession it would have to have been kept a closely guarded secret. The Armenians, though the wealthiest class of Edessans, were in a minority compared with the Greeks and Syrians, who would certainly have demanded the relic for themselves. Certainly it could not be openly flaunted. The bribe to Baldwin was probably the opportunity to see, and presumably to take over custodianship of it after Thoros' death. This would have made a nice prize, well worth the detour from Antioch.

Whatever the truth in this matter – and we will probably never know for sure – the Mandylion was certainly revered as a sacred relic at the time of the First Crusade. The association of it, in Christian minds anyway, with the story of the Crucifixion and the belief that it was impregnated with the Holy Blood of Jesus himself connects it with the Grail legend. This myth had by now developed an arcane structure all of its own, almost entirely unrelated to the earlier Arthurian tales of Wales. It is quite likely that at least part of Baldwin's reason for taking up residence in Edessa was the hope that he might find out more concerning the whereabouts of the Grail and other esoteric matters concerned with the foundations of Christianity.

I now discovered that without realizing it we had stumbled upon something else, the secret Castle of the Grail. According to the legends, the Grail was under the protection of a guardian known as the Fisher-King. It is to his castle that the hero, Percival or Galahad, has to make his way in order to find the Grail and thereby restore the wasteland which is Britain. The Fisher-King himself is an old man and though he is kept alive by the magical power emanating from the Grail, he still suffers from an incurable wound, apparently inflicted inadvertently, by the very Holy Lance which pierced the side of

Christ. He will only find peace from his suffering when a worthy knight presents himself to take over the burden of looking after the Grail. However, it is not enough for the knight to present himself at the castle and to see the Grail, he must remember to ask the question: 'whom does it serve?' Only then is it fully revealed to him and is he able to take over responsibility for it.

The Grail itself is a mysterious, other-worldly object associated with the Crucifixion. Usually it is the cup of the Last Supper but sometimes it is a large dish or platter or even a miraculous stone. The basic story has many variants according to who is telling it, but the essential ingredients are a castle, an ancient custodian, known as the Fisher-King, who is himself wounded in some way, a miraculous object associated with Christ's blood from the Crucifixion and a Knight Errant. Now as Edessa, from time immemorial, had been famous for its fish-ponds, the king who ruled over the city was in a very real sense a 'Fisher-King'. These kings had in the past mostly been called Abgar and this name, according to Professor Segal, means 'lame' in Syriac or 'having an umbilical hernia' in Arabic.[11] The Mandylion, for which Edessa was famous worldwide, was supposedly made 'by no human hands' but by Christ wiping his face on a towel. It was therefore believed to be impregnated with his blood. Not only that, but it was said to have cured the first Abgar of his lameness when first shown to him by the Apostle Thaddaeus. With all these close associations, the conclusion was inescapable: the Abgars were the Fisher-Kings, the Mandylion was the Grail and Edessa was its secret castle. If Edessa really had been the lost castle of the Grail, then there really couldn't have been a more fitting place. This was, after all, the city where Abraham, the patriarch of Arabs, Jews and Christians, was supposedly born. In sacredness it is on a par with Jerusalem, Bethlehem, Mecca or anywhere else in the Jewish, Christian or Moslem world. The Aladdin's lamp we had been shown by the Arab merchant, though probably an Assyrian representation of the Moon-god, Sin, seemed fittingly emblematic of the Fisher-King, who in a sense was Abraham himself.

By the time the Grail legend was being written down in its established form by Chrétien de Troyes and Wolfram von Eschenbach during the late twelfth century, Edessa had once more been lost to the Christians. The Frankish County had been under attack by the Turks on a regular basis for almost the entire duration of its existence. However, under

Imad ad-Din Zengi, the Atabeg of Mosul, they at last had a leader with both the leadership skills and strength of character needed to drive out the Franks. On 28 November 1144, while the then Count, Joscelin, with the main body of his army were away west of the Euphrates at Turbessel, Zengi laid siege to Edessa. The citizens and clerics who manned the walls were no match for the Turkish regulars and, on Christmas Eve, they burst through the defences. The bulk of Armenians, Greeks and Syrians were spared and allowed to carry on worshipping in their churches as normal. But perhaps in memory of the Jerusalem slaughter of nearly a half a century before, all the Frankish men that could be found in the city were rounded up and summarily executed, their women and children being taken away as slaves and their churches destroyed.

After further victories Zengi retired back to Mosul as a conquering hero and, his overlord being overthrown, he was confirmed as king by the Caliph of Baghdad. However, this honour was to be shortlived as in September 1146 he was assassinated by a Frankish eunuch. Sensing that the time might be right to counter-attack, Count Joscelin with a small contingent of men aided by some of the Christians within, tried to invade Edessa. He was unable to take the citadel however, and a few days later, Zengi's son Nur ed-Din arrived with a relieving army. Though Joscelin himself managed to escape, his army was routed near the Euphrates, the refugees accompanying him – men, women and children – being slaughtered. Without the restraining hand of Zengi, Edessa was subjected to a pillage of Assyrian proportions. As punishment for their perfidy, those Christians who survived the massacre, were driven out naked to walk to the slave markets of Mosul and Baghdad. Those who could not make it, the old, the young, the weak and the lame, were cut down where they stood. The city itself was ransacked for treasure, its great churches being used as stables and granaries or demolished to make way for mosques. Soon there was little to show that this had once been a great Christian city, the 'eye of Mesopotamia'. It was now little more than a ghost town, a place of ruins and shattered dreams. It would now sleep for the best part of a thousand years, its citizens oblivious to its extraordinary secrets.

## Guardians of the Grail

Baldwin, Count of Edessa did not long stay resident in that city. Following the capture of Jerusalem in 1099, there was much debate

about how the Holy City should be administered. After much
deliberation it was decided to offer the crown to Godfrey, Duke
of Lower Lorraine, as he possessed both the necessary aristocratic
credentials and willingness to remain in the Holy Land after most
of the other great lords had departed back to Europe. He, however,
whilst accepting the post, declined the annointing, preferring to be
referred to only as *Advocatus Sancti Sepulchri*: 'Defender of the Holy
Sepulchre'. Given the opposition of the Church to a secular office
above its own appointees, this was probably a wise move on his part.
However, Godfrey's reign', which was characterized by weakness in
the face of both the Church and powerful vassals such as Tancred, did
not last for very long. On 18 July 1100, almost exactly a year since
the seizure of Jerusalem, he died from what was probably typhoid.
Once more there was a vacancy at the top and it quickly became
clear that there was really only one man to fill it: Godfrey's brother
Baldwin. He, unlike his brother, was not bashful about receiving the
sacred crown, which many believed belonged only to Christ, and on 11
November was annointed King of Jerusalem, his County of Edessa now
being administered by his cousin Baldwin of Le Bourg. He was probably
as surprised as anyone else at the way his destiny had turned out, though
it was not entirely undeserved. As Stephen Runciman puts it:

'Of all the great leaders it was Baldwin, the penniless younger son of
the Count of Boulogne, that had triumphed. One by one his rivals had
been eliminated. Many of them had returned to the West, Robert of
Normandy, Robert of Flanders, Hugh of Vermandois and Stephen
of Blois . . . Baldwin had bided his time and had snatched at his
opportunities. Of them all he had proved himself the ablest, the
most patient and the most far-sighted. He had won his reward;
and the future was to show that he deserved it. His coronation
was a glorious one and a hopeful ending to the story of the First
Crusade.'[12]

Baldwin set about putting his new kingdom on a sure footing. One of its
most pressing problems, which was to dog it throughout its existence,
was a shortage of manpower. While Crusaders were prepared to come
out east to fight and possibly die for Christ, few of them wanted to
remain there for the duration of their lives. Most nobles had estates
and families back west in the countries from which they had come.

They were unlikely to be persuaded to give these up permanently to become vassals of Baldwin. A way had to be found around this problem and the solution seems to have been the setting up of the first military Order: the Knights Templar. Baldwin died on 2 April 1118 and was succeeded by his cousin Baldwin II, who had also done his apprenticeship as Count of Edessa. A certain Hugues de Payen, a nobleman from Champagne is said to have presented himself to this Baldwin and discussed the setting up of the Order, initially called the 'Poor Knights of Christ' soon after his inauguration. [13]

Though the Order was in time to expand to become the largest and richest in Europe, initially it was composed of just nine knights, whose numbers were not increased for nine years. Baldwin gave them the use of the Al Aqsa Mosque on the Temple Mount of Jerusalem as their headquarters, a privilege not granted to anyone else. Their close connection with the Temple Mount is shown by the way that the churches they built in Europe were nearly always circular in design, modelled on the Dome of the Rock. [14] Under Baldwin II, the Templars prospered. Their order as well as that of their rivals, the Knights Hospital of St John, came to be seen as indispensable to the security of the Kingdom. Yet they were under no direct obligation to the king, their Grand Masters having total authority and overall command over all operational matters. Back in Europe it was the same. Owing to endowments, the Order became extremely rich. They were, in fact, an international conglomerate with interests in banking, shipping, tourism, defence and much else besides. As they were outside of the jurisdiction of national kings, it is little wonder then that they soon excited envy, especially from Philip le Bel, the king of France. In 1307, Philip gave orders for all the Templars in his kingdom to be arrested and their land to be confiscated for the crown. At Philip's instigation the Pope gave similar orders to the crown heads of Europe that they should do the same. Except in Portugal, where King Denys refused, with some reluctance they complied. The Templars, on the flimsiest evidence, were condemned for heresy and for blaspheming Christ. Though most Templars survived the ordeal of torture and forced confessions that they were made to go through, the Grand Master, Jacques de Molay and Geoffrey de Charnay, Preceptor of Normandy, were publicly burnt at the stake.

One of the principal charges laid against the Order was that they worshipped a strange head. Now Ian Wilson in his fascinating study of the Turin Shroud[15] suggested that this 'head' could have been the shroud itself, folded in such way that only the head was visible. In his book *The Turin Shroud*, he tortuously argues that this cloth, believed by many to be the wrapping in which Christ's body was robed before being placed in Joseph of Arimathea's tomb, was one and the same as the Mandylion. This, he points out, was supposedly taken to Constantinople in 944 to be kept with other Imperial treasures. As these were looted during the sack of Constantinople by soldiers of the IVth Crusade, Wilson argued that the Mandylion (therefore shroud) could have fallen into the hands of the Templars at this time.

Unfortunately his, in places convincing, argument falls apart completely now that the shroud has been carbon dated and been shown to be a mediaeval fake.[16] His connection between the Mandylion and the Templars, though, is probably not far short of the mark. If either Baldwin had had a portrait of Jesus (a Mandylion), which he believed to be genuine, then he would have been concerned for its safety. The creation of a select Order, to a large extent modelled after the legendary Grail Knights of King Arthur's Round Table, to act as guardians of this treasure, would have been a sensible thing to do. Thinking about this it seemed to me that the Templars, though not in possession of the shroud as Wilson believed, did have a 'Grail' in the form of the Mandylion. By now I was beginning to understand that the real arcanum surrounding the Grail legend, at least as it was understood in mediaeval France and Germany, had little to do with the British King Arthur but derived from Gnostic Christian traditions. These were still alive in the Near East at the time of the First Crusade and at least some of the Crusaders came into contact with them as a result of that adventure. The story of the knights' quest, like that of the Magi, became a cloak under which secret, mystical knowledge was passing from East to West. Antioch, where the Lance of Longinus had been found by Peter the Hermit, was one of the places where these ideas had their origin but in the late eleventh century it was in Northern Mesopotamia that these ideas were still very much alive. Even after the lands of the East passed under different political and religious control, some elements of Gnostic Christianity continued. In ancient monasteries, grottoes and lost valleys men continued to worship in the old ways and to retain at least some contact with the Gnosis. It seems to have been a group of such people, descendants of an ancient Order called the Sarmoung Brotherhood, that Gurdjieff made contact with in the region of Nusaybin (Nisibis) some time in the 1880s or 1890s. I now had evidence of what other mysteries may have been passed back west when I was shown several coins from Edessa dating from Roman times. These, as I was to discover, indicated that someone at least was knowledgeable about the astral religions of the areas long after the advent of Christianity. I suspected I was on the trail of the lost 'School of the Persians'.

# CHAPTER 10

✳

# The Pillars of Nimrod

As we have seen, shortly after the First Crusade two military Orders were formed. One of these was the Knights Templars, who were intimately connected with the legend of the Grail and probably also the Mandylion of Edessa. The other Order, which actually came into being slightly earlier as a religious Order and is still in existence today, was that of St John the Baptist. The Order of St John, like the Templars, became immensely wealthy and powerful, however somehow it managed to avoid the opprobrium that fell on the former. The Knights Hospitallers, as they were known, built a number of immensely powerful castles in the Holy Land such as Krac des Chavaliers, Margat and Belvoir. Even after they were forced to abandon the mainland, the knights clung on to first the Island of Rhodes and later, after they were expelled from there by the Turks, after a six-month siege in 1522, Malta. When the Templars were forcibly dissolved in 1314, the Order of St John became even richer as it inherited many of its rivals former properties.

Why this Order should have been dedicated to a saint with no connection to either military or hospital service is something of a mystery. Yet, the whole role of St John in the 'Communion of Saints' is also a mystery. By tradition he stands, in the hierarchy of saints above all the Apostles and only just below the Virgin Mary herself. Most mediaeval churches had a shrine dedicated in his honour and he is often to be seen, as in the Wilton Diptych, dressed in his rough, camel-hair robe and holding the lamb of Christ in his arms.

The cult of John was very extensive in the Middle Ages and at

Damascus there was once a shrine containing his relics. Whether these were genuine or not is open to question but the Bible states that after his death his disciples collected and buried his body. These relics, or at least some of them, seem to have been moved to Edessa, as professor Segal suggests they may have been fittingly housed in the Great Baptistry there, which was built in AD 369–370.[1] It may have been these that are today on display in the Topkapi Museum in Istanbul. There, in a display case in a room close to where is kept the cloak and sword of Mohammed and to the amusement of passing tourists, can be seen a small reliquary. It is encrusted with jewels and was made to house what stands next to it, part of the Baptist's skull (plate 34). By the side of this is another gold reliquary in the shape of a right arm. This contains, so it is believed, the remains of perhaps the most honoured human limb in history: the hand that baptized Christ. In the eyes of the faithful it is probably this act more than anything else that elevates him to the very top of the saintly hierarchy but there is clearly more to his story than a simple baptism – even of Jesus Christ.

According to the Gospels, John was Jesus' cousin, being born to Mary's elderly kinswoman Elizabeth and her husband Zechariah, who was a priest in the temple. John remains an enigmatic figure, a rough outsider who lambasts the Jewish elders and through his baptism prepares the way for Jesus. His mission accomplished, he falls prey to the machinations of Herodias, Herod's vengeful wife, who conspires to have his head delivered on a plate to her daughter Salome. This macabre event, with it sensuous prologue, the 'Dance of the Seven Veils', has captured the imagination of Christians throughout the ages. Even so, John remains a mysterious figure, perhaps the strangest in the whole New Testament. Why this honey and locust-eating acsetic should stand higher than Peter, Paul and John, though made clear in the Apostle's Creed is not explained by the Church. However, I was soon to discover that this was no accident and was probably well understood by the early Church. As with the Grail legend, the key to this mystery turned out to be at Urfa.

In the first century BC, the Abgars of Edessa had a difficult task in maintaining their independence from Imperial authorities. To their east was the Parthian Empire, their nominal and sometimes actual, Suzerains. To the west was Rome, which at that time was making the transition from Republic to Empire. The first major, head-on collision between these two beasts took place, as we have seen, outside the walls of Carrhae (Harran) in 53 BC when Crassus was ignominiously defeated and killed. The role of Abgar II in this, as far as Rome was concerned, catastrophic event was at best ambiguous. He had the unenviable task of having to entertain Crassus whilst at the same time placate Surena and the Parthians. The survival of not just himself but of his dynasty depended on his maintaining a balancing act; making sure that neither side achieved overall supremacy in the region of Northern Mesopotamia.

An inkling of this dilemma, which in one way or another faced all the toparchs of Edessa, was made clear by one of the coins that were shown to us and which we also took photographs of. These were of bronze and, as it was the custom in Roman times to allow cities to mint coins themselves that were not made of silver or gold, they are an important source of knowledge for archaeologists. We were able to have this coin identified on our return as having been minted at Edessa during the reign of the Roman Emperor Severus Alexander (AD 222–235). Whilst it had his head on the obverse side, on the reverse was a curious picture of what looked like a king sitting on a throne. It was normal for cities, such as Edessa, to stamp the reverse ('tails') side of their coinage with images of local significance. Although Edessa was by now a *colonia* of Rome, having been seized by the Emperor Caracalla in 213, there was still, according to Syrian Chronicles, a king called Ma'nu: the son of Abgar the Great. As he ruled Edessa, in name at least, throughout the reign of Severus Alexander, it seems likely that he is the figure shown on the reverse side of the coin. Unfortunately, with the passage of time, the coin was badly worn but close inspection reveals that this 'king' has two faces, i.e. he is represented as the Roman god Janus. Now this god, who gives his name to our month of January, was associated

Fig. 11

Coin minted in Edessa showing Janus figure, AD 222-35.

with doorways. He was therefore the gate-keeper of both time and place. On the coin he has one face looking upwards to the left and the other downwards to the right. He sits with his legs crossed and points with his right hand upwards to what looks like a small star. Standing in front of him is a much larger 'star' that probably represents the sun. Looking at this image it seemed to me that Ma'nu, if such we may call him, is indicating that Edessa is some sort of gateway, both between East and West and between heaven and earth: a conception that fitted well with the idea of the citadel being the Grail Castle of the Fisher-King.

The second coin was in many ways very much clearer and easier to interpret. This coin is not as old as the first one and seems to date from the time of Justinian I, the Byzantine emperor who ruled between AD 527 and 565.[2] It shows what at first sight appears to be an 'M' but is, in reality, a small figure standing with arms attached to two columns. To the right of the rightmost column is the symbol of the Moon – commonly used on coins of Edessa because of its ancient connections with the Temple of Sin – whilst above the central figure is a cross representing either the Sun or Christianity.

I was at first puzzled by the central figure until I remembered what I had read in one of our guidebooks about the legends of Urfa. According to these, Nimrod was the reputed founder of Orhay, the orginal name for Edessa. He must have lived to a ripe old age as he arrested Abraham, who in the Bible is separated from him by seven generations. Nimrod first had Abraham bound between the two great columns to be seen on the Citadel Mount to this day and then, in a fit of rage, threw the patriarch off the castle wall into the valley below. However, his attempt on the patriarch's life was thwarted because God caused the fish-pools below to appear and they broke his fall. Much to Nimrod's

Fig. 12

Coin minted in Edessa showing Abraham between pillars, AD 527-65.

amazement, Abraham rose unharmed from his ordeal. The fact that the pillars weren't raised until *c*.AD 200 and the coin dates from the reign of Justinian I between AD 527 and 565, indicates that this myth must have developed between the third and sixth centuries. Though on the face of it the myth of Abraham and Nimrod is simply one of those charming legends that appeals to pilgrims, looking into the matter further, I was to discover it is the key to very much more.

Professor Segal in his illuminating book *Edessa: 'The Blessed City'*, makes reference to the way that prior to the coming of Christianity, not just in Edessa but in neighbouring cities of the area, for the ruler or *budar* to sit on a special stool. This stool was associated with at least one sacred pillar. The citadel of Edessa was called the 'Throne of Nimrod', indicating a connection between this semi-legendary king and the *budar* of the city. According to Professor Segal, the stool of the *budar* and its associated pillar were cult emblems of the god called 'Marilaha' (the Great Lord):

> Of different significance are the stool and pillar as the cult emblems of Marilaha. They appear in miniature on an Edessan coin of the reign of Elagabalus (218–22). They are also inscribed on coins of

Fig. 13

'Abraham'/Orion between the pillars of Edessa.

that Wa'el[3] of Edessa in whose reign the Sumatar[4] inscriptions were
dedicated. On these coins is shown a temple with a pediment and steps
leading up to it; inside is a "cubic cult object, on a base supported by
two curved legs". This is evidently religious furniture. A star may
be seen in the pediment of the shrine, no doubt an indication of
planetary worship.[5]

In fact, as we saw for ourselves, on top of the Citadel there are ruins
of what looks like a stepped-platform just behind (to the south) of the
pillars. As this has not been properly investigated archaeologically, it is
difficult to say what it would have been like. However, it seemed to us
that it was probably just some such building as described by Professor
Segal. Here, there could indeed have been a ceremonial throne, or
budar, with a pediment above it.

As the legendary founder of Edessa, Nimrod is associated with the
sacred stool and the fact that the Citadel is still known to this day
as the 'Throne of Nimrod' underlines this connection. I was now to
find that there were further links between this founder of cities and
astral worship. According to the Bible, Nimrod was a great-grandson
of Noah being, like Egypt, descended from Noah's son Ham:

The sons of Ham: Cush, Egypt, Put, and Canaan . . . Cush became
the father of Nimrod; he was the first on earth to be a mighty man.
He was a mighty hunter before the Lord; therefore it is said, 'like
Nimrod a mighty hunter before the Lord'. The beginning of his
kingdom was Babel, Erech and Accad, all of them in the land of
Shinar. From that land he went into Assyria and built Nineveh,
Rehoboth-Ir, Calah, and Resen between Nineveh and Calah; that
is the great city.[6]

Thus Nimrod is associated with the founding of Mesopotamian
civilization in the same way that Egypt also becomes the father
of the Egyptians. Yet it is clear, even from the above, that there
is an esoteric meaning to the passage beyond whatever genealogical
information is being conveyed. According to Professors Giorgio de
Santillana and Hertha von Dechend, Nimrod, the 'mighty hunter before
the Lord', like Hercules at Commagene, personifies the constellation
of Orion.[7] This association of astrology with Edessa at the time of the
kings is also well attested by Professor Segal:

When, now, we turn to Edessa under the monarchy, we find that its inhabitants worshipped the planets like their neighbours of Palmyra, Harran and Hierapolis. Observation of the stars was the link, indeed, between popular religion and the complex cosmological sytems of the philosophers. Baidasan [a famous poet and songwriter of Edessa] . . . was a skilled astrologer and wrote a treatise on the conjunction of the planets, and the *Book of the Laws of Countries* which was the work of his school shows familiarity with astrological concepts. One of the gates of Edessa was called Beth Shemesh, after the temple of the sun that must have stood there. The crescent moon is depicted on coins of Edessa at this period; on the tiara of King Abgar it is accompanied by one, two or three stars. The planets appear in personal names of Edessans, in Syriac texts, both at Urfa itself and in its immediate neighbourhood, on the walls of tombs, on mosaic floors, and in literature. Among them, to cite only a few are 'maidservant of Sin (the moon)', 'servant of Bel (Jupiter)', 'greeting of Atha (Venus)', 'Shemesh (the sun) has determined', 'servant of Nabu (Mercury)'.[8]

The connection with Orion and Sirius is also fairly clear as he goes on to write:

'The name Bar Kalba at Edessa and at Sumatar Harabesi [a site to the south of the city, near to Harran that was a major centre for the Sabians] suggests the worship of the Dog star. The sixth century poet Jacob of Serug, who lived most of his life at Edessa and Batnae, maintains that at Harran was a deity with the strange title of 'Mar(i) (lord) of his dogs'; perhaps this means the hunter Orion, at whose heels are the constellations of Canis major and Canis minor.'

Reading this and sensing we were on the trail of some deeper mystery, I decided to have another looking at the Greek mythology surrounding Orion the hunter to see what light this might throw on the subject of Edessa's stellar religion.

## The Hunter at the gates of dawn

According to the myths, the Greek Orion (or Oarion) was a son of Poseidon. Like Nimrod in the Bible he was a hunter and a giant. He was also exceedingly handsome but, as is so often the case, this was to lead him into trouble. When, after failing to rid the island of Chios of wild animals, Orion seduced Merope the daughter of its king, the latter had him blinded as a punishment. An oracle told Orion that he could have his sight restored if he travelled east and exposed his eyeballs to the rising sun. Accordingly he went to the island of Lemnos and there Eos (the dawn goddess) fell in love with him, his sight being restored by her brother Helios (the Sun). Later Orion joined Artemis (the Moon-Goddess) as a hunter, boasting that he would kill all wild animals. However, Apollo (also a solar deity), fearing that his twin sister Artemis might also fall for the beautiful hunter, contrived that she should accidentally kill him on one of her hunting trips.[9] Like Hercules, after his death, Orion's image was set among the stars, where, wearing a lion's skin, carrying a huge club and with a sword by his side, he forever hunts the wild bull Taurus. Beneath his feet is a hare, another of his quarries and following on his heels are his two hunting dogs, Canis Major and Canis Minor.

We can see in the Greek Orion myth a number of parallels with the Egyptian legend of Osiris. The story of his blinding by the king of Chios echoes the murder of the Egyptian god-king Osiris by his brother Seth, whilst both Isis and Eos are goddesses associated with the dawn who entreat the Sun-god (Ra/Helios respectively) to bring Osiris/Orion back to full health. In ancient Egypt the resurrection of Osiris was a matter of profound religious significance, which seems to have been connected with the annual reappearance of the Orion constellation at dawn after a period of invisibility.[10] However, Orion can also be 'blinded', i.e. his stars become invisible, when the moon (especially a full moon) passes close by.

The Greek myth does, of course, differ significantly from the Egyptian story of Osiris, not least in its portrayal of Orion as a rather wild hunter rather than a civilizing god. His primary task in the Greek myths is to rid the islands of wild animals, which though to modern ears sounds rather anti-ecological, could be interpreted as making the people more secure and therefore helping civilization. However, there is another side to the 'hunting' business and this is the sense that for a society to become civilized, something of its wild nature has to be sacrificed.

In the Bible we find the constellation of Orion mentioned by name in the Book of Job in two places. Thus we read in Job 9:9 'Which maketh Arcturus, Orion and the Pleiades, and the chambers of the south' and then in Job 38:31 'Canst thou bind the sweet influences of Pleiades, or loose the bands of Orion?'[11] In similar vein the constellation is mentioned again in Amos 5:8 'Seek him that maketh the Pleiades and Orion . . .' In all three cases the Hebrew name for Orion is *kesil* meaning 'strong'. It is evident from the above that like so many other peoples the Hebrews looked upon Orion as being a 'strong-man' and it is therefore not surprising that the constellation is also associated with that greatest of Biblical strong-men, Samson. According to Santillana and von Dechend, the story of Samson slaying the Philistines with the jawbone of an ass is to be understood astronomically. Samson is once more the strong-man constellation of Orion and the 'jawbone' which he siezes to carry out his bloody task, is the V-shaped star group which we today call the Hyades.[12] That Samson is really Orion by a different name cannot be doubted when it is realized that one of his first tasks is the slaying of a lion. Later he finds bees and a honeycomb in the corpse of the dead animal and this gives him the idea for a riddle: 'Out of the eater came something to eat. Out of the strong came something sweet.'[13] The esoteric meaning of the riddle is to be found in the sky as the lion is, of course, Leo and next to it in the constellation of Cancer is the Beehive, Praesepe. Both of these constellations are very close to Orion.

As in the Greek myth of Orion, it is a woman who proves to be Samson's undoing. His strength stems from his long hair, which he has never had cut. When he falls in love with Delilah, a Philistine, she elicits his secret from him. Then, whilst he is asleep, she cuts off his hair. This 'haircut', with its obvious sexual overtones, leads to his loss of strength and consequently his capture by the Philistines. Like Orion in the Greek myth he is blinded by his enemies and like Abraham in the mythology of Edessa, he is bound between two pillars. He cries out to God to give him back his strength one last time that he might be avenged on his enemies:

> Then Samson called to the Lord and said, 'O Lord God, remember me, I pray thee, and strengthen me, I pray thee, only this once, O God, that I may be avenged on the Philistines for one of my two eyes'. And Samson grasped the two middle pillars upon which the house rested, and he leaned his weight upon them, his right hand on the one and his left on the other. And Samson said, 'Let me die with the Philistines'. Then he bowed with all his might; and the house fell upon all the lords and upon all the people that were in it.[14]

Looking at the image of Abraham tied between the two pillars of Edessa, an event with no Biblical authenticity whatsoever, it becomes clear that what has happened is a case of cultural transference. It is not Abraham who should be tied between the pillars but Samson, who is of course mythologically identical with Orion and, therefore, Nimrod. As a further connection between the two, just as at Edessa Abraham is saved from death by the sudden appearance of a spring of water and the subsequent filling of the sacred fish-pools, so Samson also is saved by a miraculous spring:

> 'Thou hast granted this great deliverance by the hand of thy servant; and shall I (Samson) now die of thirst and fall into the hands of the uncircumcised?' And God split open the hollow place that is in Lehi, and there came water from it; and when he drank his spirit returned, and he was revived.[15]

The connection of Orion with the 'Throne of Nimrod' is borne out from other calculations. When we walked on top of the Citadel I checked out the orientation of the two pillars and found that they face exactly north. This being the case, anyone standing on the ground below the Citadel and in front of the pillars is looking directly south into the sky. They could watch the culmination of both stars and planets, a very important consideration if one's religion happens to be astral. With the use of a suitable tower, the constellation Orion itself could be seen passing through the pillars every night on his daily journey from East to West. Nimrod, not Abraham, would be seen gripping the two pillars of his Citadel, just as was represented on the second coin.

The discovery that the Citadel with its twin pillars might have been used for the observation of stars, particularly Orion, was very exciting and possibly throws some light on the etymology of the hunter's name. According to Professor Segal, the name of the province of Edessa, Osrhoene, had an orginal form Orrhoene.[16] If this is so, then Orrhoenis would mean 'man from Orrhoene'. Given that there is strong evidence there was an Orion cult at Edessa, the similarity between the words Orrhoenis and Orionis is such as to suggest that it was from here that the Greek Orion cult had its origins. This I found intriguing but what was even more startling was the connection I was beginning to see between Orion, Abraham and the Hebrew religion. This, as I was soon to find out, is one of the Bible's deepest secrets.

## Orion the Prophet

Orion in the Hebrew tradition represents not so much a hunter as a wild-man of God. As Samson he is the judge of Israel but the constellation is also linked esoterically with the ancient school of prophets. In the Old Testament the 'wild-man' who lives outside of comfortable society, possesses special powers and acts as the conscience of the nation of Israel is most clearly seen in the extraordinary figure of the prophet Elijah. Nothing is said of his parentage other than that he is 'Elijah the Tishbite, of Tishbe in Gilead . . .'[17] He appears from nowhere and straight away is performing miracles the like of which have not been seen since the time of Moses. He challenges the 450 prophets of Baal[18] to a competition to see whose god has real power, their's or his. Both he and they each sacrifice a bull and lay out its meat on a pyre. They then have to invite fire to come down from heaven to consume the offering. Needless to say, whilst the prophets of Baal spend a whole day fretting and fuming and getting nowhere, fire descends and take Elijah's offering immediately. Following their defeat, Elijah puts to death the false prophets. From this incident alone we can see that he is, like Mithras, very much a figure in the bull-slaying tradition.

Elijah, the prophet and bull-sacrificer is very distinctively dressed. When a messenger of the king is asked to describe him, his reply that: 'He wore a garment of haircloth, with a girdle of leather about his loins', is enough to identify him. The 'haircloth' has replaced the lion's pelt of Hercules and Samson but the reference to his belt links him directly to the Orion archetype. The connection is made still clearer when he prepares to make his mystic ascent to heaven. He takes his trusting apprentice, Elisha, with him when he goes to the River Jordan. Like Moses leading the Israelites over the Red Sea, he takes his rolled-up mantle and strikes the water. It parts so that they are able to cross over on dry land. As they have come from the direction of Jericho, they are evidently crossing over from the west to the east bank. There, Elijah is taken up to heaven in a fiery chariot:

And as they still went on and talked, behold, a chariot of fire and horses of fire separated the two of them. And Elijah went up by a whirlwind into heaven. And Elisha saw it and he cried, 'My father, my father! the chariots of Israel and its horsemen!' And he saw him no more.[19]

This incident is open to a number of interpretation but it does have a clear cosmological meaning in the context of esoteric astrology. In ancient Egypt the pharaohs were all, whilst alive, believed to be incarnations of the god Horus. When a pharaoh died, it was believed that his soul would ascend to join Osiris in the constellation of Orion. He himself would, in effect, become a star in that constellation. The old pharaoh having left, his earthly duties as king would then pass to his son and heir, who was now the next Horus. It seems that it was principally to assist this process that the pyramids were built.[20]

Something similar seems to be happening here, for Elisha now tears up his own clothes and puts on the mantle of his 'father' Elijah:

> Then he took hold of his own clothes and rent them in two pieces. And he took the mantle of Elijah that had fallen from him, and went back and stood on the Jordan. Then he took the mantle of Elijah that had fallen from him, and struck the water, saying, 'Where is the Lord, the God of Elijah?' And when he had struck the water, the water was parted to the one side and the other; and Elisha went over.[21]

Again in ancient Egypt, the River Nile was looked upon as a celestial counterpart of the Milky Way. As we look at the Milky Way in the sky, Orion stands on its 'bank'. It would seem in this story that the River Jordan has the same symbolic meaning for the Israelite prophets as the Nile had for the Egyptians. By crossing over the river, Elijah and Elisha were symbolically 'going over' into the celestial world, the former to stay there permanently, the latter to return back to life as a prophet.

If we look at this event from an astrological point of view it becomes clearer still. Elijah can clearly be seen by Elisha until the appearance of the fiery chariot that carries him off. Throughout the mythologies of the ancient world it was believed that the Sun-god, Helios, travelled in a chariot. The rising of the sun's chariot, drawn by his celestial horses was represented on the pediment of the Parthenon at Athens and his finely sculpted horses can still be seen in the British Museum. Thus, it seems likely that the vehicle with its 'horses of fire', whose arrival obscures Elisha's view of Elijah, is a clear reference to this chariot of the sun.

What Elisha witnesses is something else of deeply symbolic

importance to the Egyptians: the sunrise obscuring the stars of Orion from view. As the sun rises so it puts out the stars of the dawn sky, including Orion if it happens to be above the horizon at that moment. Paradoxically the morning when Orion, in his entirety, rose just before the dawn signified his rebirth. This so-called 'heliacal rising' of Orion also symbolized the resurrection of a Horus king as an 'Osiris' and again is linked to the whole idea of succession to divine office. It would seem that like Osiris, Hercules, Mithras and Samson, in the special, symbolic language of the Bible, Elijah ascended to heaven to be represented by the stars of Orion.

The connection between Orion and Elijah was both intriguing and unexpected. Immediately it set me thinking about the man who was both the last of the Old Testament prophets and herald of the New: John the Baptist. He has a very important place in church iconography and Jesus himself said that he was the reincarnation of Elijah. This is made clear in Matthew's Gospel:

> . . . Jesus began to speak to the crowd about John: 'What did you go out into the wilderness to behold? A reed shaking by the wind? Why then did you go out? To see a man clothed in soft raiment? Behold, those clothed in soft raiment are in king's houses. Why then did you go out? To see a prophet? Yes, I tell you, and more than a prophet. This is he of whom it is written, *'Behold, I send my messenger before thy face, who shall prepare thy way before thee'*[22]
> . . . For all the prophets and the law prophecied until John; and if you are willing to accept it, he is Elijah who is to come. He who has ears to hear let him hear.'[23]

The implied connection between John the Baptist and Elijah is clear from his mode of dress 'a garment of camel's hair, and a leather girdle around his waist'.[24] His 'wild-man', hunter credentials are also implicit in his diet of honey and locusts, that fits the pattern of a Samson-type prophet.

Like Samson, John's downfall is brought about by a woman (in fact two women: Herodias and her daughter Salome). Herodias had much in common with an earlier queen of Israel, Jezebel, who lived at the time of Elijah, and was his implacable enemy. She was the daughter of Ethbaal, king of Sidon and it was she who introduced the cult of Baal

to Israel. It was her priests that Elijah put to death after they failed
to bring down the fire of god on to their sacrifices and needless to
say she was very angry about it. When the matter is reported to her
she swears vengeance on the prophet:

> Ahab told Jezebel all that Elijah had done, and how he [Elijah]
> had slain all the prophets with the sword. Then Jezebel sent a
> messenger to Elijah saying, 'So may the gods do to me, and more
> also, if I do not make your life as the life of one of them by this
> time tomorrow'.[25]

Later she and her husband, King Ahab, conspire together to have an
innocent man stoned to death so that they can take possession of his
vineyard in Jezreel and turn it into a vegetable garden. For this act,
which in Biblical terms is clearly symbolic of their debasement of 'God's
vineyard', Israel, Elijah puts a terrible curse on her that: 'the dogs shall
eat Jezebel within the bounds of Jezreel'. Some time after Elijah has
departed and Ahab has been overthrown by a new king, Jehu, she is
thrown to her death from a window by her eunuchs. The story has a
gruesome end:

> So they threw her down; and some of her blood spattered on the
> wall and on the horses, and they trampled on her. Then he (Jehu)
> went in and ate and drank; and he said, 'See now to this cursed
> woman, and bury her; for she is a king's daughter'. But when they
> went to bury her, they found no more of her than the skull and the
> feet and the palms of her hands. When they came back and told
> him, he said. 'This is the word of the Lord, which he spoke by his
> servant Elijah the Tishbite, "In the territory of Jezreel the dogs shall
> eat the flesh of Jezebel; . . ."'[26]

The fate of Jezebel, one of the great witch figures of the Old Testament,
fits the 'Orion the hunter' archetype, for he is always followed by his
hunting dogs: Canis Major and Canis Minor. She who was cursed and
struck down by the hunter was eaten by his dogs.

The death of John the Baptist is equally symbolic. The Herod Antipas
that he confronts is the son of Herod the Great, who was visited by
the Magi at the time of Jesus' Nativity. John becomes embroiled in

the debate over Herod's marriage to Herodias. She is his niece but it is not so much a problem of their consanguinity that vexes John as the fact that she was already married to his brother Philip, whom she had deserted. John reproved Herod for this act because it was against Jewish law. Herod, like Jezebel's husband Ahab, was a weak man under the spell of a powerful woman. To satisfy her wishes, he had John locked up, hoping no doubt that the problem would soon blow over. However, Herodias had a deep and abiding hatred for John and would be satisfied with nothing less than his death. Her daughter Salome performs a striptease, the 'Dance of the Seven Veils', and in his excitement at this seductive performance, Herod promises the girl anything she wants, up to half his kingdom. She, to satisfy her mother's wishes, asks for nothing more than John's head on a plate (plate 35). Thus, in suitably dramatic way, ends the career of John the Baptist, last of the Hebrew prophets and, in a sense, the first Christian. However, the story of his death is redolent with deeper, symbolic meanings.

The deep-seated hatred of Herodias for John has been explained by some clairvoyants as stemming from the fact that just as he was the reincarnation of Elijah, so she was Jezebel. By this reading, John's beheading was both the outcome of Jezebel's curse on Elijah and the result of the latter's 'karma' in himself putting to death the prophets of Baal. Whether or not this is true, there is a clear linkage between the two stories and a certain astrological symbolism associated with the death of John. Salome's 'Dance of the Seven Veils' seems to be connected with the seven planetary spheres. Coming inwards, so to speak, from Saturn to the earth, the innermost sphere is that of the moon. The outer planets represent rationality, authority and maturity but the moon is connected with sleep, intoxication and hypnosis. Salome infatuates Herod who is already drunk and in this moon-like state he makes his fateful promise. Similarly, it was while Samson slept that Delilah cut his hair and it was Orion's infatuation with the Moon goddess, Artemis, that led to his death. In the John the Baptist story, Salome's plate seems to represent the moon's disc, which once more takes the life of a 'wild-man' of Orion. Even John, the forerunner of Jesus and 'reincarnation' of Elijah cannot escape his fate and dies at the hand of the moon. However, like all others of his type he must be reborn as a celestial 'god', the constellation of Orion.

*       *       *

Studying these matters it became clear to me that the esoteric connection between John and Orion must have been known by the early Church. His baptisms in the River Jordan echo Elijah, who as we have seen, departed from its banks when he was taken away from Elisha. It is very clear, then, that in New Testament terms John the Baptist is a prophet of the 'school' of Orion. However, even realizing this, I was unprepared for what I was to discover when I went back to the SKYGLOBE program and began analysing more dates, this time to do with John.

There were two important feast days of the Church associated with St John, the first of these was the Baptism of Jesus in the Jordan. It is now no longer celebrated but was, as we have seen, the original Epiphany and occurred on 6 January. The second feast, which is still shown on the Church calendar even though it is scarcely remembered today, was once, like Christmas itself, an excuse for a massive party. It is the Birth of St John and takes place on Midsummer Day, that is to say 24 June.

Looking at the astronomy of the birthday of St John, I was surprised to discover that at the time of Jesus, this was the date of the heliacal rising of Orion. Because of precessional changes during that epoch, the last of Orion's stars, though above the horizon, would probably not have been visible before the dawn light obliterated the constellation from view. However, eight or nine hundred years earlier, when Elijah would have been active, the whole constellation would have been visible. The intention was clear: St John was seen as the reincarnation of Elijah and his birthday of 24 June corresponded with the dawn rebirth of Orion after his period of invisibility.

The period around Christmas also had symbolic meaning. At this time of year the sun is in its most southerly position of the sky. Around this time Orion rises just before sunset to be followed by Sirius after the sun has gone down. In other words, Orion, the constellation associated with John the Baptist, is not seen until the star which in Egypt symbolized Isis, and in Christian times the Virgin Mary, appears above the horizon. These two travel through the sky together, visible throughout the night, but the sun passes behind the earth. Out of sight, it symbolically enters the 'waters of the abyss', passing through the deepest levels at midnight. This, in the Koreion of Alexandria, was the rebirth of the Logos and the idea seems to have been associated in Christian minds with the idea of Christ being baptized in the Jordan. The symbolism is certainly apt. John (Orion) stands visible in the night sky at the side of the 'Jordan' (Milky Way), whilst the Logos or Christ, symbolized by the sun, is immersed in the waters of the deep.

This, or something like it, seems to have been the idea behind the celebration of the Baptism at the Epiphany. Later the festival was changed to being the birth rather than the 'second birth' of Jesus and the coming of the Magi. However, as I was now to discover, this was a big mistake. Jesus already had a birthday, which is itself full of symbolic meaning. This knowledge was certainly known to the Masters of Wisdom and I was now to discover the real meaning of the Magi story and what I believe to be the true birthday of Jesus Christ.

# CHAPTER 11

✳

# We Three Kings

So who were the Magi, where did they come from and what might have been behind their mission at the stable? At last a picture was beginning to emerge and I was coming back to my original questions and the jumping off point of this long search that began in Bethlehem in 1972. The answers to these questions, I was beginning to see, lay, at least partly, in the politics of the time. The Middle East was then, as now, a highly turbulent region. Throughout most of the first century BC there was an ongoing fight between Rome and Parthia for control of what was, after all, the centre of civilization. Caught between the Sledge hammer of Rome and the Anvil of Parthia were a number of small kingdoms and principalities. These included Commagene, Osrhoene, Pontus and Armenia. It seems likely, therefore, that the 'wise men' or kings of Christian tradition came from one or more of these states.

For a short time Mithridates, King of Pontus, acted as a rallying point for the others against the encroachments of the Romans. He was a tough man and a skilful soldier, so much so that for a time he succeeded in driving them out of not only Asia Minor but Greece also. However, his rough methods won him few friends in his newly 'liberated' territories and many Greeks gave a sigh of relief when he was eventually defeated. Pompey, a key figure in the politics of the time and in many ways a greater general than Caesar, was sensible enough to come to an accommodation with Mithridates' allies. In his 'reorganization' he allowed them to retain their territories as buffer states between Rome and Parthia. He confirmed Antiochus as king of

Commagene, the Aryu Dynasty at Edessa and Tigranes in Armenia. The defeat of Crassus at Carrhae in 53 BC showed the wisdom of Pompey's strategy, for Rome was not yet ready to confront Parthia on its own territory. This devastating defeat led the Romans, for a time, to withdraw back east of the Euphrates, thereby giving the small principalities of Mesopotamia a breathing space.

This happy status quo might have persisted for a lot longer had it not been for firstly the series of civil wars between the Romans themselves and secondly the machinations of one man: Herod the Great. A terrifying mixture of Macbeth and Othello, he, unlike the other monarchs in the region, had no hereditary legitimacy. Though not a Jew himself [he was an Idumean, i.e. a descendant of Isaac's son Esau (Edom) rather than Jacob (Israel)], he usurped the kingdom of Judaea. His father Antipater, had managed to build positive relations with Pompey. Now he, riding the tiger of Roman politics, allied himself in turn with Julius Caesar, Cassius, Anthony, Augustus and finally Tiberius. Though extremely unpopular with the Jews, with Roman help he managed to stay king for thirty-three years.[1]

However, his schemes did not go entirely unchallenged. In 40 BC the Parthians sought to nip him in the bud by invading Palestine to restore Antigonus, a Hasmonean claimant to the throne.[2] Herod fled the country but not before he had kidnapped Mariamme, the granddaughter of the previous Hasmonean king, Hyrcanus II. He effectively incarcerated her under the 'protection' of his own family at the fortress of Masada. This was a virtually impregnable stronghold and the Parthians, though they laid siege, were unable to take it. Meanwhile, Herod went to Rome via Egypt and succeeded in persuading the Senate to make him king of Judaea. More importantly a Roman army was sent from Syria, the Parthians were driven out of Jerusalem and the way was made clear for him to take the throne. On his return Herod sought to legitimize his position by putting aside his first wife, Doris, and marrying Mariamme. As he later murdered her elder brother, the high priest Aristobulus, she was effectively the last of her line.

For all his fawning to the Romans, Herod was not without enemies elsewhere. With good cause he was loathed in Mesopotamia. It would seem that King Antiochus of Commagene had condoned, if not actually taken part in, the Parthian invasion of Syria and Palestine of 40 BC. In any event, in 38 BC Mark Anthony mounted an expedition against Commagene, laying siege to its capital Samosata. Herod, wanting to

ingratiate himself with the man he saw as the new force in Roman
politics, went to his aid. The incident is recorded by the Jewish historian
Josephus:

> Herod . . . when he heard that Anthony was conducting a large
> scale attack on Samosata, a well-fortified city near the Euphrates,
> he increased his speed, seeing an excellent chance of showing his
> mettle and placing Anthony under an obligation. And so it proved.
> As soon as he arrived he finished the siege for them, killing masses of
> the enemy and capturing quantities of booty, so that Anthony's old
> admiration for his prowess was greatly strengthened, and he heaped
> new honours upon him; confirming his hopes of mounting the throne;
> while King Antiochus was forced to surrender Samosata.[3]

Thus Herod had a direct hand in the overthrow of Antiochus, who, as
we have seen, was probably the head of the secret society that Gurdjieff
came across and which was known as the Sarmoung Brotherhood. To
add to the confusion of what was already a complicated situation,
Mark Anthony fell totally under the spell of Cleopatra, Queen of
Egypt. She, like Herod, was always unsure of her situation and one
by one got rid of her relatives. However, her ambitions went beyond
Egypt and she saw in Mark Anthony the opportunity to realize these
plans. As Josephus relates, this was unfortunate for her neighbours,
near and far:

> Anthony, ruined by his passion for Cleopatra, had become the
> complete slave of his desire, while Cleopatra had gone right
> through her own family till not a single relation was left alive,
> and thirsting now for the blood of strangers was slandering the
> authorities in Syria and urging Anthony to have them executed,
> thinking that in this way she would easily become mistress of all of
> their possessions. She even extended her acquisitiveness to Jews and
> Arabs and worked in secret to get their kings, Herod and Malichus,
> put to death.
>   Anthony was sober enough to realise that one part of her demands
> – the killing of honest men and famous kings – was utterly immoral;
> but he cut them to the heart by withdrawing his friendship. He sliced
> off large parts of their territory, including the palm-grove at Jericho
> where Balsam is produced, and gave them to Cleopatra along with all

the cities except Tyre and Sidon on this side of the River Eleutherus. Mistress now of this domain she escorted Anthony as far as the Euphrates on his way to fight the Parthians, and then came via Apamea and Damascus into Judaea. Herod placated her hostility with costly gifts, and leased back from her the lands broken off from his kingdom, at 200 talents a year! Finally he escorted her to Pelusium, showing her every attention. It was not long before Anthony reappeared from Parthia, bringing a prisoner – Artabazes the son of Tigranes – as a present for Cleopatra, to whom, along with the money and all the booty, the unfortunate Parthian was immediately handed over.[4]

What Cleopatra did with Artabazes, Josephus doesn't record but he was probably paraded in Alexandria before being executed. Meanwhile Mariamme was trapped in a loveless marriage to Herod. She hated him as the enemy of her family who had murdered both her brother and her grandfather but, according to Josephus, she was very beautiful and Herod was besotted with her. This 'love' extended to intense jealousy. In 29 BC, whilst he journeyed to foreign parts, he put her in the care of his brother-in-law, Joseph, who was the husband of his sister Salome. He gave Joseph strict instructions that if anything were to happen to him whilst he was away, that he should immediately put Mariamme to death. Needless to say she got to hear of this threat on her life and when Herod returned, foolishly chided him for it. Salome, who hated Mariamme both for her royal blood and looks, spread malicious gossip that she and Joseph had had an affair. Believing there is no smoke without fire, Herod immediately had them both put to death.

Mariamme had borne Herod five children, including two sons who survived childhood, Alexander and Aristobulus. Though the eldest of these, Alexander, was heir to the throne, they hated their father for what he had done to their mother. They in turn were detested by Antipater, their elder brother by Herod's first wife, Doris. He conspired against his half-brothers, persuading Herod that they were out to poison him. The youths were taken to Rome for trial but acquitted of all charges by Augustus, who was then Caesar. This, however, was not to be the end of the matter, as the intrigues went on and eventually Alexander and his brother Aristobulus were strangled on their father's orders. By now Herod was an old man and though he had a large family, with many wives, concubines and other children, he trusted no one. In fact as he lay in his sick bed, just days before his own death in 4 BC, he had Antipater, now his heir, murdered as well.

Given the character of this tyrant, the Saddam Hussein of his day, one can well imagine how he would have reacted to the news that a baby had been born who was a descendant not of the relatively recent Hasmonean line but of David himself. He must have thought that history was in danger of repeating itself. The very names Mary and Joseph would, had he been told them, have brought back awful memories of events twenty years earlier when he had killed Mariamme and her guardian who was also called Joseph. He certainly would have had no compunction about slaughtering the innocents of Bethlehem if he thought that this was going to deal with the threat.

This was the political reality at the end of the first century BC. Seen in this light, the embassy of the Magi takes on a strongly political hue. Whatever the symbolic significance behind the events described by Matthew in his charming story, the Magi of the time would have been keenly aware of the recent history of Judaea and Herod's part in the downfall of Antiochus Epiphanes of Commagene. They knew how increasingly vulnerable the regions east of the Euphrates were to Roman encroachment and may have hoped that the birth of Jesus was going to be a fresh beginning; that when he grew up, he would drive out the Romans from not only Judaea but the whole of Asia. Yet, there is more to the Magi story than the usual sorry history of wars, power politics and dynastic ambitions. Matthew's account makes it clear that these men were astrologers and that they saw something special in the sky that prompted them to make their journey to Judaea. This 'something' was a star – so big and so bright that it stayed visible long after the dawn. It was this important omen, so significant to anyone versed in Hermetic matters, that drew them on their way and it was this, so we are told, that led them to go first to Jerusalem then Bethlehem. What, then, was this star so much brighter than any other and why should it have seemed important?

Modern astronomers, able to accurately chart a horoscope for any date in the last ten thousand years, tend to agree that it was probably an important conjunction of planets. It seems likely that what the Magi saw, and what they had been anticipating, was the coming together of the two largest planets in the solar system, Jupiter and Saturn, so that their light was doubled and they could not be distinguished one from the other. This is a very rare event and occurred throughout the summer of 7 BC. Most astronomers are agreed that this is the only celestial event around that time to fit Matthew's description. Knowing this, I believe it is possible to reconstruct Jesus' horoscope and from this to learn much about his expected fate.

The Magi were from the East and they came from what was then the Parthian Empire. This was a much looser assemblage than its great rival, the Roman Empire. As we have seen, in Mesopotamia and Anatolia there were a number of more or less independent kingdoms whose people, the Romans and Jews, regarded as 'Parthian'. These were the satellite states that, at the time of Jesus' birth, formed a buffer between the two empires. The most important of these, at least from the point of view of the Magi story, were Commagene, Osrhoene (the principality containing both Edessa and Harran) and Armenia. Evidence at Edessa points to a secret tradition, with Egyptian overtones, that once existed in the area. This, as we have seen, indicates links between the pyramids, the constellation of Orion and the secret symbolism contained in the stories of Samson, Job and the prophets. This tradition has later links with traditions concerning John the Baptist.

Commagene, meanwhile, had its own sky religion based on a fusion of Greek, Persian and Egyptian ideas. Antiochus Epiphanes I instituted a new calendar based on his official 'birthday'. He constructed a shaft that points west at the place in the sky crossed each day by the star Regulus, the 'little king', also known as the lion's heart. It happens that when the sun conjuncts with this star, as it did at that time on 29 July, the star Sirius made its first dawn appearance. This day was sacred to the Egyptians marking the start of their Sothic or Sirian year. It therefore follows that Antiochus was emulating this as he sought to change the Commagene calendar from a lunar to a solar and sidereal[5] one. Clearly this new festival, which he associated with royalty and the birth of the kings of Commagene, was to be the start of the official year. It follows from this that the later kings of Commagene, including his son Antiochus II who was ruler of Commagene in 7 BC, would have been very interested in celestial phenomena at this time of year.

It so happens that on 29 July 7 BC, at the start of their new year,[6] the conjunction between the two largest planets in the solar system, Jupiter and Saturn, was still in evidence. This would have been of more than passing interest to the astronomers of Commagene and possibly elsewhere in the Near East. Knowing these basic facts, we can reconstruct the scenario.

## The horoscope of a Messiah

In looking for the correct birthday for Jesus we have to take various matters into consideration. First of all the Matthew Gospel, which is our primary source for the Magi story, states that at the time of his Nativity there was an especially bright star visible in the sky, which the wise men from the East were able to follow. This star 'came to rest' over the place where the child was. Now assuming that we are not talking about a UFO or some other extraordinary phenomenon that could be likened to an actual star, then identification of this body is relatively easy. The most likely event to have caused such interest amongst the Magi must have been this rare conjunction of Jupiter and Saturn in the constellation of Pisces, the fish. This signified to them the start of the 'New Age' of Pisces.

Now in the Book of Revelation, Jesus Christ is described as a Lion:

> Then one of the elders said to me, 'Weep not; lo, the Lion of the tribe of Judah, the Root of David, has conquered, so that he can open the scroll and its seven seals'.[7]

This description fits if Jesus himself was born under the sign of Leo but not if he was a Capricorn, as he would be with a birthday on 25 December. In fact, as we have seen, the celebration of Christmas Day was a later invention of the Church as it absorbed the Roman cults of Mithras and *Sol-Invictus*. Prior to this the winter feast was the Baptism of Jesus, celebrated on 6 January. For Matthew and other Christian initiates it was understood that Jesus was the Messiah of the New Age and that his symbolic, if not actual, birthdate should be that proper to a Horus King. This date and the one that fits all other criteria is 29 July 7 BC.

In Ancient Egypt the most important day in the year was the symbolic birth of Horus at the time of the heliacal rising of Sirius. (Just before dawn, Sirius will rise and be visible for a few minutes to be followed by the sun.) On this day the sun would have risen in conjunction with Regulus, the red-giant star in Leo whose name means 'little king'. For the Egyptians the red light of dawn symbolized the blood of the goddess Isis as she gave birth to her son. In the sky the pale light of Sirius, the soul of Isis and the brightest star in the sky, was soon to be outshone by the Sun – her son. The Sun, therefore, is symbolically the 'son' of Sirius. After his birth he becomes Ra-Harakte, the falcon son-god who was worshipped at Heliopolis and whose glyph is inscribed at the top of the XIIth Dynasty obelisk there. Following the Hermetic Dictum of 'As Above, So Below', so this awesome rebirth of the Sun each year represented the birth of the Horus Kings.

The heliacal rising of Sirius was the start of a new Sothic year and as we have seen this 'New Year' seems to have been adopted by Antiochus of Cammagene as the official birthday of both himself and his father. However, on 29 July 7 BC the two planets Jupiter and Saturn would be in conjunction, forming one very bright star. As this was the official Royal Birthday of Commagene (and possibly in some of the other small kingdoms of Mesopotamia) these portents would have been of great interest to the Magi; perhaps sufficiently

Fig. 14

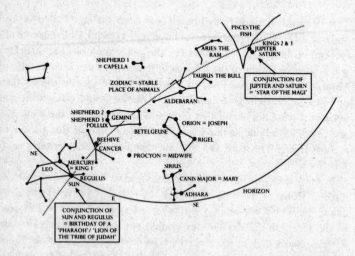

The 'Nativity' of Jesus written in the sky, 29th July 7 BC.

so that they would send out search parties to look for a divinely born child.

As can be seen from the hierothesion of Antiochus, the Commagene kings regarded themselves as being under the patronage of the great lion in the sky, Leo, and also of certain planets – most especially Jupiter. Their royal cult had strong connections with Zoroastrianism and they regarded Jupiter as being the embodiment of the Persian high god, Ohrmazd. They were also well aware of the prophecy that Zoroaster, the prophet of Persia, would have a posthumous son. Seeing the conjunction of Jupiter and Saturn in the sky on the very day that was the royal birthday of their own kings, the astrologers would naturally see this as a portent of a probable Messianic birth. Knowing that such a nativity was not expected in their own royal house, the astrologers of Commagene would naturally consult with their neighbours, the Edessans and Armenians. The royal house of Edessa was also linked to Leo as their founder was called 'Arya', a name meaning lion in both Hebrew and Syriac. Finding there was not an important birth imminent here either, they would ask where else it could be going to occur. At Edessa there was a large Jewish community and it would have been surprising if the king, Abgar, had not known that the royal house in Judea was also ruled by Leo and that the Jews were expecting a Messiah. Thus 'wise men', probably not the kings themselves, might have been sent from Edessa, Armenia and Commagene to investigate.

Arriving in Jerusalem, they would naturally have consulted the court of Herod. There they would have been treated civilly, as befitted their rank, but informed that no royal births were expected in the next few days there either. Consulting further amongst the high priests and elders of the Temple, they would have been informed that there was indeed an old prophecy that the Messiah, a scion of the House of David, would be born in a nearby town called Bethlehem. Unlike Jerusalem which stands in the lands once belonging to the Israelite tribe of Benjamin, Bethlehem was in the province of Judah. As Judah was the lion tribe of Israel, it would therefore be a lion town and astrologically an appropriate place for a king under the patronage of Leo to be born. The Magi would have been intrigued to check out this prophecy. Making their goodbyes, they would have hastened off to Bethlehem, which was only five miles down the road, to see if that was the place. Their caravan may have arrived at Bethlehem at dawn, the extraordinary conjunction of Jupiter and Saturn having symbolically guided them on their way as they made their way south from Jerusalem. Although one by one all the other stars have by now disappeared, as they arrive this 'one' is still visible, hovering over the stable where Jesus was born. With jubilation at the fulfilment of their mission, they climb down from their camels and take out birthday gifts for the young child from their saddle-bags: gold, frankincense and myrrh. They enter and, doing homage to the new Messiah, kneel before him and present him with their gifts. Then, other pleasantries having been exchanged with his parents and probably having promised to offer whatever help they can with his education, they camp down in the nearby fields. In the night they are warned by an angel not to go back to Herod, so they return to Edessa by a different route, possibly going first to Egypt to meet friends and carry out some business.

This, what we might call 'Dalai Lama'[8] scenario, is perhaps the historical story on which Matthew based his account. However, there is clearly more to the Magi legend than this. The Bible is written on many different levels and it is obvious that like everything else in his Gospel, Matthew included this story for a definite purpose. That purpose would have been understood by at least some of the audience, 'those who have ears to hear' to whom the Gospel was addressed. For them, the arrival of the Magi at the Nativity would have been understood in an entirely different manner, as a very concise way of describing Jesus' destiny.

## The Horoscope of a Messiah

Matthew, though probably not the tax-collector, for some reason referred to as 'publicans' in the King James Bible, was a Christian Gnostic. He was probably a resident of either Antioch or Alexandria and certainly understood a great deal about the pagan cults of the area. His Gospel was intended to win converts to the new faith, so he was careful to make it seem relevant. He seems to have understood the connections between the ancient mysteries and Christianity and wanted to underline these for the initiated. Thus, in the new Christian order, the original Egyptian trinity of Osiris, Isis and Horus is to be replaced by Joseph, Mary and Jesus. Thus the birth of Jesus is symbolically the same as the birth of a new 'Horus-king' on earth: He is the Aeon of the New Age replacing the old, worn-out religion of Egypt and is to be understood as such. Christian iconographers, building on the outline story as recorded in Matthew, recorded the details of Jesus' horoscope. In effect they took the story and made it into the archetypal Nativity painting, a 'legominism' which has been so successful that it has not been forgotten some two thousand years later. They did this in such a way that it would be neither forgotten nor censored, as it probably would have been had the Church authorities understood what they were doing. Knowing this, we are in a position to analyse the traditional Nativity scene and see within it a deeper meaning than would have been understood by these initiated Christian iconographers.

As we have already seen, Mary and Joseph have stellar counterparts; in a macrocosmic sense they are the star Sirius and the constellation of Orion respectively. However, the symbolism goes much wider than this. Traditionally Jesus is born in a stable: a place of animals. This seems to symbolize the zodiac, the 'animal' path of the sun as it makes its way through the sky.[9] Attending the birth, besides Mary and Joseph, are two symbolic animals who share the 'stable', i.e. that part of the zodiac which is visible. These are the ox (Taurus) and the sheep or ram (Aries). Also in attendance are three shepherds. I believe that these are three important stars that 'lead the way'. They are Capella, a very bright yellow star in the constellation of Auriga (the charioteer); and Castor and Pollux, the Gemini twins. These stars were all watched by the ancients and used for telling the time. They rise before Leo and, in a sense, act as guides. Significantly, they are are all above the line of the ecliptic in a more northerly part of the sky than Orion and Canis Major (Joseph and Mary). This seems to be what is meant by the shepherds being 'in the hills', i.e. north of the event, when they are called by the angels.

In the traditional scene, the baby Jesus lies in a 'manger', the place where the animals get their food. Now the word Bethlehem means 'House of Bread', and this city was also in the traditional holdings of the tribe of Judah. Each of the ancient tribes of Israel was ascribed to one or another of the signs of the zodiac, twelve in all. Judah was the lion tribe and its 'home' was therefore the land ruled by Leo. Thus 'Jesus in the manger' means he is in Bethlehem, and therefore in the sign of Leo. This is symbolized by the sun rising (being born) in the sign of Leo.

Another bright star, Procyon, stands midway between Mary (Sirius) and the baby Jesus (Sun conjunct Regulus). Procyon rises slightly before

Sirius and after Orion. It is therefore closer to Mary than Joseph at the time of the 'birth'. Significantly Procyon is in Canis Minor, the 'Little Dog' constellation, linking it to Canis Major, the 'Great Dog' as a smaller or younger version of it. If Canis Major represents Mary, then this constellation should be a girl. For all these reasons, I believe Procyon represents the 'midwife' who according to some traditions was the inn-keeper's daughter.

At dawn only the very brightest stars would be visible and this deals with all those in this region of the sky. There now remains only the planets to be accounted for. Planets are, according to the Hermetic philosophy, gods of the lower heavens (i.e. the Solar System). Each of them ruled over one of the 'crystal spheres' that surround the earth. It was believed that when a soul is born it receives 'gifts' from whichever planets were watching over the birth. The nature of these gifts, it was believed, would determine both the talents and fate of the person for the rest of their life on earth. It was therefore very important to know the planets of your birth, i.e. those which were above the horizon when you were born, as these would be the gods who would have the strongest influence on the native.

Assuming that Jesus was born at dawn on 29 July 7 BC, three planets would have been visible in the sky: Jupiter and Saturn, in such close conjunction that they would look like one very bright star, and Mercury, which was then visible shortly before dawn as a morning star. In the same way that Sirius represents Mary and Orion, Joseph, these three planets are clearly the astral counterparts to the three kings or Magi of later tradition. Their gifts are gold symbolizing wealth, frankincense for spiritual wisdom and myrrh[10] for longevity. These are the appropriate gifts for the three planets in question. Gold for Jupiter, myrrh for Saturn and frankincense for Mercury.

In many 'Adoration of the Magi' paintings, two of the kings stand quietly waiting their turn to pay homage to the new saviour, whilst the third kneels before the child and kisses his foot. The first two are obviously Saturn and Jupiter in conjunction, whilst this third must be Mercury. In Greek this planet was called Hermes and was associated with the Egyptian god Thoth, also known as Hermes Trismegistus: 'Thrice Greatest Hermes'. Though we are more accustomed to seeing Mercury as the youthful messenger of the gods, in the guise of the ancient prophet Hermes Trismegistus he is usually depicted as old and venerable. Thus in the Nativity paintings, the kneeling king is usually shown as the oldest of the three.

It is clear from all of this that the entire tableau of the heavens at the birth of Jesus is represented unthinkingly, in nearly all of its details, in countless paintings and nativity sets. Unfortunately, for reasons to do with calendrics and politics, Jesus' birthday was shifted by the Church to 25 December. This latter feast was originally the birthday of the Roman and Persian Sun-god, Sol-Mithras. In the early days of the Church the winter festival was the Epiphany, which was celebrated on 6 January. This feast, however, had nothing to do with Jesus' birth but rather was the celebration of his baptism by John. In the fourth century the Church turned this into the birthday of Jesus, probably because the baptism implied that Jesus needed to be initiated by John before he could begin his ministry. Church doctrine was now hardening that, as the Son of God and Second Person of the Trinity, he was omniscient and omnipotent from birth. The idea that Jesus himself went through a series of initiations before attaining his full powers was uncomfortable for a priesthood that had already forgotten, if they ever knew it, what these were. The change in date also pleased certain of the pagan Alexandrians thereby helping in their conversion. They were accustomed to celebrate the birth of the Aeon (the new year in this case) to the Kore, or Virgin goddess, on 6 January. They could accept Jesus as the Aeon and Mary as the Kore without having to change the date of their principal feast. Later still, and for probably much the same reasons, Christmas was shifted back to 25 December, the birthday of the Sun-god, and 6 January became instead the feast of the Magi.

The choice of a day near the winter solstice for the birthday of Christ had a certain logic and fitted with the Roman calendar. It meant that the Annunciation to the Virgin, the day on which she became pregnant nine months before the Nativity, could be celebrated on 25 March. Also, according to Luke's Gospel, Jesus was conceived six months after John the Baptist. This meant that John's birthday too could be comfortably celebrated on 24 June, Midsummer Day. Although according to the Bible it was Gabriel who appeared to John's father Zechariah to tell him his wife Elizabeth was pregnant, this lesser 'Annunciation' corresponds to 29 September – the feast of that other archangel, St Michael. The Church now had festivals that fitted with its teachings for the four corner days of the year: winter, spring, summer and autumn.

## Temples of the Virgin

In the teachings of the Church the star religion that connected Orion, Leo and Sirius with the birth of Jesus was disguised and modified so that it would not cause offence. The Church calendar of fixed feasts was now based around four quarter days: Christmas Day on 25 December, the feast of the Annunciation (Lady Day) on 25 March, the birth of John the Baptist on 24 June and the Michaelmas on 29 September. In mediaeval times, Lady Day was the start of the legal year, whilst Michaelmas was the beginning of the autumn term. Yet, just why these important festivals should not be celebrated exactly at the equinoxes but rather a few days later was at first a mystery to me until I began to look into the astrology of the situation.

To recap, the four quarter days concern the two 'cousins', Jesus and John the Baptist, and two archangels, Michael and Gabriel. The feast of the Annunciation, which has been marked in the Roman calendar since at least the seventh century, celebrates the event when Gabriel tells Mary of the Father's desire that, whilst still remaining a virgin, she should become the mother of the Messiah. With the memorable words, 'Be it done unto me according to thy words', she accepts her destiny and is impregnated with the seed of God. Nine months later, that is to say on Christmas Day, she gives birth to Jesus in the stable at Bethlehem. Thus, the two feasts of the Annunciation and the Nativity fit together making a pair that is both theologically and biologically meaningful. In the same way but in the eyes of the Church not important to the same extent, is the birth of John. He is born on 24 June, so it follows that his conception must be nine months earlier and therefore connected with the feast of Michaelmas. In the Gospels though, this time the story is more fully told in Luke than in Matthew, it is the same angel Gabriel who appears to John's father Zechariah and announces to him that his wife, now advanced in years, is to bear a son.

The sense, then, is that the same angel, though at different times of the year, acts as messenger to both Mary and Elizabeth, John's mother. Both women become pregnant by the will of God, though Elizabeth, unlike Mary, is a wife, not a virgin and one presumes that the seed which impregnates her is that of her husband Zechariah. Nevertheless, John is to be 'filled with the Holy Spirit, even from his mother's womb'.[11] If his birth is not quite as miraculous as that of his 'God-seed' cousin Jesus, it is still a very impressive given that his mother was previously barren and was advanced in years. In a sense then, Jesus and John are divine twins, cousins whose conceptions and births mirror one another, yet whose generation is announced by the same angel. The details in Luke's Gospel, which inform us that Gabriel appeared to Elizabeth a full six months before his meeting with Mary, implies that this seasonal difference is important.

Who then is Gabriel and what does he symbolize? In Christian iconography he, or perhaps she, is shown in traditional manner as a beautiful winged being. His mascot, which he hands to the Virgin Mary as a token of her divine calling, is a white lily symbolizing purity (plate 38). Yet this lily has a deeper meaning than simply being a token of virginity. This seems to have been understood and to have lain at the heart of European mysticism in the Middle Ages, particularly in France where the cult of the Virgin reached its apotheosis.

Once more I turned to the SKYGLOBE program and once more was in for a surprise. Setting it up for a date of around 1150 and, centring it on Paris, I soon discovered that the constellation that was most significant at both Lady Day and Michaelmas was, perhaps not surprisingly, Virgo. On 25 March Virgo would be rising at sunset. At the exact moment that Spica, the brightest and most significant star in the constellation was coming over the horizon, so the sun would sink in the west. Changing the date to 29 September was equally significant, for on this day the sun would rise actually conjunct with Spica. Thus both days, celebrated as the impregnation of Mary and Elizabeth respectively at the behest of the angel Gabriel, were linked with the constellation of Virgo.

Yet, astrologically, there was something wrong in this arrangement, tidy as it seemed. The rising of Spica conjunct with the sun at dawn was clearly the more powerful symbol of the Annunciation. This being so, it ought to relate to Jesus, as the Messiah, and not John, the prophet who goes before. In other words, because the Church had mistakenly moved Jesus' birth from summer, when the sun was conjunct with Regulus to the winter solstice, the symbolism of the Annunciation had been turned on its head. Realizing this, I decided to look into the matter further and see what parallels there might have been between the Christian feast of the Annunciation and its older, Egyptian equivalent, the 'seeding' of Isis.

In *The Orion Mystery*,[12] Robert Bauval and I had presented evidence that the southern shaft of the Queen's Chamber of the Great Pyramid was so orientated that, at the time the pyramid was built, it pointed at Sirius as it crossed the southern meridian. This, we postulated, was connected with a special ritual that we believed had at one time been carried out in the Queen's Chamber whereby Sirius, the star of Isis, was symbolically impregnated as it aligned with this shaft at dawn. As this was clearly the Egyptian equivalent of the feast of the Annunciation, I decided to see when this might have occurred at Cairo prior to the proposed Nativity of Jesus on 29 July 7 BC. To my astonishment the correct day, when Sirius would line up with the southern meridian at dawn, turned out to be when the sun would rise conjunct with Spica on 22 September 8 BC.

As this was clearly no accident, I decided to look into the symbolism of the constellation of Virgo to see who or what this had represented in Egyptian times and what connection, if any, it might have had with either the Virgin Mary or the angel Gabriel. In a book called *Astraea*

Fig. 15

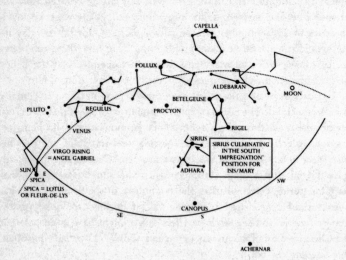

The true 'Annunciation' to the Virgin Mary written in the sky, 21st September 8 BC.

by Dame Frances Yates, I discovered that the constellation of Virgo was a Latinization of Astraea, the just Virgin of the 'golden' age. Yates elaborates on a story told in Ovid's *Metamorphoses*:

> There is a famous description in the first book of Ovid's *Metamorphoses* of the four ages. In that first golden age, under the rule of Saturn, men gathered their food without labour in an everlasting spring, all were virtuous by nature, and peace universal reigned. After the golden age of Saturn came the silver age of Jove when the eternal spring gave place to seasons, men felt for the first time the extemes of heat and cold and the labour of tillage began. The third age was the age of brass, sterner than the first two, but yet not impious. Finally came the iron age, when evil was let loose. Modesty, truth, and faith fled from the earth; men travelled greedily over the earth for gain; delved into the earth for metals. War came, and brandished in its bloody hands the clashing arms. Piety lay vanquished, and the Virgin Astraea, last of the immortals, abandoned the blood-soaked earth.[13]

Now the belief in an earlier golden age of plenty is universal. In Egypt it was characterized by the semi-mythical reign of their god-king Osiris and his wife Isis, who together established civilization. One of the fundamental pillars of society, at least as far as we can tell from this great distance in time, was a strong belief in the rule of law. The Egyptians characterized the abstract quality of truth and justice with the figure of a goddess that they called *Maat*. Her symbol was the ostrich feather, two of which were worn by the kings of Egypt in the so-called *Atef* crown of Osiris. Upholding the rule of law was the principal duty of the pharaoh as he sought to emulate Horus, who had restored order to Egypt after the murder of his father by the usurper Seth. *Maat* as truth was the principle by which the Egyptians expected to be judged after death. This is symbolized by the 'weighing of the heart' (plate 44) ceremony to be seen on countless papyri, such as that of Ani the scribe.[14] In this ceremony, which I believe may actually have been carried out in the King's Chamber of the Great Pyramid, the heart of the deceased (symbolized by the small jar in which it was placed when the body was mummified) is weighed in the balances against *Maat*, the feather of truth. Depending on the results of this trial, the soul of the deceased is either able to leave the earth to join Osiris in his heavenly world, or he is gobbled up by a monster with the body of a lion and the head of a crocodile, who lurks close to the balances. In the King's Chamber there is a south-orientated shaft that at the time the pyramid was built (*c.*2450 BC) pointed directly at the culmination point of the star Alnitak in Orion's Belt. A second shaft, from the opposite wall, was directed towards the then North star, alpha-Draconis. Whilst the court of Osiris is associated with Orion, which therefore represents heaven, the North star is symbolized by the crocodile-headed goddess Tuart. She is always shown heavily pregnant and is associated with childbirth. It therefore follows that projection of the soul through one or other of the two shafts represents the alternative outcomes of the trial. In the one case the soul joins Osiris in Paradise, in the other it has to be consumed by Tuart in order to be reborn back on Earth.

*Maat*, who is often shown standing next to the balances, (Libra in our Zodiac), is represented in the sky by the constellation of Virgo. In Egyptian mythology she was often thought of as the consort of Thoth, the god of science and writing whom the Greeks called Hermes Trismegistus. It is he who records the results of the judgement in his 'Book of life' and acts as judge and jury in the case. Both god and goddess have a role, it seems, in determining the destiny of souls, most especially their incarnations on Earth.[15]

Returning to Frances Yates and her description of the Latin Virgo, she tells us:

> Ovid is drawing on Greek sources. The golden age tradition, hinted at by Hesiod, was expanded by the Greek astronomical poet Aratos when treating of the constellation Virgo, the sixth sign of the zodiac. Aratos explains that when the virgin Justice left the world in the iron age she took up her abode in the heavens as the constellation Virgo; the figure of the just virgin now shines in the sky, bearing an ear of corn in her hand. The attribute of the ear of corn — *virgo spicifera* — is repeated in the Latin translators and imitators of Aratos, and a traditional representation of the constellation is a winged woman holding corn. The ears of corn mark the position of Spica, a particularly bright star in the constellation.[16]

In the original Egyptian version of Justitia, or Virgo as *Maat*, Spica would probably have been either a feather of justice or a lotus flower.[17] The association of the lotus with the birth of Horus as the incarnation of the Solar Logos is also clear. According to Rundle Clark:

. . . the Egyptians sometimes symbolised the appearance of the great Life Spirit out of the waters as a lotus – a water lily – rising and opening its flowers, the petals bent back to reveal the rising God of Light and Movement . . . sometimes the flower discloses a young child, the morning sun.[18]

It is very obvious from this that the child of the lotus represents the soul as Horus, the son of the Sun. This is shown in the Papyrus of Ani where a group of three lotuses are shown rising from a lily pond with a head coming out of the central, open flower.[19] It is probable that the symbol of Horus in the lily is connected with his secret birth to Isis amongst the lilies and papyrus beds of Lower Egypt.

From all of these considerations, it was now clear to me that astrally the angel Gabriel represents Justitia, the constellation of Virgo. The Annunciation to the Virgin Mary was made, at least symbolically, on 22 September 8 BC. Whether or not an angel actually appeared to her is irrelevant as far as the astral symbology is concerned. On this day, as Sirius reached the meridian at dawn, the sun was conjunct with Spica. Symbolically, the angel (Virgo) proffers the bunch of lilies with the soul of the future Horus-king sitting amongst them. Mary, symbolized by Sirius at the peak of its cycle, receives this 'seed' or rather soul into her womb. Thus it is that Jesus as an incarnating human leaves the lotus beds of the sky, i.e. the place where souls rest between incarnations, and comes into the time-frame of earth and space. In doing so he has to, like all other incarnating souls, take on a fate and destiny. All this is implicit in the Annunciation, though it is not made manifest until his birthday, again symbolized if not actual, some ten months later on 29 July.

Thus it is that the proper identification of the Annunciation as 22 September adds weight to the identification of his real birthday as having taken place in summer and not winter. His cousin John, meanwhile, who in his cosmic role as wild-man prophet is symbolized by Orion, would actually, if he were six months older than Jesus, have been born when the sun was in Aquarius, the water-bearer. What could be more appropriate for a man who was destined to be a baptiser?

By abandoning the quarter days of the Church calendar, which in any case are based not on a proper astrological understanding of the symbols they are meant to convey but rather on the Roman festival of Mithras/Sol-Invictus, I was now able to see how Christianity is indeed directly related to the ancient mysteries of Egypt. What I didn't realize, though, was that Jesus' horoscope contained even more about the story of the Magi, it revealed how closely they were involved in his astral destiny.

## The Gifts of the Magi

The Church abandoned the idea of the birthday of Jesus coinciding with the day of the heliacal rising of Sirius in 7 BC for a symbolic rebirth of the sun in winter. The July birthday would have shown all too clearly the connection between Christianity and the original Osiris religion of Egypt, for this was the start of the Sothic year and for millennia the basis of the Egyptian calendar. As late as AD 245 the 'Church Father' Origen, who was born in Alexandria and who as a bishop had dealings with Emperor Severus Alexander, decried the celebration of Jesus' birth 'as if he were a king Pharaoh'. He would not have said this had it not been understood in Egypt, even in his own day, that the true birth of Jesus corresponded with the start of the Egyptian New Year and the official birth date of Horus. Unfortunately, by losing Jesus' real birthday and the knowledge that he was born as a Leo, certain Biblical prophecies, such as in Revelation 5:5 where one of the elders says: 'Weep not; lo the Lion of the tribe of Judah, the Root of David, has conquered, so that he can open the scroll and its seven seals', become obscured. The Lion of the tribe of Judah has to be a Leo and is obviously Jesus. The seven seals that he opens are symbolic of the seven planets which seal the crystal spheres and thereby confine souls to Earth. This teaching cannot be understood without reference to the Hermetic tradition and knowledge of the astrology governing Jesus' birth.

There is also a deeper meaning to the gifts of the Magi which is not immediately obvious. According to the Hermetic philosophy, in which Matthew seems to be quite knowledgeable, the seven planets[20] were the kings or rulers of the lower heavens. Through his fall from grace, Man was brought under their dominion, which meant that he was trapped into cycles of reincarnation. It was thought that each planet, most especially those above the horizon at birth, imparted something of its nature to an incarnating soul. However, these gifts could be a blessing or a curse depending on whether or not they were used for purely selfish purposes.

Astrologically, the gifts of the three kings can be seen to symbolize the special talents given to Jesus at birth by the planetary rulers. Significantly, immediately following his baptism by John, he is tempted by the devil three times whilst fasting in the desert. The devil here seems to represent his own lower nature, or shadow side, which unlike his eternal spirit is conditioned by the astral conditions of his birth. These three temptations seem to be connected with possible misuse of each of the three gifts of the kings. He is first tempted to turn stones into bread, i.e. to carry out a magical transformation of matter. This would be a misuse of his priestly power conferred on him by Mercury, the planet of magic. He is then tempted to cast himself from a high place in the firm belief that angels will catch him and break his fall. This would be a misuse of his Saturnian power of preserving life. Finally he is tempted to make himself king of the world, a misuse of the gifts of Jupiter, the planet ruling royalty. He rejects all three temptations and, in doing so, shows that his destiny is to be higher than that of the planetary gods, symbolized by the three kings. Significantly the planets missing from his birth are Venus, Mars and the Moon. We do not hear of him being tempted by lust (Venus), by cruelty (Mars), or sloth (the Moon). The devil, or the seven-headed planetary logos that holds men's souls bound to the material world, can only tempt him according to the nature of his fate.

Later, in the course of his ministry, Jesus uses his gifts for the welfare of others. He makes use of his Mercurial powers by transforming water into wine and multiplying bread and fish, not for himself but for the needs of others. He uses his Saturnian power to heal the sick and raise the dead. His money and position, brought to him by Jupiter, he gives away by becoming a wandering mendicant. In this way the Matthew Gospel story shows how a modern Hermeticist is to behave, with humility, charity and honour. This is shown to be the very antithesis of the scribes and Pharisees, the reputed wise men of the day, who falling into the traps of the devil, spend their time in learned but empty dialogue and exhalt themselves above their neighbours. They stand accused of hypocrisy, of taking the keys of heaven (the Hermetic wisdom handed down through Abraham, Moses and the prophets) and hiding them:

'But woe to you, scribes and Pharisees, hypocrites! because you shut the kingdom of heaven against men; for you neither enter yourselves, nor allow those who would enter to go in . . .

'Woe to you, scribes and Pharisees, hypocrites! for you tithe mint and dill and cummin, and have neglected the weightier matters of the law, justice and mercy and faith; these you ought to have done, without neglecting the others. You blind guides, straining out a gnat and swallowing a camel!'[21]

At the end of his life Jesus, having fulfilled his teaching mission, hands back the gifts of the 'gods', the kings of the astral realms. At his trial he refuses to defend himself with either clever words or magic tricks. In other words he gives up Mercury. He does not seek to buy his way to freedom, which given his connections he might well have done. This is the denial of Jupiter. Thirdly, by dying on the cross he gives up his promise of a long life. In so doing he hands back the gift of Saturn. Thus he gives back to the three kings their lesser gifts, preferring to break free from the bondage of earthly existence.

There is, of course, one fourth denial that he makes: that of being a King of Judah. This was the gift of the sun-god Apollo-Helios himself, symbolized by his birth at the conjunction of the sun with Regulus. Instead he allows himself to be mocked with a crown of thorns and a reed sceptre. He is, nevertheless, crucified at Pilate's orders with the slogan 'Jesus Christ King of the Jews' nailed on his cross. Symbolically and in every respect, Jesus renounces all the temptations of the planetary world. By implication his Gnosis is superlative; he is able to break through the crystal spheres and, as all Hermetic philosophers would have wished, to take his seat at the right hand of God the Father, whose throne lies beyond our petty solar system with its minor kings the planets.

Interpreted in this way and with the understanding that the real date of the Nativity was 29 July 7 BC, the Magi story becomes one of the principal keys to understanding the rest of Matthew's Gospel. Like everyone else, Jesus the man is born with an astrological fate. He does not succumb to this, however, he fulfils his higher destiny, which involves a painful death on the cross. This was predicted for him earlier on in the Bible, with his dying breath he quotes from this:

And about the ninth hour Jesus cried with a loud voice, 'Eli, Eli, la'ma sabach-tha'ni?' that is 'My God, my God, why hast thou forsaken me?' And some of the bystanders hearing it said, 'This man is calling Elijah'. And one of them at once ran and took a sponge, filled it with vinegar, and put it on a reed, and gave it to him to drink. But the others said, 'Wait, let us see whether Elijah will come and save him'. And Jesus cried with a loud voice and yielded up his spirit.[22]

Evidently the bystanders did not include any scribes or Pharisees or they would have recognized the reference to Psalm 22:

My God, my God, why hast thou forsaken me? Why art thou so far from helping me, from the words of my groaning? . . .

But I am a worm, and no man; scorned by men, and despised by the people. All who see me mock at me, they make mouths at me, they wag their heads; "He committed his cause to the Lord; let him deliver him, Let him rescue him, for he delights in him!" . . .

I am poured out like water, and all my bones are out of joint; my heart is like wax, it is melted within my breast; my strength is dried up like a potsherd, and my tongue cleaves to my jaws; thou dost lay me in the dust of death.

Yea, dogs are round about me; a company of evildoers encircle me; they have pierced my hands and my feet – I can count all my bones – they stare and gloat over me; they divide my garments among them and for my raiment they cast lots.[23]

Reading this Psalm of David and comparing it with the Crucifixion scene as described by Matthew, it is very hard not to see it as a prophecy of the events on Calvary, right down to the piercing of the hands and feet and the soldiers casting lots for Jesus' garments. As such it throws a powerful light on the nature of destiny as opposed to fate. The whole essence of the story, often it seems lost by a Church that is unwilling to acknowledge the humanity of Jesus the man, is that he didn't have to go through with it. He could have accepted the gifts of the wise men for what they were, have lived a comfortable and even honourable life before eventually dying in a respectable way. The Crucifixion seems to be a denial of this comfortable option in favour of a harder road that would both fulfil the prophecies of a dying saviour and open the gates through the crystal spheres. It is a deep and a hard message to take that if we would like to be followers of Christ then it is not enough to idolize him. We too must confront our destinies and, if necessary, abandon our more comfortable but necessarily limited fate.

# CHAPTER 12

✳

# The Second Crusade and the Temple on the Rhine

One of, if not the, motivating factors for the First Crusade was a Millennial expectancy. The defeat of the Byzantines at Manzikert had occurred almost exactly one thousand years after the Romans had, in 70 AD, destroyed the temple of Jerusalem and expelled the Jews from the Holy Land. For Christendom, as the eleventh century drew to a close, there was a sense of foreboding. There was a widespread feeling that the return of Jesus Christ, as prophecied in the Bible, could not be very far off and, as it was expected that he would make his appearance at Jerusalem, that it was the duty of Christians to take back the Holy City and prepare the way for him. This was, no doubt, the principal reason why Godfrey of Bouillon refused to have himself crowned King of Jerusalem, preferring to take the title of *Advocatus Sancti Sepulchri*. He was, after all, simply preparing the throne for Jesus, who was expected to show up at any time in the following year of 1100.

Though Godfrey was not to know it, this was not to be. He died on 18 July while the saviour still had a few months in hand to fulfil expectations. With still over a month to go, including the most obvious date of Christmas, Baldwin I accepted what his predecessor had declined and had himself crowned on 11 November 1099, the feast of St Martin. Blasphemous as this may have seemed to some people, there was no reason why he should not keep the throne warm for the expected 'Lion of Judah'. However, his action suggests that in some quarters at least there was a realization dawning that they were in for the long haul, that the Messiah would choose his own time of return and that the year 1100 held no special magic.

As the months turned into years and Outremer, as the Frankish Crusader state in Palestine was known, began more and more to resemble any other feudal state, so some of the magic of Jerusalem began to wear thin. What had been imagined as a thoroughly exotic city, seen only in the drawings of illuminated manuscripts and embroidered on to tapestries, was now known to be like any other place. Not only that but it was far from paradisiacal; the weather was hot in summer and the land for the most part was near desert. It was not a rich country and there were few fortunes to be made there, either through trade or by conquest. To make matters worse, the kingdom was ringed about with Moslem enemies who, should they ever unite, would surely over run the fledgling state. As all these realities began to sink home so the attractions of the Holy Land as a place for emigration came to be seen as somewhat less than before and attentions began to wander elsewhere.

By now the First Crusade was almost inextricably linked with the idea of the Quest for the Holy Grail. At Antioch an old spear had been found buried under the cathedral floor, just as had previously been revealed to Peter the Hermit in a vision. This spear was believed by many to have been that which the centurion Longinus had used to pierce the side of Christ and was therefore a very holy relic. Brandishing it in battle, the Christians had been so inspired that they had driven back a relieving army of Moslems and thereby secured the city of Antioch. The search was now on in earnest for other relics.

One of the most important of these was the legendary Mandylion of Edessa which was said to bear the true likeness of Christ. Though the Byzantines believed they had it in their possession, there is a distinct possibility that what they had was a copy and that the original was still at Edessa in 1099. At any rate, Baldwin, Tancred and a small company of knights went to Edessa and Baldwin became its first Frankish Count. The castle of Edessa, with its fish-ponds and legends fits the description of the Castle of the Fisher-King in the Grail legends. A king Abgar, whose name means lame or with a hernia, invited Jesus to live in Edessa. He and his successors were guardians of the Mandylion, believed to confer a special protection on the city. Since the Mandylion was supposedly, at least in later traditions, to have been painted without human hands, it itself has Grail-like connotations.

Baldwin did not long stay in Edessa before taking on the larger role of King of Jerusalem. It seems very likely that, had he been entrusted with a Mandylion, genuine or fake, he would have taken this with him. Meanwhile his cousin, Baldwin of Le Bourg, took over the County of Edessa. He later succeeded to the throne of Jerusalem and seems to have been the king who gave a charter to the Order of Knights Templars. They were given charge of Mount Moriah, the place where Abraham had offered to sacrifice his son Isaac and where once had stood the Temple of Solomon.

Baldwin II died in 1131 and was succeeded to the throne by his son-in-law Fulk, Count of Anjou. He was an able soldier who, following the death of his first wife, had left his estates in France to his son and decided to dedicate the remaining part of his life in service to the cross. His reign was far from peaceful as he had to deal not only with the constant threat of Moslem invasion but with both the insurrection of some of his most powerful lords and increasing Byzantine assertiveness in the region. The death of Fulk from a riding accident in 1143 left a dangerous vacuum. Though his widow, Melisende, took over the reins of government with her young son Baldwin III as her colleague, it was not an altogether satisfactory solution. However, the greatest blow, one which should have been foreseen and prepared for, was the fall of Edessa in 1145. Though there had been many difficulties and setbacks in the past, this was the first important loss of territory suffered by the Crusading movement and as such marked the turning of the tide.

The loss of Edessa spurred the West once more to take action. Almost immediately an appeal went out from the Pope, Eugenius, for a Second Crusade to retake the city and bolster up the remaining states of Outremer. The driving force behind this Crusade, however, was not the Pope himself but St Bernard of Clairvaux. He was acknowledged to be the greatest churchman of his day and his fiery oratory was enough to induce even the most sceptical and lazy of Christians to do their spiritual duty by taking up the sword. He travelled through France and Germany delivering sermon after sermon, exhorting nobility and peasantry alike to make their vows to join the Crusade. The result was another mass movement, this time led not by the cadet branches of the great families but King Louis VII himself and his queen, Eleanor of Aquitaine. Unfortunately for Louis, his Crusade would not end gloriously. From start to finish it was a shambles serving only to alienate further the Byzantine Empire, to unite the Moslems in a common cause and to reveal to them the underlying disunity of their enemies. At no time did the Crusaders approach anywhere near Edessa. Instead they wasted themselves on a long march through Anatolia and a fruitless siege of Damascus.

This was not to be the end of the Crusade, though it was certainly the end of the beginning. In 1187, Jerusalem and nearly all of Palestine were once more lost to the Franks after the disastrous Battle of the Horns of Hattim. Later Crusades, such as that of Richard the Lionheart, the son of Queen Eleanor by her second husband, Henry II of England, could only postpone and not halt the day when all of the Levant as well as Anatolia would pass into Islamic hands. Finally, in May 1453, the greatest prize of all, Constantinople itself, fell to the Ottoman Turks. The great cathedral of Hagia Sophia was turned into a mosque, its murals and mosaics being covered over with plaster so that Moslem eyes should not be offended by such open displays of iconography. Thus it would stay for nearly five centuries until it was turned into a museum in 1934.

Yet, the Crusader movement had more important and long lasting effects than the retention of a relatively small parcel of land in the Levant. Crucially it opened the door to the East enabling a flood of ideas to reach parts of Western Europe, then ready and waiting to be enlightened. Directly or indirectly the key people involved in this process were the Knights Templars. Though Hugues de Payen, the leader of the first nine knights, was a relatively poor individual, they were under the powerful patronage of other more important figures. The first of these was St Bernard, who as the leading light of the Cistercian Order to which they were affiliated, wrote out their ordinances and devised the oath they had to take on joining. How far he was involved in the later development of the Order is hard to say. Certainly his intolerance of the Cathars of southern France, who were brutally suppressed in later Crusades and inquisitions, makes it unlikely that he would have been very welcoming to the importation into France of 'heretical' ideas from the East. However, the charter of the Templars set them up as an independent Order outside of all jurisdiction, religious or civil, save that of the Pope himself. They seem therefore to have had a fairly free hand to do just what they liked and though Bernard probably had a great deal of influence with them until his death in 1153, he was probably kept in the dark about their most esoteric interests.

The man who probably had the greatest sway over the Order, at least in its early days, was the liège lord of Hugues de Payen, Count Hugues of Champagne. He was one of the great barons of France and it was he who had donated the land on which Bernard's Abbey of Clairvaux was built. In 1125, he gave up his lands and family to become a Templar himself, as had always been his intention. Having no heir, the County of Champagne passed to his suzerain, Theobald II Count of Blois. This lord's eldest son, Henry, had accompanied King Louis VII on the Second Crusade. He must have made a good impression because he not only inherited the County of Champagne in 1152 but, in 1164, married Marie, the king's daughter by his first wife, Queen Eleanor of Aquitaine. He was succeeded in 1181 by his eldest son Henry II, who, in 1190, also went off to the Holy Land. Two years later he married the widow Queen Isabelle, the grand-daughter of Fulk and Melisende. Thus within two generations the lords of Champagne were now not only grafted onto the Royal House of France, but occupied the throne of Jerusalem itself. The Templar movement, which owed its origins to the court of Champagne, could now hardly be more closely linked with the seats of power in France and the East.

Troyes, the principal city in the County of Champagne, was home to a major centre of esoteric studies as early as 1070. Its most famous son, Chrétien de Troyes, wrote *Le Conte du Graal*, the first French Grail story, shortly after Henry I went off on Crusade in 1178. Chrétien, though his story remained unfinished, seems to have been in the know about certain highly esoteric matters concerning this mysterious object. The story of the Grail was taken up by other writers, notably Wolfram von Eschenbach. In his work, *Parzifal*, the connection between the Grail Quest and the Knights Templars is made crystal clear. He even claims to have first heard the story from a Templar named Kyot (probably Gyot de Provence, a well-known Troubadour, monk, poet and apologist for the Templars). From all this it seems very likely that following the disaster of the Second Crusade, something known as the 'Grail', in my opinion probably the Mandylion of Edessa, had been brought to Champagne for safe keeping. This, however, was really only a symbol for something much more important that was going on, the transference of knowledge from East to West.

## Temples of the Virgin

Accompanying King Louis and Queen Eleanor on their Crusade in 1147 was a contingent of Knights Templars. This was very fortunate as it turned out, as without their protection on one particularly hazardous part of the journey, when the rest of the army had dissolved into an undiscplined rabble, the king and queen would undoubtedly have fallen into the hands of the Turks. Around this time and possibly as a result of his close involvement with the Templars, King Louis adopted the *Fleur-de-Lys* as his heraldic device (plate 43). This was probably the symbol of an even more secret Order than the Templars to which they were attached.[1] As the king also went through a character change during the course of his Crusade, becoming ever more religious, it seems likely that his adoption of this special insignia, which quickly became the Royal Coat of Arms of France, is related to his own initiation into this Order.

As we have seen, the lily was a popular symbol not just in Egypt but Byzantium as well. The *Fleur-de-Lys*, which Louis VII adopted as his device some time in 1047 during the Second Crusade derives its name from the Fleur-de-Luce or Iris. It is the European version of the lily or lotus given to Mary by the angel Gabriel. As such it is the same as the sheaf of the Virgo figure and esoterically represents the flower from which the soul of a new king will emerge. Why the *Fleur-de-Lys* should have become so important in France has always been a mystery but further confirmation of its esoteric meaning is provided in a startling book called *The Mysteries of Chartres Cathedral*, which was published as recently as 1966. Its author is named as Louis Charpentier but as the copyright holder is Robert Laffont, this would seem to be a pen-name. Be that as it may, 'Louis the Carpenter's' book betrays knowledge of a living esoteric tradition linking the Templars with the building of the great cathedrals of France. The English translation of the French original carries a foreword by Janette Jackson, who in the sixties and seventies was well-known in Britain as the driving force behind R.I.L.K.O.[2] who published this edition. She writes:

> . . . M. Charpentier opens a fresh vista of possibilities. He says in effect that Chartres and other cathedrals, like the great monuments of Egypt and Greece, were the manifestation of a secret communicated to mankind by occult or mystical means.

What this secret is and how it was communicated is not fully revealed in the book, which was clearly written in such a way that it would provide pointers only and not give away too many secrets. It also tends to tease with wild assertions, broad generalizations and over-simplifications of some pretty complex ideas. Nevertheless, it does contain much that would suggest that Charpentier did not himself discover or invent everything he writes about. He would appear to be 'in the know', to have been instructed in at least some of the ideas he presents. This in turn suggests that he himself was (or is) an initiate of the sort of school which we have been discussing.[3]

In Charpentier's book he claims that the original nine Templar knights were charged by St Bernard with finding and bringing back to France the Ark of the Covenant. This, he suggests, had been buried somewhere on Mount Moriah prior to the destruction of the first temple of Solomon. The case for believing this story is thin indeed. There is no more reason to believe that the physical ark of Moses was brought to France than that it was taken to Ethiopia. However, if we take the ark as a symbol, which of course it is, then it is something more precious than a wooden box containing old tablets of stone: it represents the true *Gnosis* and this indeed was brought to France by the Templars. Evidence for this is provided by Charpentier in what at first appears to be something of an aside to his main theme. He shows how the Notre-Dame cathedrals of northern France were layed out to a definite plan. He argues that the ark itself contained what might be interpreted as building plans for the temple, which, after they were brought to France by the Templars, were then used by mediaeval masons as designs for the construction of such Gothic cathedrals as Chartres.

Prior to 1150 there were, in Europe, only ponderous, Romanesque cathedrals, typified by that at Durham in England. Then, following the Second Crusade an entirely new method of building was developed. This was the 'Gothic', characterized by the use of ribbed vaulting, flying buttresses, large areas of stained glass and, above all, pointed arches. These features, though developed and taken to their extremes in France, did not originate there but rather in the East. The profusion of pointed arches amongst the ruins of the old buildings of Edessa testify to the early 'Gothic' style having been known in this region before 1145 as churches were not built there after this date.

Further confirmation of this is to be seen at Mardin, a city never conquered by the Franks and under Turkish rule throughout the period that Edessa was a Crusader city. Dee and I visited Mardin curious to see what this ancient hill-top city, which had once housed a large Jacobite community, would be like. Walking up the main street we came upon a building that, though it was now a workshop, had obviously once been a church. We were surprised to see that not only did it have a pointed-arch doorway but surrounding this was zigzag tracery of the type we in Britain associate with the Normans. As neither the Normans nor Franks had built this church, this was clear evidence that the style originated not in France but in either Armenia or Northern Mesopotamia. Following this cultural transfer, in less than a century the landscape of Europe was changed as one after another these awe-inspiring structures were built. The great cathedrals of France were the skyscrapers of their day, the tallest edifices to be built anywhere in the known world since the Great Pyramid of Giza.

What was of greatest interest to me in Charpentier's book was not his appreciation of the Gothic, wonderful though it is, but rather his revelation that the Notre-Dame cathedrals of northern France were laid out to a definite plan. Each cathedral: Rouen, Chartres, Laon, Reims and others represents a different star. Taken together these 'stars' make up the main body of the constellation of Virgo.

Fig. 16

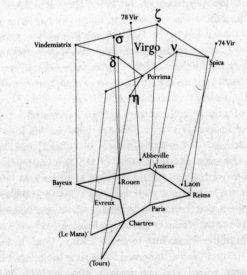

The Northern France cathedrals and the Virgo pattern. (Le Mans and Tours are the only cathedrals pictured that are not dedicated to the Virgin.)

Now though Charpentier doesn't say it, this layout plan (which can easily be checked by anyone with a map of France and a drawing of the constellation of Virgo) expresses in tangible form the Hermetic dictum: 'As Above, So Below'. As stellar correlation was also the quintessential idea behind the building of the Egyptian IVth Dynasty pyramids, this suggests a continuity of tradition. However, whereas in Egypt the execution of the architect's plan involved a relatively small area covering the pyramids fields near Cairo,[4] the Virgo figure of France is enormous.[5]

Clearly, then, the masons who built the cathedrals were highly motivated, inspired by a vision on an awesome scale. They and their benefactors, who must have included the king as well as the Counts of Champagne and Burgundy,[6] were executing a secret plan of the utmost importance. To build just one cathedral would have cost a great deal in terms of time and resources. To raise a dozen would have been not only difficult but required great perseverance and commitment. The question is, why go to all of this effort? What was it really all for?

The answer to these questions is clear when one considers the mood of the times when the cathedrals were built. The failure of the Second Crusade was a stunning blow not just to the Franks but more particularly to the Christians of the East. They now knew that the Kingdom of Jerusalem was not safe and that sooner or later it would, like Edessa before it, fall to the Turks. Some probably regarded this as no bad thing for, after all, there had been several centuries of Moslem rule in the Holy Land before and the Franks were not universally liked. Yet, others, the Armenians in particular, were more apprehensive. Many of these people, among them architects[7] who knew about ribbed vaulting and the use of pointed arches, were on good terms with the Franks. Baldwin I had encouraged inter-marriage between his followers and the local aristocracy of Edessa, and their last Count, Joscelin II, was himself half-Armenian. At least some of the Armenians, and maybe other groups as well, seem to have decided to go back to France with Philip, where they could put their building skills to good use.

It would seem that certain individuals, probably Armenians, who were also linked to the secretive Sarmoung Brotherhood were instructed to take certain of the Franks into their confidence, Louis included. The key to their mission can be discerned when one looks carefully at the map of northern France and compares it with the Virgo figure. It is striking that in the Virgo figure Reims Cathedral represents the star

'Spica', the one that seems to be symbolized both as a sheaf of wheat and a lily flower. Also that owing to its royal connections it was Reims, not Chartres, that during the Middle Ages was the most important cathedral in France; it was the place where for centuries the Kings of France were crowned. Reims, therefore, practically and figuratively represents the place of the *Fleur-de-Lys*. It signifies the Annunciation, the selection of a woman to bear the future Messiah. In a very subtle way the Virgo figure spread over northern France was indicating an expectancy, presumably shared by Louis, that the next Messiah would be French and of royal blood. It was therefore his duty to prepare the way for this advent, which was now no longer expected to occur in Jerusalem but in France. This explains his adoption of the *Fleur-de-Lys*, the symbol of Horus, as a personal insignia.

## City of the Magi

The French were not alone seeking to shift the birthplace of the Messiah from Palestine to Europe. When the Pope called for a Crusade to win back Edessa, little did he realize that his words would find a ready response east as well as west of the Rhine. Until now the Germans had taken little interest in the Crusades, prefering to do their Christian duty in subduing the pagans on their eastern borders. However, this time the Emperor Conrad was determined to take a leading role and was certainly not content to stand by and leave all the glory to Louis. His decision was to have surprising results seventeen years later far away from the Holy Land in the Cathedral City of Cologne on the Rhine.

The cathedral of Cologne is one of the Gothic masterpieces of Europe though, like the German state which it in many ways symbolizes, it was not completed until the end of the nineteenth century. The Roman city, which was founded in this far flung corner of the Empire by the Emperor Claudius at the request of his wife Agrippina, was originally called *Colonia Agrippinensis*. Christianity had probably come to Cologne quite early on and by 313 AD, following Constantine's proclamation at Milan giving freedom of worship to all Christians, it was sufficiently well established to allow the local bishop, Maternus, to build a large church complex on a hill overlooking the town. This site on which the later cathedral itself would eventually stand had previously been occupied by a small temple dedicated to Mercurius Augustus. In about 330 AD, only five years after the Council of Nicaea, disaster struck and Cologne was taken for the first time by the Franks. They did not immediately occupy the city but, in 475, it became the chief residence of King Childeric, the Franks having, in the meantime, been converted to Christianity. Over the next few centuries the church was repeatedly rebuilt. It grew in size and importance, reflecting the changing fortunes of both the city and the Frankish kingdom, which by now embraced not only France but also Germany and northern Italy.

On 23 December 800, in one of the great moments of European history, Charlemagne, king of the Franks, had himself crowned by the Pope as Emperor of the West. He moved his capital to Aachen (Aix-la-Chapelle) but the archbishop of Cologne continued to be the most senior prelate in Germany, ministering over a large See that stretched from southern Belgium to Bremen. Whilst Charlemagne lived, Aachen was the glittering capital of a renascent and reunited Western Europe. He sent envoys to Constantinople and the cathedral of Cologne continued to grow throughout this Frankish period, reflecting this increasing power. The most decisive event, however, that turned it into a major centre of pilgrimage was to occur some three and a half centuries later, during the reign of Emperor Frederick Barbarosa and it was directly connected to the story of the Nativity.

Frederick 'Redbeard', ruler of the Holy Roman Empire, was, in his day, the most powerful man in Europe. He was the son of Frederick II, Duke of Suebia (a province in the south-west corner of Germany) and Judith, daughter of Henry IX, Duke of Bavaria. Inheriting his father's title whilst still only a young man of twenty-four, he immediately went on the Second Crusade at the side of his uncle the Emperor Conrad.

Like the French, the German contingent set out in high hopes but it also was badly organized and doomed to failure. Frederick, however, profited from the experience and accounted himself well on the field. He proved that he was a capable leader of men and his uncle took a liking to him, recommending that he and not his own son should be elected to inherit the title of Emperor after his own death. This indeed happened and, on 9 March 1152, Frederick was crowned Holy Roman Emperor at Aachen. He soon began a series of campaigns in Italy to re-establish Imperial authority, which inevitably and, on more than one occassion, brought him into conflict with the papacy. In 1158, during his second Italian campaign, Milan was brought back under Imperial control.

In 1163, following a setback in his campaigns to take Sicily, then an independent Norman state, Henry turned his attentions back home to Germany. Accordingly, he robbed Milan of one of its most important collections of relics: the bones of the Magi. These were brought back to Cologne in 1164 at the behest of the Archbishop Reinald von Dassel. It was then decided to build a new shrine to house these important bones (plate 3). However, it was not until 1247 that the cathedral itself was rebuilt in the Gothic style. Work was begun in 1248 even before a fire conveniently destroyed the old church. The new building was to be in the flamboyant style and right from the start it was visualized that the new cathedral should be on a grand scale. The project, however, was plagued with delays and it was not until 15 October 1880 that the last stone, on the finial of the South Tower was laid in the presence of Kaiser Wilhelm I.

Frederick Barbarosa could not have foreseen all these consequences of his translation of the presumed relics of the Magi to Cologne but they were clearly of the highest significance to him. The failure of the Second Crusade had made all too clear the weakness of the Frankish states in Outremer. Coupled to this was a growing sense of nationhood in Europe and a desire to develop sites of pilgrimage closer to home. By turning Cologne itself into a shrine, Frederick was effectively bringing Bethlehem to Germany. Now German, French, Dutch and even English pilgrims no longer needed to make the arduous and perilous journey to Bethlehem to feel part of the Christmas story, they only needed to visit Cologne. In doing so, they brought extra wealth, trade and status to what was already a major commercial centre.

Yet was this all? Nobody today would seriously entertain the idea that the relics sent back to Cologne by Frederick really were those of the 'first Christians', the mysterious Magi who visited the stable in Bethlehem. The Middle Ages was a time of great faith and most churches had relics of some saint or other in their possession but this really was beyond belief. Frederick was no fool and he was not afraid to challenge the authority of even the Pope when it suited him. He would not easily have been taken in by claims of fake authenticity for these rather suspect relics. Yet, somehow they appealed to him. One reason for this and indeed for the great popularity of the Magi story with other mediaeval kings was that they in some way symbolized the ideals of the Crusade. For just as the foreign kings, Melchior, Caspar and Balthasar had made their way as pilgrims to worship at the feet of the newborn Jesus in defiance of the local king Herod, so

Crusading knights had brought Bethlehem back into the Christian fold. By this reasoning the Magi were the natural patrons of the Crusades and deserved as much if not more respect than later saints.

Whatever the truth behind the relics, the mediaeval ideal of three kings presenting themselves at Bethlehem very nearly did come true for Frederick. Once more disaster had struck in the East, this time threatening the whole future existence of Outremer. Always short of men and reliant on the disunity of the Moslem world, it had been all but overrun by the forces of its most deadly enemy, Saladin. In July 1187, a Christian army, the largest army ever put on the field by the little Kingdom, marched to relieve Tiberias, which was then under siege. It was a fatal error. On their way through the Galilean Hills, tired and suffering from severe thirst, they were ambushed at the Horns of Hattin. The Christian forces were annihilated and, as a consequence, Saladin was easily able to take Jerusalem as well as nearly all the other walled towns and castles in the kingdom, which had no alternative but to surrender. The Pope, Gregory VIII, preached a new Crusade to retake what had been lost and in 1190 Richard I, 'the Lionheart' King of England and Philip, King of France set out on Crusade. They were preceded by Frederick, now an old man, who was eager to take up once more the challenge of the cross. The reconquest of Palestine was not to be part of his destiny for he died in a swimming accident before his army reached Antioch. Without his strong hand, discipline and order amongst the German contingent, which up till that time had been exemplary, broke down. Had he lived, it is quite probable that the united forces of Germany, France and England would have been enough to retake Jerusalem. He, Richard and Philip would, like the three kings of old, have been able to visit the manger in Bethlehem and prostrate themselves before the crib. As it was the Crusading forces were only able to regain part of the old kingdom. Jerusalem and Bethlehem were to remain outside of the ambit of the little state which now had its capital at Acre. In time this too would be lost as would all the Frankish possessions in the Near East.

## The Prayer of Richard II

By the time Richard II came onto the throne of England in 1377 as a boy of only ten years of age, much had changed. By now the great cathedrals of northern France were more or less complete but two great tragedies, one environmental and the other political, had served to debase what should have been a golden age of French culture. The first of these was the Black Death which between 1348 and 1349 swept away up to a third of the population of Europe. The second needless tragedy was the Hundred Years' War between England and France. This, even though it involved Welsh archers and English yeomen, was really a struggle between rival French dynasties. The cause of this titanic struggle for possession of one of the richest countries in Europe was the divorce of Eleanor of Aquitaine by Louis VII following the Second Crusade and her subsequent marriage to Henry II of England. As her dowry she brought with her the valuable land of Aquitaine which was added to other French lands owned by the House of Anjou, i.e. the Plantagenets. English crown lands in France were now considerable and, within time, friction developed between the Angevins and the ruling House of Valois as to who had rightful claim over the French throne. Edward III, Richard's grandfather, invaded France and won a series of battles including Crécy in 1346. Ten years later, Edward the Black Prince defeated and captured King John of France along with his young son the Dauphin at the Battle of Poitiers. Neither battle, however, resolved the underlying conflict. How could an increasingly Anglicized House of Anjou lay claim to the throne of France? Alternatively, how could the King of France expect the King of England, as Count of Anjou, to do fealty to him as though he were merely a subject?

The crisis was still unresolved in 1377 when Richard, who was the son of the Black Prince, took his throne. Well he may have prayed to the Virgin Mary for guidance as this conflict between related Royal Houses had already poisoned relationships between the two countries for more than a generation. His marriage to Anne of Bohemia, the daughter of the German Emperor seemed to symbolize a new hope and possibility. He was himself descended through the Black Prince from Philip le Bel of France as well as Edward I of England and many other illustrious lines of kings. Now, by his union with the Holy Roman Empire, it was no doubt hoped to bring about a rebirth of Christendom.

In a startling and tangible way, this seems to have been alluded to in the famous Wilton Diptych (plate 5). Richard attended by 'Magi' Kings and John the Baptist prays to the Virgin. But there is more than one hidden meaning here. His outstretched hands invite her to pass to him the infant Jesus, whose little foot she profers. As a wearer of the *Fleur-de-Lys* as part of his insignia it is more than likely that he knew of the secret behind the building of the French cathedrals and the significance of Reims. But in his altar piece he seems to be inviting the Messiah to be his very own son. It was not to be; the history of crime saw to that. But how different the history of the Middle Ages might have been if he had been right. We might have had a Messiah king sitting on the lion throne of England, wearing the *Fleur-de-Lys* of France and crowned at Reims. We might also have avoided centuries more of warfare and seen an even greater Renaissance in Europe.

## The Masters of Wisdom

My quest for the Magi was now coming to a close. It was clear to me now that the birth of Jesus probably took place in the summer, on a date that corresponded with the heliacal rising of Sirius, the Dog Star. On that day, 29 July 7 BC, his birth would have fulfilled the prophecies of not just the Jews but of the Egyptian and Chaldaean astrologers as well. A deputation of Magi (perhaps more than one) made its way from the region of Northern Mesopotamia to seek out the place where the expected birth of a king had taken place. The people sent on this mission would have been members of a brotherhood, known as the 'Bees' or Sarman, of which Antiochus Epiphanes of Commagene had been a leading light some thirty years earlier. They were well aware of the danger posed by the paranoid, megalomaniac Herod, who thirty years before had aided Mark Anthony in his siege of Samosata. Accordingly, they were willing to do everything they could both to help Jesus and to keep the location of the stable in Bethlehem a secret. The Bible says that the visitors returned to their own country by a different route and it is possible they made a detour to Egypt first before going back home. It is not at all unlikely that in ordinary life the Magi were merchants and therefore travelled regularly to Egypt on business. There, in anticipation of the flight of Mary, Joseph and Jesus, they could have helped in the arrangements for provision of a safe house. In any event there is a strong tradition that the infant was brought by his parents to Heliopolis, the original centre of the ancient Egyptian religion. Like the expected phoenix returning to inaugurate a new age, he came to the city of the Sun.

Whilst we know nothing of Jesus' life between the ages of twelve and the start of his public ministry at the age of thirty, he does appear to have been a highly precocious boy. We are told in the Gospels that at a very early age he was able to enter into learned debate with the elders of the Temple, which he refers to as his 'Father's House'. There are other legends that as a young man he visited Persia and India as well as Egypt and there is even a persistent myth that he came to Britain as well in the company of his maternal uncle, Joseph of Arimathea. We cannot dismiss these legends out of hand. Given his inquiring nature, it is not at all unlikely that he, like Pythagoras centuries earlier, would have sought out all the wise men he could find — not just from his own country and religion, but throughout the Middle East and beyond. The unorthodox nature of his ministry and his abilities as both a healer and teacher indicate that, like Moses, he was initiated into the very highest levels of the Mysteries before beginning his work. The knowledge or *Gnosis* in which he would have been instructed by the Masters of Wisdom would have included astrology of the sort discussed in this book.

According to the Hermetic teachings, human souls are high entities that long ago became enraptured of the earth and, like flies in a cobweb, entangled in its evolutionary spirals. All this is put very beautifully in the first dialogue of the *Corpus Hermeticum*, the *Poimandres*:

But Mind the Father of all, he who is Life and Light, gave birth to Man, a Being like to Himself. And He took delight in Man, as being His own offspring; for Man was very goodly to look on, bearing the likeness of his Father. With good reason then did God take delight in Man; for it was God's own form that God took delight in. And God delivered over to Man all things that had been made.

And Man took station in the Maker's sphere, and observed the things made by his brother,[8] who was set over the region of fire; and having observed the Maker's creation in the region of fire, he willed to make things for his own part also; and his Father gave permission, having in himself all the workings of the Administrators (i.e. planets); and the Administrators took delight in him, and each of them gave him a share of his own nature.

And having learnt to know the being of the Administrators, and received a share of their nature, he willed to break through the bounding circle of their orbits; and he looked down through the structure of the heavens, having broken through the sphere and showed to downward-tending Nature the beautiful form of God.

And Nature, seeing the beauty of the form of God, smiled with insatiate love of Man, showing the reflection of that most beautiful form in the water, and its shadow on the earth. And he, seeing this form, a form like to his own, in earth and water, loved it, and willed to dwell there. And the deed followed close on the design; and he took up his abode in matter devoid of reason. And Nature, when she had got him with whom she was in love, wrapped him in her clasp, and they were mingled in one; for they were in love with one another.

And that is why Man, unlike all other living creatures upon earth, is twofold. He is mortal by reason of his body; he is immortal by reason of the Man of eternal substance. He is immortal, and has all things in his power; yet he suffers the lot of a mortal, being subject to Fate. He is exalted above the structure of the heavens; yet he is born a slave of Fate.[9]

The entrapment of mankind in the coils of nature is the Hermetic equivalent of the Adam and Eve story of the Bible. By this reading, the deadly 'fruit' of the Tree of Knowledge of good and evil is the planet earth itself. By eating of the 'forbidden fruit', i.e. entering into incarnated form, man became enmeshed in life at the planetary level and therefore subject to death. According to the Hermetic doctrine, very few souls are able of themselves to escape from the tentacles of earth's embrace. The rest, those who are not saints, go through life after life, death after death in an endless chain of rebirths. According to this teaching we need help 'from Above' if we are ever to get free from this solar system.

In his book *Deeper Man*, J.G. Bennett indicates that for souls with a high destiny, i.e. those who can provide this sort of help, special conditions are provided for their birth.[10] We see this in our own day with the intense care taken over the upbringing of a Dalai Lama, emissaries being sent out to find the child believed to be the new incarnation. A similar process seems to have been at work with the mission of the Magi. The evidence suggests that they came from the same school that centuries later made contact with Gurdjieff. If this is so, then we can expect that they would have preserved the memory of such an important event. Gurdjieff tells us that the way this was normally done was through what he calls a 'legominism', i.e. a symbol that somehow encapsulates the meaning of what it is that is to be conveyed to the future. Examples of architectural 'legominisms' are the pyramids of Egypt, the hierothesion of Antiochus and the shrine at Arsemia. Bennett recounts that Gurdjieff told him something about this process:

> He [Gurdjieff] said that from time to time from another world — 'from Above' — a Sacred Individual is incarnated in human form with a very high and special mission, the working of which is not visible in this world and which can only be perceived by the disciples or companions who are specially prepared. This mission is not performed in this world except in so far as the being who is engaged in it is incarnated in human form. A certain possibility is introduced from a realm where the impossible doesn't exist. It is something new which doesn't belong to the cause and effect of this world, and therefore changes the entire situation. The doing of this and how it is done is unseen; but, in general, it is then necessary that something should be seen, manifested, so that the particular new thing should be able to operate in the visible world amongst people with ordinary perceptions. It is to fulfil that second part of the mission that the sacred image is created and this sacred image has unlimited power in it, because its source is beyond the existing world. That sacred image we see as the founder of a religion, as a prophet or as an incarnation of God, who introduces a new hope into the life of man.[11]

The way that Christ's birth date was recorded is contained in the story of the Magi and, more especially, the Nativity Icon that has traditionally been used to illustrate the event. The power of this 'sacred image' of the Incarnation is extraordinary. It is depicted in countless paintings, sculptures and even Christmas cards. It is also re-enacted, in tableau form every time a school puts on a nativity play.[12] Always in essence the scene is the same: Mary, Joseph, the baby Jesus in the crib and attending them the shepherds and wise men. Above the stable in which they are all housed stands the star of Bethlehem. This is a five-pointed, Egyptian star[13] and not the six-pointed star of David, which really represents the Sun. However, as the 'star' guiding the Magi was in fact two planets, namely Jupiter and Saturn in close conjunction, so perhaps it would be better represented with a ten-pointed star.

Yet, hidden from view and unknown to pious Christians is the

secret meaning of the image. It is a 'legominism', and wearing the
guise of 'shepherds', 'kings' and even the Holy Family itself is Jesus'
horoscope. When its true astral symbolism is understood, it reveals the
child Messiah to be not simply a prophet of Israel but a true pharaoh or
Horus king.[14] The pharaohs of Egypt had a number of titles including
'beekeeper', which perhaps originally indicated his role as head of
the 'bees', who gather the nectar of wisdom. Their most important
title was 'Son of the Sun'. As we have seen the official birthday of
a Horus king occured on the date of the heliacal rising of Sirius and
the concurrent conjunction of the sun with Regulus. The divine nature
of such a royal birth was symbolized in ancient Egypt by the Sphinx, a
man-headed lion.[15]

The Kings of Egypt were also closely associated with the symbol of
the hawk. The hawk in Egyptian iconography is emblematic of Horus
in both his macrocosmic and microcosmic forms. Just as a hawk hovers
in the air above observing all that goes on below, so Horus the elder, the
original sky god of Egypt, flutters above our world seeing everything that
happens on earth. He symbolizes the Solar Logos or divine utterance of
the Solar Father. Within the world of our local 'universe', the sun is the
seat of creative power. As an entity or 'cosmos' in its own righ:, the
sun itself brings into being its family of planets, the solar system. The
manifestation of the sun's will, i.e. the Solar Logos, was worshipped
in Egypt as Ra-Harakte – Ra (the Sun-god) in his hawk form. As such
he is seen sculpted on the top of the XIIth Dynasty obelisk of Senusert
III at Heliopolis.

The conjunction of the hawk-headed Sun-god, Ra-Harakte, at dawn
with Regulus, the Lion star *par excellence* symbolizes the birth of 'Horus
the Younger' or 'Horus son of Isis'. He is the microcosmic Horus, the
prophet who is the Solar Logos made man. This Horus is the Sphinx
or Sphincter, the inscrutable guardian of the gateway of heaven who
prevents entry to the uninitiated. The pharaohs of Egypt were believed
to be such divine incarnations and this is represented on the wonderful
statue of Khafra, builder of the central pyramid of Giza, where the
king is shown seated with a falcon (Horus) sitting on his shoulders and
embracing the back of his head with its wings.

This in essence, I believe, is the great *Gnosis* which was taught to the
initiates of the temples of Egypt, centuries before the birth of Christ. It
is this Egyptian teaching, concerning the manifestation of the principle
of the Solar Logos coming into human form, that both attracted early

Christian philosophers, anxious to find links between the older traditions and the new religion, and scandalized their later descendants. The latter stigmatized the older revelation of the Osiris religion as the work of the Devil. Similarities between Christian and Egyptian rites and teachings were ascribed to the Devil's having 'plagiarized by anticipation' the sacred teachings and sacraments of the Church. Yet the fact remains that, historically, if any plagiarization took place it was the other way round. However, this I believe was not merely because Christianity, as it became a largely Gentile religion, took on the attributes of the religions it sought to replace but rather because Jesus Christ himself was an initiate in the tradition of the Mysteries.

Knowledge of Christianity's close links with the non-Jewish religions of the region were all but stamped out in Egypt during the persecutions of the pagans that took place in AD 390 when the last temples were closed, however the 'heresy' of Gnosticism continued to flourish further east amongst such groups as the 'Persian' Nestorians. The expulsion of the 'School of the Persians' from Edessa to Nisibis in AD 489 removed from the territory of the Roman Empire the last visible proponents of such ideas. Thereafter religious orthodoxy became the overwhelmingly dominant force throughout the Empire and people with Gnostic ideas had to keep these a closely guarded secret if they wanted to avoid persecution for heresy. Yet, in spite of persecution an undercurrent of ideas, long dead in the west, which connected the work of Jesus Christ with both the Hermetic tradition of Egypt and the Zoroastrian revelation of Persia, continued to survive. It would seem that some time in the twelfth century a decision was made at the highest level of a secret organization, which we may infer was an earlier incarnation of the Sarmoung Brotherhood later contacted by Gurdjieff, to transfer some of their knowledge to the West. This knowledge, which we may infer was given, at least in part, to the Knights of St John concerned the important role of their patron saint.

It was understood in the ancient world that the Egyptian pharaohs somehow embodied the Solar Logos, that is to say the intelligence of the Sun. As such the pharaoh or king was a living 'god' whose responsibility it was to uphold civilization on earth. With the conquest of Egypt, first by Julius Caesar and then by his nephew Augustus, this idea passed to Rome. The Caesars regarded themselves as the successors of the pharaohs, they were the new line of 'Horus kings' with the rights and responsibilities of gods. Under the preferred symbol of the eagle[16] rather than the hawk, they claimed to be the mouthpieces of the Solar Logos and created a new solar empire in its name. The Roman Empire was brutal and harsh in the extreme and in the Book of Revelation it is given the number of the beast, 666. This represents the rule of the Sun, whose number 6, is here made 'thrice-great' as ruler over body, mind and spirit.

Little wonder then that the Pope and other Church Fathers of the fourth century were appalled at the idea of Jesus being portrayed as a sort of quasi-pharaoh simply because of his birthday. However, what the West seemed not to understand was that the Christian mystery went even further than the Egyptian one. At the time of the pyramids and even later it was believed and accepted that the pharaoh, as the latest incarnation of Horus the Younger, was the 'carrier' of the Solar Logos. He was the embodiment of the intelligence of the solar system. This was the source of his power or charisma, which in Hebrew is called Baruch, in Arabic Baraka and in Persian Hvareno. The insignia of the pharaoh were the crook and flail – the first showing that he was the good shepherd to his flock, the second that he was a scourge to his enemies. Jesus, in his ministry, discarded the flail and taught the message that one must love one's enemies. He did this because, owing to what happened at his baptism, his claimed authority was even higher than that of the Solar Logos.

The special role of John the Baptist is that on the one hand he, as the last in the line of Old Testament prophets, represents the Elijah tradition. He also, as an Orion figure symbolizes the starry heaven beyond the solar system, a place beyond the reach of the Solar Logos to which the pharaohs dreamed of going after death. His baptism of Jesus therefore represents the very pinnacle of initiation into the mysteries beyond which, it seems, no one had yet gone. However, for Jesus this is just the beginning. Matthew writes:

Then Jesus came from Galilee to the Jordan to John, to be baptised by him. John would have prevented him, saying, 'I need to be baptised by you, and do you come to me?' But Jesus answered him, 'Let it be so now; for thus it is fitting for us to fulfil all righteousness'. Then he consented.

And when Jesus was baptised, he went up immediately from the water, and behold the heavens were opened and he saw the Spirit of God descending like a dove, and alighting on him; and lo a voice from heaven, saying, 'This is my beloved Son, with whom I am well pleased'.[17]

The Spirit of God, symbolized by a dove, is the Primary Logos and stands above sun and stars. It is pure and unconditioned love and as such lies beyond all created worlds. The event in the Jordan, Jesus' second birth by the Holy Spirit, is understood as being an entirely new beginning. If he was born in the stable with the rights and privileges of a pharaoh, he now transcended his fate by fulfilling a greater destiny embraced not by the falcon but the dove.

This seems to be the meaning behind the baptism story, which happens in Matthew's Gospel immediately prior to his ministry. It was better remembered in Syria where for centuries relics of St John were kept and venerated. Today these, or what purports to be them, can still be seen in the Topkapi Museum of Istanbul (plate 34). There, in, a jewelled reliquary is a fragment of the saint's skull, presumably retrieved from Herodias and Salome. More important because of its symbolism as the hand which poured the water over Christ's head and thereby began his mission, are the bones of his right hand and arm preserved in a golden, arm-shaped container. Whether King Richard II, who regarded John as his own patron, really understood these matters is open to conjecture. It is tempting to think that he did and that it is for this reason that the Wilton Diptych has such force and power even today. It is a reminder if ever we need one that the real Christmas is not 25 December or even 23 August[18] but 6 January, the feast we associate with the coming of the Magi but is really the Baptism of Christ.

# EPILOGUE

✳

In March 1996, Dee and I went back to France to look for evidence on the ground that esoteric knowledge concerning the Magi tradition had indeed been transferred from the East to France in the Middle Ages. Our first port of call was Reims, the Champagne capital, whose cathedral represents the star Spica in the Virgo pattern described by Charpentier. We had timed our visit to coincide with the start of spring and, in fact, arrived on the eve of the 25 March, the feast of the Annunciation of the angel Gabriel to the Virgin Mary. This seemed appropriate given the Virgo connection but it was, nevertheless, unseasonably cold and we had to wrap up well.

Though heavily reconstructed after the pounding it took in the First World War, Reims turned out to be still a venerable and interesting city. It was at one time the spiritual heart of France and it was here that on Christmas Day c.498 Clovis, the first Christian king of the Franks, was baptized by the local bishop, St Remi. By so doing, Remi laid the foundations for the future kingdom of France as well as ensuring the survival of the Catholic Church following the collapse of the Western Roman Empire. In 816, Louis the Pious,[1] grandson of Pippin the Short and son of Charlemagne, came onto the throne. Though his illustrious forbears had already displaced the older, Merovingian Dynasty, Charlemagne having in 800 been crowned as Emperor by the Pope himself, Louis made a conscious link between his dynasty and that of Clovis by being crowned at Reims. Thereafter, nearly all French kings followed his example and were similarly crowned at Reims, possibly the most famous coronation being that of Charles

VII who, rather unwillingly, was led to his destiny by Joan of Arc in 1429.

The cult of royalty surrounding Reims and the right of its archbishops to act as officiants at coronation ceremonies was further supported by a legend that a Holy Ampulla containing sacred oil had been brought down from heaven by a dove and given to St Remi to be used in the baptism of Clovis. This was kept in Remi's tomb in a separate basilica about a mile away from the cathedral and was brought out with much ceremonial at the start of coronation processions.[2] Reims continued to be the crowning city of France right up until 1825 when Charles X, of the restored House of Bourbon, briefly took his throne. The sumptuous coronation robes worn by himself and his son the Dauphin, as well as other royal paraphernalia, such as the splendid surcoats of his attendants and a number of elaborate tapestries, are the centrepiece of the collection in the museum that now occupies the bishops' palace next door to the great church. These were among the objects that Dee and I had now come to see.

Parking our car in a small square to the north-east, we made our way towards the cathedral which at this distance was only visible through the gaps between buildings. Gradually, as we approached, these glimpses loomed larger and larger till suddenly it was before us in all its majesty. Though by no means the largest of the French cathedrals – that title belongs to Amiens – it is a beautifully proportioned building with what was, before modern warfare and pollution took their toll, probably the finest collection of mediaeval statuary in the world. Fortunately, sympathetic restoration and, where needed, replacement have done much to heal the wounds. Today, phoenix like, the cathedral once more stands proudly like some great ship waiting to be launched free of its supporting buttressing.

Replacing an earlier building destroyed in a fire, the present cathedral was started in 1211 and mostly finished before 1275. Though never fully completed – it has always lacked most of the spires envisioned by its original architects even before it was shelled in 1914 – it remains a Gothic masterpiece. Its greatest glory, however, is still its outside statuary which, in graphic terms, illustrates the central beliefs and traditions of the Catholic Church. Reims Cathedral, it seems, was essentially a shrine of the Virgin and, as such, its art is mainly concerned with the joyous mysteries: the Annunciation, the

Nativity and the Assumption of Mary. Walking round the building it was impossible not to feel something of the joyful side of Christianity. True the sufferings of Christ are depicted in both stone and glass but these dark and often depressing images by no means dominate.

What was also clear and immediately evident even on making a cursory inspection of the statues was the esoteric nature of the iconography involved. We could sense that each and every statue had a purpose even though this was not always immediately obvious. One example of this was the connection between Reims Cathedral and the unseen, angelic world. Standing on the buttresses that support the walls of the building from the outside, was a whole battalion of angels, wings outstretched, singing the praises of the Virgin, mother of God. At the east end of the choir overlooking the whole building from his vantage point on a slender spire was a single, golden angel, holding in his hand a lightning-conducting cross of salvation. Though there was nothing in any of the guidebooks to say who or what this figure represented, I felt sure he was meant to be Gabriel, the angel of the Annunciation.

At a more personal and human level, we were to find that Gabriel is twice represented amongst the statuary that graces the three western doorways. These sculptures are amongst the finest ever produced in the Middle Ages and show traces of Byzantine influences. As P. Demouy, the author of a current guide to Reims Cathedral suggests this could be the result of the Fourth Crusade.

> The most original feature of the statuary is seen in the second school (before 1240) which, after a few test pieces for the northern transept, produced its masterpieces for the front entrance. In particular the Visitation group, in spite of traces of mosan heaviness, seems to descend from Antiquity. The bodies come alive, no longer resting squarely on two feet, the folds move, the faces express an inner life. This can be explained by the presence in the area of Gallo-Roman monuments. The fashion of imitating Antiquity might have come from Greece. In 1204, at the time of the Fourth Crusade, the Crusaders, on Venice's prompting seized the Byzantine Empire. Many lords from Champagne took part in the expedition, following the Villehardouins and the Champlittes who carved out small princedoms for themselves for some time on Greek soil.[3]

The statues of the so-called 'Visitation group' are indeed classical in both attitude and dress giving weight to the contention that the Crusaders, or rather artisans travelling with them, learnt from the Byzantines and initiated a mini-Renaissance in thirteenth century Reims. However, the finest statues of all belong to a later, indigenous school that somehow achieved a synthesis of past and present to produce some of the most subtle and spirited sculptures ever executed. The most famous of these is the so-called 'smiling angel', whose image from the northern-most of the three doorways has, curiously enough, become an icon in the marketing of Reims as a tourist destination (plate 39). Today he is to be seen depicted on everything from postcards to calendars, tea-towels and coffee mugs. That this angel is intended to be Gabriel, and therefore Virgo, is clear from his other statue immediately by the main entrance. Here he is shown, with the same smiling face, in the very act of announcing to Mary the good news of her selection to become the mother of Jesus. Both angels are today empty handed but it is almost certain that at one time they would have been holding either a lily or a herald's baton.

The connection between the cathedral and the *Fleur-de-Lys* of France was made abundantly clear to us from the many representations of that emblem to be seen on and around it. The roof ridges were covered with lines of *Fleur-de-Lys* alternating with what appear to be clover leaves – emblems representative of the Trinity. As the building was left roofless at the end of the First World War, this was clearly modern workmanship but elsewhere there were *Fleur-de-Lys* symbols carved into the stone tracery of the screens around the choir and shown on shields that are original. It seemed appropriate that there were also sprouting irises in the gardens to the side of the cathedral, the living world echoing the artistic (or perhaps it should be the other way round). In any event the proposition that in the mediaeval mind this town and building represented the earthly counterpart of the star Spica in the sky was supported and certainly not disproved by what has survived of its mystical architecture.

Inside, the cathedral turned out to be rather dark and unwelcoming. Walking through the west doorway, an icy blast greeted us as we entered. In fact so much colder was the air inside the building compared with that outside, which was relatively warm, that we could see our breath. Nevertheless, we could but marvel at the beauty and grandeur of the nave, so much larger than we had imagined. True to

the Gothic tradition, which was at its height when the present building
was begun, the columns supporting the roof were narrow and refined.
The great canopy of the roof, so high above our heads, appeared to
be floating on little more than air. The reality was, of course, that
its weight had through the masons' art been transferred to the sturdy
buttresses outside.

Walking up the nave towards the high altar was like entering a
timewarp. All around us were images belonging to another, earlier
period of French history, familiar to us from books yet divorced from
the reality of the modern Republic of France. The cult of royalty,
epitomized by the *Fleur-de-Lys* had once stood at the very centre of
French life and culture. Though similar in essence to our own British
traditions, it had in other ways been unique. One could not help but
feel that something more precious than a single man's life had been
lost with the decapitation of Louis XVIth at the time of the Revolution.
However foolish he may have been, he had been a living link with a
strange and mysterious past that had died or at least gone out of sight
when he was guillotined.

Going back out into the warming sunlight, we made our way round
to the southern aspect of the building, to the courtyard of the Tau
Museum. I was more than ever convinced that the Masters of Wisdom
had planted something here, a message perhaps more relevant to our
own day than in theirs. That the key to this was likely to be astrology
was made evident when Dee suddenly pulled my sleeve and pointed
upwards at a statue on top of the gable of the south transept. It was
a centaur in the act of firing an arrow at the ground below (plate 40).
She was delighted as it was undoubtedly her own birth sign, Sagittarius,
but what he was doing there overlooking a frieze of the Assumption of
the Virgin was not at all clear. As we were later to discover, this was
no accident and in fact, as it turned out, a vital piece of evidence for a
connection between the school of masons who built Reims Cathedral
and the Magi tradition.

## The astrology of Reims Cathedral

One of our principal reasons for coming to Reims in the first place
was to see if the building itself contained any clues to its astrological
significance. One of the most obvious of these would, of course, be
its orientation. Though all old churches were roughly orientated with

their major axis along a roughly east-west line, there is a tradition that in their layout they should face the place of sunrise on the feast of the saint to which they were dedicated. I was therefore keen to check this alignment and to see if the cathedral was indeed orientated towards sunrise on 25 March, the feast of the Annunciation. Using a simple compass, the same one which we had previously taken with us to Commagene, we quickly established that the major axis running down the aisles was directed to a point thirty degrees north of east. This was not what I had expected and would definitely not fit in with the Assumption when the sun would rise more or less due east. What could be the reason for this? A quick check with SKYGLOBE after we returned to England showed, amazingly, that the cathedral was orientated towards the rising position of Regulus as it would have appeared at the time of Christ's Nativity in 7 BC. In other words, the real dedication of the cathedral was the 'Nativity' date, 29 July 7 BC. What then was signified by the Sagittarius figure?

Since the main axis of the church pointed thirty degrees north of east, it was reasonable to suppose that the line running down through the north and south transepts was also displaced by thirty degrees. This meant that the line running under the Sagittarius figure was directed at a point thirty degrees east of south. Once more, using the computer, I was able to establish that on the date when the present cathedral was begun in 1211, it would have lined up with the rising position of the star *Caus Austral* in the tail of Sagittarius. This is a star of magnitude 1.9 and is the brightest in that rather dim constellation. This was clearly no coincidence but what was even more intriguing was that this star rose heliacally with the sun on 6 January, the feast of the Magi.

This date of 6 January was clearly connected with the legend concerning the baptism of Clovis. According to the guidebooks, this took place on Christmas Day AD 598 or 599. However, considering the Sagittarius figure as well as other symbolism involved, it was clear that this must have been 'old' Christmas, i.e. the Epiphany, and not 25 December, for this would have also been the feast of the Baptism of Christ. That the Church should prefer to keep this quiet is not so surprising when it is realized that the symbolism of Clovis's baptism is almost blasphemous in its implications. The Holy Ampulla was supposedly brought down from heaven by a dove. Thus Clovis and all succeeding kings of France were confirmed in their title by a symbol signifying the descent of the higher Logos on Christ when, during his own baptism in the Jordan, The Holy Ghost, in the form of a dove, descended on him and the voice of God announced him to be His beloved son.

The implication was clear and unequivocal: in the eyes of the Church, and certainly of Clovis and his successors, the kings of France ruled by Divine Right. In the complex and deliberate re-enactment at Reims of Jesus' Baptism in the Jordan, St Remi, it would seem, took on the role of John the Baptist. Not surprisingly, the oldest part of the church is a baptistry sited on what were originally the even older Roman baths. These are on the northern side of the church and are currently being excavated. Next to them is the triple portal of the northern entrance, richly endowed with reliefs and statues. As is traditional for this side of a cathedral, these mainly concern the Day of Judgement. Above

Fig. 17

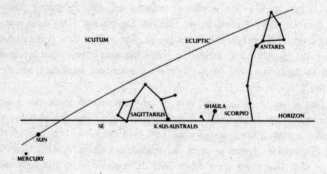

The Sagittarius rising alignment at Reims Cathedral on the Feast of the Baptism of Jesus, 6th January 1211.

the central entranceway was a large relief. In its lower registers was depicted, in graphic detail, the fate of fallen souls. These, mainly wealthy looking personages, were being led off by grotesque looking devils to be thrown into a cauldron. In the upper registers were scenes of resurrection with naked people climbing out of their tombs. Above them and occupying the uppermost portion of the tympanum was the figure of Christ as Judge. This was all a reference to the second to last chapter in the Bible:

> Then I saw a great white throne and him who sat upon it; from his presence earth and sky fled away, and no place was found for them. And I saw the dead, great and small, standing before the throne, and books were opened. Also another book was opened, which is the book of life. And the dead were judged by what is written in the books, by what they had done. And the sea gave up the dead in it, Death and Hades gave up the dead in them, and all were judged by what they had done. Then Death and Hades were thrown into the lake of fire. This is the second death, the lake of fire; and if any one's name was not found written in the book of life, he was thrown into the lake of fire.[4]

This idea of Judgement Day at the end of the age was something I had had much cause to contemplate whilst working on *The Mayan Prophecies*, my previous book which I co-authored with Maurice Cotterell. In that work we elaborated on the Maya belief that the present age would end in the year 2012 and tied this in with Cotterell's ideas concerning sunspot cycles. However, the Christian world also has its beliefs concerning the Millennium and these also seem to be connected with our own time and with the symbols surrounding the Nativity. Could it be that we ourselves will witness the second coming of Jesus, whatever that might mean, as prophecied in the Bible?

## The Second Coming and the prophecy of Nostradamus

It had been nearly twenty five years since John and I had first set out on our pilgrimage to Bethlehem and now, at last, I seemed to be finding answers to at least some of the questions which had so perplexed us then. The greatest question, however, still remained: Are we or are we not living at the end of the Aeon? Can we expect, in our own times, the second coming of Jesus Christ? These are big questions and not to be taken lightly. Yet, we cannot dodge the fact that Robert Bauval's discovery of the connection between the pyramids of Egypt and the constellation of Orion, coupled with the realization that John the Baptist/Elijah is somehow linked to this same group of stars, has provided a key for interpreting certain prophecies. In the last two verses of the Old Testament, it is announced that Elijah is to be sent to prepare the way for the Messiah.

> Behold I will send you Elijah the prophet before the great and terrible day of the Lord comes. And he will turn the hearts of fathers to their children and the hearts of children to their fathers, lest I come and smite the land with a curse.[5]

Whilst one cannot dismiss the possibility that a strange man, dressed only in a camel skin and leather belt will once more start baptizing beside the Jordan, there is an astrological interpretation to the prophecy as well. For the past twelve and a half thousand years, since the end of the last Ice Age, the constellation of Orion has been moving steadily northwards in its precessional cycle. At the time the pyramids were built, some time around 2450 BC, Alnitak, the lowest star of the Belt, aligned once a day with the southern shaft from the King's Chamber of the Great Pyramid. Today it no longer does so as the Belt has 'moved' further north. It has, in fact, reached its most northerly position in the sky, the end of a half precessional cycle. Intriguingly, Mintaka, the northern-most star of the Belt, is now poised within a few minutes of arc below the Celestial Equator, the imaginary circle running through the sky which, like its terrestrial counterpart, separates the northern hemisphere from the southern. Mintaka will never actually cross this line before it once more begins to move back south again. We are therefore living at the end of what we may call an 'Age of Orion'.

The idea that the Ages of Man are linked to the precessional cycle is one that interested Bennett. During my conversation with him I asked him whether he believed we were living at the end of the age and what this might mean for us. At the time I didn't fully understand what he meant but he asserted that this was indeed a time of change, that a process which had been initiated at the end of the last Ice Age, around 10,000 BC was now reaching its completion. He expected that there would be some other great change in the not too distant future.

Fortunately he elaborated these ideas at some length in his last book, *The Masters of Wisdom*, and the matter is well explained:

> Here I must say something about the duration of what I call the 'epochs'. There is a well-known view that associates the cycles of history with the precession of the equinox and divides the great year – or great cycle – of twenty five thousand sidereal years into twelve signs of the zodiac . . . It seems clear to me that there have been great changes in human life at intervals of twelve thousand years – that is roughly half a great cycle – going back to the origin of Adam[6] thirty-seven thousand years ago.[7]

The precession of the equinoxes has other interesting ramifications. Because Orion is now reaching his maximum elevation in the northern sky, his outstretched 'hand' or club has also moved northwards. At the time the Commagene kings were busy building their monuments the sun would pass over and 'shake-hands' with Orion on 26 May. It now does so at the summer solstice on 21 June. Again Orion seems to be pointing towards the ending of a cycle. Could it be that the ancients were so interested in Orion, whether called by that name or some other such as Hercules, Samson, Elijah or Nimrod, because they knew of its time-keeping role, that its movements marked the passage of the ages? If so the 'hand' of the celestial clock now points unshakingly towards twelve. It is noon in the great day of man.

In the Matthew Gospel, Chapter 24 is given over to portents relating to the end of the age. For centuries people have tried to interpret these cryptic writings in which Jesus purportedly tells his disciples what are the signs to look out for that indicate the end is near. A detailed interpretation of these prophecies, which are intricate and require knowledge of the Old Testament as well as the new, would go well beyond the scope of the present book. However, what is of great interest in the present context are certain astrological portents that are evidentally significant:

> . . . For as the lightning comes from the east and shines as far as the west, so will be the coming of the Son of Man. Wherever the body is, there the eagles will be gathered together.
>
> Immediately after the tribulation of those days the sun will be darkened, and the moon will not give its light, and the stars will

fall from heaven, and the powers of the heavens will be shaken; then will appear the sign of the Son of Man in heaven . . .[8]

What 'the sign of the Son of Man in heaven' might be is not at all obvious. Matthew seems to assume that we will recognize it when we see it. However, what is perhaps interesting from the astrological point of view is that on 24 August 1999 the sky will be almost as it was on 29 July 7 BC, the date which seems to be the true Nativity of Jesus. The pattern of the 'three kings', i.e. the planets Jupiter, Saturn and Mercury is not exactly the same, for although Mercury is once again 'kneeling' before the sun conjunct with Regulus, the two giants are not forming a single bright star and they are in Aries rather than Pisces. Also Venus, which was not present in the horoscope of 7 BC is this time over the horizon. These differences notwithstanding, the

Fig. 18

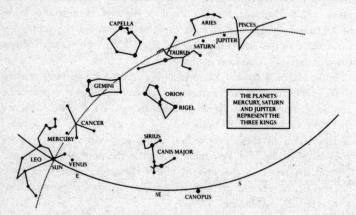

'Return of the Magi' stars, 24th August 1999. The Second Coming?

correlation between the two horoscopes is close. Such an alignment of the planets does not happen all that often and has never occurred before when Orion (symbolic of Elijah the prophet) has been at the top of its cycle, heralding some great event. Could this be the sign we have been told to look out for? We have not long to wait to find out.

Following the rediscovery of the Jesus horoscope, I was anxious to see what this would look like painted in classical manner as an 'Adoration of the Magi' painting. It was one thing to explain in words that the Bethlehem story was 'written in the stars' but quite something else to be able to show people a picture of the event according to the canons of the Hermetic Tradition. To execute the picture in oils I asked a very old friend of mine, Bengt Alfredson, Swedish artist of remarkable talent. He is a self-taught artist of the old school, a sort of modern day Rembrandt, well used to painting imaginative scenes taken from mythology. I knew that he would understand what I was talking about when I said that the stars represented different characters in the Nativity story and that he would be well capable of rendering this into light and colour. The only stipulation I made was that it had to be astronomically accurate and to ensure this I sent him a slide of the night-sky as it would have been at dawn on 29 July 7 BC (plate 37).

On 8 June 1996, after several months of work, Bengt brought over the picture. It was a tense moment for all of us as we unwrapped the protective covering to reveal a work far beyond my wildest imaginings. For not only was it technically accurate but it was beautiful too (plate 36). Here, perhaps for the first time, was a Nativity scene executed according to the Hermetic dictum: 'as above, so below' – the essence of the teaching contained in the Emerald Table of Hermes. This picture is a secret source of inspiration, still able, if we would but listen, to guide us on our way to the Millenium. It may take time but in the hidden history of the world, twenty five years or even a whole lifetime, is but a moment. I feel both privileged and grateful to have been shown at least something of the secret history. For me it is enough to have felt part of that process, if only for an instant. With Bengt's permission we reproduce here his portrait of the 'Adoration' and we leave it to the reader to judge this 'legominism' for our time.

Adrian Geoffrey Gilbert, 25 June 1996.

# APPENDIX 1

※

# The Birth of Horus
# and the Great Sphinx
# of Giza

O ne of the world's unsolved mysteries surrounds the Great
Sphinx of Giza (plate 7). Contemporary Egyptology tells us
that it is a representation of the pharoah Khephren and was
probably carved at the same time that his, the central pyramid of Giza
was built. However, this attribution is not universally accepted and
there is much speculation at the present time as to when this statue
was first sculpted. Amplifying the work of Schwaller de Lubicz on this
matter, the independent Egyptologist, John Anthony West, and his
co-researcher Robert Schoch, a geologist, have put forward evidence
to suggest that the Sphinx is much older than previously thought. By
analysing weathering patterns, both on the body of the Sphinx itself
and the surrounding rock cutting in which it sits, they have concluded
that it must have been carved at a time before Egypt became a desert.
Evidence of water erosion suggests it must date back to at least 8000
or 9000 BC. This redating of the Sphinx is highly controversial and is
not accepted by orthodox Egyptologists who insist that the Sphinx is
no older than the pyramids and would give it a date of c.2500 BC.
What is incontrovertible is that the head of the Sphinx is in the
style of a IVth Dynasty pharaoh. According to West and Schoch
this is probably because, unlike the lion's body on which it sits, it
was recarved during the pyramid age. However, even accepting this,
the question still remains: why?

Like all major religions that of Ancient Egypt was revelatory in its
nature. It was believed that at some time in the distant past civilization
had been brought to the dwellers on the Nile by a family of 'gods'.

These divine personages, led by Isis and Osiris, were the children of the sky goddess, Nut. According to the mythology of the religion, repeated endlessly in mystery plays and most especially in funereal liturgy, Osiris was the first king of a United Egypt. His rule was just and his leadership transformed what had been a barbaric nation into one of the first great civilizations. Unfortunately, his brother, Seth, became jealous and Osiris was murdered. Seth usurped the kingdom and dismembered the body of the dead king scattering the parts along the Nile. The grieving widow, Isis, who was both sister and consort to Osiris, secretly gathered the parts and bound them together to make the first mummy. Using magical rituals and invoking the intercession of the Sun-god Ra, she was able to bring Osiris back to life long enough to take his seed and thereby become pregnant. His earthly duties fulfilled, Osiris returned to the heavenly regions where he became ruler and judge of the dead. Isis, meanwhile, hid herself in the Delta marshes and, in due course, gave birth to a son called Horus. He, when he came of age, challenged his uncle to a dual and, after a very long struggle, succeeded in regaining the kingdom. The young king brought back the rule of Law, symbolized by the goddess *Maat* and brought to an end the anarchy which threatened the kingdom during the period of Seth's rule. The rule of Horus, even more than that of his father Osiris, was the archetype for that of all later pharaohs. They, whilst they were alive, were revered as living incarnations of Horus and after they died, following a series of funeral rituals, they were believed to become one with Osiris.

The legend of Osiris was the foundation for a very sophisticated sky religion. He himself was associated with the constellation of Orion whilst Isis was identified with the 'cow' constellation of Canis Major and more specifically with its brightest star, Sirius. The Hermetic dictum: 'As Above, So Below', governed Egyptian thinking on almost all matters religious and they constantly looked for parallels between life on earth and the movements of the stars in the sky. Details of this sky religion and how it was the motivation behind the building of the Egyptian pyramids need not concern us here as it is thoroughly covered in *The Orion Mystery*. However, what was not discussed in that book was the connection between the stellar religion of Osiris and the sun cult of Ra-Herakte. As this has become something of a stumbling block for many people, it is worthwhile going into this in more detail.

The ancient Egyptians do not seem to have thought of the earth as

a rotating body as we do now and, therefore, looked upon the rising
and setting of the sun, moon and stars as matters of great mystery.
They regarded the eastern sky as the place of birth and the western
one as death. Each day the sun rose at dawn, climbing the sky like a
bird before eventually coming down again to set. The daytime sun was
therefore symbolized as a hawk-god, Ra-Herakte. Unlike most other
peoples in the ancient world, the Egyptian calendar was neither solar
nor lunar but Sothic. For them the most important day in the year
was the heliacal or dawn rising of Sirius and this day, which occurred
in July, marked for them the start of a new year. It is around this time
each year that the River Nile floods its banks, due to the melting of
ice in the mountains above the great lakes which feed it. Thus, for
the Egyptians, the return of Sirius/Isis after her period of invisibility
marked for them a fresh beginning.

Fig. 19

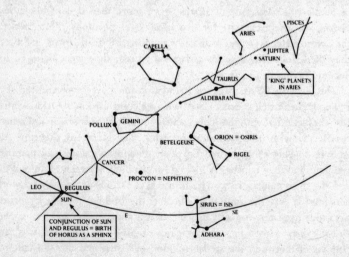

The birth of a 'Horus King' in the pyramid age, 13th July 2450 BC.

However, of equal importance was the rebirth of Horus which also occurred about this time. The conjunction of the sun with Regulus, the brightest star in Leo, symbolized the birth of the king as a 'Son of the Sun'. This is what seems to be symbolized by the Great Sphinx of Giza. Whether or not the head was resculpted, there seems little doubt that this feature of the Sphinx at least is contemporaneous with pyramids. In *The Orion Mystery* Robert Bauval and I put forward a date of *c*.2450 BC for the construction of the Great Pyramid. Robert arrived at this date from a consideration of the astronomical alignment of the so-called 'air-shafts'. It is, therefore, very interesting to note that at dawn on 13 July, the day that the sun was conjunct with Regulus in this year, the planets Jupiter and Saturn were almost conjunct in the constellation of Aries. Though the third 'king', Mercury, was invisible below the horizon, this is uncannily similar to the Bethlehem horoscope. Perhaps this actually was the birth date of a Horus king and the Sphinx was either carved from scratch or resculpted to make a permanent record of this event. In this case, it seems likely that it does indeed represent a IVth Dynasty king, though I would suspect it of being Khufu (Cheops) rather than Khafra (Khephren) as it is the former's pyramid that seems to be the key to all of these mysteries.

# APPENDIX 2

# Orion the Hunter

M iddle Easteners are not the only people to have been fascinated by the stars of Orion and to have associated them with their own mythology. Most cultures and societies, not least those of Europe, have stellar myths at the root of their traditional legends. This influence of astronomy on mythology has been well documented by Professors Giorgio de Santillana and Hertha von Dechend in their classic work *Hamlet's Mill*, which traces myths contained in Shakespeare's play *Hamlet* as far back as the Ice Ages. In doing so they were able to show, in a very convincing manner, that at the root of many ancient myths are astronomical facts and that, indeed, many of the strange details contained in the stories can only be understood when seen in this context. Orion, being such an important and bright constellation, appears, though wearing many disguises, throughout mythology; he is nearly always recognizable once one strips away the layers of cultural overlay.

We can see in the Greek Orion myth rather more than in the Hebrew one a number of Egyptian influences. The story of his blinding by the king of Chios echoes the murder of Osiris by Seth, whilst both Isis and Eos are dawn goddesses and both entreat the Sun-god (Ra/Helios) to bring Osiris/Orion back to full health. Orion's primary task in the Greek myths is to rid the islands of wild animals, which though to modern ears sounds rather anti-ecological, could be interpreted as making the people more secure and therefore helping civilization. Likewise, though not apparently a hunter, Osiris was the god the Egyptians credited with bringing about civilization. There is then the story of Orion's 'accidental' death at the hands of Artemis, who is also a Greek equivalent of Isis. Again it is the brother of Artemis/Isis who engineers the death of Orion/Osiris and, in both cases, after his death, he is placed among the stars as our familiar constellation. The Greek myth does, of course, differ significantly from the Egyptian story of Osiris, not least in its portrayal of Orion as a wild hunter rather than a civilizing god. However, there is another side to the 'hunting' business and the essence of this is if a society is to become civilized, something of its wild nature has to be sacrificed. This was probably originally at the root of the Samson myth too. Having his hair cut could symbolize having his wild nature made more civilized. At the same time, the hunter has to prove himself by his prowess in capturing and slaying wild animals. Orion is a hunter of wild animals and Samson kills a lion with his bare hands. Something of this other animal taming side to the myth seems to have originally been at the back of the Egyptian rituals surrounding the Apis Bull festivities, as indeed it was in the later Greek myths about Theseus and the Minotaur.

These bull cults were once widespread throughout the area of the Mediterranean and Middle East and, certainly in Crete, involved acrobats risking their lives jumping over the horns of charging bulls. In Roman times, the bull cults were given new life with the introduction from Iran of Mithraism. This cult, though clothed in Iranian mythology and vocabulary, is now recognized as being essentially Greek.[2] The most popular icon of the Mithras cult, the so-called *Mithra Tauroctonus* shows the figure of the god in the act of slaying a bull. According to the famous mythographer Joseph Campbell, the original statue of Mithras in the act of killing the bull was probably created by a sculptor of the school of Pergamon towards the close of the third century BC.[3] Hundreds of copies of this statue have been found all over Europe and one example can be seen in the British Museum. The symbolism of the statue is basically astrological. The figure of Mithras, who is thought to have been modelled on the likeness of Alexander the Great, represents Orion, whilst the bull that he slays is our old friend Taurus. Mithras plunges a sword into the heart of the bull and from the wound flow grains of wheat, probably representing the Milky Way. Licking up this 'blood' is a dog which undoubtedly represents Canis Major. Standing behind the bull and in the background are the divine twins, the Gemini, which is indeed the next constellation in the zodiac after Taurus. Below and attacking the bull's testicles is the scorpion, the opposite sign to Taurus and the one 'ruling' this part of the body. We, therefore, see that the whole tableau is astronomical: it represents the constellations seen rising in the east at sunset on the birthday of Mithras, which was 25 December.

The cult of Mithras was very popular amongst the Romans and was the most serious rival to Christianity before the latter was made into the state religion by Constantine. There are, of course, serious differences though, for whilst Christianity teaches that Jesus Christ allowed himself to be sacrificed on the cross for the good of the world, Mithras is a hunter who tracks down and slaughters the bull of heaven so that all life might live. There are obvious philosophical interpretations of the act of slaying the bull and the control of sensual passion but above all Mithras is a breaker of eggs to make omelettes. The wild bull has to die so that civilization can be established, only then can grain be harvested and both man and dog eat. The cult of Mithras was carried throughout Europe by the Roman legions with whom it was particularly popular and Paris became one of its chief centres. It is by no means an accident that the Phrygian cap of Mithras was adopted fourteen centuries after the fall of the Roman Empire by the *sans culottes* of the French revolution. They, like all revolutionaries, looked upon themselves as heroes charged with the task of destroying the old order so that something new could be put in its place. A more obvious survival of the cult of Mithras is the Spanish bullfight. The battle between man and bull appeals to the most primitive instincts but above all celebrates the heroism of the toreador, who acts out the role of Orion the hunter.

The vision of the constellation of Orion as a great hunter in the sky is also common throughout the mythologies of Northern Europe. Though the myth changes and evolves with time and place, certain essential elements remain the same. Orion is a hunter and hero figure and is usually a giant. He is brave, handsome, strong, attractive to women and something of a free spirit. In *Hamlet's Mill*, de Santillana and von Dechend recognize Orion in the Germanic hero Earendel, whose name is also written as Orendel, Oervandill and Aurvandil. He was a huntsman who fought giants and tackled monsters. He also went through various other adventures such as being shipwrecked before winning the hand of Breide, the fairest of women. In one curious story, which is recorded in the *Edda*, Thor narrates that he once carried Oervandill through the ice stream, Eliwagar, in a basket. Unfortunately, one of Oervandill's toes was sticking out of the basket and it got frost-bitten. Thor snapped it off and threw it into the sky where it became a bright star known as 'Oervandill's toe'. Clearly the ice flow of Eliwagar can be interpreted as the Milky Way and the 'toe' star as Sirius, which is indeed not far from the 'foot' of Orion.

The derivation of the name Orendel (in all of its various spellings) seems, according to Santillana and von Dechend to be from the Old Norse 'ör' meaning 'arrow' and a suffix 'endel':

> 'Decisive seems to us the derivation from ör=arrow, suggested by Grimm, and by Uhland, who explained Orendel as the one 'who operates with the arrow' (in contrast to his grandfather, Gerentil, who worked with the *ger*=spear.[4]

In a number of old sources de Santillana and von Dechen found references to the Milky Way as either a trackway or the footprints of some animal or the ski-tracks of the forest man. It seems the hunter is tracking some beast along the Milky Way and at least sometimes this is a deer:

> But whether the figure is the son of God, the forestman, or the Bear, he hunted a stag along the Milky Way, tore it up and scattered its limbs in the sky right and left of the white path, and so Orion and Ursa Major were separated.[5].

In this context Orion is to be seen as an archer, who having stalked his prey the stag (presumably another version of Taurus) along the Milky Way, draws back his bow and makes ready to let free an arrow.

Now Orendel was, of course, known to the Anglo-Saxons in pre-Christian times so it is tempting to see him as the original Herne (or Cerne) the Hunter, the horned god of pagan myth. We can recognize him in the familiar figure of the Dorset Cerne Abbas giant. This, probably Celtic, monument emphasizes the connection between Orion and fertility as it shows the naked giant with an erect phallus. The Herne archetype seems to have infused the myths concerning that other great archer: Robin Hood. The connection here is more straightforwardly Scandinavian as the part of England most associated with his legend (Yorkshire, Nottinghamshire and Lincolnshire) was, at one time, part of the Danelaw and had many Viking settlers. During the Middle Ages hunting was not an idle pastime but necessary for survival.

The imposition by the Normans of new forest laws, which restricted the hunting rights of ordinary yeomen, was bitterly resented by the people. In an area where the Scandinavian legends were still remembered, it is not unlikely that a local champion, such as Robin Hood, should have been confused with the myths surrounding Orendel.

The Robin Hood myth contains all of the familiar themes typical of an Orion story. There is the giant, who in this case is not Robin himself but his companion Little John; the faithful virgin/wife, Maid Marion (Isis/Eos); the wicked King John who seeks his death, (Seth/Oenopion king of Chios) and finally the Abbess of Kirklees, the woman who eventually brings about his death (Artemis/Delilah/Salome). The legend of Robin Hood's death is particularly interesting in the Orion context. He is taken by Little John to Kirklees Priory but, instead of being healed, he is slowly bled to death by the wicked prioress. Though blind through loss of blood, Robin manages, with John's help, to fire off one last arrow to mark his burial spot. The blindness and loss of virility at the hands of a woman need hardly be remarked upon but the arrow seems to be a reference to something else. In *Hamlet's Mill*, de Santillana and von Dechend point out that in many mythologies of the world, Sirius is often the target at which an arrow is aimed. We can therefore interpret Robin Hood's last arrow as representing the departure of his soul, loosed off towards the brightest of stars: Erendil's toe – Sirius.

The myth of Orion, the divine hunter has not entirely died out even in our own times, though it has taken a surprising turn. The ancient Romans had a god called Saturn whom they later identified with the Greek god, Cronos. He was the original Father Time, an 'ancient of days' with a long white beard who carried an hourglass and sickle. Though usually associated with the planet Saturn, whose orbital period of approximately thirty years is the longest of the visible planet, it doesn't take much imagination to see that this figure of time was originally Orion. As we have already seen the constellation rises at sunset on Christmas day, but it is also worth noting that it still rises around dawn during the summer months and when it rises around midnight, it is a sign that it is autumn. Orion still marks out the seasons and gives a sense of time.

Under Christian influences, it seems the cult of Orion has been superseded by a strange myth that combines both the hunter elements and those of Father Time. This is, of course the legend of Father

Christmas or Santa Claus. Stripping aside the Christian veneer of St Nicholas and his supposed generosity, we see the figure of Father Time heralding in the New Year. Father Christmas is, however, also a Scandinavian 'Orion' bringing home food and gifts, (perhaps originally the booty of Viking raids) for his wife and children. However, unlike Robin Hood, he is no longer hunting a stag along the trackway of the Milky Way, rather he has tamed the wild animal and uses its strength to pull his sleigh. Looking up in the sky after sunset on Christmas day, we see him riding over the chimney tops pulled by his favourite reindeer, Rudolph. The latter's 'red-nose' is none other than our old friend the star Aldebaran, the great red giant of the Hyades we call the eye of the Bull.

The rising and setting of the constellation of Orion and its close neighbour Sirius, the brightest star in the sky, seems to be behind many of the world's most persistent myths. The yearning to become one with these stars is expressed most strongly in the Pyramid Texts and seems to be the chief motive behind the building of the pyramids. Yet, others too seem to have a yearning for these particular stars and this is expressed most poignantly in the legend of Robin Hood's last arrow. The story of Orion is in a sense that of Everyman as he seeks to grapple with nature, come to terms with his life on Earth, his blindness to his eventual destiny after death and his yearning for a better world amongst the stars of Heaven. Our Santa Claus is a pale echo of those earlier myths but it does at least indicate that the archetype is still not completely dead in the collective subconscious.

# APPENDIX 3

# Abraham's Journey to the Promised Land

The strongly held beliefs of the people of Northern Mesopotamia that Urfa is to be identified with the Ur mentioned in the Bible caused me to have a fresh look at the early chapters of Genesis. I wanted to know if this was where Abraham had really come from and whether his legendary migration fitted with known history.

Dating anything in the Bible is problematic, not least the Book of Genesis. It is not straightforward history and is written on many levels – part allegoric, part symbolic, part race-memory. Above all, it is a religious document intended to bolster up and fortify the beliefs of a particular people, the Israelites, in their identity as the chosen people of God. As to whether or not there really was an individual family headed by a patriarch called Abraham, who made a journey from Ur to Canaan, is a matter of faith rather than of science. What we can say with some surety is that the people who wrote down this legend probably knew their geography and had some sort of memory, however vague, of real events that had occurred to their ancestors. In the Bible Abraham is a shepherd and herdsman. Taking his flocks, his wife Sarai and other followers, he travels from Ur to Haran and thence to Canaan, the Biblical 'Promised Land'. However, because of famine, for a time he moves on from there to Egypt, where, because he lies about Sarai being his sister and not his wife, she is 'taken into Pharaoh's house'. When the deception was found out, the house of Abraham is sent packing, out of Egypt and back to Canaan.

Now, according to most scholars, the 'Ur of the Chaldees' mentioned in the Bible is to be found in Southern Mesopotamia, 140 miles south of Babylon. This Ur was the capital city of Sumer, the earliest known civilization in the region. Its ruins at Tell el Mukayyar in Iraq were first excavated by Taylor in 1854 but a proper investigation was not made until after the First World War. However, it was not until the mid-1920s, under the directorship of Leonard Woolley, that the most important finds were made. He excavated a great *ziggurrat*, or stepped tower, as well as revisiting the remains at nearby Tell el Obeid of an ancient temple of the Moon-god, Sin, which had first been dug by H.R. Hall in 1919. His findings, now exhibited at the British Museum, turned out to be of extreme antiquity. In April 1925 Woolley was to write in *The Illustrated London News*:

> What makes this temple and everything found in connection with it of quite extraordinary interest is its age. From the foundation tablet we learn that it was built in honour of the goddess Nin-Khursag by A-an-ni-pad-da, who was the second king of the First Dynasty of Ur, a dynasty which, until this material proof of its existence came to light, was commonly regarded as mythical. It is too early to fix the king's actual date, for the Babylonian lists of dynasties are not free from error, and other evidence is yet to seek; but his reign certainly falls within the fourth millennium BC, and the most conservative estimate would assign to our temple an antiquity of some 5,400 years.

Woolley's greatest discoveries, however, were yet to come. In 1928, he published a series of articles relating to finds of important funerary objects, including the intact tomb of a queen and the mass burial of an entire harem of slaves, servants and bodyguards to accompany a dead king on his way to the next world. The tomb of Queen Shub-ad itself contained a magnificent gold head-dress, which is now also on display at the British Museum as well as many other objects made of gold, silver and precious stones. Woolley, perhaps because of its implicit connection with the story of Abraham and Isaac in the Bible, was more than a little intrigued by his discovery of evidence of human sacrifice at Ur and writes:

> No less remarkable than the objects found last winter in the royal graves at Ur was the discovery of the rites of human sacrifice which accompanied the burial of a king. In all the literature of Babylonia

there is no hint of any such custom as having been practised at any time; long before the historic period from which our written records date it had been discontinued and the memory of it either forgotten or carefully concealed by writers grown ashamed of the barbarities of an earlier day. But now we have definite proof that in the Fourth Millennium before Christ the Sumerian king went to his tomb in company with a whole following of soldiers, courtiers and women, who, like the vases of food and drink, the weapons and tools set in his grave, should minister to his needs and pleasures in another world.

At the time Woolley was digging at Ur there was not a little rivalry between archaeologists working in Egypt and Mesopotamia as to who could find the oldest and most extraordinary treasures. It was still only a few years since Howard Carter's discovery of the tomb of Tutankhamun in the Valley of the Kings and finding such important graves at Ur must have come as a great fillip to the pride of all those working in Sumeria. Naturally, Woolley was pleased that his discoveries indicated that Ur had been highly civilized for several hundred years at least before the foundation of the Egyptian Old Kingdom, who built the pyramids. However, were the archaeologists overstating their case in claiming a Biblical connection between this golden city of Ur and the patriarch Abraham?

The academic competiveness between Egyptologists on the one hand and Sumeriologists on the other extended to more than just simply trying to prove that one or the other civilization was of greater or lesser antiquity than the other, it also concerned funding. Major digs often depended upon the support of quite wealthy benefactors, such as Lord Carnarvon in the case of Howard Carter and the discovery of Tutankhamun, but there were other interested groups. Foremost amongst these were societies dedicated to proving the authenticity of the Bible. Under such names as the 'Egypt Exploration Fund' or the 'Palestine Exploration Fund' they provided a lot of the money needed to keep a Woolley or a Petrie active in the field. Naturally, these sponsors expected a pay-off: where possible finds were to be given a Biblical interpretation, to support rather than counter the word of God. Often they were to be disappointed as time and again dirt archaeology produced evidence that was either neutral or antipathetic to Biblical chronology. However at Ur, Hall, Woolley and others were happy to oblige. Tell el Mukayyar became 'Ur of the Chaldees' and it was taken for granted that this must have been the place from which Abraham and his father Terah began their journey to the Land of Canaan. The discovery of important royal graves and the enormous antiquity of the site added to this romantic vision, for it supported the idea that Abraham was not really a rough herdsman leading a tribe of itinerant Bedouin but was a city dweller, maybe even a royal personage, from the regions most ancient capital. The dating of Ur to the Fourth Millennium also fitted with ideas of a seven thousand year 'redemptive cycle' from the time of Abraham to the end of the Millennium. Thus, there would be four thousand years from Abraham to Jesus, a sort of preparatory period; two thousand years of 'latter days' from the time of Jesus to the 'end of days'; and finally the one thousand years of the Millennium that would follow his return around AD 2000. By this reckoning, Abraham had to live around 4000 BC – not long before the date of archaeological Ur. By associating Abraham with this 'Ur of the Chaldees' the archaeologists, or so they thought, were offending no one and bringing a lot of cheer to their Jewish and Christian benefactors. But was this the truth?

In 1953, during his peregrinations in Iraq, Syria and Turkey, J.G. Bennett visited the sites of Woolley's digs. He loved Ur and it is evident from his writings that he regarded Sumeria as the birthplace of civilization.

Conversely, he seems to have had little, if any, interest in Egypt and, indeed, there is no published record of his ever having visited that country. Yet, even he adds a note of caution when extrapolating the evidence from archaeological digs. He records in his diary:

> . . . here I was at the threshold of the Tombs of Ur gazing into the dark cavity from which such treasures had come. My strongest impression was of the gulf that separates us from the remote past. By chance, we find this or that trace of the ancient world. According to what we find we reconstruct by guesswork the conditions of life. I am very sure that if the inscriptions had not been deciphered and if the tombs had not been discovered, no one would have ascribed a high level of culture to these ancient cities.[1]

Abraham's journey makes very little sense if he was a Fourth Millennium city dweller from Southern Iraq. Even supposing that there were some shepherds in the region of Southern Mesopotamia, animal husbandry would not have been the predominant way of farming the land. In the fertile plain of the Lower Tigris-Euphrates it was possible to grow more than one crop a year of wheat and vegetables. To have had large flocks of sheep wandering around grazing these arable lands would have been impractical. This sort of farming is far more appropriate to hilly or mountainous districts where sheep and goats can make use of land that would otherwise be unproductive. Also, for Abraham's father Terah to have taken his family from Tell el Mukayyar to Harran when their real destination was Canaan makes little sense. There would have been quicker ways for them to have travelled from Sumeria to Canaan that would not have necessitated a detour to Harran. However, if Abraham had lived, as is now generally accepted, in the Second rather than the Fourth Millennium BC and come not from Ur in Sumeria but from Urfa (Edessa), then this gives us a historical scenario that makes much more sense and, moreover, fits with Islamic traditions still alive in the region.

Though he wouldn't quite admit as much, Professor Segal hints that this may in fact be what he believed as in a footnote in his *Edessa, 'The Blessed City'*. He quotes a Jacobite Metropolitan, called Michael the Syrian – a friend of Zengi, who conquered Edessa in 1044. Michael apparently says that the name 'Orhay' is derived from 'Ur', meaning 'town', and 'hay' meaning 'of the Chaldaeans', this latter epithet because it was they who populated it. The name *Chaldini* is what the people of Uratu, i.e. the country later called Armenia, called themselves in ancient times. They came from the region of Mount Ararat and, at some time around 1500 BC, migrated into the fertile plains of Northern Mesopotamia. Here they established a powerful kingdom called Mitanni. Orhay was one of their cities and was Chaldaean, unlike Ur in Sumeria, which in its golden age was not.

The Mitanni, who dominated Northern Mesopotamia in the middle of the Second Millennium BC, were part of a larger group of peoples known as the Hurrians, whose position in history is gradually becoming better understood. Around 1670 BC a people known as the Hyksos or 'Shepherd Kings' invaded Egypt. This invasion took place during what is called the Second Intermediate Period. The Hyksos took over the Delta region, their kings becoming the XVth and XVIth Dynasties. There are sculptured friezes of the Hyksos to be seen in the Egyptian Museum at Cairo, which show them with thick beards and Semitic rather than

Egyptian features. This would seem to indicate that their invasion of Egypt was part of the much larger migration of peoples from the regions of Eastern Turkey, around Mount Ararat into the 'cradles' of civilization: Mesopotamia and Egypt. The people who carried out this invasion were warriors from the steppes of Russia that we now call the Hurrians.

Though almost forgotten, the Hurrian invasion of Mesopotamia and Egypt was one of the most significant events in history. They were the first to introduce the sleepy civilizations of the Middle East to the war chariot, an invention they brought with them from the steppes of Russia.[2] With the aid of this new introduction, the Mitanni carved out for themselves an Empire, which though short lived[3] was, nevertheless, significant as the first known Syrian Kingdom. The Hurrians either built or took over a number of important cities in the region including Carchemish, Urfa and Harran. The last of these is mentioned in the Bible as the place where Abra(ha)m's family first settled after leaving Ur of the Chaldees:

> Terah took Abram his son and Lot the son of Haran, his grandson, and Sarai his daughter-in-law, his son Abram's wife, and they went forth together from Ur of the Chaldeans to go to the land of Canaan; but when they came to Haran they settled there. The days of Terah were two hundred and five years; and Terah died in Haran.

Given these circumstances, it is not unreasonable to see that Abraham must have been either a refugee, first driven out from his home of Ur (Urfa) by these insurgents and then again later from neighbouring Harran, or his family were themselves migrating Hurrians. Some evidence for this last assertion seems to be provided further back in Genesis with the earlier account of Noah, whose family make a similar migration from Armenia into Mesopotamia.

## Mesopotamia, place of origins

The civilizations that grew up in the lands watered by the river systems of the Tigris and Euphrates are even older than the Old Kingdom of ancient Egypt. Though in a narrow sense the land of Mesopotamia is the flood plain between the two rivers that was once called Babylonia and is now contained in modern day Iraq, the rivers themselves have their sources quite far to the north of this flat, alluvial plain, in the mountainous plateau of Eastern Turkey. This plateau, dominated by Mount Ararat seems to have been the site of the Biblical Eden.

> A river flowed out of Eden to water the garden, and there it divided and became four rivers. The name of the first is Pishon; it is the one which flows around the whole land of Havillah, where there is gold; and the gold of that land is good; bdellium and onyx stone are there. The name of the second river is Gihon; it is the one which flows around the whole land of Cush. And the name of the third river is Tigris, which flows east of Assyria. And the fourth river is the Euphrates.[4]

The Genesis narrative concerning the four great rivers of Eden has a clearly symbolic meaning related to the idea of the cross, its arms pointing towards the cardinal points of the compass. Nevertheless, it does seem that a definite geographical location was intended for Eden and that the inclusion of the Tigris and Euphrates in the list indicates that the rivers themselves were real and not just abstract ideals. The problem for commentators has always been to identify the first two, Pishon and Gihon. Abandoning all sense of geography, they have felt free to identify them with such diverse river systems as the Nile, the Ganges and even the Yangtse. However, if we accept what the Bible says as being based on some sort of real tradition, then all four rivers must have had their sources fairly close together. Thus, these two, like the Tigris and Euphrates, must have their sources in the Eastern Anatolian Plateau.

In fact, there are two large rivers that have their sources quite close to those of the Tigris and Euphrates in this very region. The first of these is the Arax which rises near Erzerum. This is probably the Biblical Pishon and it flows more or less eastwards to the Caspian Sea. Today, it marks the border between Armenia, Turkey and Iran. The name Pishon means 'free-flowing' and, indeed, this river is a turbulent stream that in winter time is virtually impassable and dangerous to navigate yet, in summer, can easily be forded. The land of Havillah is probably to be identified with Georgia, not far to the north of this river and once the mythical land of Colchis. It was here that Jason and the Argonauts are said to have gone in search of a golden fleece. The other river is called Gihon, which means 'stream'. This is probably the River Halys (Kizil

Irmak), which is the longest river in Asia Minor and is fed by springs on Kizil Dag, not far to the north of the sources of the Euphrates. This river flows westwards before curving to the north and emptying into the Black Sea. The River Halys divides eastern from western Anatolia and once embraced the heart of the ancient Hittite Empire that had its capital at a place called Bogazkoy (Hattusa).

The mountainous area of eastern Anatolia where these four great rivers arise seems to be the mythical Eden. Not far to the east of this 'Eden' is Lake Van, perhaps the original 'garden' and to the north of here, overlooking the valley of the Arax some four thousand metres below, is Mount Ararat where Noah is said to have landed his ark. Whether or not we believe in the story of the flood and the ship-wrecking of Noah's Ark on Mount Ararat, all the evidence points to this region as being the place of origins from which the wider 'family' of Noah fanned out to conquer the known world. One branch or tribe of this group were the Abrahamites. Another, perhaps larger group, were the *Chaldini* (Chaldaeans), who looked upon a mythical ancestor, in the Bible the great-grandson of Noah, called Nimrod as their patriarch.

Taking all these matters into consideration, it seems likely that the tribe of Abraham were indeed Hurrians belonging to a different branch of the family from the Chaldaean Mitanni. The legends still preserved by the people of Urfa to this day of a conflict between Abraham and the local king, whom they identify with the Biblical Nimrod may indeed be based on some real historical event. Furthermore the linguistic similarities between 'Hurrian', Harran (the city), Haran (Abraham's brother), point towards some sort of connection. An impartial observer would be forced to admit that maybe Abraham really was born at Urfa and forced to migrate with his family, first to neighbouring Harran and then onwards to Canaan. Short of finding inscriptions to this effect, we will probably never know the truth for certain. However, this does seem a more likely scenario than the consensus view that he came from Ur in Sumeria. It also goes a long way towards explaining why the region of Northern Mesopotamia should have continued to be an important reservoir of esoteric knowledge, much of it connected with the Bible, right up until our present time.

# APPENDIX 4

# The Ascension of Jesus

S t Matthew's Gospel ends with an entreaty by the risen Jesus to his eleven remaining disciples (Judas having hanged himself) that they should go forth and teach all nations, 'baptizing them in the name of the Father, and the Son and the Holy Ghost'. Mark, however, takes the Jesus story further and tell us of his 'Ascension into Heaven':

> So then after the Lord had spoken unto them, he was received into heaven, and sat on the right hand of God.[1]

Luke, in his Gospel, gives slightly more detail to the story of the Ascension, telling us that it took place at Bethany, the village near Jerusalem where his friends Martha, Mary and Lazarus had their home:

> And he led them out as far as Bethany, and he lifted up his hands and blessed them.
>
> And it came to pass that while he blessed them, he was parted from them, and was carried from them.
>
> And they worshipped him, and returned to Jerusalem with great joy:
>
> And were continually in the temple, praising and blessing God. Amen.[2]

The fullest account of all and the one on which the traditional image of the Ascension is based is to be found in *The Acts of the Apostles*:

To them [the Apostles] he presented himself alive after his passion by many proofs, appearing to them during forty days, and speaking of the kingdom of God . . .

So when they had come together, they asked him 'Lord, will you at this time restore the kingdom to Israel?' He said to them, 'It is not for you to know the time or the seasons which the Father has fixed by His own authority. But you shall receive power when the Holy Spirit has come down on you; and you shall be my witnesses in all Judea and Samaria and to the end of the earth'. And when he had said this, as they looked on, he was lifted up, and a cloud took him out of their sight. And while they were gazing into heaven as he went, behold, two men stood by them in white robes, and said, 'Men of Galilee, why do you stand looking into heaven? This Jesus, who was taken up from you into heaven, will come in the same way as you saw him going into heaven'.[3]

This story of Jesus' ascension into heaven is one of the essential dogmas of the Church and it is still celebrated as a major festival that occurs forty days after Easter. At first sight this interval appears to be symbolic, rather like the forty days he spent fasting in the wilderness. However, closer analysis reveals something quite extraordinary: Jesus' ascension has a definite, astrological meaning.

There is considerable debate concerning the exact year the events of the Crucifixion, Resurrection and Ascension are supposed to have taken place. In an exhaustive article, covering both documentary and astronomical evidence, *The Encyclopaedia Britannica* arrives at the year 29 AD as the most likely:

To sum up: the various dates and intervals, to the approximate determination of which this article has been devoted, do not claim separately more than a tentative and probable value. Perhaps their harmony and convergence give some additional claim to acceptance, and at any rate do something to secure each one of them singly – the Nativity in 7–6 BC, the Baptism in AD 26–27, the Crucifixion in AD 29 – from being to any wide extent in error.[4]

The Last Supper, which took place on the first Maundy Thursday, was in reality the Jewish feast of the Passover. This meal is always celebrated on the eve between the fourteenth and fifteenth day of the

Hebrew month of Nisan. In modern terms this means on the day of the first full moon following the spring equinox. In the year of Jesus' death, this seems to have occurred on the day before the sabbath, which would begin at sunset on the Friday. The Resurrection, our modern festival of Easter took place two days later on the following Sunday and the Ascension forty days after that.

There is some vagary about dates, varying by up to three days, depending on how one calculates the full moon. However, in AD 29 Passover would have occurred some time between 14–16 April Good Friday on the 15–17 and Easter Sunday on 16–18 April. Counting on forty days brings us to 26–28 May. Using SKYGLOBE it is possible to see that on all three of these days the sun would be in the 'shake-hands' position, above the outstretched, right arm of Orion. It would seem that just as the Nativity chart of Jesus (29 July 7 BC) fits the birthday of the Commagene kings, so also his 'Ascension' fits with the orientation of the shaft at Arsameia and took place on the appropriate date for a Royal Ascent to the stars.

In *The Mayan Prophecies*, I drew attention, curtesy of *Hamlet's Mill*, to the belief prevalent throughout the ancient world that at either 'end' of the Milky Way there was a star gate. According to de Santillana and von Dechend these were to be found where the ecliptic, or annual pathway of the sun, intersected with the Milky Way. the southern gateway was near the tail of Sagittarius, whilst the northern was in Gemini, close to the 'shake hands' position above Orion. This idea was well-known in the Roman world and is recorded by Macrobius, a writer from the late fourth and early fifth centuries AD.[5]

The conclusion, though perhaps shocking for many Christians, is that just as Orion symbolized Osiris, the 'Father' of the Egyptian pharaohs, so it also now represents Jesus' 'Father in Heaven' by whose right hand he now sits. This is not to suggest that God the Father himself is a constellation any more than that Jesus is the sun but that once more the Hermetic dictum, 'As Above, So Below', is apposite. It would seem that Jesus' ascension into heaven, like that of Elijah, is intricately linked with Orion and that it was towards this part of the sky that he was believed to have departed. This being so, then we have further reason to take note of the fact that Orion, 'Father Time', is now reaching its maximum elevation in the sky. Could it be that a star-gate is about to be opened?

# NOTES

## Prologue

1 By 'esoteric' is meant knowledge that is restricted to the few as opposed to 'exoteric' or public knowledge.

## Chapter 1. A Pilgrimage to the City of David

1 P.D. Ouspensky, *A New Model of the Universe* (London, Routledge & Kegan Paul Ltd, 1967), pp.344–345.

2 Matt. 1:18–2:12.

3 John Harvey, *The Plantagenets*, (Glasgow, Penguin Books, 1976), pp.149–150.

4 Hone, W. (Trans.), *The Lost Books of the Bible* (New York, Gramercy Books, 1979), p.40.

5 Ibid. p.40.

6 Matt. 3:13–17.

7 Jonathan Riley-Smith, *Oxford Illustrated History of the Crusades* (Oxford, Oxford University Press, 1995), p.1.

## Chapter 2. Meeting with a Magus

1 J.G. Bennett, *Deeper Man* (London, Turnstone Press, 1978), p.148.

2 Ibid. pp.148–149.

3 This was one of over a dozen foreign languages including Greek, Indonesian, Tibetan and Sanskrit, he was to master.

4 The Chatalja Lines were a fortified position 25 miles west of and protecting Constantinople.

5 The *Mevlevi*, known as the 'whirling dervishes' on account of their peculiar, entranced dance, are the most famous of a number of Sufi brotherhoods.

Today, although their convents are still officially closed, they are making something of a comeback.

6 The Theosophical Society founded by Madame Blavatsky was the forerunner of the many 'New Age' groups of today. It was and is a very broad church, embracing Eastern and Western mysticism.

7 The name *Tertium Organum* was an oblique reference to Aristotle's *Organon*, meaning 'instrument of thought' and Roger Bacon's *Novum Organum* or 'new instrument of thought'. By calling his book 'third instrument of thought' Ouspensky was provocatively implying that his book updated the work of these philosophers.

8 See P.D. Ouspensky, *A New Model of the Universe* (London, Routledge & Kegan Paul Ltd, 1967), pp.xiii–xiv.

9 Ibid. p.32.

10 According to Bennett this is an alternative spelling, Sarmoung being the Armenianized version of the name.

11 Gurdjieff makes veiled references to this in *Beelzebub's Tales to his Grandson*, Chapter XXX, where he refers to it as the 'Club of Adherents' to Legominism'.

12 Kenneth Guthrie (Trans. & Compiler), *The Pythagorean Sourcebook and Library* (Grand Rapids, Michigan, Phanes Press, 1987), p.61.

13 Ibid. p.125.

14 Ibid. p.124.

15 J.G. Bennett, *Gurdjieff Making a New World* (London, Turnstone Press, 1973), p.59.

16 The ruins of Ani are extensive and straddle the border between Turkey and the new republic of Armenia; it is, at the time of writing, quite a dangerous place to visit as the border is politically highly sensitive.

17 Alexandropol is now called Leninakan and since the break-up of the Soviet Union has become the capital city of the new Armenian republic.

18 G.I. Gurdjieff, *Meetings with Remarkable Men* (London, Picador, 1978), p.96.

19 Ibid. p.99.

20 Ibid. p.120.

21 J.G. Bennett, *Gurdjieff Making a New World* (London, Turnstone Press, 1973), p.274.

22 P.D. Ouspensky, *In Search of the Miraculous* (London, Routledge & Kegan Paul Ltd, 1977) p.30.

23 J.G. Bennett, *Gurdjieff Making a New World* (London, Turnstone Press, 1973), pp.56–57.

## Chapter 3. A Search among the Sufis

1 Sufi *Tekkes* bear some comparison with Christian monasteries, except that the dervishes, the equivalent of Western monks, are usually family men with ordinary jobs and do not live in a closed community. They are,

however, bound in obedience to their sheikh who, as the 'abbott' of the *Tekke*, acts as a *murshid* or guide to the holy life.

2  J.G. Bennett, *Witness* (London, Turnstone Press, 1975), p.289.

3  In 1986, following in Bennett's footsteps, I visited the Konya *Tekke* myself. It turned out to be one of the most curious buildings I have ever visited: a holy shrine pretending to be a museum. Outside, in the courtyard fronting the building were the usual lustral facilities that one associates with Islam and several old men busying themselves with their *zikr*. This is the main, spiritual practice of the Sufis. Usually it involves breath control coupled with repetitive prayer, though the exact form this takes differs from order to order and is a matter of initiation. Its purpose is to raise consciousness, ultimately to enable union with God. Inside the *Tekke* was the most extraordinary atmosphere of love and peace. Near the doorway was the tomb of Rumi himself, an elaborate affair covered with expensive brocades in a chapel covered from floor to ceiling with calligraphic designs. Nearby were the tombs of several of his most important followers, each surmounted by an elaborate turban showing his rank. The *Sema Hané* itself was smaller than I had expected and was occupied by display cases filled with instruments, writings and other memorabilia of the Order. Even so, the memory of the whirling dance seemed to be so strongly imprinted into the fabric of the room that I had an overwhelming urge to spin round and round and abandon myself to the dance. It was a strange feeling and what I think Bennett was hinting at when he wrote about the building focusing psychic energies.

4  J.G. Bennett, *Witness* (London, Turnstone Press, 1975), p.290.

5  J.G. Bennett, *Journeys in Islamic Countries*, (Glos., Coombe Springs Press, 1977), vol.2, p.49.

6  According to the Avesta (Yasna, 9, 17), Zoroaster came from Airyanem Vaejo, on the River Daitya. In the Bundahish (29, 32 and 24, 15) it states that the River Dareja was in Airan Vej and it was on its banks that his father had his house. The Bundahish also says that Airan Vej was located in Atropatene, the district of northern Media to the west of the Caspian Sea. It is therefore generally accepted that the River Daitya (Dareja) is the Arax and that he came from this area.

7  Some commentators believe he may have lived much earlier: *c.*1400–1200 BC. The confusion is not surprising given that many of the original writings of Zoroastrianism were destroyed at the time of Alexander's conquest of the Persian Empire in 334 BC. Even more of the oral tradition was lost as many of the Magi perished when the conquering Macedonians plundered their temples and shrines. Enough, however, survived for the faith to flicker on during the, for them, dark days of Greek domination before bursting forth in revived form once more as the state religion of the Sassanian Empire.

8  The Holy books of today's Zoroastrian Parsees.

9  J.G. Bennett, *The Masters of Wisdom* (Santa Fé, Bennett Books, 1995), p.51.

10 Just as Buddhists look forward to the coming of Maitreya and Christians to the 'Second Coming' of Jesus Christ, so Zoroastrians believed that at the end of time, a posthumous son of Zoroaster, called Saoshyans ('saviour') would be born and he would save the world.

11 A successor state to the old Persian Empire that was re-founded around 248 BC.

12 The name Aryan is generally applied to the tribes of people emanating from Persia and India and speaking a common Indo-European language. The relationship between these ancient tribes and modern Europeans is a problematic and contentious issue.

13 G.I. Gurdjieff (Meetings with Remarkable Men), p.66.

14 Hatra was a desert fortress to the south of Mosul with a largely Aramaean population. Inscriptions indicate that at one time the North Mesopotamian god Be'elshamin (king of the gods – probably to be equated with Ahura Mazda) was worshipped there along with Sin-Marilaha, the local Moon-god.

15 J.G. Bennett (Journeys in Islamic Countries, vol.2) p.49.

16 Mithra, Mitra, Mihr are other variations on the name.

17 Indeed Mithraism has been described as Greek philosophy wearing Persian clothing but this definition is inadequate.

18 Presumably the tree of life.

19 The second 'Adam' is Jesus Christ, who undoes the sin of the first.

20 Joseph Campbell, The Masks of the Gods – Occidental Mythology (London, Souvenir Press, 1974), p.261.

21 Ibid, pp.261–262.

22 R.C. Zaehner, The Teachings of the Magi (London, Sheldon Press, 1975), p.15.

23 In India it developed, via the Vedas, into the Brahmanic religion of today. Curiously, in the sub-continent the Asuras (equivalent of the Iranian Ahuras) were demonized whilst the Devas (devils in Zoroastrianism) were elevated to the position of important gods. Later, Indian polytheism was refined and modified by such enlightened teachers as Krishna and Buddha so that the original substructure of Vedic thought is almost invisible in the religion as practised in the subcontinent today. Yet it is still there and is the inspiration at the root of what could perhaps be called the Yogic tradition.

24 E. Wynn-Tyson, Mithras, The Fellow in the Cap (London, Rider, 1958), p.40.

25 Joseph Campbell, (The Masks of God – Occidental Mythology), p.255.

26 The Kabbalistic 'tree of life' with its ten sephiroth or 'lights' is really an extension of the seven-branched, Jewish candlestick or Menorah.

27 For example, individuals imbued with the power of Mars made good soldiers. It gave them the courage, drive, forcefulness and dynamism needed to undertake dangerous ventures. But it would also give an angry temperament and incline the person towards cruelty.

28  Joseph Campbell, *The Masks of God — Occidental Mythology*, p.255.
29  Rev. 1:20.
30  Aeon means literally 'age' but it also stands for the spirit of an age or period of time personified as a 'god'.
31  Once for each planetary sphere?
32  G.R.S. Mead, *Thrice Greatest Hermes* (London, John M. Watkins, 1964), vol. III, p.99.
33  Ibid. vol 1. p.144.
34  Ibid. p.146.
35  Ibid. p.157.
36  Ibid. p.157.
37  John: 1:1–5
38  G.R.S. Mead, *Thrice Greatest Hermes*, Vol I, p.161.

## Chapter 4. Hermes Trismegistus

1  A.G. Gilbert, *The Cosmic Wisdom Beyond Astrology* (Shaftesbury, Solos Press, 1991).
2  Gen. 11:31–32.
3  *See* G.R.S. Mead, *Thrice Greatest Hermes*, vol 1 p.5 & W. Scott (ed.), *Hermetica*, pp.218–219.
4  The *Hermetica* collection contains more than just the *Corpus Hermeticum*.
5  Kabbalah is an esoteric form of Judaism involving meditation on certain images coupled with astrology and the names of God. Suitably modified it becomes Christian Kabbalah.
6  *See* Frances Yates, *Giordano Bruno and the Hermetic Tradition* (Routledge & Kegan Paul Ltd, 1982), p.63.
7  Ibid. pp.351–352.
8  Walter Scott (ed.) *Hermetica* (Solos Press), pp.34, 41.
9  G.R.S. Mead, *Thrice Greatest Hermes*, vol. 1, p.19.
10  The Adytum is the most sacred part of a temple, church or shrine; e.g. the Holy of Holies of the Temple of Jerusalem or the King's Chamber in the Great Pyramid.
11  G.R.S. Mead, *Thrice Greatest Hermes*, vol. 1, p.30.
12  Horus is here being addressed by his mother, Isis.
13  W. Scott (ed.) *Hermetica*, p.179.
14  Ibid. p.47.
15  Ibid. p.190.
16  Ibid, pp.191–192.

## Chapter 5. The Orion Mystery

1  The culmination of a star is the point in the sky, directly south, where, in its daily apparent movement across the sky, it reaches its highest elevation above the horizon.

2 See *The Orion Mystery* for full details of this extraordinary discovery.

3 Matt. 1:17.

4 Gen. 12:10–20.

5 Gen. 41:44–45.

6 Jacob's first two sons by Rachel's sister Leah.

7 The plain around Harran between the Tigris and Euphrates rivers.

8 Gen. 48:7.

9 Aaron was Moses' elder brother.

10 Exod. 2:1–10.

11 King of Israel.

12 2 Kgs. 17:5–6.

13 1 Chr. 5:26.

14 R. Young, *Analytical Concordance to the Bible* (Guildford, Lutterworth Press, 1975).

15 Jer. 43:12–13.

16 'Him' is generally reckoned to be Antiochus IV of Syria.

17 Dan. 11:30–31.

18 Ruled AD 63–40, died 30 BC.

19 Matt. 2:13–15.

20 Matt. 2:16.

21 *The Lost Books of the Bible*, p.47.

22 Ibid: p.38.

23 R.T. Rundle Clark, *Myth and Symbol in Ancient Egypt* (London, Thames & Hudson, 1978), pp.87–98.

24 Isa. 11:1–2; 10.

25 See Rom. 15:12.

26 R.T. Rundle Clark, *Myth and Symbol in Ancient Egypt*, p.246.

## Chapter 6. A Search for the Secret Brotherhood

1 See above.

2 e.g. the inability of Yezidis to exit a circle when one is drawn around them in the dust. See above.

3 Much more will be said about this city later.

4 These Greek names mean 'dual-form' and 'mono-form' respectively.

5 The national god of the Assyrians, who though originally the local deity of the city of Assur, later took on many of the divine attributes of both the sun and storm gods.

6 D. Luckenbill, *Ancient Records of Assyria and Babylonia – Part One* (London, Histoire & Mysteries of Man Ltd, 1989) p.74.

7 Ibid. p.75.

8 Ibid. p.217. As 20 minas of silver is a paltry amount, only a quarter of a talent, it would seem that Commagene was richer in timber than metals.

9 The name of the city has recently been changed to SanliUrfa – 'Urfa the

illustrious' – because of its heroic resistance against the French in the aftermath of the First World War.

10 The smallest of the three pyramids of Giza.

## Chapter 7. The Lion of Commagene

1 See *The Orion Mystery* (London, William Heinemann Ltd., 1994), p.91.

2 *Greek Horoscopes*, an article by O. Neugebauer and H.B. van Hoesen.

3 The stadium or furlong was an ancient unit of measure. Its length varies from place to place but Eratosthenes' is approximately 1/10 of a British mile.

4 Astronomers always give BC dates as minus numbers. In their method of computation there is no year '0', the calendar going straight from –1 to +1. This means that an extra year has to be subtracted from astronomical dates to turn them into BC dates; e.g. –61 becomes 62 BC.

5 Because of precessional changes, 0° Aries, the point where the ecliptic or path of the sun cuts the celestial equator, gradually slips backwards. Because of this slippage, astrological 'signs' of the zodiac no longer correspond to their constellations. Even in Antiochus' day this precession was noticeable.

6 In fact the Moon overtakes Mercury as the day progresses.

7 Details of this journey, which was largely concerned with Urfa/Edessa, follow in the next chapter.

8 W. Scott (ed.), *Hermetica*, pp. 52–53.

9 Ibid. p.206.

10 A small city on an isolated rock at the east side of the Plain of Argos in the Peloponnese.

11 In fact in some versions of the myth it is stated clearly that the dead lion was turned by Zeus into the constellation of Leo. In the relief at Arsameia Hercules is shown with the Nemean Lion's skin, which he used to wear as a distinctive costume, thrown over one arm.

12 Today, because of precession, it takes place between Gemini and Taurus.

13 Again because of precession it has slipped back a sign and is now almost in Scorpio.

14 The birthday of Mithras was 25 December, just after the winter solstice.

15 There is a constellation named Hercules made of rather inconspicuous stars between Lyra and Corona Borealis. This second or even third division constellation cannot have been the one the Greeks originally had in mind when they said that Zeus had honoured the greatest of his demi-gods by putting him among the stars.

16 There will, in fact, be two points on the ecliptic that align with this shaft. The first in spring when the sun is moving north the second in late summer when it is retreating back south again. The Regulus alignment, after the summer solstice, is the second of these. I was looking now for the first, the one which would occur in spring.

17 See *The Orion Mystery* for details.

18 In Zoroastrianism two of the greatest sins are telling lies and polluting the

elements. As dead bodies are considered to be highly polluting for the earth, it was the custom of the Persians (and still is amongst the Parsis of India) to first leave corpses to be picked over by scavenging birds before entombing the remaining bones.

## Chapter 8. The City of the Patriarchs

1 Daisan means 'leaping' in Syriac, the same as its Greek translation, Scirtos, that was also used. This is probably a reference to the turbulent nature of the river which was prone to flooding a well as drying out.

2 The name 'Aryu' means 'lion' in Syriac.

3 Pliny, Tacitus and Plutarch refer to the Edessans as Arabs.

4 A corruption of Aramaean. It was Abgar.

5 *The Lost Books of the Bible*, pp. 62–63.

6 'So his fame spread throughout all Syria, and they brought him all their sick, those afflicted with various diseases and pains, demoniacs, epileptics, and paralytics, and he healed them.' [Matt. 4:24].

7 In Luke Chapter 10, Jesus sends out 70 disciples in pairs to spread the word.

8 The date given seems to be according to the local calendar based on the accession of Seleucus. The start of his dynasty was officially taken as his return to Babylon in 312 BC. Thus a date of 340 would correspond to AD 18. This, as we will see, is a little early to be the correct date for an event after the Crucifixion but it is not far out.

9 See J. B. Segal, *Edessa 'The Blessed City'* (Oxford, Oxford at the Clarendon Press, 1970), p. 76.

10 Ibid. p. 77.

11 A somewhat similar situation exists in Mexico today. There is a sacred icon of the Virgin Mary 'miraculously' imprinted on an Indian peasant's gown in the sixteenth century. This now hangs in splendour in the Basilica of Guadalupe in Mexico City. Copies of it, however, are to be found in every Catholic church throughout the country and the Virgin of Guadalupe is the centre of a major, Christian cult.

12 There are still caves and springs associated with these prophets that are venerated by the local Moslem population to this day.

13 St Paul made Antioch his base for his evangelizing missions amongst the Gentiles and St Peter is also believed to have lived there for a time.

14 W. Kingsland, *The Gnosis in the Christian Scriptures* (Solos Press, 1993), p.84.

15 These rather technical terms mean that Jesus Christ embodied the 'spirit of the age'. He was the Logos, or word of God, made flesh.

16 Interestingly, the Moslems believed the Mandylion to be a relic not of the Crucifixion but of the Baptism. They subscribed to the theory that it was the towel Jesus had used to dry himself after his immersion in the Jordan.

17 See Lynn Picknett and Clive Prince, *Turin Shroud, in whose image?* (London, Bloomsbury, 1994).

## Chapter 9. A Tale of Two Cities

1 As described in chapter 7 we returned to Arsameia to measure the direction of the shaft at Base Site 3.

2 The importance of water, particularly wells, in the life of Harran is indicated in the few references to the city in the Bible. When Abraham sent his chief servant to Harran to find a wife for his son Isaac, the latter made a pact with God that the first woman to offer water from the well outside the city for both himself and his animals would be the one. The story has a happy ending for she, of course, turns out to be Isaac's cousin Rebekah and in due course they were married.

3 D. Luckenbill (trans.), Ancient Records of Assyria and Babylonia —. Part 2, p.45.

4 The Black Obelisk is now in the British Museum.

5 D. Luckenbill (trans.), Ancient Records of Assyria and Babylonia — Part 2, p.353.

6 Ibid, p.354.

7 J. Riley-Smith (ed.) The Oxford Illustrated History of the Crusades, p.6.

8 See J.B. Segal, Edessa 'The Blessed City' (Oxford at Clarendon Press, 1970).

9 This was the name applied to the Syrian Monophysite Church after its founder: Jacob Baradaeus, a former Bishop of Edessa.

10 The Melkites were the 'royalist' Church (Melcha meaning King) that adhered to the official teachings supported by the Byzantine court.

11 See J. Segal, Edessa 'The Blessed City', p.16.

12 S. Runciman, A History of the Crusades, vol I, p.326.

13 There is some reason to believe that Baldwin I may have met up with Hugues some years earlier, see M. Baigent, R. Leigh and H. Lincoln, Holy Blood and Holy Grail (London, Jonathan Cape, 1982), p.37.

14 This is a Moslem building covering the site of the original Holy of Holies of the Temple of Soloman, which for Jews, Christians and Moslems alike was and still is an extremely holy place. It is octagonal in shape with a golden dome.

15 The Turin Shroud is a long piece of cloth on which is imprinted the form of a man who appears to have been crucified. Its provenance has always been highly suspect since it first came to light in the fourteenth century and it gets its name from the city in Italy where it currently resides.

16 See L. Picknett and C. Prince, Turin Shroud, In whose image?

## Chapter 10. The Pillars of Nimrod

1 J.B. Segal, Edessa 'The Blessed City', p.174.

2 This is the same emperor who built the great Hagia Sophia Cathedral of Constantinople and he carried out some very importnt improvements at Edessa. Following the great floods of AD 525 it was he who had built

a dam and a new channel to take away excess water from the River Daisan. His system has prevented major floods since then and is still in use to this day.

3 Name of a Toparch.

4 Sumatar Harabesi is an archaeological site south-east of Urfa. Here important remains have been found relating to the Sabian cult of Harran.

5 J.B. Segal, *Edessa 'The Blessed City'*, p.58.

6 Gen. 10:6–12.

7 G. de Santillana and H. von Dechend, *Hamlet's Mill* (Boston, Gambit Inc., 1969), p.166.

8 J. B. Segal, *Edessa 'The Blessed City'*, p.50.

9 In another version of the myth she kills him after he attempts to rape her.

10 The constellation becomes invisible, of course, because during this time of the year it is above the horizon during daylight hours. After his dawn reappearance, Osiris/Orion is steadily visible for more and more of the night until around nine months later it begins to set around sunset and therefore once more becomes invisible. *See The Orion Mystery* for further details.

11 It is perhaps interesting to note that there is a well (*Bir Eyüp*) outside the south wall of Urfa where it is believed that Job bathed and was healed of his terrible afflictions. Nearby once stood the Christian shrines of two popular, local saints, Cosmas and Damian, who were physicians. The healing waters of Job's Well were and still are resorted to by suffering pilgrims, most especially for curing skin complaints.

12 Giorgio de Santillana and Hertha von Dechend, *Hamlet's Mill*, pp.165–166.

13 Judg. 14:14.

14 Judg. 16:28–30.

15 Judg. 15:18–19.

16 J. B. Segal, *Edessa 'The Blessed City'*, p.9 n.

17 1 Kgs. 17:1.

18 Baal was the Phoenician name for the Babylonian Bel. Both mean 'Lord' and can refer to any god, including, at times, Yahweh, the God of the Hebrews. More usually Baal or Bel is associated with the cult of the planet Jupiter. However, Baalism as opposed by the prophet Elijah was nature worship involving idols, sacrifices and sexual magic.

19 II Kgs, 2:11–12.

20 See *The Orion Mystery* for details concerning all these matters.

21 2 Kings 2:12–14.

22 This is a reference to the last two verses of the Old Testament. 'Behold I will send you Elijah the prophet before the great and terrible day of the Lord comes. And he will turn the hearts of fathers to their children and the hearts of children to their fathers, lest I come and smite the land with a curse.' Malachi 4:5–6.

23 Matt. 11:10–15.

24 Matt. 3:4.

25  1 Kgs 19:1–2.
26  2 Kgs 9:33–36.

# Chapter 11. We Three Kings

1  From 37 BC to his eventual death in 4 BC.
2  The Hasmonean Dynasty, also known as the Maccabees, were descended from the family of freedom fighters who brought independence to the Jewish state in the second century BC. Their position somewhat parallels that of the Royal Family of Commagene, which gained independence at about the same time.
3  Josephus, *The Jewish War* (London, Penguin Books, 1977), p.64.
4  Ibid. p.69.
5  The sidereal calendar is based on the cyclical movements of the stars, especially Sirius, rather than on the sun and moon.
6  The Commagene New Year.
7  Rev. 5:5.
8  A year or two after a Rinpoche, such as the Dalai Lama, dies, search parties are sent out to find the child who is his reincarnation. Special provision is then made for the child's education and upbringing to prepare him for his heavy destiny.
9  According to the Oxford Dictionary, zodiac comes from the Greek *zoidion*, meaning sculptured animal.
10  Myrrh was used by the Egyptians for embalming corpses in the mummification process.
11  Luke 1:15.
12  See Chapter 12.
13  Frances A. Yates, *Astraea* (London, Pimlico, 1975), p.30.
14  This is in the British Museum.
15  It is noteworthy that in the Greek system of astrology, most of which was adapted from early Egyptian sources, Mercury (Hermes) is the ruler over the constellation of Virgo.
16  Frances A. Yates, *Astraea*, pp.30–31.
17  In the zodiac of Denderah, where Virgo is clearly represented, she seems to be holding some sort of long-stemmed plant that could be a reed or a lily.
18  R.T. Rundle Clark, *Myth and Symbol in Ancient Egypt*.
19  There is an extra layer of meaning in that the cluster of lotuses also represent the Delta area of Lower Egypt where Horus and his mother Isis had to hide at the time of his birth.
20  Anciently these included the Sun and Moon but left out Uranus, Neptune and Pluto, which had not then been discovered.
21  Matt. 23:13; 23–24.
22  Matt. 27: 46–50.
23  Psalms 22:1; 6–8; 14–18.

## Chapter 12. The Second Crusade and the Temple on the Rhine

1 Following the book *The Holy Blood and Holy Grail* by Baigent, Leigh and Lincoln, there has been much speculation concerning a shadowy Order known as the 'Priory of Sion' and its possible association with the Templars. This Order, they suggest, was not only the driving force behind the Crusading movement but was intent on displacing the Capetian Dynasty (from which Louis VII sprang) with the more ancient but by then pretender line of the Merovingians. By this analysis, the Templars were no more than a front for this movement. This I find unbelievable. It seems more likely to me that the Templars were a mystical rather than political brotherhood and that the secret Order with which they were in contact was the Sarman and that their symbol at that time was the lily or *Fleur-de-Lys*.

2 Research into Lost Knowledge Organization.

3 A clue to what this school might have been is provided in the 'appreciation' of the translator, Sir Ronald Fraser, which is printed immediately after the Publisher's Foreword. In this it is noted that the original, French version of the book was put into the hands of Mrs Jackson by none other than J.G. Bennett.

4 An area roughly 20 km by 10 km.

5 Roughly a diamond shape of 210 by 160 km.

6 The Cistercian order, to which the Templars were affiliated, began in Burgundy under the patronage of the Count.

7 The Armenians were well known as architects in the region. Their great cathedral of Ani was among the finest buildings in the world and it was Armenian architects who were called in by the Byzantines to repair the collapsed roof of Haghia Sophia in Constantinople.

8 This is the demiurgic intelligence, the equivalent of the Biblical Elohim.

9 Scott, *Hermetica*, p.50.

10 See chapter 2 above.

11 J.G. Bennett, *Sacred Influences*, pp.38–39.

12 This is also a worldwide phenomenon and I personally have seen how even in Tropical Mexico people are moved to build huge, life-size nativity sets and place them on street corners.

13 In Egypt all stars were shown as five pointed. Examples of these can be seen on the ceiling paintings of both some of the later pyramids and tombs in the Valley of the Kings.

14 Though later pharaohs, such as Rameses II, were often cruel autocrats, the title itself was originally applied to the palace and means 'the Great House'.

15 Recent work by author John Anthony West and geologist Robert Schoch indicates that the Great Sphinx of Giza is probably very much older than the pyramids. However, the head is definitely carved in the style of the IVth Dynasty, indicating that this feature at least is contemporaneous with

the building of the pyramids in c.2450 BC. It would seem that the head, which may originally have been simply that of a lion, was resculpted. The model for it was probably Khufu, builder of the Great Pyramid.

16 The imperial eagle dates back to Babylon and was the equivalent symbol to the Egyptian hawk as used by the empires of Assyria, Persia and Greece.

17 Matt. 3:13–17.

18 Because of precessional changes over the centuries, the solar conjunction with Regulus now takes place in late August and not July.

## Epilogue

1 The name Louis, so popular with French kings, is derived from Clovis.

2 It would seem that this Sacred Ampulla, along with many other treasures, was either looted or hidden away during the French Revolution. If its location is known today, it is a closely guarded secret.

3 P. Demouy, Reims Cathedral, p. 44.

4 Rev. 20: 11–15.

5 Mal. 4: 5–6.

6 In Bennett's system 'Adam' represents the evolutionary birth of intelligence into the human race.

7 J.G. Bennett, The Masters of Wisdom, p. 30.

8 Matt. 24: 27–30.

## Appendix 2 Orion the Hunter

1 Giorgio de Santillana and Hertha von Dechend, Hamlet's Mill (Boston, Gambit Inc., 1969), pp. 165–166.

2 Bulletin of the Egyptological Seminar 3, (1981), p.20

3 Campbell, J., The Masks of the Gods – Occidental Mythology (London, Souvenir Press, 1974), p.257.

4 Giorgio de Santillana and Hertha von Dechend, Hamlet's Mill, p.357.

5 Ibid. p.247.

## Appendix 3 Abraham's Journey to the Promised Land

1 J.G. Bennett, Journeys in Islamic Countries, vol. 2, p.21

2 It is difficult for us to appreciate the significance of this development in terms of the science of warfare as understood at the time, but in many ways, chariots were the ancient equivalent of modern day tanks. They were the armour that gave an attacking force its punch and could change the course of a battle. Whereas an infantry soldier had to carry his weapons and shield with him wherever he went and could, therefore, only bear a single sword and spear, a charioteer could bring with him a whole arsenal of weapons allowing him the option of fighting close up or firing projectiles from a distance. Even mounted cavalry were in many

ways disadvantaged compared with charioteers, for the chariot could carry more than one person. Thus, whilst the driver was steering, the passenger could be firing off a stream of arrows at pursuing cavalry, the chariot itself providing at least some protection from returning fire. The advent of the war chariot into Middle Eastern politics must have produced a great deal of turmoil as the whole balance of power was changed almost overnight.

3 Within a couple of hundred years it was overwhelmed by the neighbouring Hittites and incorporated into their kingdom.

4 Gen 2:10–14.

# Appendix 4

1 Mark 16:19
2 Luke 24:50–53
3 Acts 1:3–11
4 *Encyclopaedia Britannica*, vol 3, 1951, p.527
5 See *The Mayan Prophecies* p.155–8 and *Hamlet's Mill* pp.243–5.

Fig. 20

## The Family tree of the kings of Commagene.

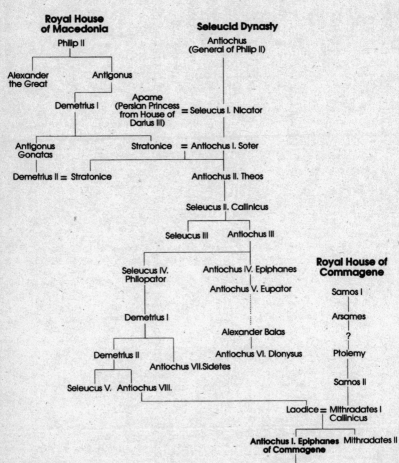

Fig. 21    King Herod and the Hasmonean and Herodian Succession

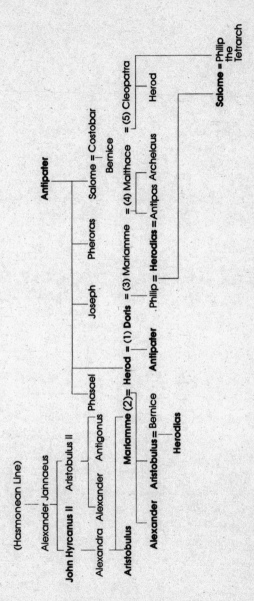

Not all branches of this highly convoluted and, at times incestuous, family tree are shown.
Important characters in the present story are shown in bold.

# BIBLIOGRAPHY

Baigent, M., Leigh, R. and Lincoln, H., *The Holy Blood & Holy Grail*, London, Jonathan Cape, 1982.

Bauval, R. and Gilbert, A. G., *The Orion Mystery*, London, William Heinemann Ltd, 1994.

Bennett, J.G., *Deeper Man*, London, Turnstone Press, 1978.

Bennett, J.G., *Gurdjieff Making a New World*, London, Turnstone Press, 1973.

Bennett, J.G., *Journeys in Islamic Countries*, Glos., Coombe Springs Press, 1977.

Bennett, J.G., *Sacred Influences*, Glos., Coombe Springs Press, 1982.

Bennett, J.G., *The Masters of Wisdom*, Santa Fe, Bennett Books, 1995.

Bennett, J.G., *Witness*, London, Turnstone Press, 1975.

Boyce, M., *Zoroastrians*, London, Routledge & Kegan Paul Ltd, 1987.

Campbell, J., *The Masks of the Gods – Occidental Mythology*, London, Souvenir Press, 1974.

Charpentier, L., *The Mysteries of Chartres Cathedral*, London, R.I.L.K.O., 1976.

de Santillana, G. and von Dechend, H., *Hamlet's Mill*, Boston, Gambit Inc., 1969.

Gilbert, A.G., *The Cosmic Wisdom beyond Astrology*, Shaftesbury, Solos Press, 1991.

Gordon, D., *The Wilton Diptych*, London, National Gallery Pubs., 1993.

Gurdjieff, G.I., *All and Everything, Series I, Beelzebub's Tales to his Grandson*, 3 vols., London, Routledge & Kegan Paul Ltd., 1976.

Gurdjieff, G.I., *Meetings with Remarkable Men*, London, Picador, 1978.

Guthrie, K. (Trans. & Compiler), *The Pythagorean Sourcebook and Library*, Grand Rapids, Michigan, Phanes Press, 1987.

Harvey, J., *The Plantagenets*, Glasgow, Fontana, 1976.

Hone, W. (Trans.), *The Lost Books of the Bible*, New York, Gramercy Books, 1979.

Josephus, *The Jewish War*, London, Penguin Books, 1977.

Kingsland, W., *The Gnosis in the Christian Scriptures*, Shaftesbury, Solos Press, 1993.

Luckenbill, D., *Ancient Records of Assyria and Babylonia — Parts I-II*, London, Histories and Mysteries of Man Ltd., 1989.

Mead, G.R.S., *Fragments of a Faith Forgotten*, New York, University Books Inc., 1960.

Mead G.R.S., *Thrice Greatest Hermes*, vols I-III. London, John M. Watkins, 1964.

Millar, F., *The Roman Near East — 31 BC-AD 337*, Harvard University Press, 1994.

Ouspensky, P.D., *A New Model of the Universe*, London, Routledge & Kegan Paul Ltd., 1967.

Ouspensky P.D., *In Search of the Miraculous*, London, Routledge & Kegan Paul Ltd., 1977.

Picknett, L. and Prince, C. *Turin Shroud, in Whose Image?* London, Bloomsbury, 1994.

Riley-Smith, J. *Oxford Illustrated History of the Crusades*, Oxford, Oxford University Press, 1995.

Runciman, S., *A History of the Crusades* vols. I-III, London, Penguin Books, 1990.

Rundle Clark, R.T., *Myth and Symbol in Ancient Egypt*, London, Thames & Hudson, 1978.

Scott, W. (Trans. and ed.), *Hermetica*, Shaftesbury, Solos Press, 1992.

Segal, J.B., *Edessa: 'The Blessed City'*, Oxford, Oxford at the Clarendon Press, 1970.

Tacitus, *The Histories*, London, Guild Publishing, 1992.

Walker, J., *Armenia — the Survival of a Nation*, London, Croom Helm, 1980.

Wilson, I., *The Turin Shroud*, London, Victor Gollancz, 1978.

Wynn-Tyson, E., *Mithras, The Fellow in the Cap*, London, Rider, 1958.

Yates, F.A., *Astraea*, London, Pimlico, 1975.

  *Giordano Bruno and the Hermetic Tradition*, London, Routledge & Kegan Paul Ltd, 1982.

Young, R. *Analytical Concordance to the Bible*, Guilford, Lutterworth Press, 1975.

Zaehner, R.C., *The Teachings of the Magi*, London, Sheldon Press, 1975.

# ACKNOWLEDGEMENTS

I would like to thank the following people and institutions for their
help in bringing this project to fruition.

My old friend John Harvey, who accompanied me on many
saddle-sore miles and witnessed the beginning of the quest; the
staff of the British Museum, who have always been most helpful
– most especially Dr Dominique Collon; the Warburg Institute; the
Sanliurfa Museum of archaeology; a big thanks to Mark A. Haney of
KlassM Software for his SKYGLOBE computer program which made
the unravelling of the Magi mystery possible. (Anyone wanting to
obtain a shareware version of the program should contact him at
PO Box 1067, Ann Arbor, MI 48106, USA). To John Baldock, who
put me onto the amazing Magi sculptures at Autun cathedral; Ann
Walker and 'White Arrow', for their constant encouragement; Bengt
Alfredson, for his extraordinary, astronomically correct painting of *The
Adoration of the Magi*; Bill Hamilton and Sarah Fisher of A. M. Heath &
Co. for looking after an at times exhausted author; Kathy Rooney and
all at Bloomsbury for their faith and patience over the last two years;
and last but not least my wife Dee, who has accompanied me on most
of my journeys and been steadfast throughout.

Thanks are due to the following organization for permission to
quote from their published works.

To Bennett Books for quotations from the following titles by J.
G. Bennett: *Deeper Man; Gurdjieff making a new world; Journeys in
Islamic Countries; Sacred Influences; The Masters of Wisdom; Witness*. To
Penguin/Arcana for quotations from P. D. Ouspensky's books, *A New*

*Model of the Universe; In Search of the Miraculous;* G. I. Gurdjieff's *Meetings with Remarkable men;* Josephus, *The Jewish War;* and S. Runciman's, *A History of the Crusades.* To Routledge & Kegan Paul for M. Boyce's, *The Zoroastrians;* Dame Frances Yates' *Giordano Bruno and the Hermetic Tradition* and *Astraea.* To Harvard University Press for F. Millar's *The Roman Near East.* To Oxford University Press for J. Riley-Smith's *Oxford Illustrated History of the Crusades.* To Oxford at the Clarendon Press for J. B. Segal's *Edessa, 'the Blessed City'.* To Thames and Hudson Ltd for R. T. Rundle Clark's *Myth and Symbol in Ancient Egypt.* To Souvenir Press London for Joseph Campbell's *The Masks of God — Occidental Mythology.* To Collins/Fontana for J. Harvey's *The Plantagenet's.* Thanks also to the many other authors and publishers not listed above whose books have inspired the present work and helped to fertilise my thoughts.

Picture credits.

Thanks are due to the National Gallery, London, for permission to reproduce the following: *The Wilton Diptych* (artist unknown); *The Baptism of Jesus* by Piero della Francesca, *St Veronica with the Sudarium* and *The Annunciation* by Fra Filippo Lippi. To Bengt Alfredson for the Star-correct *Adoration of the Magi.* All other pictures and diagrams are the copyright of Dee and Adrian Gilbert.

# INDEX